Zen Masters

Zen Masters

Edited by
STEVEN HEINE
and
DALE S. WRIGHT

UNIVERSITY PRESS

2010

UNIVERSITY PRESS

Oxford University Press, Inc., publishes works that further
Oxford University's objective of excellence
in research, scholarship, and education.

Oxford   New York
Auckland   Cape Town   Dar es Salaam   Hong Kong   Karachi
Kuala Lumpur   Madrid   Melbourne   Mexico City   Nairobi
New Delhi   Shanghai   Taipei   Toronto

With offices in
Argentina   Austria   Brazil   Chile   Czech Republic   France   Greece
Guatemala   Hungary   Italy   Japan   Poland   Portugal   Singapore
South Korea   Switzerland   Thailand   Turkey   Ukraine   Vietnam

Copyright © 2010 by Oxford University Press, Inc.

Published by Oxford University Press, Inc.
198 Madison Avenue, New York, New York 10016

www.oup.com

Oxford is a registered trademark of Oxford University Press

All rights reserved. No part of this publication may be reproduced,
stored in a retrieval system, or transmitted, in any form or by any means,
electronic, mechanical, photocopying, recording, or otherwise,
without the prior permission of Oxford University Press.

Library of Congress Cataloging-in-Publication Data

Zen masters / edited by Steven Heine and Dale S. Wright.
   p. cm.
Includes bibliographical references and index.
ISBN 978-0-19-536764-5; 978-0-19-536765-2 (pbk.)
1. Zen priests—Biography. I. Heine, Steven, 1950–   II. Wright, Dale Stuart.
BQ9298.Z36   2010
294.3092'2—dc22
[B]   2009029582

Printed in the United States of America
on acid-free paper

Preface

In contrast to most other forms of Buddhism, sacred literature in Chan or Zen consists primarily of religious biographies, or stories about the lives of Zen masters. The emergence of these narratives, often in anecdotal style, concerning the practices and teachings of Zen masters in the late Tang and early Song dynasties in China, provided new and vivid models for what it meant to be awakened. Iconic images of these often irreverent, blasphemous patriarchs spread quickly, and became the basis of a new school that rose to prominence throughout East Asia.

In this sense, Zen masters in China, and soon thereafter in Korea and then Japan, were among the cultural leaders of their times. Stories about their personal powers and radical styles of comportment were circulated and studied, gaining popularity with the scholar-officials and literati of that era. Poets and writers, as well as statesmen and even emperors, traveled great distances to meet the famous teachers, to witness firsthand their unusual forms of discourse and behavior, and to hear the teachings and practices they initiated. The practice of these Zen patriarchs and the literature that valorized them created, in effect, a new kind of Buddhism and a novel image of enlightenment that held inspirational power for centuries.

Moreover, it was the image of the Zen master that first focused the attention and interest of the literary and cultural avant-garde on Buddhism in the United States and Europe during the twentieth century. Beat writers such as Jack Kerouac in the 1950s, in addition to creative artists and musicians of various stripes, were inspired by stories about Zen masters that had begun to emerge from translations and descriptive accounts of how Zen was practiced in premodern East Asia. Contemporary artists and thinkers were intrigued by the disruptive, transgressive, and sacrilegious behavior of Zen patriarchs, the unusual and dynamic language in which their teachings were expressed, and the transformations of mind and character that were thought to have given rise to these distinctive styles of comportment.

Although there are various kinds of genealogical continuity that have identified Zen in relation to other forms of Buddhism over the centuries, there is also an evolutionary narrative to be told about the image of the Zen master, the way it has unfolded over the centuries. In each era of Zen history, we can see the emergence of new personality or behavioral features that alter the identity of Zen to some extent. What it means to be a Zen master changes over time. Essays in this volume highlight which elements of Zen identity came into focus in the various periods of history by showing how each of these factors stands in relation to earlier and subsequent models of the ideal teacher.

The focus of these essays is on the "image" of the Zen master as it has been projected over the past millennium by the classic literature of this tradition. More than anything else, this image is what has made Zen Buddhism famous, both throughout East Asia since the ninth century and now around the globe as Zen spreads into every major cultural center in the world. For this purpose, we have selected ten important Zen masters from different historical periods and different geographical areas ranging from medieval China to modern Japan and contemporary America.

Among the issues addressed by the essays in this volume are: the personality and charismatic elements that define each Zen master; the relationships each master is thought to have had with teachers, rivals, and disciples; the lines of transmission that were received and then granted to disciples; the forms of behavior and comportment that have shaped the image of the Zen master; the primary teachings for which the Zen master has become known; the main practices that the Zen master taught and emphasized; the sayings, slogans, and catchphrases that epitomize the approach of the Zen master; the historical and social context in which the Zen master lived and taught; the representations, icons, and symbols with which the Zen master has been identified; the enduring influences and contemporary images that have derived from each Zen master; and the techniques and methods used by the classic texts to project and maintain the image that has made each of these Zen teachers famous.

Each essay in this volume undertakes an analysis of one Zen master in terms of how he represents certain ideals and the ways these have at once affected and been received by the tradition. The Zen masters that we have chosen to structure this volume begin with four of the most famous Chinese patriarchs. Mario Poceski examines Baizhang, traditionally credited with formulating the code of behavior that regulates life in a Zen monastery. Dongshan, who is dealt with by Taigen Dan Leighton, was the traditional cofounder of what is known today as the Sōtō (C. Caodong) sect, one of two primary forms of Zen Buddhism in Japan. Albert Welter evaluates the Zen image of Yanshou, a famous medieval master known for philosophical prowess as well as his efforts to incorporate devotional practices into Zen. Dahui, perhaps the most famous master in the later history of Chinese Zen, known for his systematization of kōan or gongan study, is explicated by Miriam Levering.

Following this section on famous Chinese patriarchs, we take up four different images of the Zen master in Japan and two East Asian missionaries who helped Zen spread in the West. First, Steven Heine assesses the image of Dōgen, Japan's most famous thinker and founder of the Sōtō tradition in Japan. Moving through Japanese history, David Riggs takes up the renowned Menzan, formulator of many of the practices that have come down into contemporary Japanese Sōtō Zen. Michel Mohr treats Shaku Sōen, Japan's representative from the Rinzai sect to the World Parliament of Religions in 1893 and the first to champion Zen in the West. Hisamatsu Shin'ichi, the twentieth-century Zen master who most effectively inspired a global Zen movement, is examined by Christopher Ives. Dale Wright puts a contemporary Zen master in the context of this history of Zen images by assessing the extent to which Maezumi Roshi of the Los Angeles Zen Center typifies the image of the Zen master that has been formulated in the classical model. Finally, Sorching Low discusses Seung Sahn, who was the first Korean Zen master to found a Zen school in the West.

The following sums up the book's coverage of masters in historical perspectives:

Tang China	Baizhang, Dongshan
Song China	Yanshou, Dahui
Kamakura Japan	Dōgen
Tokugawa Japan	Menzan
Modern Japan	Sōen, Hisamatsu
Asians in America	Maezumi, Seung

Further, this represents five masters of the Rinzai school (Baizhang, Dahui, Sōen, Hisamatsu, Seung), four of the Sōtō school (Donghshan, Dōgen, Menzan, Maezumi), and one syncretist (Yanshou).

Acknowledgments

The editors acknowledge with gratitude the wealth of expertise that Oxford University Press brings to its projects; many thanks to Cynthia Read and her staff for their efficient and expert assistance in bringing this volume to publication. We also thank several people who contributed to the editing of the manuscript, including Christina Donahue, Liettel Ortega, Anna Scharnagl, Jennifer Garcia, and Therese Sollien.

Contents

Contributors, xiii

Abbreviations, xvii

Note on Terminology, xix

1. Monastic Innovator, Iconoclast, and Teacher of Doctrine: The Varied Images of Chan Master Baizhang, 3
   Mario Poceski

2. Dongshan and the Teaching of Suchness, 33
   Taigen Dan Leighton

3. Yongming Yanshou: Scholastic as Chan Master, 59
   Albert Welter

4. Dahui Zonggao (1089–1163): The Image Created by His Stories about Himself and by His Teaching Style, 91
   Miriam L. Levering

5. Dōgen, Zen Master, Zen Disciple: Transmitter or Transgressor? 117
   Steven Heine

6. The Zen of Books and Practice: The Life of Menzan Zuihō and His Reformation of Sōtō Zen, 147
   David Riggs

7. The Use of Traps and Snares: Shaku Sōen Revisited, 183
   Michel Mohr

8. True Person, Formless Self: Lay Zen Master Hisamatsu Shin'ichi, 217
   Christopher Ives

9. Humanizing the Image of a Zen Master: Taizan Maezumi Roshi, 239
   Dale S. Wright

10. Seung Sahn: The Makeover of a Modern Zen Patriarch, 267
    Sor-Ching Low

Index, 287

Contributors

Steven Heine is professor of religious studies and history and director of the Asian Studies Program at Florida International University. Heine has published numerous books and articles dealing with the life and thought of Dōgen and the history and philosophy of Zen Buddhism, including *Dōgen and the Kōan Tradition: A Tale of Two Shōbōgenzō Texts*; *Shifting Shape, Shaping Text: Philosophy and Folklore in the Fox Kōan*; *Opening a Mountain: Kōans of the Zen Masters*; *Did Dōgen Go to China? What He Wrote and When He Wrote It*; and *Zen Skin, Zen Marrow: Will the Real Zen Buddhism Please Stand Up?*

Christopher Ives is professor and chair of religious studies at Stonehill College; his scholarship focuses on modern and contemporary Zen ethics. His publications include *Imperial-Way Zen: Ichikawa Hakugen's Critique and Lingering Questions for Buddhist Ethics* (2009); *Zen Awakening and Society* (1992); a translation of philosopher Nishida Kitarō's *An Inquiry into the Good* (cotranslated with Abe Masao, 1990); a translation of Hisamatsu Shin'ichi's *Critical Sermons of the Zen Tradition* (co-translated with Tokiwa Gishin, 2002); *The Emptying God* (coedited with John B. Cobb, Jr., 1990); and *Divine Emptiness and Historical Fullness* (edited volume, 1995).

Taigen Dan Leighton teaches at Loyola University, Chicago and online at the Institute of Buddhist Studies of the Graduate Theological Union, Berkeley, and is also a Soto Zen Priest and Dharma heir. Leighton is author of *Faces of Compassion: Classic Bodhisattva*

Archetypes and Their Modern Expression and *Visions of Awakening Space and Time: Dōgen and the Lotus Sutra*. He is editor and cotranslator of *Dōgen's Extensive Record: A Translation of the Eihei Kōroku; Cultivating the Empty Field: The Silent Illumination of Zen Master Hongzhi;* and *Dōgen's Pure Standards for the Zen Community: A Translation of Eihei Shingi;* as well as writing or translating various other books and articles.

Miriam Levering is professor of religious studies at the University of Tennessee. Her area of specialization is in Song dynasty Chan literature. Her publications include the edited volume *Rethinking Scripture: Essays from a Comparative Perspective* (1989), and *Zen: Images, Texts, Teachings* (2000).

Sor-Ching Low is an assistant professor of religion studies at Muhlenberg College. She focuses on contemporary Buddhism in the diaspora, as well as art and religion. Her current research is in the indigenizing of Buddhism in America. Low's publications include *Romancing Emptiness*, and *Shakubuku in a Global Age* (forthcoming). She also reviews for *Philosophy East and West*.

Michel Mohr is an assistant professor of religious studies at the University of Hawaii. His research focuses on Japanese religions and intellectual history, with a special emphasis on the Tokugawa and Meiji periods. Recent publications include the contribution "Beyond Awareness: Tōrei Enji's Understanding of Realization in the Treatise on the Inexhaustible Lamp of Zen, Chapter 6" for *Buddhist Philosophy: Essential Readings* (2009), and chapters for three volumes in this series: *The Kōan* (2000), *Zen Classics* (2006), and *Zen Ritual* (2008).

Mario Poceski is an associate professor of Buddhist studies and Chinese religions at the University of Florida. A specialist in the history of Chinese Buddhism, he is the author of *Ordinary Mind as the Way: The Hongzhou School and the Growth of Chan Buddhism* (2007) and *Introducing Chinese Religions* (2009). Poceski's publications also include two other books and a number of articles and chapters on various aspects of Buddhist studies.

David E. Riggs is currently a research associate at Oberlin College, where he has taught in the Religion Department. He has also taught at the University of California Santa Barbara and the University of Illinois. He received his Ph.D. from the University of California Los Angeles, where his dissertation was entitled, "The Rekindling of a Tradition: Menzan Zuihō and the Reform of Japanese Sōtō Zen in the Tokugawa Era."

Albert Welter is professor of religious studies at the University of Winnipeg, specializing in Chinese Buddhism. His previous publications include *The Linji lu and the Creation of Chan Orthodoxy: The Development of Chan's Records of Sayings Literature;* and *Monks, Rulers, and Literati: The Political Ascendancy of Chan Buddhism*. He is currently working on a book on Yongming Yanshou's view of Chan.

Dale S. Wright is David B. and Mary H. Gamble Professor of Religious Studies and Asian Studies at Occidental College. His area of specialization is Buddhist philosophy, particularly Huayan Buddhism and Chan/Zen Buddhism. His publications include *Philosophical Meditations on Zen Buddhism*; *The Six Perfections: Buddhism and the Cultivation of Character*; and coedited with Steven Heine, *The Kōan: Texts and Contexts in Zen Buddhism*; *Zen Canon: Understanding the Classic Texts*; *Zen Classics: Formative Texts in the History of Zen Buddhism*; and *Zen Ritual: Studies of Zen Buddhist Theory in Practice*.

Abbreviations

C.   Chinese
DZZ   *Dōgen zenji zenshū*, edited by Kagamishima Genryū, Kawamura Kōdō, Suzuki Kakuzen, Kosaka Kiyū et al. 7 vols. Tokyo: Shunjūsha, 1988–1993.
FKM   Fukuzawa Kankei monjo (unpublished microfilms).
J.   Japanese
K.   Korean
S   Sōtōshū Zensho Kankōkai, edited by *Sōtōshū zensho*. Revised and enlarged ed. 18 vols. Tokyo: Sōtōshū Shūmuchō, 1970–1973.
Skt.   Sanskrit
SZ   *Shaku Sōen zenshū*, edited by Matsuda Take no shimabito. 10 vols. Tokyo: Heibonsha, 1929–1930.
T.   *Taishō shinshū daizōkyō*, ed. Takakusu Junjirō and Watanabe Kaigyoku, 100 vols. (Tokyo: Taishō issaikyō kankōkai, 1924–1932).
XZJ   *Xu zang jing* (rpt. J. *Dai Nihon zoku zōkyō*), 150 vols. (Taipei: Shin wen fang, n.d.).
ZS   Zoku Sōtōshū Zensho Kankōkai, edited by *Zoku Sōtōshū zensho*. 10 vols. Tokyo: Sōtōshū Shūmuchō, 1974–1977.
ZZ   *Zoku zōkyō* [*Dai Nihon zokuzōkyō*]. Kyoto: Zōkyō shoin, 1905–1912.

Note on Terminology

There are a number of terms in this volume, both English and foreign words that are common in Buddhist studies, that are used in various ways by the contributors, either italicized or romanized, with caps or in lowercase, as one word or separated, or with or without hyphens. Rather than enforcing uniformity in style, we have left these as the author intended. In addition, please note that some authors have chosen to use diacritical marks for Sanskrit terms but others have not.

Zen Masters

1

Monastic Innovator, Iconoclast, and Teacher of Doctrine: The Varied Images of Chan Master Baizhang

Mario Poceski

Over the centuries, diverse Chan or Zen traditions throughout East Asia have venerated Baizhang Huaihai (749–814) as one of the greatest Chan teachers of the Tang era (618–907). Baizhang (known in Japanese as Hyakujō Ekai) is widely recognized as the leading disciple of the renowned Mazu Daoyi (709–788), the "founder" of the Hongzhou school that came to dominate the Chan movement during the mid-Tang period. Because of his broad renown and perceived historical importance, Baizhang's name and religious persona are often featured in various Chan texts and other pertinent sources, most of them composed from the early Song period (960–1279) onward. Baizhang's high standing in the pantheon of Chan worthies is primarily based on broad appreciation of his putative roles as the originator of Chan monasticism and key exemplar of an iconoclastic ethos celebrated in traditional Chan lore. Even today, he is still widely evoked as a source of religious authority or inspiration, and he remains one of the most recognized Chan teachers of all time.

  As subsequent generations of Chan/Zen writers and adherents formulated and wrote down their visions of Chan orthodoxy, they imputed aspects of their ideological agendas and religious sentiments back to Baizhang and other Chan teachers from the same era. In so doing, they refashioned Baizhang's image in light of changing religious, institutional, and historical circumstances. Although some elements of that hagiographic transformation were unique to Baizhang, on the whole they closely mirrored the ways in which communal remembrances of the great monks from the Tang period were repackaged as part of an ongoing rewriting of Chan history. Accordingly, critical examination of the hagiographic transformations of leading Chan teachers, such as Mazu and Baizhang, provides us with valuable insights about the Chan school's larger historical trajectories and ideological repositionings. That includes improved appreciation and understanding of the socioreligious predicaments and cultural constraints that shaped the growth and diffusion of Chan beyond the Tang era—in China, Japan, and elsewhere.

This chapter is a study of those kinds of changing perceptions and shifting images, in addition to being a source of information about the historical person that is behind those images. I focus on three key hagiographic transmutations of Baizhang's religious persona: paradigmatic Chan iconoclast, patron saint of Chan monasticism, and sophisticated teacher of Chan doctrine and contemplative practice. The chapter includes five main sections. I start with a biographical summary of the life of Baizhang, which includes a survey of his early life as a scion of one of the most powerful clans of Tang China, early study of Buddhism and training under Mazu, subsequent creation of a monastic community at Baizhang mountain, and training of disciples during the last two decades of his life. The second section explores the general ways in which the Chan tradition remembered or reconstituted its past, in large part by creating and revising hagiographic narratives about Chan teachers such as Baizhang. The next three sections each takes separately one of the aforementioned hagiographic transformations of Baizhang. These evolving representations of Baizhang's religious persona, I argue in the conclusion, mirror the multifaceted and far-reaching changes that marked the Chan school's historical trajectory as a major tradition of East Asian Buddhism.

Baizhang's Life

Baizhang was born into a privileged background in 749, toward the end of the glorious reign of Emperor Xuanzong (r. 712–756).[1] He was a scion of the prominent Wang clan of Taiyuan (now the capital of Shanxi province), although at the time his family resided in Fuzhou (now the capital of Fujian province).[2] His clan had a long and illustrious history, and was among the most prestigious aristocratic clans in the Tang empire. Although we do not have detailed information about Baizhang's childhood, it is safe to assume that he received at least some classical education, as was common for sons of families of that social standing. He was still in his teens when he entered monastic life as a novice (*chujia*, literally, "leave home"). At that time he was given the monastic name Huaihai (Embracing the Sea). His tonsure master was a little-known monk called Huizhao, who originally hailed from Guangdong province in the south of China. Another famous disciple of the same monk was Yaoshan Weiyan (745–828), who later also became a student of Mazu and a leading Chan teacher of his era.[3]

Baizhang received the full monastic precepts in 767 from a Vinaya teacher called Fazhao. His ordination as a full-fledged monk (Skt. *bhiksu*; C. *biqiu*) took place at a monastery in Nanyue (literally, "The Southern Peak"), the famous mountain in Hunan that was the location of many Buddhist and Daoist monasteries. Also known as Hengshan, the mountain was also a popular site of pilgrimage and was one of the Five Sacred Peaks of China, a grouping of religiously important mountains that were especially associated with Daoism. After his ordination, Baizhang traveled northeast and settled in what is now Anhui province. There he dedicated himself to scriptural reading and doctrinal study. After doing that for two or three years, around 770 he traveled to southern Jiangxi. There he met Mazu for the first time at Gonggong Mountain, where Mazu had already been residing for well over a decade. At that point, the young Baizhang joined the growing monastic community as a disciple of Mazu.[4]

Soon after Baizhang's arrival at Gonggong Mountain, Mazu was invited by the provincial governor to move to Hongzhou, the capital of Jiangxi (present-day Nanchang). Baizhang and other disciples followed Mazu to his new position as the abbot of Kaiyuan Monastery in Hongzhou. Mazu's new monastery was an official monastic establishment, part of a network of monasteries with the same name that was established by Emperor Xuanzong and was supported by the imperial government. Baizhang remained at Kaiyuan Monastery until Mazu's death in 788, by which time Mazu had become arguably the best known and most influential Chan teacher in China.

Mazu had many disciples, more than any other Chan teacher of the Tang era. His disciples came from virtually all parts of China, and after their study with him many of them went on to establish new monastic congregations all over the sprawling Tang empire.[5] At the time of Mazu's death, Baizhang did not particularly distinguish himself, nor did he stand out among the most senior and prominent disciples. His relatively modest standing among Mazu's surviving disciples at that point is acknowledged in his stupa inscription. While the inscription is full of praise about Baizhang's virtue and wisdom, it also offers a rather lame excuse for the omission of Baizhang's name from the list of prominent disciples that was included at the end of the prose section of Mazu's stele inscription. The reason for the omission, we are told, was that Baizhang was very humble and completely unconcerned about fame or status:

> Baizhang's words were succinct and his reasoning was insightful. His physical appearance was affable and his spirit was lofty. He was respectful to all those he encountered and he slighted himself wherever he stayed. Being virtuous, he did not seek any renown. Therefore, in the stele inscription of his late teacher Mazu, only his name did not appear in the list of main disciples.[6]

Initially Baizhang's elder dharma brother Xitang Zhizang (735–817), who was among Mazu's most senior and respected disciples, took the leadership of the remaining monastic community in Hongzhou.[7] Baizhang then moved to Letan monastery at Shimen (Stone Gate) Mountain (also situated in Hongzhou prefecture), which was Mazu's resting place and the site of his memorial pagoda. From there he later moved to Baizhang (Hundred Zhang) Mountain, at the invitation of local patrons.[8] Also known as Daxiong (Great Hero or Greatly Imposing) Mountain, Baizhang Mountain was located in the vicinity of Shimen. At the time, that was a fairly isolated area, and Baizhang was the first monk associated with the Chan school to establish a monastery there.

During the final two decades of his life, Baizhang remained at the mountain. There he trained numerous disciples, although not nearly as many as his teacher Mazu. Some of his disciples became prominent Chan teachers and established their own monastic congregations. Among them, by far the best known are Guishan Lingyou (771–853) and Huangbo Xiyun (d. 850?), both of whom were widely recognized by the later tradition as being the leading Chan teachers of their generation. After Baizhang's death, the abbotship of the monastery on Baizhang Mountain was passed on to one of his senior disciples, and for a long time it remained a major center of Chan practice. Seven years after Baizhang's passing away, in 821, the Tang imperial government granted him the posthumous appellation of "Chan teacher of great wisdom" (Dazhi chanshi). Subsequently Baizhang came to be recognized as the foremost disciple of Mazu, although Chan sources from the post-Tang period usually list him and Xitang together as Mazu's two main disciples, with Nanquan Puyuan (748–834) also joining the exclusive list at a later stage, to form a troika of chief disciples.[9]

Along with his fame as the patron saint of Chan monasticism (see below), Baizhang's prominent standing within the later Chan tradition was to a large extent based on his inclusion (along with Huangbo) in the direct ancestral line of transmission that linked Linji Yixuan (d. 866), the "founder" of the Linji school of Chan (known as Rinzai in Japanese), with Mazu. That established the notion of an "orthodox" line of transmission, with the names of four dominant Chan teachers from the Tang era at its core:

Mazu → Baizhang → Huangbo → Linji → all later Chan masters in the Linji/Rinzai line of transmission

During the Song era, the Linji school became the most influential Chan faction and the main line of transmission. It was also transmitted to Korea and Japan, where it assumed dominant positions. These developments further buttressed Baizhang's position as a prominent Chan figure, whose image and persona are indelibly linked with the (real and imagined) glories of the Tang era. Over the centuries Baizhang remained a permanent fixture in traditional Chan lore, and to this day his name is frequently evoked in diverse Chan or Zen circles.

Hagiography in Three (or More) Keys

Remembering, recording, and reconfiguring of the past were all essential elements in the broad historical processes by way of which the Chan school fashioned its identity as a distinct tradition within Chinese Buddhism. That was especially the case during the Tang-Song transition, but it is also applicable to subsequent periods in Chan history. At different historical junctures, Chan writers and adherents created new or revised quasi-historical narratives by selectively remembering or reimagining their tradition's past. Often that was undertaken in response to specific institutional developments or changing socioreligious predicaments. This process was influenced by established traditions of Buddhist historiography, which played important roles in the demarcation of orthodoxy and the shaping of religious identities in medieval (and later) Chinese Buddhism. Within that context, the positioning of Chan "history" as the central narrative within a broader chronicling of the Buddhist past was as concerned with legitimizing the present and reshaping the future of the Chan school as it was with the compiling of factually accurate accounts of bygone events.

Communal remembrances or ingenious reinventions of the past have traditionally played important roles in the construction of religious identities across a broad spectrum of religious traditions—past and present, in China and elsewhere. Although these processes are not unique to the Chan school, in general they have played an especially important role in its historical growth and transformation, and have often taken forms that are unique to it. Accordingly, a useful way of understanding the Chan school and situating it within a broad historical framework is to look at it as a community of memory, in which the past and the present are closely interlinked and mutually reinforcing. Throughout the whole sweep of Chan history, an enduring feature that underscored virtually all of its beliefs, ideological suppositions, ritual observances, and spiritual practices was the perpetual looking backward in time, with a focus on the lives of paradigmatic figures such as Baizhang and on seminal events in which they were allegedly involved.

The tendency to look back toward the past became especially predominant during the early Song period—although elements of it were already present in the Tang era—and remained a major factor from that point onward. That was reflected in the continuous invocation or allusion to the Buddha's awakening, which was domesticated and integrated into the Chan school's myth of origins. With an adroit, mythologizing sleight of hand, Chan writers and historians brought into China the central event and high point of Buddhist spirituality—symbolized by the image of Buddha sitting under the *bodhi* tree in India—via a putative lineage of patriarchs that featured seminal figures such as Bodhidharma (fl. late fourth and early fifth centuries), who was widely celebrated as the first Chan patriarch in China.[10] The focal point of the historical gaze, however, were the great glories of Tang Chan, chiefly represented by the words and deeds of such luminaries as Huineng (638–713), the celebrated "sixth patriarch," Mazu, and Baizhang. During the early Song era, when the Chan movement as a whole was reconfigured and repositioned as the main tradition of elite Buddhism in the newly reunified empire, this propensity was expressed in the form of an ongoing dialogue—or rather a monologue—with the past, as evident in the important Chan chronicles and other records compiled during that period. Within that context, the past was interpreted in light of cumulative traditions, but also in terms of current concerns and exigencies.

When looking at the Chan school as a community of memory, we can readily appreciate the inherently conservative tendencies that usually lurk behind its habitually lofty rhetoric and iconoclastic posture. As we carefully examine the provenance, character, and function of traditional historical narratives, we begin to see how the larger historical trajectories of Chan Buddhism can be construed as a series of creative interpretative distortions, which were both expressions of religious piety and tools of ideological dominance. The main medium for such creative remembrance and reconstitution of the past were the monastic hagiographies of great Chan teachers such as Baizhang, which from the mid-tenth century onward increasingly came to feature quaint stories—some perhaps real, but for the most part invented—about their dramatic acts and inscrutable statements.

Hagiographic elements are copiously included in a broad range of texts composed in the various Chan genres and in other sources used for the study of Tang (and Song) Chan. Hagiographic modes of narration are especially central in the Chan records of sayings (*yulu*) and the transmission of the lamp (*chuandeng*) histories, which contain a wealth of information about Chan history and doctrine, albeit often of an uncertain provenance.[11] They also perform important functions in the various *gong'an* (or *kōan* in Japanese) collections, such as *Biyan lu* (Blue Cliff Record) and *Wumen guan* (Gateless Pass). The Chan monastic codes (*qinggui*, literally, "rules of purity") represent the only major Chan genre that does not prominently incorporate hagiographic components, although in the case of Baizhang his hagiography is a major part of most texts associated with this genre.[12] Hagiographic retellings of the monastic lives of noted Chan teachers are also central to other important textual sources, such as the stele inscriptions (*beiming*) composed for individual monks and the collections of biographies of eminent monks (*gaoseng zhuan*), which by the Song era came to be dominated by the hagiographies of Chan teachers, as evident in Zanning's (919–1001) influential *Song gaoseng zhuan* (Biographies of Eminent Monks from the Song Era), composed in 988.[13] Hagiographic pieces also appear in various local gazetteers (*difangzhi*), especially those that cover areas where major monasteries led by Chan monks were situated.

When we look at the various texts that provide information about Baizhang's life and his teachings, we can uncover several layers of materials that present different images of him. Although it is possible that a medieval monk such as Baizhang could have had a complex and multifaceted personality, a closer examination of the texts where these contrasting images appear reveals that they were composed at different times, and in response to different needs and circumstances. Therefore, these assorted modulations or revisions of Baizhang's religious persona convey distinct images of him as a major historical actor that left notable imprints on Chan history. As was suggested in the introduction to this chapter, my analysis of the extant literature ascertained several textual strata and distinct narrative modes. These can be organized into distinctive images or modes of representation of Baizhang, each with its own provenance. Consequently, we are faced with divergent hagiographic portrayals of Baizhang's life and his role as a Chan teacher, presented in three distinctive keys: Chan iconoclast in the classical mold; patron saint of Chan monasticism; and learned teacher of doctrine and contemplative practice. At times, two or even all three of them are mixed together into a single text—for instance, in Baizhang's biography in *Jingde chuandeng lu* (Jingde Era Record of the Transmission of the Lamp) published in 1004—which points to the origins of such texts as compilations that drew on a variety of sources.[14]

The depictions of Baizhang as a paradigmatic Chan iconoclast are primarily found in the kind of popular stories that form the central element of traditional Chan lore. This mode of representation is not unique to Baizhang, as it was applied to virtually all prominent Chan teachers from the second half of the Tang era, starting with Mazu, as well as to their spiritual descendants who lived during the Five Dynasties era (907–960). In contrast, the traditional image of Baizhang as the creator of a unique pattern of monastic life and patron saint of Chan monasticism is unique to him, although the legend in which it is imbedded played important functions in later Chan history that transcended the singular significance of Baizhang as a historical individual. Finally, the divergent image of Baizhang as a sophisticated teacher of doctrine, who is at ease with both the philosophical and contemplative aspects of Buddhism, is based on the earliest strata of sources about his teachings.[15] Although this representation of Baizhang has been largely ignored within Chan and Zen circles over the centuries—and still continues to be largely unknown and unacknowledged at the present—in my recent study of the Hongzhou school I showed that it was not unique to Baizhang, but was representative of the lives and teachings of other noted Chan teachers from the same period, especially those affiliated with the Hongzhou school.

If we were to look beyond Baizhang's hagiographic representations, there are a few further interpretive possibilities. The records of his teacher Mazu and other Tang monks suggest additional ways in which Chan masters were remembered or envisaged, for instance as thaumaturges, poets, or popular religious figures. A case in point is the depiction of Mazu as a thaumaturge, albeit of a peculiar Chan type, presented in his biographies in *Song gaoseng zhuan* (Song Biographies of Eminent Monks) and *Zutang ji* (Hall of the Patriarchs Collection). In one of these stories he is depicted as a tamer of malevolent demons that dwelled on Gonggong Mountain and terrorized the local populace at the time of his arrival in the area.[16] In another story, he saves the learned but arrogant and spiritual undeveloped abbot of Da'an monastery in Hongzhou from the demon of death.[17] Furthermore, the image of an exemplary Chan poet is amply represented in the records about the life of Mazu's disciple Pang Yun (d. 808), who came to be celebrated not only for his poetic achievements but also for his role as a paradigmatic Chan layman.[18]

Paradigmatic Iconoclast

The most common and best-known cluster of imagery associated with the orthodox or classical Chan tradition, especially in the style that purportedly flourished during the Tang era, revolves around dramatic portrayals of Chan teachers' iconoclastic acts and outlandish statements. In their standard variety, these representations of notable Chan monks from the Tang period come to us in the form of numerous short stories and vignettes. These kinds of accounts, which inhabit unstable or alterable intersections of legend and history, constitute a literary format that contemporary scholarship often refers to as "encounter dialogue" (*jiyuan wenda* or *kien mondō* in Japanese). These stories are prominently featured in a wide range of classical Chan texts, especially the various *gong'an* collections, transmission of the lamp histories, and records of sayings. The main heroes of the encounter dialogue anecdotes are Chan teachers such as Mazu and Baizhang, who typically are depicted as incorrigible iconoclasts bent on subverting conventional mores and rejecting established religious traditions. The Chan teachers featured in these stories dispense their wisdom in an array of peculiar or unconventional ways, which include shouts and beatings that are meted out to their eager disciples.

The encounter dialogue stories embody a unique iconoclastic ethos that by the early Song period came to be portrayed as a central element of Chan spirituality. In the course of the subsequent historical growth and transformation of Chan teachings and institutions across East Asia, such depictions of Chan iconoclasm were canonized and refracted via the interpretative prisms of later Chan/Zen traditions in China, Japan, and elsewhere. The popular images of Chan iconoclasts found especially receptive audiences in the West, ever since they were first introduced by D. T. Suzuki (1870–1966) during the early twentieth century as a crucial component in his repackaging of Zen for Westerners. They became accepted as emblematic expressions of a timeless and unique form of Chan spirituality among Western audiences that were largely unfamiliar with the historical forms or expressions of Chan institutions, beliefs, and practices. For a variety of reasons, such representations resonated with the intellectual or religious sensibilities of Zen practitioners and aficionados, and they remained with us even as Zen became an integral part of popular culture, along with being a viable topic of intellectual enquiry or artistic expression.

As is the case with other prominent Chan monks from the Tang era, classical Chan texts often present Baizhang as an embodiment of the aforementioned iconoclastic ethos. In classical Chan literature there are a number of encounter dialogue stories that feature him either as the main protagonist or in a supportive role. These stories span his whole life, from the first childhood visit to a local Buddhist temple to his final days as an abbot of a sizable monastic congregation and an influential Chan teacher. Here is one well-known example from his early years, which purports to depict his formative training under Mazu's tutelage:

One day as the Baizhang accompanied Mazu for a walk, they heard a cry of wild duck. Mazu asked, "What kind of sound is that?"

Baizhang replied, "It is a cry of wild duck."

After a while, Mazu asked, "Where is the sound gone?"

Baizhang said, "It has flown away."

Mazu turned his head, grabbed Baizhang's nose, and pulled it out. Baizhang cried out with pain. Mazu then said, "And yet, you said it has flown away." On hearing that, Baizhang had an insight.[19]

This story contains most of the main elements of the encounter dialogue format. Here we have a Chan teacher and his student engaged in a spirited exchange that incorporates enigmatic statements and dramatic acts, including certain amount of symbolic and physical violence. In a familiar Chan fashion, the story ends with the student's insight into the profound truth that was supposedly communicated by the teacher's unconventional pedagogical technique (if it can be called that).[20] Some Chan texts also include a couple of follow-ups to this exchange between Mazu and Baizhang, which adhere to a similar pattern. The related exchanges are filled with conventional tropes and incorporate dramatic elements often encountered in stories of this kind. In one of them we find Baizhang both crying and laughing at the monks' residence in the company of a fellow monk. That is followed by another seemingly bizarre incident that features Baizhang rolling up his bowing mat in front of Mazu, which in a later version of the story elicits a shout from Mazu.[21]

There are variations among the different extant versions of these exchanges, which is quite common among encounter dialogues of this kind. Generally speaking, later versions of the stories tend to be more elaborate and to include a greater number of illogical or iconoclastic elements.[22] Here is an example of another well-known story that once again features Mazu and Baizhang:

When Baizhang went to see Mazu again, Mazu took his whisk and held it upright. Baizhang said, "It is that function; it leaves that function." Mazu put the whisk back at its old place.

After a while, Mazu asked, "Later, when you open your mouth, what are you going to tell other people?" Baizhang took the whisk and held it upright.

Mazu said, "It is that function; it leaves that function." Baizhang put the whisk back at its old place.

Mazu gave a shout, which made Baizhang temporarily deaf for three days.[23]

In other stories we come upon Baizhang as a mature Chan teacher who interacts with his own disciples. Below I present a couple of such examples. The first case comes in the form of a dialogue between Baizhang and his disciple Guishan, who became one of the most prominent Chan teachers of the late Tang era. Subsequently, Guishan also came to be known as the "cofounder" of the Guiyang school of Chan.[24] That was the earliest of the so-called Five Schools of Chan, which during the Song era were recognized as the core orthodox lines of transmission:

> Once when Baizhang and Guishan were engaged in manual labor, Baizhang asked, "Do you have any fire?"
> "I have," replied Guishan.
> Baizhang then asked, "Where is it?"
> Guishan took a branch of brushwood, blew into it, and then gave it to Baizhang.
> After receiving it, Baizhang said, "This is like an insect gnawing on wood."[25]

The second illustration is an oft-quoted exchange between Baizhang and an anonymous monk that is meant to convey Baizhang's fondness for Daxiong Mountain, where his monastery was located. This time the story does not conclude with the student's spiritual awakening, but at the end we witness the by now familiar act of beating:

> A monk asked Baizhang, "What is the most special thing?"
> "Sitting alone on Daxiong Mountain," replied Baizhang. The monk bowed, and Baizhang then hit him.[26]

During the Song era, stories like these were subjected to extensive elaboration and exegesis, prime examples of which are preserved in the influential *gong'an* collections, perhaps best represented by *Biyan lu*. This widely used text was compiled by Yuanwu Keqin (1063–1135) on the basis of an earlier collection composed by Xuedou Zhongxian (980–1052). Xuedou's original text featured a hundred well-known "cases," which were primarily exchanges between noted Chan teachers (mostly from the Tang era) and their disciples, composed in the encounter dialogue format. To these he attached his poems, which were supposed to serve as running commentaries of sorts on the original cases. Yuanwu introduced additional layers of literary complexity by adding commentaries on both the original cases and Xuedou's poems, along with interlinear glosses and introductory pointers. The end result of these literary endeavors was an intricate and multilayered work, written in an ornate language and replete with oblique allusions and obscure metaphors.

The utilization of such elaborate style and involved structure by Yuanwu (and by other authors of similar collections) was to a large extent aimed at meeting the literary tastes, cultural sensibilities, and horizons of expectation of the Song literati, who were major patrons of Chan monasteries. In the process, the historical personage of earlier Chan teachers like Baizhang receded into the background, becoming approachable only via thick layers of meandering poetic and prose commentary or interpretation. This kind of exegesis often seems to have a tenuous connection even with the (mostly) apocryphal contents of the original stories, let alone with the actual lives and teachings of the historical figures that are featured in them. To illustrate that, let us look at what happens with the aforementioned image of Baizhang sitting alone on Daxiong Mountain when it is appropriated and integrated into a text such as *Biyan lu*. In this short passage extracted from case twenty-six in *Biyan lu*, we have Xuedou's commentary in the form of a four-line verse, along with Yuanwu's interlinear glosses (set in parenthesis), which are supposed to be explaining the original exchange between Baizhang and the anonymous monk who asked him about the most special thing:

> In the ream of the patriarchs gallops a heavenly colt. (Such a person is born only once in every five hundred years. Among a thousand or ten thousand individuals, there is but one or a half. The son [Baizhang] takes on the work of the father [Mazu].)
>
> Among the expedient teachings, rolling out and rolling up are not the same paths. (It is already so before any words have been uttered. Baizhang gains freedom, which is a matter of his adepts' methods.)
>
> In a flash of lightening or a spark coming from stone, he retains the ability to change in accord with circumstances. (He came head-on, turning to the left, turning to the right. Do you still see if Baizhang is helping people or not?)
>
> How laughable: a person comes to grab the whiskers of a tiger! (He deserves thirty blows. Where there is a great reward, there must be a valiant person. He does not shy away from losing his body and his life. I leave this move to you, venerable sir.)[27]

The earliest examples of Chan stories composed in the encounter dialogues format can be traced back to the middle of the tenth century, as we can see from their inclusion in *Zutang ji*, composed in 952 in the kingdom of Min (909–945), located in southeastern China (corresponding to present-day Fujian province). In Baizhang's case, that is about a century and a half after his death. The earlier sources about his life and teachings, including his stupa inscription, do not contain any stories of this kind. As I have shown in a previous publication, none of the encounter dialogue stories or exchanges, neither those that feature Baizhang nor any other Chan monk, can be traced back to the Tang period.[28] From what we know, the encounter dialogue format was not even known during the Tang dynasty. Consequently, it is erroneous to assume that it was a major mode of instruction or communication used in Chan circles, which until recently was the operative assumption in both popular and scholarly writings on Chan history and literature.

The initial emergence of the encounter dialogue model as the quintessence of an iconoclastic ethos that was unique to the Chan school occurred during the Five Dynasties–Song transition. Popular stories that feature the outlandish acts or inscrutable ramblings of Baizhang and other noted Chan teachers from the Tang era became key elements of traditional Chan lore only during the Song period. Subsequently they remained focal points in an ongoing process of reimagining or reconfiguring Tang Chan, within (and also beyond) the various Chan/Zen milieus that grew and thrived across East Asia. The stories about Baizhang recounted above—and all other similar stories—thus need to be read as apocryphal or legendary narratives, in the sense of being reflections of Song-era efforts at creating a new image of Baizhang that fit into a particular religious prototype, which was communicated via a predetermined and formulaic mode of narration.

The fashioning of that iconoclastic image was linked to the growth of a nascent Chan orthodoxy that became dominant during the Song era, which had its own institutional concerns and ideological suppositions. Accordingly, the stories recounted above need to be placed within the relevant historical context, and interpreted in relation to the traditions that produced and disseminated them. At its core, the fashioning of the iconoclastic image of Baizhang presented here involved a creative hagiographic process, which conveyed novel religious ideals and reflected a far-reaching reformulation of Chan orthodoxy. An important part of that change was the legitimization of Song Chan by retroactive attribution of assorted religious ideals and images back to Baizhang and other great Chan teachers from the Tang era.

Patron Saint of Chan Monasticism

One of the best-known sayings associated with Baizhang is the dictum "a day without work is a day without food." This oft-cited statement is said to succinctly convey the Chan school's embrace of manual labor as an essential part of its monastic paradigm, as well as an integral aspect of its comprehensive program of spiritual cultivation. In the institutional arena, the egalitarian ideal conveyed by Baizhang's dictum is linked with the Chan school's presumed spirit of economic self-sufficiency, which is often taken to be a cornerstone of its unique style of monastic life. The context in which Baizhang purportedly came up with the "a day without work is a day without food" dictum is told in a story that dates back to the Song era. Set at the monastic community on Baizhang Mountain, the story describes how the elderly Baizhang refused to eat when his disciples tried to prevent him from unduly exerting himself in the fields, as was his habit, by hiding his work tools:

> Baizhang toiled hard whenever he was engaged in [manual] labor, always going ahead of the monastic congregation. All the monks could not endure that, so they secretly took away his tools and asked him to take rest. Baizhang said, "I am a person without any virtue. How can I cause trouble for others?" He then went on to look for his tools everywhere, but was unable to find them. Consequently, he failed to take his meal. Because of that, there is the saying, "a day without work is a day without food," which became widely known all over the world.[29]

This story is part of a well-known legend about Baizhang, which depicts him as the originator of a new system of rules and procedures for organizing monastic life. According to the legend, at his monastery Baizhang established the first autonomous monastic community that marked the Chan school's incipient independence from the rest of Buddhism. That was accompanied by his codification of new monastic rules that were unique to the Chan tradition. Because of that, over the last millennium generations of Chan adherents have celebrated Baizhang as the founding father and patron saint of "Chan monasticism," even though the symbolic meanings associated with the Baizhang legend assumed broader significance, as its multifaceted connotations transcended the historical reality of a single person. As a result, the assumed role of an important monastic leader and legislator became a key part of Baizhang's religious persona. His accomplishments in that area were linked with the belief that he composed an influential monastic code, usually referred to by the title *Baizhang qinggui* (Baizhang's Rules of Purity), which was subsequently lost. Later Chan monastic codes composed during the Song and subsequent dynasties evoked the spirit of Baizhang's original code and alleged to contain elaborations of its basic ideals and principles.

The earliest mention of Baizhang's founding of a distinct Chan monastery goes back to the late tenth century. That seminal event is recalled in a passage embedded in Baizhang's biography in *Song gaoseng zhuan*.[30] The same information is also presented, in a somewhat modified form, at the beginning of "Chanmen guishi" (Rules for the Chan School), a short but influential text that is appended to Baizhang's biography in *Jingde chuandeng lu*. Here is the *Jingde chuandeng lu* version of the traditional account about the events and considerations that led to Baizhang's decision to establish a separate Chan monastery:

> From the initial establishment of the Chan school [in China] by [the first patriarch] Bodhidharma until after the time of [the sixth patriarch] Huineng, its followers mostly resided in Vinaya monasteries.[31] Although they occupied separate monastic compounds, they did not yet have their own system of rules regarding [such matters as] preaching the Dharma or [procedures associated with] abbotship. Being constantly concerned with such state of affairs, Baizhang stated, "I wish for the way of the patriarchs to spread widely and enlighten the multitudes. If we are to hope that in the future it will not come to an end, how can we afford to follow the practices of the various Hīnayāna traditions?"[32] . . . Baizhang then said, "Our [Chan] school does not belong to either the Mahāyāna or the Hīnayāna tradition. Neither does it differ from either Mahāyāna or Hīnayāna. We should carefully consider both of them, and then establish monastic rules that will include them both in a harmonious way, while also being appropriate to the needs of the present situation." With that in mind, Baizhang initiated the establishment of a separate Chan community.[33]

The same text then goes on to briefly describe Baizhang's introduction of supposedly innovative features in the structuring of Chan practice and the organization of monastic life. While generations of Chan scholars and adherents have interpreted that as a major paradigm shift in the history of Chinese monasticism, on closer inspection Baizhang's assumed innovations turn out not to be revolutionary or unique to the Chan school. During the Song era, the notion that Baizhang was the first Chan teacher to institute separate rules, meant for a new type of a monastic community, became a central element of Chan belief and ideology. Furthermore, the supposed rejection of the hallowed Vinaya tradition—which, being imported from India, had canonical basis and sanction—came to be perceived as a seminal event in the history of Chinese Buddhism. That has been construed as a key point in the Chinese transformation of the "foreign" religion, when monastic institutions and observances at long last became truly Sinicized.

The Baizhang legend was subsequently picked up by the various Chan abbots who wrote comprehensive monastic codes for the running of their and other Chan monasteries, which became a distinct and officially recognized type of Buddhist establishment only during the Song era. The author of the earliest and one of the most important texts in that genre, Changlu Zongze (d. 1107), evoked the Baizhang legend as a source of inspiration for his monastic code. In his *Chanyuan qinggui* (Rules of Purity for Chan Monasteries) he linked his rules to those contained in the code composed by Baizhang.[34] The same sort of connection is also implied in *Chixiu Baizhang qinggui* (Imperial Edition of the Baizhang Rules of Purity), compiled by Dongyang Dehui in 1338, which was more comprehensive than its predecessors and became widely used in Chinese monasteries throughout the late imperial period.[35] Because of that connection, Baizhang came to be perceived as one of the historically most significant Chan figures. Some later Chan text even compared his stature to those of Bodhidharma and Huineng, arguably the two most revered Chan patriarchs of all time.[36]

On the basis of widespread beliefs about Baizhang's important role in the development and codification of Chan monastic life, from the Song period onward his image was featured prominently in the hall of patriarchs (*zu tang*), just to the right of Bodhi-dharma, who occupied the central position as the founding Chan patriarch.[37] That building was an important element in the architectural layout of Chan monasteries. It served as an ancestral hall for the resident monastic community, which was represented by the current abbot, and housed the ancestral tablets of the previous abbots of the monastery. This practice was grounded in traditional religious culture, as the hall of patriarchs performed functions similar to those of Confucian temples or ancestral shrines built by well-heeled families.

Because of his status as a key monastic ancestor, Baizhang was given special memorial services. These were important ritual occasions in the monastic calendar. The main ceremonial observances were presided over by the abbot and were attended by the whole congregation. *Chixiu Baizhang qinggui* contains fairly elaborate description of the various liturgical elements that were included in the memorial service dedicated to Baizhang, which took place in the Dharma hall. That included the setting up of a special altar that contained the image of Baizhang, along with the making of sacrificial offerings, the chanting of scriptures, the ritualized offering of incense, the performance of prostrations, and the intoning of special prayers and invocations.[38] The same text also contains flowery words of praise that extol Baizhang's virtue and highlight his importance, which in part read as follows:

When he spoke, that became the law of the land. It marked the norm and established the standard [for all to follow]. Over the course of myriad generations, the Way he instituted is known as being worthy of reverence. It contains [key] principles and precedents on the basis of which a harmonious way of life has ever since flourished in [Chan] monasteries, which have produced many notable religious personalities. . . . Regardless of whether one follows a particular norm or departs from it, the words avoid the weight and subtlety [of thought?]. Regardless of whether one departs from a particular occasion or enters into it, the principle permeates the multitude of wonders. It is proper to worship him in the company of the Chan patriarchs.[39]

The Baizhang legend and its connection with the emergence of Chan monasticism have received sustained and substantial amounts of scholarly attention. Early scholarship, most of which was presented by Japanese scholars, took for granted the historicity of Baizhang's role as a monastic innovator and presumed that there was an actual code that he composed for his monastic community.[40] That led to various efforts to reconstruct the contents of the lost Baizhang code, typically on the basis of later sources, which were read in light of normative Zen views and romanticized imagining of Tang Chan. Eventually some scholars started to doubt the existence of Baizhang's code, and even question Baizhang's historical role in the codification of Chan monastic life.[41] We now know that the story about Baizhang's creation of a unique system of Chan monasticism is the stuff of legend, and is not connected in any meaningful way with Baizhang as a historical person. Similarly, the search for establishing the contents of his lost code turned out to have been a futile academic exercise, since by now it is fairly clear that no such text ever existed.

There is no evidence from the Tang era about Baizhang's creation of distinctive Chan monastic rules, nor is there any intimation of the existence of a new system of Chan monastic life that was institutionally separate from mainstream Buddhist monasticism.[42] Furthermore, *Guishan jingce* (Guishan's Admonitions), an important text on Chan practice and monastic discipline composed by Baizhang's disciple Guishan, reveals how after Baizhang's death his disciples and other monks associated with the Hongzhou school continued to adhere to traditional monastic mores and ideals.[43] The same attitudes remained prevalent during the final decades of the Tang dynasty, as can be seen from "Shi guizhi" (Teacher's Regulations), the earliest monastic code written by a Chan teacher that is still extant, composed in 901 by Xuefeng Yicun (822–908).[44] Even the actual rules and monastic innovations that are attributed to Baizhang in "Chanmen guishi," and are further elaborated and expanded in *Chanyuan qinggui*, turn out for the most part to be based on various Vinaya rules, to be derived from monastic customs that were not unique to the Chan tradition, or to be influenced by common Chinese cultural practices and ritual observances.[45]

To sum up, the legend about Baizhang's creation of a new system of Chan monastic rules had tenuous connection at best with actual events in the life of Baizhang. It also tells us little about the historical realities of Tang Chan. During the Song era the legend gradually became a centerpiece of an expansive narrative about the consolidation of Chan into a distinct Buddhist tradition with its own institutional moorings and a distinct pattern of monastic life. Accordingly, the hagiographic transmutation of Baizhang into the patron saint of Chan monasticism is indicative of important changes that took place within the Chan school in the course of its historical growth and transformation during the Tang-Song transition. Here we have a prime illustration of how the Chan school, or at least some of its influential leaders, responded to changing historical predicaments and navigated key ideological and institutional realignments. A central element of that was the creative reconfiguring or reinventing of its past, a notable expression of which was the hagiographic transmutation of Baizhang into the patron saint of Chan monasticism.

Teacher of Doctrine and Contemplative Practice

If the depictions of Baizhang as an indomitable iconoclast and patron saint of Chan monasticism were developed and disseminated by later generations of writers and Chan adherents, what about the historical person to whom that kind of imagery was retroactively ascribed? As we transpose ourselves into the medieval world of Tang China, what can we say about the actual religious personas of Baizhang and other Chan teachers like him, or at least about their perception among contemporaries? And what about their teachings and the responses they elicited among select Tang audiences? Some of the recent Western scholarship about Chan has exhibited a tendency to question the traditional reliance on textual sources and the objectivist historians' quest for factual knowledge about early Chan figures and teachings. That has resulted in thinking about Chan history as a literary artifact, in which noted Chan patriarchs such as Bodhidharma and Huineng are treated as textual paradigms rather than as historical persons.[46]

To some degree, the introduction of these kinds of critical perspectives has been useful in terms of moving scholarship away from naïve reliance on traditional sources and interpretations. It has also helped shed light on slanted historical reconstructions of Chan history in terms of normative interpretative templates or ideological supposition that exude latent sectarian biases. However, at times these trends have led to broad mischaracterizations of key features of Tang Chan, which usually go together with a tendency to gloss over the actual lives and contributions of notable historical actors. While it is, of course, important to trace the development of key literary transmutations of major Chan figures such as Baizhang, or of the movements they belonged to, that should not lead to scholarly neglect of historical analysis of their lives and teachings, set against the backdrop of the appropriate social, religious, intellectual, and institutional contexts. In addition, we cannot fully understand or appreciate the Song (or later) perceptions and imaginings of Tang figures—or of the whole of Tang Chan as the tradition's golden age—if we do not have adequate knowledge about the historical actualities of Chan monks, or if we are unable to ascertain the contours of their teachings, as they existed during the Tang era.

It is true that Baizhang's religious persona is somewhat elusive, as we can only approach it on the basis of limited literary artifacts. The same applies to his teachings. At the same time, by making good use of the available sources, and by situating them within the pertinent religious, intellectual, and social milieus, we can arrive at a clearer picture of Baizhang's life and teachings, as they unfolded during the mid-Tang period.[47] The picture that emerges from the early sources, especially Baizhang's stupa inscription and his *Extensive Record* (*Baizhang guang lu*) represents a striking contrast with the hagiographic representations surveyed in the previous two sections.[48] The *Extensive Record* is an especially valuable source of information about Baizhang's teachings, and it is also among the most valuable resources for the study of Chan doctrine from the Tang period.

The image of Baizhang conveyed by the Tang-era sources is that of a learned and sagacious monk who is well versed in both the theoretical and contemplative aspects of medieval Chinese Buddhism. Here we encounter Baizhang as a teacher of a particular Chan brand of Buddhist doctrine, formulated in a manner and idiom that are unique to him and to the Hongzhou school as a whole. Nonetheless, he also comes across as someone who is cognizant of major intellectual trends in Tang Buddhism, as well as deeply steeped in canonical texts and traditions. His discourses are filled with scriptural quotations and allusions. He also often resorts to technical Buddhist vocabulary, of the kind one usually finds in the texts of philosophically oriented schools of Chinese Buddhism such as Huayan, Faxiang, and Tiantai. Here the primary mode in which Baizhang communicates his teachings is the public Chan sermon, presented in the ritual framework of "ascending the [Dharma] hall [to preach]" (*shangtang*).[49]

In the Tang context we find Baizhang assuming a traditional role of Dharma teacher, albeit of a peculiar kind that developed within the religious milieu of the Chan school. Seated on a high seat in the main hall of his monastery, he offers fairly detailed instructions about Chan doctrine and practice. From what we can gather, the solemn audience to whom his teachings and exhortations were directed was primarily constituted of his monastic disciples, although he also preached to laymen. In form and content, the sermons he gives represent idiosyncratic modulations of prevalent forms of preaching rituals, which collectively constituted a key element of medieval Chinese Buddhism. On the whole, here we are on familiar Buddhist ground. Furthermore, in this narrative context, Baizhang operates within a fairly conventional institutional framework.

Elsewhere I have written in some detail about Baizhang's teachings, so here I will provide only a brief summary of some of the key themes and basic religious outlooks communicated in the extant redactions of his sermons.[50] A central idea that infuses most of Baizhang's sermons is the ineffability or indescribability of reality. Ultimate reality cannot be predicated in terms of conventional conceptual categories, as it transcends the familiar realm of words and ideas. Nonetheless, it can be approached or realized—as it truly is, without any accretions or distortions—as it manifests at all times and in all places. That is done by means of intuitive knowledge, whose cultivation is one of the cornerstones of Chan soteriology.

Since the essence of reality cannot be captured or conveyed via the mediums of words and letters, according to Baizhang it is pointless to get stuck in dogmatic assertions, or to attach to a particular doctrine or practice. Like everything else, the various Chan (or more broadly Buddhist) teachings are empty of self-nature. They simply constitute expedient tools in an ongoing process of cultivating detachment and transcendence that supposedly free the mind of mistaken views and distorted ways of perceiving reality; to put it differently, they belong to the well-known Buddhist category of "skillful means" (*fangbian*, or *upāya* in Sanskrit). Holding on rigidly or fetishizing a particular text, viewpoint, or method of practice—even the most profound and potent ones—can turn out to be counterproductive, as it becomes a source of attachment that impedes spiritual progress. The perfection of the Chan path of practice and realization, therefore, does not involve the attainment of some particular ability or knowledge. Rather, in Baizhang's text it is depicted as a process of letting go of all views and attachment that interfere with the innate human ability to know reality and experience spiritual freedom. Here is a passage from one of Baizhang's sermons in which he elaborates on the ineffability of reality and the subtle processes of mental restructuring and contemplative discernment that lead to its realization:

Fundamentally, this principle is present in everyone. All the Buddhas and Bodhisattvas are called persons who point out a jewel. Originally, it is not a thing. You need not know or understand it; you need not affirm or deny it. Just cut off dualism. Cut off the supposition that it exists and the supposition that it does not exist. Cut off the supposition that it is nonexistent and the supposition that it is not nonexistent, so that there are no traces of either side. Then, when the two sides are brought up, you are unattached to them, and no measures can control you. [In reality,] there is neither deficiency nor sufficiency, neither profanity nor holiness, and neither light nor darkness. That is not having knowledge, yet not lacking knowledge. It is neither bondage nor liberation. It is not any name or category at all. Why is this true speech? How can you carve and polish empty space to make a Buddha image? How can you say that emptiness is blue, yellow, red, or white?[51]

One of the particular doctrinal innovations presented in Baizhang's sermons is his ingenious schematization of a progressive Chan path of spiritual cultivation that involves the perfection of three distinct mental states or ways of knowing (or relating to) reality. In Baizhang's *Extensive Record* they are referred to as the "three propositions" (*sanju*), which can also be understood as three distinctive stages of spiritual realization. The three propositions are: thoroughgoing detachment from all things and affairs; nonabiding in the state of detachment; and letting go of even the subtlest vestiges of self-referential awareness or knowledge of having transcended detachment. They mark key points in a spiritual continuum, which culminates with the realization of ultimate detachment, whereas the mind becomes devoid even of the subtlest elements of ignorance and self-centered awareness.

Taken as a whole, the three propositions are hierarchical and progressive, implying dialectical ascent to increasingly rarefied states of awareness, distinguished by gradually more subtle levels of detachment and transcendence. While each stage rectifies the imperfections and limitations of the preceding stage(s), it also integrates the qualities characteristic of the previous stage(s). This soteriological scheme visibly diverges from normative models that are typically associated with Chan orthodoxy, which prioritize the notion of "suddenness" as the central ordering principle of classical Chan doctrine. Instead of refuting the validity of canonical formulations of the Buddhist path in terms of diverse stages and practices, as we are led to expect from leading Chan teachers of the Tang (and subsequent) eras, Baizhang is introducing an innovative conceptual scheme that takes into account the inevitably gradual character of actual Chan practice. Let us have a closer look at one of Baizhang's explanations of the third and final stage (or proposition):

> Once one does not abide in nonattachment anymore, and does not even engender any understanding of not abiding in it either, then that is the final good. That is the full-word teaching. Such a person avoids falling into the formless realm, avoids falling into meditation illness, avoids falling into the way of the bodhisattvas, and avoids falling into the condition of king of demons. Because of hindrances of knowledge, hindrances of stages, and hindrances of practice, seeing one's Buddha nature is [as difficult as] seeing shapes at night. As it has been said [in the scriptures], at the stage of Buddhahood one obliterates two forms of ignorance: the ignorance of subtle knowledge and the ignorance of extremely subtle knowledge. Therefore, it has been said [in the *Huayan Sutra*] that a man of great wisdom smashes an atom to bring into the world a volume of scripture.[52]

The first sentence defines the third proposition in relation to the first and second propositions (denoted by the expressions "nonattachment" and "not abide in nonattachment," respectively). The text then goes on to describe the genuine and accomplished Chan adept as someone who has realized such rarefied state of wisdom and awareness of reality. There are a couple of things that are striking about this passage, which overall is representative of the form and contents of Baizhang's sermons. First, there is a profusion of technical Buddhist terms, of the kind one usually encounters in canonical sources and exegetical literature: formless realm, meditation illness, way of bodhisattvas, hindrances of practice, Buddha nature, and ignorance of subtle knowledge, to name a few. It is quite remarkable that Baizhang is able to cram so much technical vocabulary into such short passage. That is indicative not only of Baizhang's extensive learning but also of the fact that the monks in his monastery, as well as at least some of the lay disciples who came to hear his sermons, were reasonably familiar with such specialized terminology.

Second, Baizhang's description of the third proposition is capped with a quotation from a well-known canonical text, the *Huayan Sutra* (also referred to as the *Avatamsaka Sūtra* or the *Flower Ornament Scripture*). This kind of scriptural use and invocation of canonical authority are common occurrences in Baizhang's sermons, as well as in the sermons of his teacher Mazu and his disciple Huangbo. The passage in question appears in the "Manifestation of the Tathagata" chapter of the *Huayan Scripture*, and is part of one of the most often quoted sections in this immensely important and popular text.[53] It introduces the metaphor of a limitless scripture—said to be as expansive as the great universe, and to contain knowledge about everything in it—being enclosed within a particle of dust, just as the infinite Buddha wisdom inheres in the mind of each person. As the wise person in the scripture's simile breaks out the particle of dust and releases the mysterious scripture into the world for the benefit of all, likewise by his wise and effective teachings the Buddha enables each person to release the inherent Buddha wisdom from within and manifest it in the world for the sake of all beings.

Concluding Remarks

In this chapter I explored the broad issues of historical remembrance and representation within the Chan tradition by looking at key hagiographic depictions of Baizhang, as revealed in various Chan texts and other pertinent sources. The shifting images and evolving hagiographic representations of Baizhang that were surveyed in the previous pages are reflections of the multifarious and momentous changes that marked the Chan school's historical trajectory as a major tradition, first of Chinese and then of East Asian Buddhism. The ongoing fashioning and transformation of the images of famed Chan teachers like Baizhang had significant ramifications within and beyond the complex evolution of Chan as a distinct Buddhist tradition. It also affected the reception of Chan ideas and teachings among varied audiences in China and elsewhere. In the process, the image and persona of Baizhang underwent notable transformations: from the learned and wise teacher of Chan doctrine and contemplative practice that existed during the Tang era, into the indomitable iconoclast and patron saint of Chan monasticism that became dominant in later Chan lore, starting with the early Song period. As the later images of Baizhang took hold and captured the popular imagination, the learned monk of the Tang era, along with his recondite yet refreshingly direct and perennially relevant teachings, were all but ignored by generations of Chan scholars and practitioners.

Astute analysis of the hagiographic transformations of Baizhang and other Chan monks from the Tang era points to the malleability and fallibility of religiously inflected memories, both individual and communal. It aptly illustrates the prevalence of mythologizing tendencies, historical distortions, pious embellishments, or (dis)ingenuous fabrications in the collective recollections and representations of various Chan groups—as well as their parallels among other religious traditions—as preserved in diverse oral and written narratives. Understanding of these historical and literary processes helps us go beyond traditionalist and homogenizing discourses that highlight the mythos of Chan's uniqueness. Instead, the various sources reveal great diversity and historical complexity, a mélange of elements that span the popular and the elitist, the court-oriented and the localized. By tracing the inventive reimaginings of Tang Chan in light of changing religious predilections, institutional predicaments, and cultural suppositions, we also add nuance to our knowledge of the larger historical trajectories and gradual paradigm shifts that shaped East Asian Buddhism.

The constituting of Chan as a distinct community of memory within Chinese Buddhism involved the development of particular historical patterns of remembering, recording, and reconfiguring the past. That was part of a larger tradition of Buddhist historiography, which reflected the great importance of chronicling and evoking the past in Chinese culture as a whole. Buddhist writers and adherents imaginatively fashioned essential quasi-historical narratives by selectively evoking or reimagining their tradition's past, especially at key junctures in the historical growth of their tradition. That was part of a continuing process that unfolded within the confines of a particular religious tradition, which reflected the inner dynamics of its growth and transformation. At the same time, it was also a response to specific institutional developments and changing socioreligious predicaments that were very broad in scope, going well beyond the confines of Chan or even Buddhism as a whole. For instance, during the early Song period there was a reconfiguration of the social and religious landscapes in the aftermath of the establishment of the new dynasty. That contributed to the institutional and ideological transformations of the Chan school, which amid such circumstances was able to secure its preeminent status as the main tradition of elite Buddhism. It also set in motion far-reaching changes in other key areas, most notably the prevalent forms of literary expression and contemplative practice.

Although I have primarily focused on the key hagiographic transformations of Baizhang that were created during the Tang and Song eras, the same type of analysis can also be extended to subsequent periods and applied to the reception and growth of Chan or Zen in other cultures. To a large extent, subsequent Chan/Zen history can be seen as a series of interpretative distortions, shaped by distinct ideological agendas and centered on creative remembrances or imaginings of Mazu, Baizhang, and the other great sages of yore. That is evident when we look at the revival of Chan that took place in the seventeenth century, during the Ming-Qing transition.[54] The same is largely true of the Kamakura period (1192–1333), when Chan was transmitted into Japan by pioneering figures such as Dōgen Kigen (1200–1253) and Myōan Eisai (1141–1215), as well as of the Tokugawa era (1603–1868), when both the Rinzai and Sōtō sects experienced important revivals and reformations under the dynamic leadership of influential priests such as Hakuin Ekaku (1686–1769) and Manzan

Sōhaku (1636–1715). Similar tropes and hagiographic processes continue to shape the various contemporary manifestations of Chan/Zen across East Asia, for instance, within the Buddhist traditions that presently flourish in Korea and Taiwan.

Key elements of the hagiographic representations of Baizhang continue to crop up not only in East and Southeast Asian contexts but also everywhere else where traditional Chan stories are read, discussed, and reflected upon. We are thus witnessing the continued addition of peculiar new wrinkles to long-standing historical processes, especially in the context of the ongoing globalization of Zen (along with other forms of Buddhism) that increasingly implicates America and Europe into intricate cultural flows that contravene traditional cultural categories and ingrained religious boundaries. In the present age, which is marked by increased connectivity, complexity, and fluidity, we can observe how emerging transcultural frameworks shape current reinterpretations of traditional Chan/Zen teachings and related imagery.[55] For instance, nowadays we might come across a lecture on *kōan* that features Baizhang given at a Zen center in California, or perhaps witness an evoking of the "a day without work is a day without food" adage within the context of a Zen retreat in France.

Consequently, the stories and imagery about the spiritual exploits of Baizhang and other Tang figures continue to be given new meanings in the course of Zen's participation in variable flows of religious ideas, symbols, and practices. Amidst changing personal and communal identities, which are increasingly shaped by global networks that foster cosmopolitan hybridity, the hagiographic transmutations of Baizhang continue to be subjected to new interpretations, but perhaps that is a good topic for another publication.

NOTES

1. This section is based on my previous study of Baizhang's life, included in chapter 2 of my comprehensive study of the history and teachings of the Hongzhou school of Chan; for more details and fuller annotation, see Mario Poceski, *Ordinary Mind as the Way: The Hongzhou School and the Growth of Chan Buddhism* (New York: Oxford University Press, 2007), pp. 49–52.

2. The earliest extant source with reliable information about Baizhang's life is the inscription for his memorial stupa, which was composed by the official Chen Xu soon after Baizhang's passing away; see "Tang hongzhou baizhangshan gu huaihai chanshi taming," in *Quan tang wen* 446 (Shanghai: Shanghai guji chubanshe, 1990), p. 2014a–b, and *Chixiu baizhang qinggui* 8, T. 48.1156b–57a.

3. For Yaoshan's biographies, see *Song gaoseng zhuan* 17, T. 50.816a–c; *Zutang ji* 4 (Changsha: Yuelu shushe, 1996), pp. 102–110; and *Jingde chuandeng lu* 14, T. 51.311b–12c.

4. For Mazu's life, see Poceski, *Ordinary Mind as the Way*, pp. 21–43. The earliest source about his life is his stele inscription, composed in 791 by the famous official and literatus Quan Deyu (759–818); see "Tang gu hongzhou kaiyuansi shimen daoyi chanshi beiming bingxu," preserved in *Quan tang wen* 501, pp. 5106a–07a, and *Tang wenzui* 64 (Hangzhou: Zhejiang renmin chubanshe, 1986), pp. 1058–1059. Another helpful source that contains early data is his biography in *Song gaoseng zhuan* 10; see T. 50.766a–c.

5. See Poceski, *Ordinary Mind as the Way*, pp. 234–236.

6. *Quan tang wen* 446, p. 2014a; translation adapted from Poceski, *Ordinary Mind as the Way*, p. 50.

7. For Xitang, see Poceski, *Ordinary Mind as the Way*, pp. 47–49; Ishii Shūdō, "Kōshūshū ni okeru Seidō Chizō no ichi ni tsuite," *Indogaku bukkyōgaku kenkyū* 40/1 (1991), pp. 280–284; and Ishii Shūdō, *Chūgoku zenshū shiwa* (Kyoto: Zen bunka kenkyūjō, 1988), pp. 199–211.

8. Zhang is a traditional Chinese unit of length; it is roughly equivalent to 3.6 meters or 11 feet 9 inches.

9. See *Jiangxi mazu daoyi chanshi yulu*, XZJ 119.813a; *Jingde chuandeng lu* 6, T. 51.249b–c; and Poceski, *Ordinary Mind as the Way*, p. 59.

10. Notable texts from the Tang era that exemplify this trend include *Lengqie shizi ji* (Record of the Teachers and Disciples of the Lankavatara, compiled in the early part of the eighth century), *Lidai fabao ji* (Record of the Dharma Jewel through Successive Generations, compiled c. 774), and *Baolin zhuan* (Record of the Precious Grove, compiled in 801).

11. For the records of sayings, see Mario Poceski, "Mazu yulu and the Creation of the Chan Records of Sayings," in Steven Heine and Dale Wright, eds., *The Zen Canon: Understanding the Classic Texts* (New York: Oxford University Press, 2004), pp. 53–79; and Albert Welter, *The Linji Lu and the Creation of Chan Orthodoxy: The Development of Chan's Records of Sayings Literature* (New York: Oxford University Press, 2008).

12. For the main texts that belong to the rules of purity genre, see Yifa, *The Origins of Buddhist Monastic Codes in China: An Annotated Translation and Study of the "Chanyuan Qinggui"* (Honolulu: University of Hawaii Press, 2002); Ishii Shūdō, "Hyakujō shingi no kenkyū," *Komazawa daigaku zenkenkyūjo nenpō* 6 (1995): 15–53; and Theodore Griffith Foulk, "*Chanyuan qinggui* and Other 'Rules of Purity' in Chinese Buddhism," in Heine and Wright, eds., *The Zen Canon*, pp. 275–312.

13. For the biographies of eminent monks, see John Kieschnick, *The Eminent Monk: Buddhist Ideals in Medieval Chinese Hagiography* (Honolulu: University of Hawaii Press, 1997).

14. See *Jingde chuandeng lu* 6, T. 51.249b–50c.

15. Each of these distinctive images of Baizhang is described in more detail in the following three sections.

16. *Song gaoseng zhuan* 10, T. 50.766a–b.

17. *Zutang ji* 14, pp. 304–305.

18. See Mario Poceski, "Lay Models of Engagement with Chan Teachings and Practices among the Literati in Mid-Tang China," *Journal of Chinese Religions* 35 (2007): 63–97 (esp. pp. 87–92).

19. *Gu zunsu yulu* 1, XZJ 118.161b; translation adapted from Cheng Chien Bhikshu (Mario Poceski), trans., *Sun-Face Buddha: The Teachings of Ma-tsu and the Hung-chou School of Ch'an* (Berkeley: Asian Humanities Press, 1992), pp. 100–101. See also *Tiansheng guangdeng lu* 8, XZJ 135.655a.

20. For examples of scholarly articles that present the encounter dialogues format as a distinctive pedagogical technique or path of spiritual practice, see John R. McRae, "Encounter Dialogue and the Transformation of the Spiritual Path in Chinese Ch'an," in Robert E. Buswell Jr. and Robert M. Gimello, eds., *Paths to Liberation: The Mārga and Its Transformations in Buddhist Thought* (Honolulu: University of Hawaii Press, 1992), pp. 339–369; and Robert E. Buswell Jr., "The 'Short-cut' Approach of *K'an-hua* Meditation: The Evolution of Practical Subitism in Chinese Ch'an Buddhism," in Peter N. Gregory, ed., *Sudden and Gradual: Approaches to Enlightenment in Chinese Thought* (Honolulu: University of Hawaii Press, 1987), pp. 321–377 (esp. pp. 334–338). This kind of viewpoint also resonates with the views of Yanagida and other contemporary Japanese scholars.

21. See *Gu zunsu yulu* 1, XZJ 118.161b–62a, and Cheng Chien, *Sun-Face Buddha*, pp. 101–102. See also the similar version of the story in *Tiansheng guangdeng lu* 8, XZJ 135.655a.

22. See Yanagida Seizan, "Goroku no rekishi: Zen bunken no seiritsu shiteki kenkyū," *Tōhō Gakuhō* 57 (1985): 570–571; and Mario Poceski, "The Hongzhou School during the Mid-Tang Period," Ph.D. dissertation, University of California, Los Angeles, 2000), pp. 108–110.

23. *Guzunsu yulu* 1, XZJ 118.161b–62a; translation adapted from Cheng Chien, *Sun-Face Buddha*, p. 102. For different versions of this exchange, see *Baizhang huaihai chanshi yulu* (in *Sijia yulu* 2), XZJ 119.817b, and *Jingde chuandeng lu* 6, T. 51.249c.

24. For traditional accounts of Guishan's life and teachings, see *Jingde chuandeng lu* 9, T. 51.264b–66a; *Zutang ji* 16, pp. 359–363; and *Song gaoseng zhuan* 11, T. 50.777b–c. For a study of the Guiyang school, see the series of articles by Ishii Shūdō: "Igyōshū no seisui (1–6)," *Komazawa daigaku bukkyō gakubu ronshū* 18–22, 24 (1985–1991, 1993).

25. *Baizhang huaihai chanshi yulu*, XZJ 119.819b–20a; *Zutang ji* 14, p. 317; and *Jingde chuandeng lu* 6, T. 51.249c–50a.

26. *Baizhang huaihai chanshi yulu* (in *Sijia yulu* 2), XZJ 119.818b. See also *Tiansheng guangdeng lu* 8, XZJ 135.655b; and *Biyan lu* 3, T. 48.166c. The last one is translated in Thomas Cleary and J. C. Cleary, trans., *The Blue Cliff Record* (Boston: Shambala, 1992), pp. 172–175.

27. *Biyan lu* 3, T. 48.167a; translation adapted from Cleary and Cleary, *The Blue Cliff Record*, p. 174.

28. Poceski, "Mazu yulu and the Creation of the Chan Records of Sayings."

29. *Baizhang huaihai chanshi yulu*, XZJ 119.820b. See also *Zutang ji* 14, p. 317; *Tiansheng guangdeng lu* 8, XZJ 135.658a; *Wudeng huiyan* 3, XZJ 138.91a; and *Chixiu*

baizhang qinggui 2, T. 48.1119b. The same quote appears in many other classical Chan texts, and the "a day without work is a day without food" dictum is also often mentioned in modern Chan/Zen literature.

30. *Song gaoseng zhuan* 10, T. 50.770c. See also Zanning's brief remark about the same event in his historical survey of Chinese Buddhist monasticism, *Da song sengshi lüe*, T. 54.240a–b.

31. "Vinaya monasteries" is a literal translation of *lüsi*. Here it is used in the sense of monasteries regulated by the Vinaya, that is, conventional Buddhist monasteries. This is sometimes misinterpreted to mean monasteries that belonged to a separate Vinaya school or sect.

32. The text refers to Hinayana by the alternative term Agama, which is usually used to denote the various collections of "Hīnayāna" scriptures.

33. *Jingde chuandeng lu* 6, T. 51.250c–51a. For a complete English translation of "Chanmen guishi," see Martin Collcutt, "The Early Ch'an Monastic Rule: *Ch'ing kuei* and the shaping of Ch'an Community Life," in Whalen Lai and Lewis Lancaster, eds., *Early Ch'an in China and Tibet* (Berkeley: Asian Humanities Press, 1983), pp. 165–184. The account of the same event that is included in Baizhang's biography in *Song gaoseng zhuan* adds the following remark: "Everywhere the Chan school was like grass bending under the blowing of [strong] wind. The independent practice of the Chan school started with Huaihai [i.e., Baizhang]." T. 50.270c.

34. For an English translation of the first seven fascicles of this text, see Yifa, *The Origins of Buddhist Monastic Codes in China*.

35. For an English translation, see Shohei Ichimura, trans., *The Baizhang Zen Monastic Regulations* (Berkeley: Numata Center for Buddhist Translation and Research, 2006).

36. For instance, see the comparison with Bodhidharma in *Chixiu baizhang qinggui* 8, T. 48.1157b–c.

37. See *Chixiu baizhang qinggui* 2, T. 48.1117c; Ichimura, *The Baizhang Zen Monastic Regulations*, p. 50; and Foulk, "Myth, Ritual, and Monastic Practice in Sung Ch'an Buddhism," in Patricia Buckley Ebrey and Peter N. Gregory, eds., *Religion and Society in T'ang and Sung China* (Honolulu: University of Hawaii Press, 1992), pp.172–173.

38. *Chixiu baizhang qinggui* 2, T. 48.1118b; Ichimura, *The Baizhang Zen Monastic Regulations*, pp. 56–57.

39. *Chixiu baizhang qinggui* 2, T. 48.1118b–c; the translation is adapted from Ichimura, *The Baizhang Zen Monastic Regulations*, pp. 57–58.

40. The scholarly works that presume the existence of Baizhang's code are too numerous to list all of them. Here are some of the more notable examples: Ui Hakuju, *Zenshū shi kenkyū*, vol. 2 (Tokyo: Iwanami shoten, 1941), pp. 375–395; Kagamishima Genryū, "Hyakujō shingi no seiritsu to sono igi," (Aichi Gakuin Daigaku) *Zen kenkyūjo kiyō* 6 and 7 (1976): 117–134; Kagamishima Genryū et al., trans., *Yakuchū: Zennen shingi* (Tokyo: Sōtōshū Shūmuchō, 1972), pp. 1–3; Yanagida Seizan, "Chūgoku zenshū shi," in Nishitani Keiji, ed., *Zen no rekishi: Chūgoku* (Tokyo: Chikuma shobo, 1967), pp. 58–60; Suzuki Tetsuo, *Tō-godai no zenshū: Konan, kōsei hen* (Tokyo: Daitō shuppansha, 1984),

pp. 142–143; Sato Tatsugen, *Chūgoku bukkyō ni okeru kairitsu no kenkyū* (Tokyo: Mokujisha, 1986), pp. 479–489; Tanaka Ryōshō, *Tonkō zenshū bunken no kenkyū* (Tokyo: Daitō shuppansha, 1983), pp. 469–476; Kenneth Ch'en, *The Chinese Transformation of Buddhism* (Princeton: Princeton University Press, 1973), pp. 148–151; and Shohei Ichimura, *The Baizhang Zen Monastic Regulations*, pp. xiii–xix.

41. For instance, see Kondō Ryōichi, "Hyakujō shingi seiritsu no yōin," *Indo tetsugaku bukkyōgaku* 2 (1987): 231–246; Ishii Shūdō, "Hyakujō shingi no kenkyū," pp. 15–53; Theodore Griffith Foulk, "Myth, Ritual, and Monastic Practice in Sung Ch'an Buddhism," pp. 147–208 (esp. pp. 156–159); and Mario Poceski, "Xuefeng's Code and the Chan School's Participation in the Development of Monastic Regulations," *Asia Major, Third Series* 16/2 (2003): 33–56 (esp. pp. 35–41).

42. There is a set of five rules that were allegedly inscribed next to Baizhang's stūpa inscription, which appear in a post-Tang source. See *Chixiu baizhang qinggui* 8, T. 48.1157a, and Yifa, *The Origins of Buddhist Monastic Codes in China*, 34. The five items are narrow in scope, and they consist of fairly conventional regulations that are not in any way unique to Chan.

43. For an analysis of this text, see Mario Poceski, "*Guishan jingce* (Guishan's Admonitions) and the Ethical Foundations of Chan Practice," in Steven Heine and Dale Wright, eds., *Zen Classics: Formative Texts in the History of Zen Buddhism* (New York: Oxford University Press, 2005), pp. 15–42. For the original Chinese text, see XZJ 114.928a–39b, and XZJ 111.284a–296b.

44. For a study and translation of this text, see Poceski, "Xuefeng's Code and the Chan School's Participation in the Development of Monastic Regulations." For the original Chinese text, see XZJ 119.972b–73a, and Yanagida Seizan, ed., *Zengaku sōsho*, vol. 3 (Kyoto: Chūbun shuppansha, 1973), pp. 278–279. A modern Japanese translation can be found in Ishii, *Chūgoku zenshū shiwa*, pp. 480–482.

45. See Yifa, *The Origins of Buddhist Monastic Codes in China*, pp. 53–98.

46. For example, see Bernard Faure, *Chan Insights and Oversights: An Epistemological Critique of the Chan Tradition* (Princeton: Princeton University Press, 1993), pp. 110–135. Echoes of some of the same ideas can also be found in John R. McRae, *Seeing through Zen: Encounter, Genealogy, and Transformation in Chinese Chan Buddhism* (Berkeley: University of California Press, 2003), esp. pp. 1–15, 24–28.

47. An example of that is the brief biographical reconstruction of Baizhang's life presented at the beginning of this chapter.

48. For the Chinese text of Baizhang's *Extensive Record*, see *Baizhang guang lu*, in *Guzunsu yulu* 1, XZJ 118.164b–71b, and XZJ 119.821a–22b; it is translated into English in Thomas Cleary, trans., *Sayings and Doings of Pai-chang* (Los Angeles: Center Publications, 1978). For more on the provenance and history of this text, see Poceski, *Ordinary Mind as the Way*, pp. 241–242.

49. For a study of the *shangtang* rituals that covers the Tang as well as later periods of Chan/Zen history, see Mario Poceski, "Chan Rituals of Abbots' Ascending the Dharma Hall to Preach," in Steven Heine and Dale Wright, eds., *Zen Ritual: Studies of Zen Theory in Practice* (New York: Oxford University Press, 2008), pp. 83–111, 299–304.

50. See Mario Poceski, *Ordinary Mind as the Way*, pp. 131–132, 162–168, 203–219. In the book, the discussion of Baizhang's teachings is integrated into a large study of the Hongzhou school's doctrines and practices.

51. *Baizhang guang lu*, XZJ 118.166a; quoted in Poceski, *Ordinary Minds as the Way*, p. 182. See also Cleary, *Sayings and Doings of Pai-chang*, pp. 34–35.

52. *Baizhang guang lu*, XZJ 118.165a; quoted in Poceski, *Ordinary Minds as the Way*, p. 209. See also Cleary, *Sayings and Doings of Pai-chang*, p. 31.

53. See *Dafang guangfo huayan jing* 51, translated by Śikṣānanda (652–710), T. 10.272c; and Cheng Chien Bhikshu (Mario Poceski), *Manifestation of the Tathāgata: Buddhahood According to the Avatamsaka Sūtra* (Boston: Wisdom, 1993), pp. 105–106.

54. For a comprehensive study of Chan during this period, see Jiang Wu, *Enlightenment in Dispute: The Reinvention of Chan Buddhism in Seventeenth-Century China* (New York: Oxford University Press, 2007).

55. For an insightful theoretical discussion of the study of contemporary mobile religion in terms of networks, see Manuel A. Vásquez, "Studying Religion in Motion: A Networks Approach," *Method and Theory in the Study of Religion* 20 (2008):151–184.

2

Dongshan and the Teaching of Suchness

Taigen Dan Leighton

Dongshan Liangjie (807–869, J. Tōzan Ryōkai), one of the most prominent teachers of Tang dynasty Chan, is considered the founder of the Caodong lineage, one of the Chan "five houses."[1] After it was transmitted to Japan by Eihei Dōgen (1200–1253), this lineage was known as Sōtō Zen, and it is now a significant factor in the transporting of Buddhism to the West. As founder of one of the five houses, Dongshan has a major impact in the classic Chan/Zen literature attributed to the legendary Tang dynasty masters. It is generally accepted by modern scholars that the *Recorded Sayings* and *Transmission of the Lamp* documents attributed to Tang masters are often not historically reliable, as many of them, including Dongshan's record, were not recorded until well after the teacher lived.[2] But in this chapter, rather than analyzing the historicity of the material attributed to Dongshan, I will consider material in his *Record Sayings* and in major kōan collections as it has been transmitted as exemplary of Chan lore.

The *Recorded Sayings* attributed to Dongshan include many stories of encounter dialogues between Dongshan and his teachers, and then with his students. Many of these stories also appear in varied forms in the classic kōan collections (many published before the various *Recorded Sayings* anthologies). Dongshan's *Recorded Sayings* also includes various teaching verses attributed to Dongshan. Dongshan is perhaps best known for the teaching poem, "The Jewel Mirror Samadhi" (C. *Baojing Sanmei*, J. *Hōkyō Zammai*), which is also considered the first enunciation of the teaching of the five ranks or degrees that is the dialectical philosophy underlying much of Caodong, and indeed Chan discourse as a whole. Most discussions of Dongshan focus on this five ranks teaching.[3] One modern Chinese commentator, just before presenting an extensive discussion of the five ranks and Dongshan's related teachings, ironically states, "This doctrine and others like it are not of central importance in the teachings of Tung-shan's school [Tung-shan is the Wade-Giles transliteration for Dongshan]. They are merely expedient means or pedagogical schemata for the guidance of the less intelligent students. It is regrettable that historians of Chan have a tendency to treat these incidents as essentials and to ignore the true essentials altogether."[4] Indeed, although the five ranks stand as an important theoretical product of Dongshan's teaching, there is much more to the practical unfolding of the teachings attributed to Dongshan. "The Jewel Mirror Samadhi," still chanted as an important part of the liturgy in modern Sōtō Zen, begins, "The teaching of suchness is intimately transmitted by buddhas and ancestors." Selected passages from this poem will be discussed at the end of this chapter (and the five ranks more briefly), but its first line provides two of the central issues in the writing and stories attributed to Dongshan, which will be the two focal topics addressed here.

The first topic is the nature of suchness, and the Zen process of engaging this level of reality through the practice of meditative attention. Many of the central stories about Dongshan relate to recognizing, exploring, or expressing reality, or the suchness of things. Known in Sanskrit as *tathata*, this suchness is described in Indian Buddhism as ultimate truth, reality, the source, or the unattainable.[5] This classic Buddhist teaching becomes an important touchstone in the material related to Dongshan.

The second issue will be the teaching itself, how this reality is "intimately transmitted." Many of the stories about Dongshan concern his subtle style of teaching, the Zen pedagogy for conveying the truth of suchness. The approaches to the teaching that Dongshan experienced with his teacher Yunyan Tansheng (781–841; J. Ungan Donjō), and that are later reflected in Dongshan's own engagement with his students, are especially elusive and slippery. This reflects both the subtle nature of the reality to be conveyed and the importance of the student's own personal experiential realization of this reality.

These two main issues of suchness and approaches to its teaching will be addressed in three contexts. First, I will closely explore the stories about Dongshan's own training, his relationship to his teachers, and the circumstances of his own awakening and receiving of Dharma transmission. These stories focus explicitly on the issues of the nature of reality, and the complexity of the relationship of Chan student and master. The second section will more briefly discuss a number of the encounter dialogues about Dongshan and his own disciples, and how they elucidate the issues of suchness and Chan teaching. Finally, this chapter will briefly describe how these two issues are reflected in passages from "The Jewel Mirror Samadhi," and as they are related to the five ranks teaching.

Dongshan's Training in Suchness

The story of his first meeting with his teacher Yunyan involves Dongshan's questioning as to whether nonsentient beings could expound the Dharma. The story, as presented in Dongshan's *Recorded Sayings*, is extensive and rather elaborate, and is distinctive and even eccentric in how it emphasizes the issues of the nature of Dharma, or reality, and the strategies for conveying it. The story can be summarized as follows. Dongshan first inquired about this question with the great teacher Guishan Lingyou (771–853; J. Isan Reiyū), who is considered the founder of one of the other five houses of Chan. Dongshan repeated to Guishan a story he had heard about a lengthy exchange with a student by National Teacher Nanyang Huizhong (d. 776; J. Nan'yō Echū), who maintained that nonsentient beings did indeed expound the Dharma, constantly, radiantly, and unceasingly.[6] Huizhong states, perhaps ironically, that fortunately he himself cannot hear the nonsentient beings expounding, because otherwise the student could not hear his teaching. The National Teacher provides a scriptural source for the expounding by nonsentient beings from the *Avatamsaka Sutra* (Flower Ornament; C. *Huayan*, J. *Kegon*), citing the passage, "The earth expounds Dharma, living beings expound it, throughout the three times, everything expounds it."[7]

After narrating this story, Dongshan asked Guishan to comment, and Guishan raised his fly-whisk. When Dongshan failed to understand and asked for further explanation, Guishan averred that, "It can never be explained to you by means of one born of mother and father." Dongshan would later refer to such nonexplanation with appreciation. Guishan finally suggested that Dongshan visit Yunyan for further illumination on this question.

This issue of nonsentient beings' relation to the Dharma had arisen over the previous couple centuries in Chinese Buddhist thought in relationship to the teaching of buddha-nature, which describes the potentiality for awakening in beings. This potentiality of buddha-nature is also sometimes presented as an aspect of the nature of reality itself. A century before Dongshan, Tiantai scholar Zhanran (711–782; J. Tannen) articulated the teaching potential of grasses and trees, traditionally seen as inanimate and thus inactive objects.[8] Zhanran devoted an entire treatise to explicating the buddha-nature of nonsentient things, though previously the Sanlun school exegete Jizang (549–623; J. Kichizō) had argued that the distinction between sentient and nonsentient was empty, and not viable.[9] Jizang says that if one denies buddha-nature to anything, "then not only are grasses and trees devoid of buddha-nature, but living beings are also devoid of buddha-nature."[10] Zhanran's view of nonsentient beings' Dharmic capacity reflected in part his interest in Huayan cosmology, with its vision of the world as a luminous ground of interconnectedness and with the mutual nonobstruction of particulars. This anticipated Guishan's citation of the *Huayan* or *Avatamsaka Sutra* to Dongshan. Zhanran cited the Huayan school patriarch Fazang's dynamic view of "suchness according with conditions" to support his own teaching of the buddha-nature of nonsentient beings, and was the first to connect "the co-arising of suchness and the essential completeness of Buddha nature."[11] For Zhanran, "the very colors and smells of the world around us constitute the Assembly of the Lotus [Sutra]; they are the immediate and undefiled expression of buddhahood."[12] Thus a central inference of the discussion of nonsentient beings expounding the Dharma presented in Dongshan's stories is the limitation, and ultimate inaccuracy, of usual and conventional human notions of sentient and nonsentient, and of awareness.

The teaching of suchness involved in this story is not a matter of mere human psychological or perceptual realities, but is grounded in ontological reality as a primal expression of buddha-nature. We might also hear, in this question about the Dharmic capacity of nonsentient beings, modern concerns about our human relationship to the environment, and even ecological consciousness. What is the role of the phenomenal world and the world of nature to human spirituality? How might one discern the value of supposedly nonsentient elements of the natural order to a vision of spiritual wholeness and awakening?

A noteworthy implication of the historical context to this story is the degree to which Chan discourse responds to and comments on scholarly Chinese Buddhist teaching. This is so despite the widely proclaimed Chan slogan of "going beyond words and letters," attributed to Bodhidharma long after his lifetime. Robert Sharf claims that the Chinese native philosophical concern with human "nature" contributed to this discussion in Chinese Buddhism. "I do not know of any Indian references to mundane objects such as roof tiles or stones becoming buddhas and preaching the dharma. In other words, the extension of buddha-nature to the *insentient* appears to have been a distinctively Chinese innovation."[13] According to recovered documents from Dunhuang, as early a Chan figure as the fourth patriarch, Daoxin (580–651; J. Dōshin), proclaims that walls, fences, tiles, and stones preach the Dharma and so must possess buddha-nature.[14] Nanyang Huizhong, cited by Dongshan, was considered the greatest Chan exponent of the Buddha nature of nonsentient beings. When asked whether "mind" and "nature" were different or not, he replied that, "To the deluded mind they are different; to the enlightened they are not different."[15]

Returning to Dongshan's story, when he finally arrived at Yunyan after leaving Guishan, he asked who was able to hear the Dharma expounded by nonsentient beings. Yunyan said that "Nonsentient beings are able to hear it." When asked if Yunyan could hear it, he told Dongshan that if he could, then Dongshan could not hear him. Then Dongshan asked why he could not hear it. Yunyan raised his fly-whisk, and then asked if Dongshan heard it yet. When Dongshan replied that he could not, Yunyan said, "You can't even hear when I expound the Dharma; how do you expect to hear when a nonsentient being expounds the Dharma?"[16]

Although there is no indication of any communication between Guishan and Yunyan aside from the person of Dongshan inquiring before them, Yunyan intriguingly performed the same action as Guishan by raising his fly-whisk. Rather than seeing this as an exotic example of mystical accord or extrasensory perception between Guishan and Yunyan, this exemplifies simply using what was at hand, literally. Such whisks were symbols of teaching authority and Dharma, commonly carried by Chan masters. But more directly, the whisk was the conventionally inanimate object most immediately at hand. If all nonsentient beings proclaim the Dharma, there was no need to seek further.

After the above exchange, Yunyan gave as scriptural citation for Dongshan not the *Huayan Sutra*, as did Nanyong Huizhong, but, interestingly for a Chan teacher, the Pure Land *Amitabha Sutra*: "Water birds, tree groves, all without exception recite the Buddha's name, recite the Dharma."[17] Thereupon Dongshan reflected on this, and composed a verse that he presented to Yunyan:

> How marvelous! How marvelous!
> The Dharma expounded by non-sentient begins is inconceivable.
> Listening with your ears, no sound.
> Hearing with your eyes, you directly understand.[18]

A slightly different version of this exchange from the one from the *Recorded Sayings*, given above, occurs in the *Jingde chuandeng lu*, the most prominent lamp transmission text, and is cited by Dōgen in his *Eihei kōroku* (Extensive Record) with his own comment. In this version, the whisk and the citation to the *Amitabha Sutra* are not included, suggesting that they might have been colorful accretions in the later *Recorded Sayings* text.[19] However, in this version, when Yunyan initially states that if he, Yunyan, could hear nonsentient beings then Dongshan would not hear him, rather than asking why Dongshan could not hear it, Dongshan responds that then he, Dongshan, could not hear Yunyan. This implies that Dongshan is admitting that he can indeed hear the expounding of nonsentient beings, contrary to the other version. Such hearing might have impelled Dongshan's related questions in the first place.

In his closing verse, the same in both renditions, Dongshan goes beyond merely inquiring into whether or how nonsentient beings might expound the Dharma, and demonstrates his apprehension. This hearing with eyes is a description of synesthesia, the mingling of senses so that sensation in one mode occurs from stimulus in another sense mode. This synesthesia might be related to the Buddhist *dharani*, incantations commonly chanted in Sanskrit or, in East Asia, in transliterations of the Sanskrit into Chinese or Sino-Japanese. In such *dharani*, particular sounds are supposed to have particular, beneficial spiritual outcomes. Signified meaning is not the point, but the active aural signifying of Dharma effects is useful. The actual ritual experience of proclaiming these sounds is said to have somatic benefits, and to aid memory and analytic faculties, fostering eloquent expounding, and so to connect the senses of speech or sound and mind.[20]

Dongshan uses synesthesia to present experiential evidence of an awareness of suchness beyond the conventional limitations of sensation and the familiar routines of human conceptualization. His description may also be taken as a meditative or *samadhi* instruction. A quality of presence is indicated, usually defined in Zen practice traditions in terms of uprightness and qualities of *mudra* or postures. The practitioner's openness to the phenomenal world is not narrowly defined in terms of particular sense media but, rather, awareness of phenomena occurs within a more primal wholeness, not separated into sight, sound, smell, taste, touch, or thought. All of the senses might be seen as part of a single instrument for perceiving, engaging, and practicing suchness. This multifaceted embrace of sensation also suggests radical awareness and acceptance of the phenomenal world of karma, the causes and conditions that allow one's presence.

This extended story about Dongshan's meeting with Yunyan and its background demonstrates aspects of the subtlety of teaching that is characteristic of the tradition of Dongshan. Guishan's statement to Dongshan, "It can never be explained to you by means of one born of mother and father," as well as the instructions by the National Teacher and from Yunyan, all indicate that this realm of teaching is beyond the usual human conceptual categories, and challenges the student to his own experiential realization, beyond any theoretical "explanations."

Probably the most pivotal and emblematic story about Dongshan concerns his departure from Yunyan, rather than their first meeting, just discussed. After some period of practice with Yunyan (its duration unspecified in extant records, as far as I know), just before departing to visit other teachers, Dongshan asked Yunyan, "Later on, if I am asked to describe your reality, how should I respond?"[21] After a pause, Yunyan said, "Just this is it."

The narration states that Dongshan was lost in thought, and Yunyan said, "You are now in charge of this great matter; you must be most thoroughgoing." Dongshan departed without further comment. Later while wading across a stream, he looked down, saw his reflection, and "awakened to the meaning of the previous exchange."[22] He then wrote the following verse:

> Just don't seek from others, or you'll be far estranged from self.
> I now go on alone; everywhere I meet it.
> It now is me; I now am not it.
> One must understand in this way to merge with suchness.[23]

This story is informative about the nature of this suchness, or reality, and also for the teaching about it. Yunyan's "Just this is it" evokes meditative or mindfulness practices of bare attention from early Buddhism.[24] "This" certainly might be envisioned in the context of their dialogue as referring simply to the presence together of Yunyan and Dongshan, or as referring back to Dongshan's directly prior inquiry. But "just this" also refers more universally to the simplicity and immediacy of reality beyond human conceptualizations. Such an ultimate utterance neither requires nor suggests any quick rejoinder from Dongshan, and none was forthcoming. But Yunyan sealed his conveyance of the Dharma to Dongshan saying, "You are now in charge of this great matter; you must be most thoroughgoing."

Dongshan's subsequent revelation upon gazing at his reflection in the stream presents an inner dynamic overcoming the familiar subject-object division, a primary hindrance to the apprehension of suchness. His verse response does not merely concern discerning a description of some external reality. Dongshan speaks to the complex dialectic that goes beyond the estrangement of self and other, and integrates his personhood with the omnipresence of the reality of suchness. This reality is unavoidable: "Everywhere I meet it."

The subtle key line that suggests the inner nature of this interrelationship is, "It now is me; I now am not it." This dynamic interaction may be viewed from many perspectives. Gazing at his reflection in the stream, Dongshan could see that this image was him, yet he could not be reduced to this representation. The relationship of true reality to image, reflection, or depiction is at work in various ways here.

Further, the "it" of "just this" is a totally inclusive experience, incorporating everything. So "it" truly was him, the totality of his being, and yet he could not personally claim to encompass it all. This depicts the relationship of the limited "I," including its egoistic self-clinging, to the all-encompassing universal nature, of which any "I" is simply a particular partial expression. This dialectic echoes the Huayan Fourfold Dharmadhatu, which encompasses: the universal, the particular, the mutual nonobstructive interaction of universal and particular, and, finally, the mutual nonobstructive interaction of particulars with "other" particulars.[25] This dialectic between universal and particular would be developed as the Caodong five ranks teaching, introduced by Dongshan in his "Jewel Mirror Samadhi." In that teaching poem, this line from Dongshan's awakening verse celebrating the stream reflection, "It now is me; I now am not it," would be echoed as, "You are not it; it truly is you."

One of the seminal writings of Eihei Dōgen, who brought the Caodong/Sōtō lineage to Japan, includes a line that might be taken as a revealing commentary to Dongshan's, "It now is me; I now am not it." In his essay "Genjōkōan" (Actualizing the Fundamental Point) from one of his masterworks, *Shōbōgenzō* (True Dharma Eye Treasury), Dōgen says, "To carry yourself forward and experience myriad things is delusion. That myriad things come forth and experience themselves is awakening."[26] In this case the "You are not it" is amplified as the self carrying forward or projecting some constructed self on to one's experience, defined by Dōgen as delusion. The constructed "you" is not it, or reality. Dongshan's "It now is me" is expressed as the myriad things of the phenomenal world interdependently co-arising and mutually experiencing themselves, described as awakening. This mutual arising of all would, of course, include the particular self, but now seen as merely one of the ten thousand particular aspects of reality, rather than imposing its desires and human presuppositions on to reality. This total interconnected dependent co-arising is exactly you. This description from Dōgen in terms of the dynamic process of self, the projection of the constructed egoistic self, and nonself as the wholeness of reality including the provisional person, illuminates the dynamic of Dongshan's five ranks and its integration of the particular, including each and every self, with the ultimate universal, to be further discussed in this chapter.

In addition to its relevance to issues concerning the nature of suchness, Dongshan's verse and Yunyan's primary response also pertain to the student-teacher relationship, and the "intimate transmitting" of this truth. In both Yunyan's statement, "Just this is it," and in the middle lines in Dongshan's verse above, there is an indefinite pronoun that could be read as either "it" or as a personal pronoun, such as "him." So Yunyan's statement might be read, "Just this person." And the reading of Donghsan's verse would then be:

I now go on alone, but everywhere I meet him.
He now is me; I now am not him.

Yunyan's statement and this verse are often translated in this way, and both the readings of "it" to imply "suchness," and of "him" as the teacher, are certainly implicit and valid in these lines of Dongshan's verse, as well as in his "Jewel Mirror Samadhi."[27] Clearly some of the comments on this story by Dongshan himself infer reading this as a personal pronoun, indicating the intricacy of his relationship to his teacher.

In Dongshan's *Recorded Sayings*, in the story immediately preceding the narrative in which Yunyan tells Dongshan, "Just this is it" or "Just this person," Dongshan is already described as taking his leave from Yunyan. Yunyan said, "After your departure, it will be hard to meet again." Dongshan replied, "It will be hard not to meet."[28] Even before he gazed at his reflection in the stream, Dongshan felt the enduring imprint of his teacher Yunyan's presence; "everywhere I meet him."

The story that Hongzhi Zhengjue (1091–1157; J. Wanshi Shōgaku) later used as case 49 of the kōan collection that would become the *Book of Serenity* (C. *Congrong lu*, J. *Shōyōroku*) is actually a follow-up comment on Yunyan's stating, "Just this is it." In that text, the original story and Dongshan's verse after seeing his reflection in the stream appear only in Wansong's later commentary on the case. The story featured in the case involves Dongshan some time later as leader of an assembly making offerings to an image of Yunyan as his teacher. He was making offerings to his teacher Yunyan, probably on the occasion of a monthly memorial service for a teacher or temple founder, still part of Sōtō liturgy. A monk came forward and asked, "When Yunyan said 'Just this is it,' what did he mean?"

> Dongshan responded, "At that time I nearly misunderstood my late teacher."
>
> The monk said (somewhat impudently), "Did Yunyan himself know it is, or not?"
>
> Dongshan said, "If he didn't know it is, how could he be able to say this? If he did know it is, how could he be willing to say this?"[29]

The first half of this comment is clear. Yunyan had to have personally experienced the suchness of "just this" in order to be able to state as the heart of his teaching, "Just this is it." However, it is significant that Dongshan responded to the monk with a question, "If he didn't know it is, how could he be able to say this?" The other half of the question expresses the problematic of stating this directly. To really see "just this" includes the awareness that such realization cannot be "intimately transmitted" simply through verbiage. Dongshan needed to gaze into the reflection in the stream to realize that, "It now is me; I now am not it." Dongshan asked that if Yunyan really knew just this, then how could he have been willing to say "just this" so explicitly? Dongshan presented an unanswerable question about whether Yunyan could really have known suchness. And this deep questioning is what is most helpful toward provoking the student's own realization of the dynamics of suchness. Dongshan refused to give any direct answer to the monk questioning about Yunyan.

In the *Recorded Sayings*, immediately after the preceding exchange, presumably on a different occasion when Dongshan was making offerings for Yunyan, another monk inquired as to why Dongshan so honored Yunyan, who was fairly obscure, as opposed to other renowned teachers Dongshan had studied under, such as Nanquan Puyuan (748–835: J. Nansen Fugan). Dongshan replied, "I do not esteem my late teacher's virtues or his Buddhist teaching; I only value the fact that he didn't explain everything for me."[30] Here Dongshan strongly emphasizes a pedagogic style of indirectness, and the crucial importance of the student's personal experience rather than intellectual or ideological presentations of inner truth. At the end of this dialogue, Dongshan evinced his own indirectness by replying to the monk's further questioning that Dongshan only half agreed with Yunyan because, "If I completely agreed, then I would be unfaithful to my teacher."[31] Just as Yunyan did not explain everything (or especially the most important things) for Dongshan, Dongshan would not be willing to blindly agree with Yunyan about everything. This is a retrospective nonexplanation regarding the memory of his teacher. Even if Yunyan now is Dongshan, and Dongshan meets Yunyan everywhere, Dongshan cannot fully be, and indeed is not, Yunyan. Thus, in such a way, Dongshan becomes Dongshan.

In an earlier story about Dongshan, when he was still a young monk studying under Nanquan, the complex relationship of student and teacher is already prefigured. In the story, Nanquan was preparing for the memorial service for his own teacher, Mazu Daoyi (709–788; J. Baso Dōitsu), a great and important teacher sometimes said to have had 139 enlightened disciples. Nanquan asked his assembly, "Tomorrow we will pay homage to Mazu. Do you think he will return or not?" When nobody else responded, young Dongshan came forward and said, "He will come as soon as he has a companion."[32] Already Dongshan realized that the reality of a teacher was in the interaction with a worthy student. Nanquan complimented the young monk as being suitable for training. Dongshan then said, "Master, do not crush what is good into something mean." Here Dongshan rejected the view of Zen teaching as being a matter of molding, perfecting, or improving the student. In his later meeting with Yunyan, Dongshan would recognize the reality of teaching as the mutual recognition of suchness, and the relationship that expresses the dynamic of suchness.

Dongshan's Kōans

Among the encounter dialogues or stories attributed to Dongshan, which are numerous in his *Recorded Sayings*, several will be discussed here that are revealing of Dongshan's considerations of the nature of suchness, and of skillful approaches to its teaching. Developing from these themes and their dynamics, some of the stories also focus on the interrelationship of the ultimate, unconditioned truth with the particulars of the phenomenal, conditioned world (the focus of the five ranks teaching), and approaches to the practice of that relationship. The following comments and partial exegeses of these kōans, as well as those given earlier, hardly explain, much less exhaust, the complexities and lively spiritual challenges they present.

There is a later story from Dongshan in his *Recorded Sayings* that is related to the story of hearing or not hearing nonsentient beings expounding Dharma, through which he met Yunyan. This story also relates to the practice of receiving the awareness of suchness. Dongshan instructed his assembly by saying, "Experiencing the matter of going beyond Buddha, finally capable we can speak a little." An intrepid monk inquired, "What is speaking?" Dongshan said, "At the time of speaking you do not hear." The monk asked, "Master, do you hear or not?" And Dongshan replied, "Just when I do not speak, then I hear."[33]

Even though he previously recommended hearing with the eyes, Dongshan here recommends not using the tongue to hear. This implies silence and the practice of silent meditation as the context for "going beyond Buddha." Such going beyond signifies not attaching to prior awareness or conceptions of awakening, but fully and ongoingly sensing and simply meeting the present suchness. And yet there is still the suggestion of speaking "a little" to subtly convey this awareness. Silence alone is not sufficient to go beyond Buddha. And suchness is an unending, not static, reality.

In commenting on this dialogue, Dōgen says in his kōan verse commentaries in his *Extensive Record*:

> Seeing words we know the person like seeing his face.
> Three direct pointers are tongue, sharp wit, and writing.
> Fulfilling the way, wings naturally appear on the body.
> Since meeting myself, I deeply respect him.[34]

Dōgen here is praising Dongshan. Since meeting the constructed illusory self, his own "myself," Dōgen says he deeply respects this teaching, and the so-called other. Dongshan's Record includes numerous subtle stories about how to convey this silence, or hearing with the eyes, that is engagement and practice of suchness. Dongshan and Dōgen are both concerned here with how one meets this Dharma of suchness; how one might hear, taste, touch, enjoy its fragrance, and then how engage this sensing of reality. Still, despite its elusiveness, Dongshan says one must "speak a little" to convey this reality. And Dōgen is even willing to praise "tongue, sharp wit, and writing."

In a story that occurs at the end of his leading a summer practice period, Dongshan seems to criticize sensory engagement with suchness when he enigmatically recommends that his monks now go where there is no grass for ten thousand miles (li). This story appears as case 89 in the *Book of Serenity*, framed by Hongzhi Zhengjue with later comments from two other teachers:

> Dongshan spoke to the assembly, "It's the beginning of autumn, the end of summer, and you brethren will go, some to the east, some west; you must go where there's not an inch of grass for ten thousand miles."
>
> He also said, "But where there's not an inch of grass for ten thousand miles, how can you go?"
>
> Shishuang said, "Going out the gate, immediately there's grass."
>
> Dayang said, "I'd say, even not going out the gate, still the grass is boundless."[35]

This is an example of Dongshan's difficult, challenging teaching. What does it mean to go where there's not an inch of grass for ten thousand miles? The ten thousand grass tips are a conventional Chan expression for the whole phenomenal world—all the myriad things of the world. All of the sense objects, our possessions, all of our physical experiences are all just grass. Dongshan's directions imply a place beyond conditions, beyond karma, beyond this phenomenal world. He encourages travel into the realm of the unconditioned, beyond desires and aversion and habitual patterns of seeing things. The unconditioned nirvanic realm is juxtaposed with the realities of the temporal world in which the grasses grow. But could one also see suchness as grass, or grass as suchness?

The version of this story in the *Recorded Sayings* includes the later response from Shishuang Qingzhu (807–888; J. Sekisō Keisho), a Dharma heir of Yunyan's Dharma brother and also biological brother, Daowu Yuanzhi (769–835; J. Dōgo Enchi). In this version, Shishuang's statement criticizes

Dongshan's monks, as he said, "Why didn't someone say, 'As soon as one goes out the door, there is grass'?" Dongshan heard of this comment and approved, saying, "Within the country of the Great T'ang such a man is rare."[36]

Dongshan is tricky. Even though students may glimpse or imagine a realm beyond the phenomenal sense world, Dongshan's encouragement may help them to see that this is not the whole reality of suchness he saw in the stream. He asks, "Where there's not an inch of grass for ten thousand miles, how can you go?" Yunyan in his statement, "You are now in charge of this great matter; you must be most thoroughgoing," and Dongshan in his conclusion to "The Jewel Mirror Samadhi," "Just to do this continuously is called the host within the host" (see below), are encouraging an engagement with suchness that can be sustained in the long term, right in the realm of sense awareness and the unavoidable grasslands, but unobstructed by attachments.

As indicated in the *Book of Serenity* case, a later teacher in Dongshan's lineage, Dayang Qingxuan (d. 1027; J. Taiyō Kyōgen), commented, "Even not going out the gate, still the grass is boundless."[37] The phenomenal world is ever-present, even within the monastic container and its enterprise of turning within and going beyond current self-awareness. The balancing of a fundamental practice polarity is implicit here. Intuitive insight or wisdom is usually seen in Mahayana or Chan as the product of meditative turning within, glimpsing the unconditioned realm, empty of all grasses. Traditionally this is balanced in practice with going out into the realm of diverse suffering beings, the myriad grass-tips, extending awareness with compassion. Dongshan's initial admonition to the departing monks in this case might suggest retaining their meditative insight as they travel. Hongzhi's verse comment to the case begins:

> Grass boundless;
> Inside the gate, outside the gate, you see by yourself.
> To set foot in the forest of thorns is easy,
> To turn the body outside the luminous screen is hard.
> Look! Look!
> How many kinds?[38]

This story shows Dongshan subtly suggesting the suchness that encompasses both the luminous screen and the many kinds. And yet in another related story, Dongshan seems more emphatic about going where there is no grass. His disciple Huayan Xiujing (n.d.; J. Kegon Kyūjō) confessed to Dongshan that he was still caught by "the vicissitudes of feelings and discriminating consciousness," and Dongshan told him to go to the place without an inch of grass for ten thousand miles. Xiujing humbly asked if it is all right to go to such a place, perhaps concerned to not disregard the grasses. Yet Dongshan replied,

"You should only go in such a way."[39] Dongshan uncompromisingly insisted that his students experience this fully on their own.

Dongshan challenged his monks in an even more immediate, personal manner in another story that appears in both the *Recorded Sayings* and as case 43 of the important kōan collection, *The Blue Cliff Record* (C. *Biyanlu*; J. *Hekiganroku*). A monk inquired, "How does one escape hot and cold?" Dongshan retorted, "Why not go where it is neither hot nor cold?" When the monk asked what place that was, Dongshan confided, "When it's cold, you freeze to death; when it's hot, you swelter to death."[40]

Here Dongshan is challenging his monks not merely to avoid all of the worldly affairs described somewhat abstractly via the metaphor of grasses, but to go beyond their own personal, physical comfort zones. First, he says to go to a place with no heat or cold, which may have been intense at times in his monastery up in the mountains. Even more, he says, to accomplish this the monks must be willing to give up their very lives. Although Dongshan does not engage in the shouts or blows famously employed by his closely contemporary Chan masters Linji Yixuan (d. 867; J. Rinzai Gigen) and Deshan Xuanjian (780–865; J. Tokusan Senkan), Dongshan's subtle teaching is no less challenging to his students. From these stories, the misimpression of the notion that Caodong does not engage in gongan/kōans like the Linji tradition should also be obvious.[41]

The intensity of this story of no hot or cold certainly might apply simply to the weather. But aside from complaining about the temperature, this monk might have entered the contemplative life to escape the inner heat and intensity of human rage or passions. And he may have realized that the icy chill of uncaring dullness or of lifelessness was an equally pernicious alternative. Where is the place with no such emotional heat or frozenness?

In his verse for the story in the *Blue Cliff Record*, Xuedou refers to Dongshan's five ranks, asking, "Why must correct and biased be in an arrangement?"[42] Correct and biased are the two sides of the polarity whose interrelationship is elaborated in the five ranks. These two might also be described as the real and apparent, upright and inclined, universal and particular, ultimate and phenomenal, oneness and many, or absolute and relative, and they are also frequently suggested in Chan discourse by the metaphors of host and guest or lord and vassal. Yuanwu in his commentary on the *Blue Cliff Record* case proceeds to elaborate the fivefold arrangements of correct and biased. He analyzes the story in terms of correct and biased, and even quotes in full Dongshan's own five verses on their five interactions: the biased within the correct; the correct within the biased; coming from within the correct; arrival within the biased; and arrival within both at once.⁴³ Although these categories might indeed be employed analytically here, this story of hot and cold also simply informs Dongshan's expression of suchness with the intensities of hot and of cold, and also with the surpassing of hot and cold, whether from climate or emotion.

Dōgen later devoted a whole essay called "Shunju" (Spring and Autumn) to this dialogue of Dongshan in his *Shōbōgenzō* (True Dharma Eye Treasury).⁴⁴ Tanahashi evocatively translates Dongshan's final line of the dialogue as, "When it's cold, cold finishes the monk. When it is hot, heat totals the monk," suggesting the fullness as well as the finality of Dongshan's place without hot or cold, where these conditions are faced rather than evaded. In this essay Dōgen cites eight comments on the story by later masters, and adds his own comments on these, most at least somewhat approvingly. A full discussion of all these is beyond the scope of this chapter. But the eight do include Xuedou's verse used in the *Blue Cliff Record* and a few others that reference the five ranks polarity. Dōgen clearly criticizes such analysis, by saying, "If buddha-dharma had been transmitted merely through the investigation of differentiation and oneness, how could it have reached this day?" and "Do not mistakenly say that Dongshan's buddha-dharma is the five ranks of oneness and differentiation."⁴⁵ In his introduction, Dōgen extols Dongshan's summit of cold or heat, and says that "Cold is the vital eye of the ancestor school. Heat is the warm skin and flesh of my late master."⁴⁶ This concerns direct experience beyond systematic formulations such as the five ranks. Dōgen requires "understanding cold or heat in the everyday activities of Buddha ancestors."⁴⁷ Both Dongshan and Dōgen suggest one face rather than avoid the reality of heat or ice.

The verse comment by Hongzhi, cited and commented on by Dōgen, emphasizes the byplay of Dongshan and this specific monk, and thus more generally appreciating the importance of the particular persons portrayed in encounter dialogues, as opposed to seeing them as representations of ideological propositions. Hongzhi discusses the dialogue about hot and cold as if it was "you and I playing *go*," and then Dōgen asks, "Who are the two players?"⁴⁸ *Go* is an ancient Chinese (and Japanese) game played on a board, slightly analogous to chess. Two players take turns placing black and white stones on the board to delineate and mark off territory, although either side's stones may at times fully envelop and capture the other's stones, thus acquiring more territory. Dōgen references the equalizing handicaps that can be given in the game, and rejects seeing such a discussion as merely a game.

In another story in the *Recorded Sayings*, a monk demonstrates the subtlety of realization of suchness that Dongshan encourages. This unnamed monk has incorporated the ultimate in his own experience, and engages in appropriate expression to confirm it with Dongshan. Dongshan asked the monk, "Where have you come from?" and the monk said, "From wandering in the mountains." Dongshan asked, "Did you reach the peak?" and the monk said, "Yes." Dongshan asked if there was anyone on the peak, and the monk said, "No there wasn't." Dongshan said, "If so, then you did not reach the peak." Here Dongshan indicates that if nobody was there then neither was the monk. If this peak experience was true emptiness in which not a thing exists, then neither did the monk. But the indomitable monk replied, "If I did not reach the peak, how could I have known there was no one there?"

After this revelation, Dongshan asked why this monk had not remained there, and the monk replied that he would have been so inclined, but that there was someone from the West (perhaps referring to the Buddha or Bodhidharma) who would not have approved. Dongshan then praised the monk by saying, "I had wondered about this fellow."[49]

In his response, the monk did not hesitate or fade away, indicating that he was indeed present as a witness to the space without a blade of grass, without heat or cold, and by his presence therein he demonstrated the subtlety of Dongshan's teaching of suchness. His engagement with the suchness of the phenomenal world of causes and conditions through his own experience beyond conditioning was verified in his "speaking a little" with Dongshan. The monk understood that the buddhas required him to take responsibility and return from the peak to share the awareness from his experience.

A briefer dialogue appearing fairly late in the *Recorded Sayings* is included as case 98 in the *Book of Serenity*. A monk asked, "Which of the three bodies [of buddhas] does not fall into any category?" Dongshan responded, "I am always close to this."[50] The final "this" may refer to such a buddha body, but also to the whole question of not falling into any category. The reading above is based on the Chinese characters given by Hongzhi for the case that was used in the *Book of Serenity*. The characters in the *Recorded Sayings* version, the earliest extant version of which did not appear until some five hundred years after Hongzhi, reads, "I was once [or formerly] concerned with this." The variant reading basically differs only in putting Dongshan's concern or closeness in past tense, as opposed to being ever present, and remaining.[51]

The three bodies of buddhas is a teaching that describes different aspects of what "Buddha" came to signify in the development of the Mahayana. First, the Dharmakaya or reality body is the Buddha as the nature of reality itself, also seen as the body of the whole phenomenal universe, seen from the viewpoint of reality. Second is the Sambhogakaya, or the "bliss" body of buddhas existing in meditative pure lands, such as the Buddha highly venerated in East Asian devotion, Amitabha (C. Amitofo; J. Amida). Third is the Nirmanakaya, the incarnate or manifested body of a buddha in history, such as Sakyamuni Buddha, who lived as an historical personage in sixth- or fifth-century B.C.E. in northern India, although future and past buddhas also are said to appear incarnated in history. This incarnate body of Buddha is the primary subject of early Buddhist views of Buddha. The teaching of three bodies, or at least that of the Dharmakaya, appeared in early Perfection of Wisdom texts, and later was articulated as three or sometimes more bodies in texts associated with the Cittamatra branch of teachings, also called Yogacara.[52]

This question asked of Dongshan is ironic. Even to distinguish bodies of Buddha is to create categories. One point of the question is the search for that which might go beyond categories, conditions, limitations, or stages of spiritual development. Dongshan's response successfully avoids grasping onto any category or explanation that might settle this monk's questioning. Yet Dongshan acknowledges the importance of the question by saying "I am always close to this." The quality of not focusing on stages of practice seems to be characteristic of Dongshan's teaching. Although some of the secondary presentations of the five ranks seem to indicate a progression in practice accomplishment, these five ranks or positions are most often viewed as the ontological interrelationship of universal and particular.

Hongzhi's verse comment in the *Book of Serenity* case for this dialogue includes the unconditioned as a topic of this question of not falling into categories. He begins, "Not entering the world, not following conditions." But then he says, "In the emptiness of the pot of ages there's a family tradition," acknowledging the reality of a teaching praxis and a living tradition of such from Hongzhi's vantage point nine generations after Dongshan. Hongzhi further envisions, "evening on an autumn river;/An ancient embankment, the boat returns—a single stretch of haze."[53] In Dongshan's effort to remain close to that which is beyond categories emerges a way of seeing suchness with the ears, or perhaps with the touch on the skin of the cool haze of an autumn evening.

The several stories of Dongshan's teaching recounted here are a mere smattering of the many dialogues recorded and attributed to him. But these provide some context for Dongshan's presentation of suchness, and his subtle style of teaching. Another image used on several occasions by Dongshan is that of the bird's path, which he encourages his students to follow, leaving no traces.[54] This is a provocative image for selfless practice, reminiscent of the space with no grass or without heat or cold. However, birds can actually follow the same migratory paths for centuries, so something must remain to be followed. Another later Caodong school presentation of Dongshan's teaching includes the bird's path among "three roads" of Dongshan, which also include "extending the hands" of helpfulness as an image not separate from the bird's path, "Traveling the bird's path by yourself, yet you extend your hands."[55]

The Jewel Mirror Samadhi

"The Jewel Mirror Samadhi" is a long teaching poem, one of a number of such in the Chan/Zen tradition. It is generally attributed to Dongshan, although in the *Recorded Sayings*, Dongshan presents it to one of his successors, Caoshan Benji (840–901; J.: Sōzan Honjaku), and tells him that this teaching was secretly entrusted to Dongshan by his teacher Yunyan.[56] This may be a way of recognizing his teacher's inspiration, but there exists no other indication that this text was drafted by Yunyan. This verse presents many suggestions about suchness and its teaching, and fairly cryptically incorporates the five ranks. Here is this verse by Dongshan in its entirety:

> The teaching of suchness is intimately transmitted by buddhas and ancestors; Now you have it; preserve it well.
> A silver bowl filled with snow; a heron hidden in the moon.
> Taken as similar, they are not the same; not distinguished, their places are known.
> The meaning does not reside in the words, but a pivotal moment brings it forth.
> Move and you are trapped; miss and you fall into doubt and vacillation.
> Turning away and touching are both wrong, for it is like a massive fire.
> Just to portray it in literary form is to stain it with defilement.
> In darkest night it is perfectly clear; in the light of dawn it is hidden.
> It is a standard for all things; its use removes all suffering.
> Although it is not constructed, it is not beyond words.
> Like facing a precious mirror; form and reflection behold each other.
> You are not it, but in truth it is you.
> Like a newborn child, it is fully endowed with five aspects:
> No going, no coming, no arising, no abiding;
> "Baba wawa"—is anything said or not?

In the end it says nothing, for the words are not yet right.
In the illumination hexagram, inclined and upright interact,
Piled up they become three, the permutations make five,
Like the taste of the five-flavored herb, like the five-pronged vajra.
Wondrously embraced within the real, drumming and singing begin together.
Penetrate the source and travel the pathways; embrace the territory and treasure the roads.
You would do well to respect this; do not neglect it.
Natural and wondrous, it is not a matter of delusion or enlightenment.
Within causes and conditions, time and season, it is serene and illuminating.
So minute it enters where there is no gap, so vast it transcends dimension.
A hairsbreadth's deviation, and you are out of tune.
Now there are sudden and gradual, in which teachings and approaches arise.
When teachings and approaches are distinguished, each has its standard.
Whether teachings and approaches are mastered or not, reality constantly flows.
Outside still and inside trembling, like tethered colts or cowering rats,
The ancient sages grieved for them, and offered them the Dharma.
Led by their inverted views, they take black for white.
When inverted thinking stops, the affirming mind naturally accords.
If you want to follow in the ancient tracks, please observe the sages of the past.
One on the verge of realizing the Buddha Way contemplated a tree for ten kalpas,
Like a battle-scarred tiger, like a horse with shanks gone grey.
Because some are vulgar, jeweled tables and ornate robes;
Because some are wide-eyed, cats and white oxen.
With his archer's skill Yi hit the mark at a hundred paces,
But when arrows meet head-on, how could it be a matter of skill?
The wooden man starts to sing; the stone woman gets up dancing.

> It is not reached by feelings or consciousness, how could it
> involve deliberation?
> Ministers serve their lords, children obey their parents;
> Not obeying is not filial, failure to serve is no help.
> With practice hidden, function secretly, like a fool, like an idiot;
> Just to do this continuously is called the host within the host.[57]

This verse has many references to the two issues of the nature of suchness and approaches to its teaching that are the focus of this article, and which are also highlighted in the first line of the verse. The whole text might be seen as referring back to the topic of teaching of suchness and how it is intimately transmitted. A full exegesis of this lengthy and stimulating text is beyond the scope of this article, but I will very briefly discuss selected lines that are informative about suchness and Chan pedagogy related to it, followed by mentioning how the five ranks appear in this text.

The first thing Dongshan says about this teaching of suchness is that "You now have it," with the admonition to "preserve it well." This expresses that the reality of suchness is not something that needs to be calculated or acquired. It is already present, but needs to be personally discerned, realized, expressed, and maintained. As for the subtlety required and the inadequacy of language for conveying this suchness, the verse says, "The meaning does not reside in the words, but a pivotal moment brings it forth." This "pivotal moment" can also be read as the energy brought forth by the inquiring student, to which the reality of suchness does indeed respond, according to Dongshan. "Turning away and touching are both wrong, for it is like a massive fire," indicates that this suchness cannot be ignored or evaded, but also that it cannot be grabbed or grasped, other meanings of the character here for "touching." "The Jewel Mirror Samadhi" also claims about suchness and its teaching that their "use removes all suffering," making the very nature of reality a soteriological agent.

Unlike some Chan interpretations of the slogan of "direct pointing to the mind, beyond words and letters," Dongshan avows that the teaching of suchness can be effectively taught or discussed, "Although it is not constructed, it is not beyond words." In the line, "Wondrously embraced within the real, drumming and singing begin together," the drumming and singing refers to instant, unmediated inquiry and response or, literally, hitting and yelling back. Again, suchness responds to sincere inquiry, without any mediation through analysis or deliberation. Clearly, for this text this is not a matter of arduous study or mastery since, "Whether teachings and approaches are mastered or not, reality constantly flows." The problem, and the need for highly subtle teaching, is the habit of conditioned patterns of thinking and attachment. But, according to

Dongshan, this can indeed be seen through and put aside. "When inverted thinking stops, the affirming mind naturally accords." This "affirming mind" is an appealing image for the awareness propounded by "The Jewel Mirror Samadhi."

Another provocative image proclaims, "The wooden man starts to sing; the stone woman gets up dancing." This echoes many traditional Chan/Zen images of life arising from stillness, the revival of spirit promoted by samadhi practice, such as "a dragon howls in a withered tree," or "the plum blossoms on a dead branch." Suchness connects with the source of creative energy. Dongshan again emphasizes the inner, alchemical nature of this reality as, "It is not reached by feelings or consciousness, how could it involve deliberation?" Dongshan's long verse ends with the exhortation to "preserve it well," as he states that, "Just to do this continuously is called the host within the host," an image for complete fulfillment and realization.

The Five Ranks in the Jewel Mirror Samadhi

It is apparent from the previous considerations that Dongshan's teaching about suchness, and about teaching itself, can be presented and discussed without recourse to the five ranks teaching. Although a great deal of Chinese Caodong scholarship as well as much in Japanese Sōtō history have addressed technical aspects of the five ranks formula, it appears only at the end of Dongshan's *Recorded Sayings* and is downplayed by many teachers in his lineage, including Dōgen.[58] Immediately before "The Jewel Mirror Samadhi" in the *Recorded Sayings* text, Dongshan presents verses on five ranks, which are relationships between the real, true, or upright (C. *zheng*; J. *shō*), and the partial, particular, or inclined (C. *pian*; J. *hen*). Another version of the five is mentioned above as given in the *Blue Cliff Record* commentary on the kōan about Dongshan's place with no hot or cold. In the *Recorded Sayings*, the five are: the partial within the real, the real within the partial, coming from within the real, going within together, and arriving within together. These are generally understood as ontological interrelationships of the two fundamental aspects of upright and inclined, rather than "ranks" in the senses of stages of development. But right after these five verses, and just before "The Jewel Mirror Samadhi" in the *Recorded Sayings*, Dongshan presents verses on five other qualities: looking upon, serving, accomplishing, accomplishing mutually, and accomplishment of accomplishment.[59] These do seem to represent stages of practice development.

Elaborate presentations and implications of this teaching have been offered in Caodong and Sōtō history, and sometimes they describe "The Jewel Mirror

54 ZEN MASTERS

Samadhi" as presenting the five ranks. In addition to various references to fiveness, this long verse includes five lines with the Chinese character for truth or reality used in the five ranks, and these lines might be taken as referring to these five. First the partial within the real appears as, "In darkest night it is perfectly *clear* (real); in the light of dawn it is hidden" (although this might sound as if the second, and indeed the first two ranks are interactive). The second of the real within the partial occurs as, "You are not it, but in *truth* it is you."

The third rank of coming from within the real is depicted in the incomplete emergence described as, "In the end it says nothing, for the words are not yet *right*."

The fourth rank of going within together describes both aspects in cooperation, "In the illumination hexagram, inclined and *upright* interact," with a reference to the ancient Chinese classic, the *Yi Qing* or *Book of Changes*, whose traditional analysis includes a fivefold interplay of changing lines. The fifth rank of arriving within together, the two aspects of real and apparent (or upright and inclined) functioning together without any separation or sense of distinction, is depicted in, "Wondrously embraced within the *real*, drumming and singing begin together."

Aside from the five ranks teaching, the dialogues attributed to Dongshan both as a student and then in his teaching convey the subtle nature of the reality of suchness, and his ingenious approach to conveying this reality. Further study of how this style is sustained in the Caodong/Sōtō teaching tradition that Dongshan initiated will reveal more about the figure of Dongshan and his teaching.

NOTES

1. It is often suggested that the name Caodong is based on Dongshan's name combined with that of one of his main disciples, Caoshan. However, Caoshan was not the successor whose line was predominant in Caodong's development. More to the point, the order of the name Caodong implies the "Cao" preceding "Dong," so it is more likely that the Cao in Caodong actually referred to Caoxi, the teaching site and thus a name used for the famed Chan sixth ancestor Dajian Huineng (638–713; J. Daikan Enō). The name Caodong might thereby refer to all six teachers in the lineage from the sixth ancestor to Dongshan. For later Song dynasty questions about this lineage, see Morten Schlütter, *How Zen Became Zen: The Dispute over Enlightenment and the Formation of Chan Buddhism in Song-Dynasty China* (Honolulu: University of Hawaii Press, 2008), pp. 140, 173.

2. See, for example, John R. McRae, *Seeing through Zen* (Berkeley: University of California Press, 2003); Griffith Foulk, various articles, including "Controversies Concerning the 'Separate Transmission,'" in Peter Gregory and Daniel Getz, Jr., eds.,

Buddhism in the Sung (Honolulu: University of Hawaii Press, 1999), pp. 220–294; Albert Welter, *The Linji Lu and the Creation of Chan Orthodoxy: The Development of Chan's Records of Sayings Literature* (New York: Oxford University Press, 2008); and Schlütter, *How Zen Became Zen*. This questionable historicity is especially true for Dongshan, whose earliest extant discourse record was not compiled until eight centuries after his death. See William Powell, *The Record of Tung-shan* (Honolulu: University of Hawaii Press, 1986), pp. 3–4. Exceptions include the *Recorded Sayings* texts of Huangbo and Yunmen, which were supposedly compiled by direct students of the masters. We may note that oral traditions might sometimes be reliable, so the historicity of these records can be highly suspect, but not necessarily disproved except where contradictions with reliable historical records are found. The *Recorded Sayings* of Dongshan, in Chinese, *Ruizhou Dongshan Liangjie Chanshi Yulu*, or *Dongshan Yulu* for short, can be found in T. 47.519b–526b.

3. See, for examples in English, Chang Chung-yuan, trans., *Original Teachings of Ch'an Buddhism* (New York: Vintage Books, 1969), pp. 41–57; John Wu, *The Golden Age of Zen* (Taipei: United Publishing Center, 1975), pp. 171–190; and Alfonso Verdu, *Dialectical Aspects in Buddhist Thought: Studies in Sino-Japanese Mahayana Idealism* (Lawrence: Center for East Asian Studies, University of Kansas, 1974), pp. 115–187.

4. Wu, *The Golden Age of Zen*, p. 177.

5. Sangharakshita, *The Eternal Legacy* (London: Tharpa Publications, 1985), pp. 218–220, which includes citations from the *Lankavatara Sutra*.

6. Powell, *The Record of Tung-shan*, pp. 23–25; T. 47.519b–c. See also Yi Wu, *The Mind of Chinese Ch'an (Zen): The Ch'an School Masters and Their Kung-ans* (San Francisco: Great Learning Publishing, 1989), pp. 99–101.

7. Powell, *The Record of Tung-shan*, p. 24; T. 47.519b.

8. For Zhanran, see Linda Penkower, "T'ien-t'ai during the T'ang Dynasty: Chan-jan and the Sinification of Buddhism," Ph.D. dissertation, Columbia University, 1993; and Robert Sharf, "How to Think with Chan Gong'an," in Charlotte Furth, Judith Zeitlin, and Ping-chen Hsiung, eds., *Thinking with Cases: Specialist Knowledge in Chinese Cultural History* (Honolulu: University of Hawaii Press, 2007), pp. 213–214.

9. Robert Sharf, *Coming to Terms with Chinese Buddhism: A Reading of the Treasure Store Treatise* (Honolulu: University of Hawaii Press, 2002), p. 247.

10. Sharf, "How to Think with Chan Gong'an," p. 212. This article by Sharf has a thorough discussion of the history of this discussion.

11. See Jacqueline Stone, *Original Enlightenment and the Transformation of Medieval Japanese Buddhism* (Honolulu: University of Hawaii Press, 1999), pp. 9, 14, 170; and Penkower, "T'ien-t'ai During the T'ang Dynasty: Chan-jan and the Sinification of Buddhism," pp. 371, 404, 430 n.68.

12. Sharf, "On the Buddha-nature of Insentient Things: How to Think about a Ch'an Kung-an," section II of online, preliminary version of portions of the already cited essay, second to last paragraph (http://kr.buddhism.org/zen/koan/Robert_Sharf-e.htm).

13. Sharf, "How to Think with Chan Gong'an," p. 222.

14. Sharf, "How to Think with Chan Gong'an," p. 216.

15. Sharf, "How to Think with Chan Gong'an," p. 220.
16. Powell, *The Record of Tung-shan*, p. 25; T. 47.519c.
17. Powell, *The Record of Tung-shan*, p. 26; T. 1986: 47.519c–520a.
18. Powell, *The Record of Tung-shan*, p. 26; T. 47.520a.
19. For a rendition from the Jingde Transmission of the Lamp anthology (C. *Jingde chuandeng lu*; J. *Keitoku dentōroku*, published in 1004), see Chang, *Original Teachings of Ch'an Buddhism*, pp. 58–59. For Dōgen's version with his commentary, see Taigen Dan Leighton and Shohaku Okumura, trans., *Dōgen's Extensive Record: A Translation of Eihei Kōroku* (Boston: Wisdom Publications, 2004), pp. 405–407, 570–571.
20. See Hirakawa Akira, *A History of Indian Buddhism: From Sakyamuni to Early Mahayana* (Honolulu: University of Hawaii Press, 1990), pp. 300–301.
21. This story can be found in Powell, *The Record of Tung-shan*, pp. 27–28; T. 47.520a; Chang, *Original Teachings of Ch'an Buddhism*, pp. 59–60; and in the commentary to case 49 in Thomas Cleary, trans., *Book of Serenity* (Hudson, N.Y.: Lindisfarne Press, 1990), pp. 206–207. The *Book of Serenity* is a major kōan collection initiated by the important Caodong lineage master Hongzhi Zhengjue (1091–1157; J. Wanshi Shōgaku), who selected and ordered the cases and wrote the verse comment. Following the pattern of the earlier *Blue Cliff Record*, further commentaries were added in the thirteenth century by another Caodong teacher, Wansong Xingxiu (1166–1246: J. Banshō Gyōshū). It should be noted that in the phrase "describe your reality," this reality, or "genuine image" might also be read as someone asking whether Dongshan received Yunyan's "portrait" (J. *chinzō*), which later in Chan history was bestowed as an insignia of Dharma transmission. That this word is used here is evidence of the later provenance of this story in the *Recorded Sayings*. But in context, the story indicates something deeper, the actual Dharma, or teaching of reality, represented by Yunyan.
22. Powell, *The Record of Tung-shan*, p. 27; T. 47.520a.
23. Cleary, *Book of Serenity*, p. 206.
24. See, for example, the Satipatthana Sutta: Bhikku Nanamoli and Bhikku Bodhi, trans., *The Middle Length Discourses of the Buddha: A Translation of the "Majjhima Nikaya"* (Boston: Wisdom, 1995), pp. 145–155. For a modern treatment, see Mark Epstein, *Thoughts without a Thinker* (New York: HarperCollins, 1995), pp. 109–128.
25. For the Huayan Fourfold Dharmadhatu, see Thomas Cleary, *Entry into the Inconceivable: An Introduction to Hua-yen Buddhism* (Honolulu: University of Hawaii Press, 1983), pp. 24–42, 147–169; and Garma C.C. Chang, *The Buddhist Teaching of Totality: The Philosophy of Hwa Yen Buddhism* (University Park: Pennsylvania State University Press, 1971), pp. 18–21, 136–170.
26. Kazuaki Tanahashi, ed., *Moon in a Dewdrop: Writings of Zen Master Dōgen* (New York: North Point Press, 1985), p. 69. This has also been translated as, "Acting on and witnessing myriad things with the burden of oneself is 'delusion.' Acting on and witnessing oneself in the advent of myriad things is enlightenment." Thomas Cleary, trans., *Shōbōgenzō: Zen Essays by Dōgen* (Honolulu: University of Hawaii Press, 1986), p. 32.

27. See Powell, *The Record of Tung-shan*, pp. 27–28; T. 47.520a; and Chang, *Original Teachings of Ch'an Buddhism*, p. 60, for translations as "him."

28. Powell, *The Record of Tung-shan*, p. 27; T. 47.520a.

29. Cleary, *Book of Serenity*, p. 206; see also Chang, *Original Teachings of Ch'an Buddhism*, pp. 60–61; Powell, *The Record of Tung-shan*, p. 28; and T. 47.520a–b. Powell translates the final comment as, "If he knew reality, why did he go to the trouble of answering that way?"

30. Cleary, *Book of Serenity*, p. 207; see also Chang, *Original Teachings of Ch'an Buddhism*, pp. 61–62; Powell, *The Record of Tung-shan*, pp. 28–29; and T. 47.520b.

31. Cleary, *Book of Serenity*, p. 207; see also Chang, *Original Teachings of Ch'an Buddhism*, pp. 61–62; Powell, *The Record of Tung-shan*, pp. 28–29; and T. 47.520b.

32. Powell, *The Record of Tung-shan*, p. 23; T. 47.519a; see also Chang, *Original Teachings of Ch'an Buddhism*, p. 58.

33. See Chang, *Original Teachings of Ch'an Buddhism*, p. 65; or Powell, *The Record of Tung-shan*, p. 52; T. 47.524b.

34. Leighton and Okumura, *Dōgen's Extensive Record*, p. 569.

35. Cleary, *Book of Serenity*, pp. 382–384. See also Powell, *The Record of Tung-shan*, p. 48; T. 47.523b–c.

36. Powell, *The Record of Tung-shan*, p. 48; T. 47.523b–c.

37. For Dōgen's further comment related to this case, including Dayang's comment, see Leighton and Okumura, *Dōgen's Extensive Record*, p. 542.

38. Cleary, *Book of Serenity*, p. 383.

39. Powell, *The Record of Tung-shan*, p. 44; T. 47.522c.

40. Powell, *The Record of Tung-shan*, p. 49; T. 47.523c; Thomas and J.C. Cleary, *The Blue Cliff Record* (Boston: Shambhala, 1977), vol. 2, pp. 306–311. *The Blue Cliff Record* was initiated with a hundred cases selected and ordered with his own appended verse comments by Xuedou Chongjian (980–1052; J. Setchō Jūken) from the Yunmen lineage. *The Blue Cliff Record* collection was created later by the important Linji lineage master, Yuanwu Keqin (1063–1135; J. Engo Kokugon), who wrote introductions to the cases, and commentaries and added sayings to both the cases and Xuedou's verses. This collection was the model for the later *Book of Serenity*, cited previously.

41. For comparison of Dongshan and the Caodong tradition with Linji, see Schlütter, *How Zen Became Zen*, pp. 157–158.

42. Cleary and Cleary, *The Blue Cliff Record*, p. 309.

43. Cleary and Cleary, *The Blue Cliff Record*, pp. 307–308. See also Powell, *The Record of Tung-shan*, p. 49; T. 47.523c.

44. Tanahashi, ed., *Moon in a Dewdrop*, pp. 108–113.

45. Ibid., pp. 109, 111.

46. Ibid., pp. 108–109.

47. Ibid., p. 113.

48. Ibid., p. 110.

49. Thomas Cleary, *Timeless Spring: A Soto Zen Anthology* (Tokyo: Weatherhill, 1980), p. 45. See also Powell, *The Record of Tung-shan*, p. 49; T. 47.523c; Chang, *Original Teachings of Ch'an Buddhism*, pp. 62–63; Lu K'uan Yü [Charles Luk], *Ch'an and Zen*

Teaching: Series Two (London: Rider, 1961), pp. 144–145; and Andy Ferguson, *Zen's Chinese Heritage: The Masters and Their Teachings* (Boston: Wisdom, 2000), p. 185. I note that the Powell translation indicates that at the end of the dialogue, Dongshan disapproved of the monk. Although I can understand Powell's interpretation as "I've been suspicious," from my reading of the original in context, I read it as *formerly* having "questioned" or "doubted" this monk. This positive reading is given by Cleary, Ferguson, and Lu cited above, while the Chang version omits that line.

50. T. 47.524c–525a; Cleary, *The Book of Serenity*, pp. 422–424; Powell, *The Record of Tung-shan*, p. 56; Chang, *Original Teachings of Ch'an Buddhism*, p. 68; and Lu, *Ch'an and Zen Teaching*, p. 146.

51. For dating of Dongshan's *Recorded Sayings*, see Powell, *The Record of Tungshan*, pp. 3–4. The Transmission of the Lamp reading accords with Hongzhi's. Interestingly, Chang renders Dongshan's response as, "I often think about it"; and Lu offers, "I am always keen about this." See citations in the previous note.

52. See Paul Williams, *Mahayana Buddhism: The Doctrinal Foundations* (London: Routledge, 1989), pp. 168–179, 123; and Donald Mitchell, *Buddhism: Introducing the Buddhist Experience*, second edition (New York: Oxford University Press, 2002, 2008), pp. 131–132.

53. Cleary, *Book of Serenity*, p. 423.

54. See, for example, T. 47.524c; Powell, *The Record of Tung-shan*, p. 55; and also Powell's note, p. 85, providing earlier Buddhist references to this image.

55. Cleary and Cleary, *The Blue Cliff Record*, vol. 2, pp. 463–464.

56. T. 47.525c–526a; Powell, *The Record of Tung-shan*, pp. 63–65. For questions about the source and age of "The Jewel Mirror Samadhi," see Schlütter, *How Zen Became Zen*, p. 158.

57. T. 47.525c–526a. The version in the text is close to the one (initially translated by Taigen Dan Leighton, Shohaku Okumura, Carl Bielefeldt, and Griffith Foulk and reviewed in conference) in Sōtō Zen Text Project, *Soto School Scriptures for Daily Services and Practice* (Tokyo: Sōtōshū Shūmucho, 2001), pp. 33–37, and for roman letter transliterations of the Japanese, pp. 110–113. For other renditions, see Powell, *The Record of Tung-shan*, pp. 63–65; Sheng-yen, *The Poetry of Enlightenment: Poems by Ancient Ch'an Masters* (Elmhurst, N.Y.: Dharma Drum, 1987), pp. 75–78; and Lu, *Ch'an and Zen Teaching*, pp. 149–154.

58. The fullest exposition of this five ranks scholarship tradition in English is the somewhat obscure work already cited, Verdu, *Dialectical Aspects in Buddhist Thought*.

59. T. 47.525c; Powell, *The Record of Tung-shan*, pp. 61–63.

3

Yongming Yanshou: Scholastic as Chan Master

Albert Welter

Western discourses on Zen, highly influenced by the Japanese Rinzai tradition, rarely mention Yongming Yanshou (904–975). Where Yanshou's name is mentioned, it is often used pejoratively as the antithesis of a "real" Zen master. Given Rinzai's propensity for idealized Zen masters as convention-defying iconoclasts, this comes as no surprise. Yanshou's reputation as a scholastic and his renown for syncretism, whether between Zen and Pure Land or between Zen and doctrinal teaching, brand him in the eyes of many as unworthy of the Zen title, prompting some to question whether he even deserves to be included among the ranks of Zen masters.

In the history of Zen, Yanshou is usually dismissed as the harbinger of decline, the architect of an impure Zen that modern Zen purists have relegated to a decidedly inferior status. The Zen traditions of China, Korea, and Vietnam, however, tend to look upon Yanshou quite differently. Rather than being marginalized, Yanshou emerges in these traditions as a central figure through which indigenous Chan, Sŏn, and Thiên teachings and practices are validated. How does one come to terms with these disparate images of Yanshou? Should he be included as a Zen master? If so, what meaning does this designation carry?

Any inclusion of Yanshou among the ranks of Zen masters, as this chapter argues, forces a reevaluation of the very meaning of the term Zen and how it has been commonly (mis)represented in contemporary discourse. An examination of Yanshou's Zen identity compels us to rethink the notion of what Zen is, and to come to terms with living Zen traditions that value Yanshou as the founding patriarch of the traditions they represent. If, indeed, Yanshou is the "typical" Zen master rather than a marginalized figure; if his teaching represents "true" Zen rather than some scholiast's aberration—in other words, if Zen syncretism rather than some hypothetical pure Zen represents "true" Zen—then Yanshou emerges as a central figure in the mainstream Zen tradition, and so-called "radical" Zen is marginalized as the ill-conceived aberration. This chapter considers the struggle to appropriate Yanshou as a Zen master who is indicative of contradictions that lie at the heart of Zen.

Included in the discussion will be a description of the textual images of Yanshou, how these textual images compare with the style of Zen promoted in his own writings, and how textual images of Yanshou evolved over time according to the forces that shaped them. The evolution of Yanshou's identity is reviewed in three phases: as "promoter of blessings," as Chan master, and as Pure Land advocate. Finally, I propose another image of Yanshou, drawn from his own writings, as advocate of bodhisattva practice. Before beginning this review, I open with a discussion of the problems associated with addressing Yanshou's identity.

The Problem of Yanshou's Identity, Past and Present

The Buddhist identity of Yongming Yanshou has long been problematic. Yanshou's devotion to Buddhism has never been questioned, nor his commitment to Buddhist teaching. Difficulties frequently arose, however, in trying to determine what type of Buddhist Yanshou was. Questions concerning Yanshou's identity are rooted in the original records of Yanshou's life. They are reiterated during the centuries following his death in the attempts to construct an image of Yanshou relevant to contemporary Buddhist practitioners. These questions continue down to the present day, when Yanshou is highly regarded in some Buddhist circles while virtually ignored or denigrated in others.[1] Why has the image of Yanshou, a popular figure of immense importance in Chinese Buddhist history, continued to be so controversial? The present study is an attempt to reflect on circumstances contributing to the problem that Yanshou's image represents in Buddhist circles.[2]

Generally speaking, the difficulty in assigning identity to Yanshou is rooted in historical changes occurring within Chinese Buddhism. As a product of the revival and promotion of Buddhism in the quasi-independent principality of Wuyue during the Five Dynasties period (907–959), Yanshou sought to preserve the Buddhist legacy of the Tang dynasty. As a harbinger of change,

Yanshou tried to integrate the elements of past Buddhist teaching into a comprehensive system that reflected challenges Buddhism faced in China. In this sense, Yanshou was rooted in the traditions of Tang Buddhist scholasticism, but provided the framework and impetus from which Song and subsequent Buddhist developments grew. Thus, the root problem in determining Yanshou's identity is that he is the product of the scholastic Buddhism of the Tang, although he attempted to shape it in new ways, but his identity was determined by Buddhists in the Song who defined themselves outside of parameters established by their Tang forebears. It is somewhat surprising, given this circumstance, that Yanshou continued to be honored as a central figure in a tradition that developed in ways largely unanticipated by Yanshou himself. It is not surprising, however, that Yanshou's image began to resemble less the man of history and more the figure of legend. It took a remarkably long time, one might add, for the figure of legend to settle into an established form. The activity surrounding the legend-making process attests to the potency of Yanshou's image through the ages.

It is also hardly surprising to find Yanshou's image manipulated in this way. Figures throughout history, regardless of period or culture, have often acquired characteristics that reflect the time and place of the people who honor them. In this, Yanshou is no exception. As he became a leading figure within Song Buddhist circles, his image began to take on the shape of the communities that honored him. As these communities changed, so did the image of Yanshou.

During the Song, two interpretations of Buddhism came to dominate: Chan and Pure Land.[3] Yanshou became closely connected to both groups. In Chan circles, Yanshou was cast as a paradigmatic Chan monk, composing enlightenment verses and responding to questions from students with enigmatic replies. Among Pure Land practitioners, as interpreted through the writings of Tiantai monks who were promoting the Pure Land movement, Yanshou became the consummate advocate of Pure Land teaching and practice. Throughout these developments, Yanshou's identity provoked considerable, sometimes heated debate. The content of these debates exposes two things about Yanshou's identity. First, it shows that Yanshou did not easily fit the sectarian categories that came to dominate Buddhism in the Song; second, the controversy over Yanshou's image in Song Buddhist circles suggests his overwhelming importance. However contentious Yanshou's identity became, he could not be ignored.

Yanshou as "Promoter of Blessings" (*xingfu*)

The earliest known biography of Yanshou was compiled by Zanning (919–1001) in the *Song gaoseng zhuan* (Song Biographies of Eminent Monks), compiled in

988, a mere thirteen years after Yanshou's passing.[4] In addition to being written shortly after Yanshou's own life, other factors attest to its reliability. Like Yanshou, Zanning hailed from the Wuyue region and initially achieved fame for his activities there. Like Yanshou, he was a product of the Wuyue Buddhist revival, and had intimate knowledge of Yanshou and the circumstances and events of his life.[5] In spite of these compelling factors that favor its reliability, however the information contained here must be viewed critically in light of the conventions governing biographies compiled in the *gaoseng zhuan* (biographies of eminent monks) format. A source used for many of the biographies in these collections was the tomb-inscription (*taming*) compiled as a kind of eulogy memorializing the memory of deceased Buddhist masters.[6] Although the content of Yanshou's tomb-inscription is unknown, one can assume that it was a source for Zanning's biography of Yanshou in the *Song gaoseng zhuan*, especially given that Zanning makes specific reference to its existence at the end of the biography.[7]

Buddhist biographies followed both general conventions governing Chinese biographies such as place of birth and family backgroundand other conventions specifically related to the monks' careers as Buddhists. In Yanshou's case, these include the circumstances through which he became a monk, the Buddhist teachings and scriptures he was most devoted to, the masters who served as his teachers, the temples with which he was associated throughout his career, episodes in his life that reflect key aspects of his character, his major written works, and the account of his death. I have dealt with these details of Yanshou's life elsewhere.[8] Here I will focus on aspects relating to how individual compilers identified Yanshou, the image of Yanshou that individual biographies project.

Unlike future biographies of Yanshou that identified Yanshou in terms of his sectarian affiliation, Zanning identifies Yanshou as simply "Song dynasty [monk] Yanshou of Yongming Monastery in Qiantang."[9] Even this apparently innocent appellation, however, suggests that the circumstances of Yanshou's life had already begun to be extracted from their original context to serve the needs of the compilation in question and the circumstances under which it was being written. Yanshou was not really a Song dynasty monk. He lived and died in an independent Wuyue kingdom, received the patronage of a series of monarchs provided by the Qian family, the ruling warlords (*jiedu shi*) of the region. There is no evidence that Yanshou had any interactions with the Song court. Wuyue was among the last of the autonomous kingdoms during the so-called "Five Dynasties and Ten Kingdoms" period to be absorbed into the new Song hegemony in 978, three years after Yanshou's death. Zanning, on the other hand, served as Wuyue ambassador, personally accompanying Prince Zhongyi

(Qian Chu) to the Song court during the tense negotiations that officially relinquished control of the region. While Yanshou did not live to see these developments, they were an important factor in Zanning's career. Zanning became the highest ranking member of the Buddhist clergy at the Song court, and was personally acquainted with the Song emperor and leading members of the imperial bureaucracy.[10] Not only did it serve Zanning's interests in promoting Buddhism at the Song court to include Yanshou among the ranks of prominent Song Buddhists but it was also impossible to ignore the official beginning of the Song dynasty in the year 960. To suggest otherwise would be viewed not only as presumptuous but also offensive to the sensibilities of the new dynasty.

The power and prestige of Wuyue was considerable during Yanshou's lifetime. Qiantang, the capital city of Wuyue, became a thriving commercial and cultural center at this time, the hub of an economic transformation that propelled the lower Yangtze Valley area into the most dynamic region in China during the Song. Under the name Hangzhou, Qiantang served as the capital of China during the Southern Song (1127–1279), after the north was abandoned. As a center of Chinese culture, it exerted considerable influence over the entire East Asian region. Monasteries revived through Wuyue patronage on Mount Tiantai, the principle sacred mountain of the region, and other Buddhist centers throughout Wuyue, became leading institutions for the study of Buddhism during the Song.[11] Monks from Japan such as Eisai (a.k.a. Yōsai) and Dōgen who studied at these monasteries became founders of the Japanese Zen movement. Even in Yanshou's day, the king of the major Korean kingdom of Koryo (or Goryeo, C. Gaoli) sent a delegation of monks to study under Yanshou. The fame of Buddhist institutions in Wuyue was widespread, both within China and outside its borders. Appointed to head prestigious monasteries in Qiantang, Yanshou stood at the pinnacle of the Wuyue Buddhist establishment.

Zanning's identification of Yanshou was based on criteria specific to the *gaoseng zhuan* genre. *Gaoseng zhuan* works commemorated the contributions of Buddhist monks in ten categories, on the basis of nonsectarian criteria. In the first of these works, the *Gaoseng zhuan* compiled c. 520 by Huijiao, these were: translators (*yijing*), exegetes (*yijie*), miracle workers (*shenyi*), meditation practitioners (*xichan*), elucidators of discipline (*minglu*), self-immolators (*wangshen*), cantors (*songjing*), promoters of blessings (*xingfu*), hymnodists (*jingshi*), and sermonists (*changdao*).[12] The *Xu gaoseng zhuan* (compiled in 667 by Taoxuan) and *Song Gaoseng zhuan* altered the order and names of the categories slightly, but retained the nonsectarian spirit of the genre.[13] Under these circumstances, Buddhist monks were not identified according to sectarian affiliation, but categorized according to the area of expertise within Buddhism through which they achieved eminence. As such, a monk is noted for his achievements as a *xichan* (meditation) practitioner, for example, not for his membership in a Chan school lineage. The categories themselves are free of sectarian bias.

As is the case with *Song gaoseng zhuan* biographies generally, the actual account of Yanshou's life is sparse. The strongest impression left by the account is of Yanshou's affinity for reciting the *Lotus Sutra*, intensive meditation practice, and performing meritorious deeds. He was noted as a prolific writer.[14] He is distinguished by his austere and frugal lifestyle; sincerity and honesty of character; connections to the Qian family rulers of Wuyue as well as his Buddhist mentors, Cuiyan and Deshao; and the honors bestowed upon him by the Korean king.

Yanshou's association with *Lotus Sutra* recitation, with meditation, and with the performance of meritorious deeds suggests the basis for the three ways in which Yanshou came to be identified in biographical records: as Pure Land master, as Chan practitioner, and as "promoter of blessings" (*xingfu*). Of these three, Zanning chose promoter of blessing as most appropriate for designating Yanshou's identity. What evidence exists in Yanshou's own writings to support Zanning's designation?

The best evidence in support of Zanning's characterization is contained in Yanshou's work promoting the practice of myriad good deeds, the *Wanshan tonggui ji* (Anthology on the Common End of Myriad Good Deeds).[15] It is interesting to note that in Zanning's biography, this work is mentioned prior to Yanshou's other major work, the *Zongjing lu* (Records of the Source Mirror), a much larger work containing Yanshou's anthology of Chan sources. The order in which Zanning mentions them in his biography seems intentional. Tradition suggests that Yanshou compiled the *Zongjing lu* prior to the *Wanshan tonggui ji*, while living in relative obscurity, first as a student of Cuiyan at Longce Monastery (from 937), then as a student of Deshao on Mount Tiantai (until 952), and finally as a teacher in his own right on Mount Xuedou (a.k.a. Mount Siming) (952–960), where he is said to have attracted students in large numbers. This implies that the *Zongjing lu* was completed during Yanshou's tenure on Mount Xuedou, and his appointment as abbot of the newly rebuilt Lingyin Monastery in Qiantang by Prince Zhongyi in 960 was made, in part, as a recognition of Yanshou's achievement. The Lingyin Monastery is generally regarded as a Chan monastery, however defined. The following year, Yanshou was appointed as abbot of Yongming Monastery. The Yongming Monastery was conceived of as having a broader mission to promote Buddhism among lay patrons in Wuyue. One can imagine the different congregations served at the two establishments. Lingyin Monastery, located at the outskirts of the city, was primarily an urban center for monastic training. Yongming Monastery, located in the city proper on the shores of the famed West Lake, focused on ministering to the needs of the Wuyue state and lay public. Following this line of speculation, the *Wanshan tonggui ji* was compiled by Yanshou during his tenure at Yongming Monastery, in response to the broader role Buddhism was playing in Wuyue.

On the basis of available evidence, there is no way to confirm or deny this speculation. What is undeniable is the endorsement the *Wanshan tonggui ji* provides for Zanning's characterization of Yanshou as a promoter of blessings. In the *Wanshan tonggui ji*, Yanshou supports a broad range of Buddhist activities, free of sectarian concerns. The list of activities promoted includes the following:[16]

- adorning, worshiping, and engaging in the adoration of Buddhas and bodhisattvas;
- preaching the Dharma, promoting Dharma assemblies (*fahui*), and a whole range of activities in support of the Dharma;
- reading, memorizing, and chanting sutras, especially the *Lotus Sutra*;
- constructing and maintaining stupas;
- supporting the precepts and practicing repentance, especially the *Fahua* (Lotus) *samadhi* repentance of the Tiantai school;
- following a wide range of standard Buddhist practices drawn from scriptural accounts, including the *paramitas*, the eightfold path, and so on;
- adopting a wide range of meditation techniques, including breath control, *zuochan* (seated meditation), *chanding* (*samadhi*), contemplating images of the Buddha, techniques associated with Tiantai *zhiguan* (cessation and contemplation) practice, and so on;
- invoking the Buddha (*nianfo*) for rebirth in the Pure Land, usually in conjunction with
- stupa worship, sutra chanting, circumambulatory meditation practice, and contemplation;
- self-immolation, or surrendering one's body, or a portion thereof, as the supreme act of almsgiving;
- building and maintaining temples;
- pursuing public works projects, such as clearing and repairing roadways; building bridges and ferries; planting flowers and trees and constructing hills for parks; digging wells and latrines for public use; and providing clothing, medicine, and shelter for the less fortunate;

- conducting altruistic activities inspired by Buddhist teaching: setting fish and birds free; refraining from activities like hunting or fishing; avoiding harm to sentient beings; freeing prisoners; releasing people facing the death penalty by purchasing their freedom; providing refuge to those escaping tax burdens or military conscription;
- abiding by Confucian-inspired virtues, such as loyalty and filial piety, to aid and reform the kingdom and to order and protect the household.

Zanning's characterization of Yanshou gives priority to the *Wanshan tonggui ji* as representative of Yanshou's identity as a Buddhist free of sectarian identity and as a promoter of blessings broadly conceived. This depiction later proved problematic in light of the strong sectarian character of Song Buddhism. To later members of the Chan community, Zanning's choice amounted to an unpardonable oversight. Contesting Zanning's depiction, Chan advocates rallied to rehabilitate Yanshou and claim priority for his identity as a Chan master.

Yanshou as Chan Master (*Chanshi*)

Less than twenty years after Zanning compiled Yanshou's biography in the *Song gaoseng zhuan*, the Chan monk Daoyuan claimed Yanshou as a member of the Chan school. The *Jingde chuandeng lu*, compiled in the fourth year of the *Jingde* era (1004) and issued under imperial sanction in 1011, marks a major advance in official recognition of Chan lineages in China. Unlike the *Song gaoseng zhuan*, the *Jingde chuandeng lu* was compiled on strict sectarian lines to promote the independent identity of Chan lineages within Song Buddhism. The style and content of the *Jingde chuandeng lu* implicitly distinguished Chan from its scholastic forbears in several ways. It did not focus on abstract doctrine or textual exegesis, but rather placed emphasis on the concrete experiences of Chan monks. As a result, Chan biography and hagiography, as a record of these experiences, took on enhanced meaning.[17] Dialogue and encounters between masters and disciples became a central feature of the biographies. Poetic utterances, enlightenment verses, and enigmatic remarks became the hallmark of Chan monks who disdained logical analysis and wordy explanations as mistaking the true nature of words and the inherent limitations on their utility.

Chan lineage records also acknowledged kinship ties as a fundamental motif of Chinese culture and society. Leaving one's natural home to enter a Buddhist monastery had long been legally acknowledged in China as a kind of adoption, whereby the official registration of the person in question was transferred from their family roster and added to the roster of the monastery in question. In effect, one legally became a member of a new Buddhist "family." Chan took this process in new directions, by making lineage the organizing framework of its membership.[18] Thus, not only were individual temples maintained through a succession of abbots but Chan lineages were also maintained through a succession of patriarchs independent of individual temple affiliation. In this way, Chan came to represent a series of lineages, branches, and subbranches, in affiliation with, but not directly dependent on, an existing temple-institution structure.

It is interesting to note how this new arrangement fits the circumstances of increasing government control over abbacy appointments. Although further investigation is required, it suggests that temple lineage alone was inadequate for acknowledging monks of national prominence. Temples are by nature local, and generally have no influence beyond their particular region. Temple abbots would be similarly restricted. Chan lineages, on the other hand, assume a Chan influence transcending regional limitations.[19]

The *Jingde chuandeng lu* was not the first record to assert the universal history of Buddhism from a Chan perspective. It was compiled to counter the claims of the *Zutang ji*, a multilineal Chan transmission record compiled in 952.[20] Both works openly acknowledged each other's lineages. The issue was not legitimacy, but one of primacy in understanding Chan teaching.

Little is known of Daoyuan, compiler of the *Jingde chuandeng lu*.[21] He also hailed from the Wuyue region and is presumed to have been, like Yanshou, a student of Deshao, indicating a strong likelihood of personal contact between them.[22] The compilation of the *Jingde chuandeng lu* is clouded by the role of Yang Yi (974–1020), a powerful Song official, in bringing the work to publication.[23] Yang Yi's preface indicates that Daoyuan's original text was reedited by leading scholar-officials at the Song court, under the direction of Yang Yi.[24] Lacking Daoyuan's original compilation, it is impossible to tell what effect Yang Yi's editorial work had on the text's contents. We do know that Yang Yi was heavily influenced by Linji Chan masters and played an active role in promoting that school at the Song court. We also know that his conception of Chan as a "separate *practice* outside [Buddhist] teaching" (*jiaowai biexiu*) was consistent with the emerging Song Chan self-definition as "a separate *transmission* outside [Buddhist] teaching" (*jiaowai biechuan*), especially as conceived of by members of the Linji lineage.[25] Daoyuan's own preface suggests that he conceived his work in different terms. His original title, *Fozu tongcan ji* (Collection of the Common Practice of the Buddhas and Patriarchs), indicates commonality between the practice of the buddhas and Chan patriarchs. Chan, in other words, was not conceived as unique or separate from Buddhist teaching and practice, but in fundamental accord with it. The question emerging from the two prefaces was not over the status of Chan as the preeminent teaching of Buddhism, but the kind of Chan promoted.

Yanshou was destined to become a controversial figure in the debate over the nature of Chan teaching. The questions regarding Yanshou's Buddhist identity in the *Jingde chuandeng lu* are twofold. In the first place, there is the question of Yanshou's status as a Chan master, which the *Jingde chuandeng lu* claims unequivocally. The second question concerns the true or orthodox nature of Chan teaching. In the *Jingde chuandeng lu*, Yanshou's image is cast in typically Chan terms, befitting the emerging identity of Chan orthodoxy at the Song court. In the *Jingde chaundeng lu*, Yanshou is presented as a Chan master in the fashion that this text helped standardize. His experience as a Buddhist practitioner is punctuated by sudden insight accompanied by poetic reflection, and by critical encounters with students, through which the essence of his insight into the nature of Chan is made evident.

The *Jingde chuandeng lu* biography acknowledges Yanshou as third patriarch in the Fayan lineage, one of the "five houses" (*wujia*) of medieval Chan. The title of the biography claims Yanshou as "the tenth generation heir of Chan master Xingsi," a disciple of the famed sixth patriarch Huineng and "the Dharma-heir of former National Preceptor (*guoshi*) Deshao of Mount Tiantai."[26] Earlier in the *Jingde chuandeng lu*, Daoyuan claimed that Deshao was the ninth-generation heir of Xingsi, and Dharma-heir of Fayan Wenyi (885–958).[27] The titles themselves reveal the new way Yanshou's life was cast as a prominent member of a leading lineage in the Chan movement. In his own writings, Yanshou pays little regard for Chan lineage as a mark of Buddhist identity and makes no mention of any Fayan factional identity. Nor is any special role assigned to Tiantai Deshao, the master from whom the *Jingde chuandeng lu* suggests Yanshou received a special mind-to-mind transmission and upon whom his identity as a Chan master rests.

Like the *Song gaoseng zhuan*, the *Jingde chuandeng lu* biography of Yanshou emphasizes his devout nature, frugal character, fondness for chanting the *Lotus Sutra*, and so on. These characteristics point to areas of overlap in the depiction of Yanshou in the two sources, which is attributable to the familiarity both compilers had with Yanshou's life and their temporal proximity to the events in question. In spite of this commonality, the *Jingde chuandeng lu* was conceived of for different purposes than the *Song gaoseng zhuan*, and this changed the way Yanshou was identified. The overwhelming impression left by the *Jingde chuandeng lu* biography is of Yanshou as a Chan master. After taking up residence as a teacher at Mount Xuedou, for example, Yanshou reportedly addressed his followers in typically Chan style: "Here on Mount Xuedou, where the water of a dashing waterfall plunges thousands of feet, even the tiniest chestnut has nowhere to rest. On the awesome crag ten thousand feet high, there is no place for you to stand. I ask each and every one of you, where are you going?"[28]

Later on, after assuming the abbacy of Yongming Monastery, a monk reportedly asked: "What is the subtle essence of your teaching here at Yongming Monastery?" Yanshou responded, "Put more incense on the burner." Following the exchange, Yanshou composed a poem:

> If you want to know the teaching at Yongming:
> In front of the gate there lies a lake;
> When the sun shines, bright light is reflected off it;
> When the wind blows, waves arise.[29]

As in examples like this, Yanshou's teaching bears the typical mark of an enigmatic Chan master who employs the unexpected and seemingly trite example or turn of phrase to reveal the profound nature of his understanding.

The problem with this characterization is that it bears no resemblance to the Chan teaching Yanshou displays in his writings. Yanshou's compilations are known for the extensive use of materials drawn from classic Buddhist sources, but as a Chan master, it is odd that Yanshou makes such sparse mention of prominent Chan figures. In the *Wanshan tonggui ji*, for example, Bodhidharma is not mentioned. Huineng is mentioned but once, as are Nanquan Puyuan, Baizhang Huaihai, and Layman Pang. Niutou Farong is mentioned twice. There is no mention at all of Yanshou's supposed lineal forbears, Tiantai Deshao and Fayan Wenyi. Zongmi, on the other hand, is mentioned five times. To help put these figures in perspective, Tiantai master Zhiyi is mentioned seven times. Yanshou's mention of Chan or other prominent Buddhist figures pales in comparison to his references to classic Buddhist scriptures: the *Huayan Sutra* is cited fifty-one times, and the *Lotus Sutra* is cited twenty-nine times. Chan figures and sources, as currently defined, are noticeable by their absence and seem to have exerted little influence on Yanshou.[30]

One might expect the *Zongjing lu*, Yanshou's compilation of "Chan" sources, to reveal a different picture. Yet this is not the case. While Yanshou does refer to Chan lineage masters more frequently and more prominently in the *Zongjing lu*, their presence is still greatly overshadowed by his reliance on traditional scriptural sources. For example, on the one hand, the *Huayan Sutra* and commentaries on it are cited over 360 times, the *Lotus Sutra* and commentaries on it are cited over 130 times, and the *Nirvana Sutra* and commentaries on it cited over 140 times. On the other hand, there are only seven references to the sixth patriarch, Huineng, seven references to Bodhidharma, and six references to Mazu and Huangbo. In contrast, there are nine references to Zhuangzi.[31] To be fair, Chan *yulu* texts, the major sources of the Chan school, were not yet published in Yanshou's day, and Chan lineage masters had not achieved the status and credibility that they would later enjoy.[32] Nevertheless, it is clear that Yanshou favored an understanding of Chan as an integral part of the Buddhist scriptural and doctrinal tradition. In fact, the evidence suggests that Yanshou was highly critical of the style of Chan that many classic Chan figures are said to represent.

In the *Wanshan tonggui ji*, Yanshou responds critically to those who base their understanding of Buddhism on common Chan sayings. For example, when a questioner cites a famous saying attributed to Huineng in the *Jingde chuandeng lu*, "When things are not considered in terms of good and evil, one naturally gains entrance into the essence of the mind (*xinti*),"[33] Yanshou chides him for his partial understanding of Buddhism and biased understanding of Chan.[34] In another instance, a questioner cites the Chan saying, "Everything that comes into contact with one's eye is in the state of *bodhi*, whatever comes into contact with one's feet is the Way (*dao*)" as a basis for criticizing Yanshou's more formal and conventional approach to Buddhist practice.[35] Yanshou's response to exclusive reliance on such an approach to Chan is unequivocal, "You should not, because of some idiosyncratic interpretation of the void (*xu*), obliterate virtue and destroy good deeds [only] to be haphazardly reborn in some evil transmigration, or deny existence and cling to emptiness [only] to become haplessly implicated in a net of evil."[36] The position of so-called Southern Chan, which came to represent an orthodox Chan position, held otherwise. In the *Platform Sutra*, Huineng claims: "Building temples, giving alms, and making offerings are merely the practice of seeking after blessings. One cannot make merit with blessings. Merit is in the Dharma-body, not in the field of blessings . . . Merit is created from the mind; blessings and merit are different."[37]

Yanshou's aim in the *Zongjing lu* makes clear his belief in the authority of Buddhist scripture. In the preface to this work, Yanshou states explicitly his goal of establishing true, or correct, *zong*.[38] The term *zong* is problematic, owing to its different meanings. It can refer to a doctrinal interpretation, particularly the underlying theme or essential doctrine of a text, or to a "school," which in Chinese Buddhism refers to a tradition tracing its origin back to its founder.[39] In this case, Yanshou is closer to the first meaning, suggesting a unified underlying theme or essential doctrine of Buddhist teaching as a whole, and is clearly countering narrower interpretations favored by sectarian lineages. The means to accomplish this aim are also made clear: using the question-and-answer method to dispel doubts, and citing writings that make explicit true principle, in other words, the central, unifying source (*zhengzong*) of Buddhist teaching. The suggestion that such a unifying doctrine underlies all Buddhist teaching is essentially antithetical to sectarian concerns.

According to Yanshou, the citation of authoritative scriptures, the teachings of the buddhas and patriarchs, makes clear that the one, all-encompassing, universal mind (*yixin*) is the *zong*, the central, unifying source of Buddhist teaching. The myriad dharmas of phenomenal existence (*wanfa*) are the mirror, or reflections (*jing*) of the mind.[40] Hence the title of the work, *Zong jing lu*, refers to a record (*lu*) of sources which reflect or mirror (*jing*) the essential, underlying doctrine of Buddhist teaching (*zong*).

Although the aim of Yanshou's work is to provide comprehensive unity and harmony for Buddhist teaching, it is also important to read it as a reaction to divisive sectarian tendencies in Chinese Buddhism. In this sense, it may be suggested that Yanshou's choice of the term *zong* for inclusion in the title of his work was not simply a bland assertion of the obvious, but rather a polemical counter to sectarian developments as antithetical to true Buddhist aims.

Yanshou's conception of Chan is heavily indebted to Huayan teaching.[41] He speaks of Buddhist practice as being dependent on the natural interplay between *li* and *shi*, noumena and phenomena. Enlightenment, the truth, and so forth, must be actualized and performed. Only Buddhist practice makes this possible. As a result, Yanshou is disdainful of claims to enlightenment based on the renunciation of Buddhist teaching and practice. The appropriate role of Chan is to foster the actualization process by encouraging Buddhist practices. The response by Yanshou to the following question illustrates this point:

> Question: ... The still waters of meditation (*dingshui*) would become pure if people would abruptly stop becoming entangled in vexing circumstances. Of what use are assorted good deeds? Dashing about to confront external [circumstances] and turning one's back on true cultivation only causes exhaustion and worry.
>
> Answer: The tranquil manifestation of "no-mind" (*wuxin*)—this is the criterion for realization. Solemn, adorning practices (*zhuangyan*) for the accumulation of blessings and virtues (*fude*) are necessary on account of the nature of conditioned arising (*yuanqi*). Equipped with both ["no-mind" and adorning practices] functioning as a pair, the essence of Buddhahood (*foti*) is complete. None of the scriptures of the greater vehicle fail to record this in detail.[42]

The biography of Yanshou in the *Jingde chuandeng lu* and the approach to Buddhism in his writings created a major discrepancy between the image of Yanshou as Chan master and his actual Chan teaching. Dealing with this discrepancy resulted in major rifts in the Chan community. The *Tiansheng guangdeng lu*, compiled shortly after the *Jingde chuandeng lu* in 1036, responded by passing over Yanshou in its roster of Chan masters. This is remarkable, given that the Fayan lineage is acknowledged, but without acknowledging Yanshou's association with it.[43] This called into question the identity of Yanshou as a Chan master by a compiler who represented the interests of Chan lineages and who acknowledged the legitimacy of the Fayan faction. The *Tiansheng guangdeng lu* was compiled under the influence of Linji Chan at the Song court, and is particularly noteworthy for documenting previously unpublished teachings of masters in the Linji lineage.[44] The teachings of these Linji masters would eventually dominate Chan, and continue to define notions of the Chan school down to the present day.

Others continued to champion the cause of Yanshou as Chan master. Yanshou is included as a master in the Fayan lineage by Qisong, compiler of the *Chuanfa zheng zong ji* in 1061.[45] Qisong, a well known proponent of Chan-Buddhist syncretism, had close affinities with Yanshou's interpretation of Chan. Another proponent of scholastic (*wenzi*) Chan, Huihong, openly challenged those who questioned Yanshou's Chan identity by criticizing Zanning's classification of him as a promoter of blessings:

> Zanning compiled the extensive *Song gaoseng zhuan*, utilizing ten categories for the purpose of classification. He placed "exegetes" at the top [of the list]. This is laughable. Moreover, he presented Chan master Yendou Huo as a "practitioner of asceticism," and Chan master Zhijue [i.e., Yanshou] as a "promoter of blessings." The great master Yunmen is chief among monks. He was a contemporary of these people, but astonishingly [Zanning] did not even mention him.[46]

In addition, Huihong compiled a biography of Yanshou, recorded in both the *Chanlin sengbao zhuan* and the *Lingyin sizhi*.[47] This biography affirms Yanshou's Chan identity by asserting his association with the famous Chan temple, the *Lingyin si*, where he briefly served as abbot. This was the culmination of the "Chan phase" of Yanshou's career. Subsequently, he was reassigned to the Yongming Monastery where, according to speculation, he began to interpret Buddhism for a wider audience. Huihong's biography also features materials from the *Zongjing lu*, the work most closely associated with Yanshou's Chan teaching. It demonstrates Yanshou's conception of Chan as based on the essential harmony between Chan and scholastic Buddhist teaching. The style of the presentation substitutes the staid question-and-answer format typical of Chinese Buddhist scholastic discourse, taken from Yanshou's actual writings, for the emotionally charged exchanges attributed to Yanshou in the *Jingde chuandeng lu*.

Yanshou as Pure Land Master

Huihong's biography apparently settled the issue of Yanshou's identity in favor of Yanshou as a Chan scholastic who integrated Chan with the larger tradition of Mahayana Buddhism. New developments associated with key events in Yanshou's life, however, made the issue of Yanshou's identity even more complicated. Less than forty years after Huihong published Yanshou's biography in the *Chanlin sengbao zhuan* (1123), a new image of Yanshou as Pure Land practitioner was projected in the *Longshu jingtu wen* (1160). Over the next century, this new image of Yanshou became predominant in Chinese Buddhist circles. It persists as the dominant image of Yanshou down to the present day.

Two factors made Yanshou an attractive model for these new developments. Zanning had already indicated Yanshou's strong propensity for *Lotus Sutra* recitation, and identified him as a promoter of blessings. Even given Yanshou's strong Chan credentials, his style of Chan included performing myriad good deeds, activities he viewed as an inherent part of being Buddhist. Theory and practice fit together for Yanshou as two necessary parts of an integrated and harmonious approach to Buddhism. While meditation was an integral part of Yanshou's practice, and "Chan" was the moniker through which he touted his brand of Buddhism, there is no denying the broad array of practices—worship, recitation, invoking of Buddha names, mystical chants, adornments, and so forth—that characterized Yanshou's approach.

The second factor that made Yanshou an attractive candidate as a model Pure Land practitioner was the emergence of the Pure Land movement in the Song. During the Southern Song (1127–1279), the Pure Land movement was formally recognized and organized by historians of the Tiantai school, with which the movement was closely associated. Biographies of Pure Land masters were compiled by Tiantai historians, and a lineage of Pure Land patriarchs was established.[48] A significant portion of Yanshou's career was spent on Mount Tiantai as a student under Tiantai Deshao, a monk who played a major role in the revival of Mount Tiantai and of Buddhism generally in Wuyue. Yanshou's own writings were heavily influenced by the *Lotus Sutra* and Tiantai scholasticism. As Tiantai historians began promoting the Pure Land, it is easy to see how Yanshou emerged as a prime candidate for inspiration.

The elevation of Yanshou to Pure Land status was prompted by new accounts of Yanshou's life. In this sense, the *Longshu jingtu wen* represents a major departure in how the story of Yanshou's life had come to be regarded. It is the first source to document the new Pure Land tendencies that came to dominate the characterization of Yanshou's life. As a work designed to promote Pure Land doctrine and faith, the *Longshu jingtu wen* was critical of both Chan practitioners who promoted "Mind-Only" (*weixin*) Pure Land, and Pure Land practitioners who emphasized salvation in an afterlife to the neglect of performing meritorious works in the present world.[49] "Mind-Only" Pure Land followed the principles of the Consciousness-Only (*weishi*) school of Buddhism, which posited that all of reality, including the notion of the Pure Land, is simply a product of one's own mind and therefore devoid of substantial reality. Pure Land practitioners who neglected meritorious deeds in the belief that salvation could be won by invocation alone ran the risk of running into moral jeopardy without a prescribed routine of activities to guide them.

Yanshou's biography in the *Longshu jingtu wen* appears in a fascicle entitled "Records of Miraculous Communications" (*ganying shiji*), implying divine communications beneficial for those seeking rebirth in the Pure Land. Two noteworthy aspects characterize the *Longshu jingtu wen* record of Yanshou; both involve events predicated on miraculous communication. One is the assertion that Yanshou had a vision of Guanyin at a crucial juncture in his career, shortly after leaving his official duties and becoming a monk. In the vision, Guanyin sprinkles Yanshou's mouth with "sweet dew," in what amounts to an anointment of Yanshou. As a result, Yanshou is said to have obtained the eloquence of Guanyin.

Guanyin, of course, is a major figure in the Pure Land cult, appearing prominently in the *Lotus Sutra* and the *Wuliang shoujing* (*Sukhāvatāvyūha sūtra*).[50] In effect, Yanshou's vision connects his career to the divine assistance provided by the compassionate Guanyin, a major premise of Pure Land thought. The *Wanshan tonggui ji* and the *Zongjing lu* are both mentioned in the *Longshu jingtu wen* biography, so that one of the functions of this episode is to provide an integrated sense of Yanshou that accounts for both his Chan and Pure Land personae, albeit within a Tiantai/Pure Land framework. But even though an aspect of Yanshou as Chan practitioner is incorporated in the *Longshu jingtu wen* biography, the type of *chan* meditation that Yanshou engages in here is Pure Land *chan*, the purpose of which is to produce miraculous visions, not the awakening experience common to works dedicated to Chan factional lineages. The effect of the episode is to claim Yanshou unequivocally as a model Buddhist for Pure Land practitioners.

The second noteworthy aspect of the *Longshu jingtu wen* biography is the evidence it provides for a cult associated with the worship of Yanshou's stupa. The story related here is about a monk who daily worshiped the stupa of

Yanshou. When asked his reason for doing so, the monk replied that when he was consigned to the underworld in a previous life, he noticed the image of a monk in the corner of the palace King Yama, the king of the underworld. He also observed King Yama himself come before the image and prostrate himself before it. His curiosity was aroused by this strange sequence of events: a monk in the palace of the king of hell, who the king himself worshiped! The monk (in his previous incarnation as a denizen of hell) asked the caretaker of the palace about the identity of this monk that even King Yama worshiped. The caretaker informed him that this was none other than the Chan master Yanshou of Yongming Monastery. The caretaker also added that while normally people have to pass through the palace (to be judged) after they die, Yanshou was able to directly attain a most favorable rebirth in the Pure Land, without subjection to King Yama's judgment and wrath. The episode concludes with a statement to the effect that striving for the Pure Land is deemed valuable even in the underworld. In other words, salvation in the Pure Land remains possible for all, even those in the most dire of circumstances. Yanshou is the emissary of this salvation.

This episode provides the rationale for Yanshou's high status among Pure Land aspirants. Because of his special affinity with the Pure Land, Yanshou became the object of a cult that worshiped his stupa. In this capacity, Yanshou not only is honored as an object of admiration but also assumes the role of recipient of the supplications of others striving for rebirth in the Pure Land. The above story demonstrates that Yanshou's value to the Buddhist community at some point began to transcend the events, real or imagined, associated with his life on earth. Yanshou came to be regarded as a sacred presence, with qualities normally associated with Buddhist deities who serve as intermediaries on behalf of the petitions of others to help them gain rebirth in the Pure Land.[51]

Later Pure Land–inspired biographies continued to develop the story of Yanshou's life in ways that reflected the aspirations of the Pure Land faithful. The *Lebang wenlei*, compiled in 1200 by Zongxiao, included a number of miraculous episodes suggesting that Yanshou's entire career developed around incidents involving divine intervention.[52] The point of these stories is essentially the same as was seen with the *Longshu jingtu wen*—to connect Yanshou's life with the miraculous intercession of Buddhist deities and to present Yanshou as a model for emulation to those seeking such salutary effects.

One episode from the *Lebang wenlei* is particularly illustrative of the way divine intercession is used to explain key points of transition in Yanshou's career, particularly for affirming Yanshou's reputation as a Pure Land devotee. According to the episode, while he was circumambulating an image of

Samantabhadra (Puxian) during the night, a lotus flower that had been offered to the image suddenly appeared in Yanshou's hand. This prompted Yanshou to recall two vows he had made regarding the practice of Buddhism. The first was to recite the *Lotus Sutra* throughout his life. The second was to devote his life to saving sentient beings. The *Lebang wenlei* claims Yanshou yearned to carry out these two vows, but was prevented from doing so because he also enjoyed the tranquility of meditation (*chan*). This resulted in uncertainty in Yanshou's practice, and he could not resolve which course to follow: the one suggested by the two vows, the other based on devoting himself to *chan* meditation. The suggestion that such a tension was in need of resolution is the result of rising sectarian identities within Buddhism, particularly between Chan and Tiantai/Pure Land. In order to resolve this dilemma, Yanshou went to the meditation hall of Zhiyi (*Zhizhe chanyuan*) and wrote out two divination lots: "practice *chan-ting* (*chan samadhi*) exclusively" or "recite sutras, perform myriad good deeds, and solemnly adorn the Pure Land." If one of these two options was to be followed, Yanshou determined, it would be drawn seven times in succession. According to the story, Yanshou prayed to the buddhas and patriarchs for assistance, and then drew the second lot, "recite sutras, perform myriad good deeds, and solemnly adorn the Pure Land," the required seven times. This was interpreted as a clear indication of divine will. Yanshou's prayers had been answered and his dilemma resolved. Accordingly, Yanshou reportedly carried out the practices suggested by the second lot for the rest of his life. In the context of Chan and Pure Land sectarian dominance over Chinese Buddhism, this episode clarified Yanshou's allegiance in favor of Pure Land. The remaining episodes associated with Yanshou's life in the *Lebang wenlei* provide a decidedly Pure Land interpretation to his career.

In the meantime, Chan biographies of Yanshou continued to appear, but these records too followed the new image of Yanshou that Pure Land devotees had established. The *Rentian baojian*, compiled in 1230 by Tanxiu, acknowledged the new developments in Yanshou's life stemming from Pure Land sources.[53] Amid these changes, the *Rentian baojian* record reflects an attempt to reestablish Yanshou's Chan identity while conceding that divine intervention played a major role in Yanshou's life. It attempted to portray Yanshou as harmonizer of disputes, a task that Yanshou is eminently qualified for, given the character of his own thought, but one that did little to restore his tarnished image as a Chan master. It also recorded the miraculous story involving Samantabhadra referred to above. In the *Rentian baojian* version, we are simply told that as a result of the flower suddenly appearing in Yanshou's hand, he decided to scatter flowers as an offering to Samantabhadra throughout his life. This version avoids the decisive climax that affirmed Yanshou's Pure Land identity in the *Lebang wenlei* account, but does little to redeem an image of Yanshou as Chan master in the classic style.

In the end, the *Rentian baojian* did little more than concede that the battle over Yanshou's Buddhist identity has been decided in favor of the Pure Land. This is confirmed with the appearance of the *Shimen zhengtong* in 1237 and the *Fozu tongji* in 1269.[54] In the former, Yanshou is designated a "Dharma protector" (*hufa*). His biography is presented in the most systematic and comprehensive manner to date, indicating that it is beginning to achieve a standard form. Any remaining Chan proclivities are successfully expunged from his image. Episodes are added to Yanshou's life on Mount Xuedou, hitherto associated with the "Chan phase" of his career, presenting him as a Pure Land practitioner. In the *Fozu tongji*, Yanshou is designated a Pure Land patriarch, the crowning achievement in the transformation of his image by Pure Land devotees.

Many impulses contributed to Yanshou's elevation in Pure Land circles. Pure Land practices do play a role in Yanshou's own thought, as we have seen, but not to the degree suggested by Yanshou's Pure Land image makers. An examination of *Wanshan tonggui ji*, the text most often cited by Pure Land advocates as the source for Yanshou's Pure Land thought, clarifies the role that Pure Land plays, which is not as great as is usually suggested.[55]

This brings us to the question of what kind of *nianfo* (Buddha-invocation) practice Yanshou actually advocated.[56] Formal *nianfo* practice for Yanshou is based on the teaching of the fourfold *samadhi* in the Tiantai school.[57] This teaching makes provisions for the practice of *nianfo* either while sitting in meditation (*zuochan*) or while circumambulating the image of the Buddha. In addition, there is good indication that Yanshou intended *nianfo* recitation and contemplation to be used as an integral part of the *Fahua* repentance ritual. In the text of the *Fahua* repentance, cited by Yanshou, it is stated that there are two kinds of cultivation: "cultivation amid phenomena (*shi*)," which involves worshiping (*li*) and invoking the Buddha (*nianfo*) while circumambulating (*xingdao*), and "cultivation amid noumena (*li*)," contemplation which recognizes the nonduality of mind and nature and shows that everything is an aspect of the mind.[58]

In the same manner that Tiantai teaching includes *nianfo* in its teaching of the fourfold *samadhi* as a practice harmonious with the aims of contemplation and meditation, Yanshou views *nianfo* as compatible with the aims of *chanding*. For Yanshou, the aims of *chanding* are understood in terms of Buddhist ideational theory, which claims that all realms of existence are creations of mind-only (*weixin*). *Nianfo* is analogous to what mind-only creates; the Pure Land of mind-only (*weixin jingtu*) is the creation of the storehouse-consciousness. Thus, what is created through the cultivation of Pure Land practice is analogous to any existence that mind-only creates, including this world that we inhabit.

In this way, capitalizing on the creative capacity of the mind according to *weixin* theory, Yanshou is able to emphasize the positive function of the mind which, of its own nature, is able to create provisional existence. Though provisional and ultimately unreal, a Pure Land thus created is of positive value in the quest for enlightenment. As a state of existence, it is neither more nor less real than the external condition of the physical world, which according to *weixin* theory is ultimately a reflection of the same creative processes of our mental capacities. As such, the mind can be utilized in a similar manner to further Buddhist aims. This is not to suggest, however, that the existence of the Pure Land be taken literally. Yanshou is quite explicit in stating that in reference to the fundamental absolute, one should never suggest that buddhas and buddha lands actually exist, much less talk about arriving there.[59] By the same token, Buddhist ideational theory would never suggest that the existence of the physical world be taken literally, either. The Pure Land, as a provisional existence for the assistance of sentient beings in their quest for enlightenment, represents a skillful means. Understood in its broadest sense, the Pure Land may be seen as a function of *wanshan* practice in the *Wanshan tonggui ji* as a whole.

Mind cultivation, or mediation practice (*chanding*, *zuochan*, *zhiguan*, *guanxin*, etc.), constitutes the cornerstone of traditional Buddhist practice. It aims at attaining enlightenment in this life through the realization that all objects are but manifestations of the mind. With this realization, the practitioner aims at curbing, or extinguishing, the mind's manifesting power, thus emptying it of mind-objects, and nullifying the causes and conditions which life and death (that is, *samsara*) depend on. It is the cultivation of this realization that breeds enlightenment, wisdom, and eventually, Buddhahood.

For Yanshou, the cultivation of *wanshan* operates within the same set of assumptions utilized in different, somewhat contrary ways. *Nianfo* practice represents a concrete expression of *wanshan* cultivation. Instead of suppressing the manifesting power of the mind, the practitioner is encouraged to utilize it to create those causes and conditions which will result in favorable circumstances (that is, the Pure Land or some other buddha land) in their next incarnation. These circumstances are designed to assure one's salvation in the next life. The Pure Land, then, is none other than the favorable circumstances created by the manifesting power of one's own mind in this life.

By stressing the positive function of the mind rather than curbing its manifesting power, Yanshou is able to supply a structure that supports the activity of the myriad good deeds and validates practice designed for attaining birth in the Pure Land. In doing so, he tends to regard existence in a positive and meaningful way despite its essentially provisional nature. The theoretical basis for the relationship between *chanding*, on the one hand, and *nianfo* and sutra recitation, on the other, is described by Yanshou in various terms: the silence of meditation and the sound of recitation, tranquility (*jing*) and motion (*dong*), silence and words.[60] The point here is again the same as for the relationship between *chanding* and *wanshan*. These do not represent duality; they are complimentary aspects of the same reality. Conditioned activities in the realm of *shi* are complimentary and harmonious with the unconditioned realm of *li*. The sound of recitation and the silence of mediation, the activity of *wanshan* and the tranquility of *chanding*, when cultivated together with equal emphasis, reflect the harmony and equilibrium of these two realms.

In the final analysis, Yanshou conceived *nianfo* within the parameters of *wanshan*, and not the other way around. Nor did he conceive of *nianfo* as in any way the focal point of *wanshan*. As a result, it is inappropriate to isolate Yanshou's Pure Land practice, as has traditionally been done, as indicative of his Buddhist sectarian affiliation. This assumption stems from the Buddhism of a later age, and is insupportable on the basis of Yanshou's own writings.

Yanshou as Advocate of Bodhisattva Practice

It is clear that a more accurate view of Yanshou is needed. This is evident, for example, from the way that modern textbooks on Chinese Buddhism treat Yanshou.[61] Textbook accounts of Yanshou leave students with a number of erroneous impressions. In the first place, Yanshou is marginalized as a peripheral figure, even in cases that suggest his important contributions. Yanshou has received little attention in recent scholarship, in part because his contributions came during an "age of decline," based on the assumption that the Tang dynasty represented the "golden age" of Buddhism in China and that subsequent periods represent a fall from this pinnacle.

Within the assumptions that cast him as a marginal figure, Yanshou is typically regarded in one of two ways. The first regards Yanshou as a Chan syncretist, and in this capacity he is often cast as exemplifying the decline of Chan in China on the presumption of a "pure" and uncompromising form of Chan orthodoxy. The other way Yanshou is frequently regarded is to highlight Chan and Pure Land practice as the specific focus of Yanshou's syncretism.[62] These images are deeply indebted to the way Yanshou has been cast in traditional sources. As reviewed above, the development of this image of Yanshou is quite late, and bears little resemblance to the style of Buddhism projected through his own writings.

How should we regard Yanshou? The above analysis suggests that the common ways of understanding Yanshou, whether as "promoter of blessings," or as "Chan master," or as "Pure Land devotee," however justifiable, fail to capture the comprehensive vision of Buddhism Yanshou promoted in his own writings. At the risk of further complicating an already complicated picture, I would like to suggest another image of Yanshou, drawn from his writings, that does more justice to his comprehensive Buddhist vision: to reclaim Yanshou as an "advocate of bodhisattva practice." This appellation has the merit of presenting Yanshou as a devout, trans-sectarian Buddhist, whose main interest was promoting Mahayana Buddhism, free of sectarian intent. It is not meant to deny the other images drawn of Yanshou, but rather to suggest that the prevailing images are limited and do not do full justice to the comprehensive way Yanshou understood Buddhism. The image of Yanshou as advocate of bodhisattva practice has the advantage of overcoming these limitations while at the same time incorporating the prevailing views of Yanshou into a larger, more comprehensive framework.

The model of the bodhisattva suggests a Buddhist practitioner free of sectarian bias, one who fully understands scriptural and doctrinal teachings, and applies this understanding in the actual circumstances provided through conventional Buddhist ritual practice. The impulse here is to encourage all to participate as their capacities allow, rather than to discourage an activity as misguided based on the presumption of superior insight. Evidence suggests that Yanshou intended his promotion of individual Buddhist practices to be understood in this way. For example, in the case of Yanshou's promotion of the Pure Land, he writes: "When contemplation is shallow and the mind wanders, sense-objects are overpowering and the force of habit is oppressive, one needs to be reborn in the Pure Land. By relying on the excellent circumstances there, the power of endurance is easily attained, and one quickly practices the way of bodhisattvas."[63]

Elsewhere, as a warning to Chan practitioners who assume that insight alleviates the need for conventional Buddhist practice, Yanshou asserts:

> Myriad good deeds (*wanshan*) are the provisions with which bodhisattvas enter sainthood; the assorted practices are gradual steps with which buddhas assist [people] on the way [to enlightenment]. If one has eyes but no feet, how can one reach the pure, refreshing pond [i.e., nirvana]? If one obtains the truth but forgets expedients, how can one soar to the spontaneous, free land? On account of this,

skillful means and *prajna*-wisdom always assist each other; true
emptiness and wondrous existence always complement each other.
In the *Lotus Sutra*, the three vehicles are joined and unified with the
one vehicle, just as the myriad good deeds all propel one toward
enlightenment.[64]

In support of this view, I would like to draw attention to a lesser known work by Yanshou, a "Preface to the Teaching on Induction into the Bodhisattva Precepts" (*Shou pusa jiefa bingxu*).[65] The text itself is no longer extant, and only the preface remains. The compilation of the original text appears to have been based on the *Brahmajala Sutra* (*Fanwang jing*), an influential work concerning the bodhisattva precepts.[66] The preface is divided into nine sections, an introduction and eight brief questions followed by responses varying in length. The style of the preface is reminiscent of that used by Yanshou in his other major works: an introductory section setting forth the main principles, followed by question-and-answer sections in which doubts are resolved with responses based in scriptural sources. One of the functions of this method is to illustrate the authoritative nature of Buddhist scripture as the record of the teachings of the buddhas and learned Buddhist sages.

The preface suggests that "bodhisattva practice" was a centralizing motif in Yanshou's thought. We know that administering the bodhisattva precepts was a major activity for Yanshou. The *Jingde chuandeng lu* notes how Yanshou regularly administered the bodhisattva precepts to the Buddhist faithful, specifically to over ten thousand people on Mount Tiantai in the seventh year of the *Kaibao* era (974).[67] The introduction to the preface begins: "The various bodhisattva precepts establish stages [of progress] for the thousand sages, produce the foundation for the myriad good deeds (*wanshan*), open the gateway to nirvāna[68] and set [practitioners] on the path to bodhi. The *Brahmajala Sutra* says, 'When sentient beings are inducted into the Buddhist [i.e., bodhisattva] precepts, they enter the ranks of the Buddhas.'"[69] Yanshou comments:

> [The *sutra*] wants us to understand that the Buddhist precepts are none other than the mind of sentient beings; there is no Buddhist teaching separate from them. Because they awaken one's mind, they are called the "Buddha." Because they make it possible to follow and support [Buddhism], they are known as the "Dharma." Because they make the mind inherently harmonious [toward others] and nondivisive, they are known as the "Sangha." Because of the mind's inherent perfection and purity, they are known as the "precepts." Because they [foster] tranquility and wisdom, they are known as "prajna." Because they make the mind fundamentally quiet and tranquil, they are

known as "nirvana." The bodhisattva precepts are the supreme
vehicle of the tathagata, and the reason why the patriarch
[Bodhidharma] came from the west.[70]

This makes clear the priority of bodhisattva precept practice for Yanshou. They are the basis for sagely practice and the foundation for the myriad good deeds, setting practitioners on the path toward enlightenment. In this capacity, the bodhisattva precepts function as the framework from which Yanshou was traditionally regarded as a "promoter of blessings," as they "produce the foundation for the myriad good deeds."

In addition, the emphasis on understanding the precepts as "the mind of sentient beings" suggests that they serve as Yanshou's framework for understanding Chan. The precepts are responsible for awakening one's mind (Buddha), making it possible to follow Buddhist teaching (Dharma), and for making the mind harmonious and nondivisive (Sangha). In like fashion, the precepts are linked to moral cultivation via precept observance, *prajna*-wisdom, and nirvana. They are "the supreme vehicle of the tathagata," suggesting a link to Buddhist doctrine as revealed in the sutra-teachings of the Buddha, and "the reason why Bodhidharma came from the west," suggesting a linkage to the Chan lineage. This parallel treatment of the Buddha and Bodhidharma affirms Yanshou's interpretation of Chan as viewed in the *Zongjing lu*, to the effect that Chan patriarchs revealed the principles of Chan (*chanli*), transmitting the true, underlying doctrine of Buddhism (*zhengzong*) tacitly to one another in secret, while Buddhas made explicit doctrinal teachings (*jiaomen*), establishing the main points through written texts. A similar parallel is struck elsewhere in Yanshou's preface, again in connection with the *Brahmajala Sutra*.

According to the *Brahmajala Sutra:* "Anything possessing mind
has no choice but to uphold the Buddhist precepts."[71] Of those born
in human form, who does not have mind? When common
people attain Buddhahood they always manifest it from the mind.
As a result, Sakyamuni appeared in the world to open the minds
of sentient beings to the knowledge and insight of a Buddha.
Bodhidharma came from the west, pointed directly to the human
mind, to see one's nature and become a Buddha. On account of this,
a patriarch said: "Mind is Buddha; Buddha is mind. There is no
mind apart from Buddha; there is no Buddha apart from mind."[72] As
a result, all physical and mental forms, whether they pertain to the
emotions or to the mind, are without exception included in the
bodhisattva precepts (*foxing jie*).[73] The mind of sentient beings and
the mind of Buddha-nature (i.e., the bodhisattva) are both inherent

in the Buddha-mind precepts (*foxin jie*). How different the bodhisattva precepts, which cherish saving others, are from the rules of the lesser vehicle, which bind one to external circumstances! As a result of this [difference], bodhisattvas provide numerous blessings [for others].[74]

The content of these passages indicate how the bodhisattva precepts function as a framework for incorporating Chan with the promotion of blessings stemming from the practice of myriad good deeds. Can the image of Yanshou as promoter of bodhisattva practices also be made to incorporate his image as a Pure Land practitioner? This is a topic raised in the last question-and-answer section of the preface.[75]

The thrust of Yanshou's message in this section is that the practice of *nianfo* is efficacious for attaining rebirth in the Pure Land, but exclusive reliance on this practice alone is not advisable. Transferring merit gained from invoking the Buddha enables one to be reborn in the Pure Land, but only at the lowest ranks.[76] Only after twelve kalpas will such practitioners begin to develop awareness; even then they will not have developed sufficiently to actually meet the Buddha (a precondition according to Pure Land teachings for attaining enlightenment oneself). In other words, rebirth in the Pure Land, according to Yanshou, does not preclude the necessity of progressing through the ascending stages of Buddhist teaching and practice. Gradually, practitioners advance through lesser vehicle teachings and practices. Those who are inducted into the bodhisattva precepts have distinct advantages over practitioners who are not. Having conceived of supreme enlightenment as defined by the teachings of the greater vehicle, they follow a set of practices and regulations designed to foster their progress while curbing the effects of evil karma. In short, the practice of invoking the Buddha (*nianfo*), like confession of sins (*chanhui*) and assisting living beings (*zhusheng*), functions as an aid to help one from violating the precepts. The point is that the bodhisattva precepts are cast by Yanshou as the central program of Buddhist practice; invoking the Buddha, confessing sins, and assisting living beings function as auxiliary practices augmenting the bodhisattva precepts. Rebirth in the upper ranks of the Pure Land, moreover, can only be achieved through following the bodhisattva precepts and practicing myriad good deeds, including *chanding*. The implication of this section and the preface as a whole is that while great variety exists among sentient beings to understand and advance on the path to enlightenment, and while Buddhist teaching employs a multitude of opportunities for advancement in accordance with the notion of expediencies, the bodhisattva precepts function as a centralizing framework around which various Buddhist practices derive their meaning and purpose.

Concluding Remarks

Returning to questions asked at the outset of this inquiry—is Yanshou a Zen master? if so, what kind of Zen master is he?—I offer the following reflections. The attempt to define the parameters of Zen identity, especially with sectarian motives in mind, is always rooted in claims to orthodoxy. The exclusion of Yanshou from the Chan and Zen ranks is predicated on the rhetorical claims of Linji and Rinzai orthodoxy as "a special transmission outside the teaching." Yet this claim, as we have seen, need not be as exclusive as it is often interpreted. Another, lesser known interpretation of this phrase is to couple the secret, esoteric transmission allegedly stemming from Sakyamuni's initiation of the Chan patriarchy with his public, exoteric preaching, documented through the canon of Buddhist scriptures. Iconographically, this is represented in the Buddhist triad of Sakyamuni flanked by Mahakasyapa, the successor to the Chan patriarchy on one side, and Ananda, the deliverer of the Buddha's oral teachings, on the other. This is not an image normally seen in Japan, but is common in other parts of East Asia. If Chan exclusivity is a function of Linji and Rinzai factional rhetoric with limited applicability "on the ground" to the actual conduct that constitutes the everyday reality of Chan, Sŏn, and Zen practice, how should Chan, Sŏn, and Zen be understood? The marriage of Chan factionalism, exhibited through lineage construction, and Mahayana orthodoxy, represented through the array of conventional Buddhist practices, is a nuptial over which Yanshou presided. Whenever a divorce occurred, Yanshou's reputation suffered. The legacy of Yanshou's identity as Chan master and a practicing Mahayanist is caught between these polarities.

NOTES

1. In addition to the general neglect of Yanshou, the attitude toward Yanshou in Rinzai circles is indicated in a conversation that I had with Nishiguchi Yoshio of the Institute for the Study of Zen Culture at Hanazono University in Kyoto, Japan, a scholar whose work I otherwise admire greatly. When asked why so little scholarly work was done on Yanshou by Zen scholars in Japan, I was told, matter-of-factly, that it was because Yanshou was not a Zen master.

2. For my previous work on Yanshou's biography, see Albert Welter, "The Life of Yung-ming Yanshou: The Making of a Ch'an and Pure Land Patriarch," in *The Meaning of Myriad Good Deeds: A Study of Yung-ming Yenshou and the Wan-shan t'ung-kuei chi* (New York: Peter Lang, 1993), pp. 37–108; and "The Contextual Study of Chinese Buddhist Biographies: The Example of Yung-ming Yanshou (904–975)," in Phyllis Granoff and Koichi Shinohara, eds., *Monks and Magicians: Religious Biographies in Asia* (Oakville, Ont.: Mosaic Press, 1988), pp. 247–268. Shih Heng-ching, "The

Ch'an-Pure Land Synthesis in China: With Special Reference to Yung-ming Yen-shou" (Ph.D. diss., University of Wisconsin, 1984) (subsequently published as *The Syncretism of Ch'an and Pure Land Buddhism*, New York: Peter Lang, 1992), pp. 132ff., reconstructs Yanshou's life following the literal reading of traditional sources, without sufficient regard for the circumstances and motivations of the documents in question.

3. This is not to deny the power wielded by a revived Tiantai school, which was also indebted to Yanshou. Ikeda Rōsan, in "Eimei enju no *Kishinron* kenkyū," *Indogaku bukkyōgaku kenkyū* 47/1 (1998): 201–204, argues for the need to reevaluate Yanshou's underestimated and ignored influence over Song Tiantai figures such as Zixuan and Zhili. Song Tiantai scholars were also responsible for creating the Pure Land "school," attesting to the close identification of both during this period. On this, see Daniel Getz, "T'ien-t'ai Pure Land Societies and the Creation of the Pure Land Patriarchate," in Peter Gregory and Daniel Getz, eds., *Buddhism in the Sung* (Honolulu: University of Hawaii Press, 1999), pp. 477–523.

4. T. 50.887a–b. For a translation of Zanning's biography of Yanshou, see Welter, *The Meaning of Myriad Good Deeds*, pp. 193–194.

5. See Hatanaka Jōen, "Goetsu no bukkyō—toku ni tendai tokushō to sono shi eimei enju ni tsuite," *Indogaku bukkyōgaku kenkyū* 2/1 (1953): 322.

6. On the use of tomb-inscriptions as sources for Chinese Buddhist biographies, see Koichi Shinohara, "Two Sources of Chinese Buddhist Biographies: Stūpa Inscriptions and Miracle Stories," in Phyllis Granoff and Koichi Shinohara, eds., *Monks and Magicians: Religious Biographies in Asia*, pp. 119–228.

7. T. 50.887b15–16. Arthur F. Wright, in his study of Huijiao and the *Gaoseng zhuan*, drew the same conclusion: "We are perhaps safe in assuming that as a general rule, when he mentions the existence of a memorial inscription as a biographical fact, he had access to the data it contained"; "Biography and Hagiography: Hui-chiao's Lives of Eminent Monks," in *Silver Jubilee Volume of the Jimbun Kagaku Kenkyujō* (Kyoto, 1954), p. 427.

8. Welter, *The Meaning of Myriad Good Deeds*, pp. 37–108.

9. T. 50.887a29.

10. See Welter, "A Buddhist Response to the Confucian Revival: Tsan-ning and the Debate over *Wen* in the Early Sung," in Peter Gregory and Daniel Getz, *Buddhism in the Sung*, pp. 21–61.

11. Regarding the revival of Buddhism in Wuyue, see Abe Jōichi, *Chūgoku zenshūshi no kenkyū: seiji shakai teki kosatsu*, revised edition (Tokyo: Seishin shobō, 1987), pp. 125–210.

12. T. 50–2059.

13. T. 50–2060 and 2061. The ten categories here are: translators (*yijing*), exegetes (*yijie*), meditation practitioners (*xichan*), elucidators of discipline (*minglu*), protectors of the Dharma (*hufa*), miracle workers (*gantong*), self-immolations (*yishen*), hymnists (*dusong*), promoters of blessings (*xingfu*), and miscellaneous invokers of virtue (*zake shengde*).

14. For the list of sixty-one works attributed to Yanshou and the eleven extant ones, see Welter, *The Meaning of Myriad Good Deeds*, pp. 113–118.

15. T. 48(2061).958a–993c.

16. The summary here is based on *The Meaning of Myriad Good Deeds*, pp. 132–137.

17. This is not to suggest that the materials recorded in these biographies are in any way factual. In the guise of actual events, Chan biographies are actually highly dramatized portrayals of fictional episodes, set against the background of historical circumstances. Yanagida Seizan has suggested that Buddhist "historical" records such as Chan transmission records are unlike other historical sources in that they are connected to literature in their composition, more akin to narrative stories in what amounts to a kind of historical fiction, in "Shinzoku tōshi no keifu," *Zengaku kenkyū* 59 (1978): 5.

18. John Jorgensen, "The 'Imperial' Lineage of Ch'an Buddhism: The Role of Confucian Ritual and Ancestor Worship in Chan's Search for Legitimation in the Mid-T'ang Dynasty," *Papers on Far Eastern History* 35 (1987): 89–133, demonstrates how the original formation of Chan lineages is connected to the Confucian-inspired ancestral lineages of Tang emperors.

19. Koichi Shinohara, "From Local History to Universal History: The Construction of Sung T'ien-t'ai Lineage," in Gregory and Getz, eds., *Buddhism in the Sung*, pp. 524–576, shows a similar process at work in the formation of Tiantai lineages in the Song, where local records tied to specific temples were transformed into universal genealogical histories of Buddhism based on the idea of Dharma transmission.

20. The *Zutang ji* survives only in a Korean edition (*Chodang chip*), published by Yanagida Seizan in an edited and punctuated format, with concordances, *Sodōshū sakuin*, 3 vols. (Kyoto: Meibun shain, 1984), and by the Zenbunka kenkyūjō: Yoshizawa Masahiro and Onishi Shirō, et al., eds., *Sodōshu* (Kyoto: Kibun tenseki sōkan, 1994).

21. For a review of what is known of Daoyuan, see Ishii Shūdō, *Sōdai zenshūshi no kenkyū* (Tokyo: Daitō shuppansha, 1987), pp. 26–44.

22. Ishii Shūdō, "Eimei enju den—toku ni hōgenshū sansō to rensha shichi den," *Komazawa daigaku daigakuin bukkyōgaku kenkyūjō nenpō* 3 (1969): 78.

23. This is discussed in Albert Welter, *Monks, Rulers, and Literati: The Political Ascendancy of Chan Buddhism* (New York: Oxford University Press, 2006), pp. 172–186.

24. The *Jingde chuandeng lu* was officially adopted in 1011 after being edited and abbreviated by leading Song scholar-bureaucrats Yang Yi, Li Wei (*jinshi* 985), and Wang Shu (963–1034). Both Daoyuan's original preface and Yang Yi's preface to the edited text are contained in Ishii Shūdō, *Sōdai zenshūshi no kenkyū*, pp. 21–23.

25. Albert Welter, *Monks, Rulers, and Literati*, and "Mahākāśyapa's Smile: Silent Transmission and the Kung-an (Kōan) Tradition," in Steven Heine and Dale Wright, eds., *The Kōan: Texts and Contexts in Zen Buddhism* (New York: Oxford University Press, 2000), pp. 75–109.

26. The *Jingde chuandeng lu* biography is found in ch. 26 (T. 51.421c6–422a20). English translations are found in Welter, *The Meaning of Myriad Good Deeds*, pp. 194–198; and Chang Chung-yuan, *Original Teachings of Ch'an Buddhism* (New York: Pantheon, 1969), pp. 250–253.

27. T. 51.407b5–6.

28. T. 51.421c20–21.

29. T. 51.421c25–29.

30. On the sources cited by Yanshou in the *Wanshan tonggui ji*, see Welter, *The Meaning of Myriad Good Deeds*, pp. 121–127 (referred to as the *Wan-shan t'ung-kuei chi*). An appendix (pp. 177–189) traces the sources cited.

31. The number of citations in the *Zongjing lu* is based on Ishii Shūdō's unpublished manuscript, "Eimei enju no chōsaku no kōsei to inyō kyōten," completed as part of his graduate work at Komazawa University (n.d.).

32. Published Chan sources were cited with slightly more frequency, such as the "Inscription on Believing Mind" (*Xinxin ming;* 13 times), "Song of Realization" (*Chengdao ke;* 10 times), and the poems of Hanshan (10 times).

33. With slight variation, these lines appear in the context of a discussion between Huineng and Xue Jian, a palace attendant dispatched by the emperor to invite Huineng to the palace to discourse on Chan. As a result of Huineng's statement, Xue Jian is said to have achieved awakening (T. 51.236a). Freedom from conceptualizing things in terms of good and evil (i.e., in moral terms) is a common theme among Chan masters; see, for example, the teaching attributed to Huangbo. See, as an example, Iriya Yoshitaka, *Zen no goroku 8: Denshin hōyō & Enryōroku*, Zen no goroku, vol. 8 (Tokyo: Chikuma shobō, 1969), pp. 85 and 133.

34. T. 48.958c4ff.; Welter, *The Meaning of Myriad Good Deeds*, pp. 208–211.

35. T. 48.961a25–26; Welter, *The Meaning of Myriad Good Deeds*, p. 213. The first line of this saying, "everything that comes into contact with one's eyes," is cited in the *Jingde chuandeng lu*, in a conversation recorded in the biography of Chan master Fuqing Zuanna (flourished in the tenth century) (T. 51.356b19–20). The same line also came to be associated with the awakening of Chan master Shixiang Qingzhu (807–888), occurring in the context of a conversation with his master Daowu, also cited in the *Jingde chuandeng lu* (T. 51.356b11).

36. T. 48.961b25–26.

37. Philip Yampolsky, *The Platform Sutra of the Sixth Patriarch* (New York: Columbia University Press, 1967), pp. 156–157.

38. T. 48.417a19–21.

39. See Stanley Weinstein, "The Schools of Chinese Buddhism," in Joseph Kitagawa and Mark Cummings, eds., *Buddhism and Asian History: Religion, History, and Culture: Selections from the Encyclopedia of Religion* (New York: Macmillan, 1989), pp. 257–265.

40. T. 48.417b20–21.

41. Especially noteworthy is the influence of Huayan master Chengguan's (738–839) subcommentary on the *Huayan jing*, the *Yenyi chao* (T. 36–1737) over the contents of the *Zongjing lu*; see Ishii Shūdō, "*Sugyōroku* ni oyoboshita chōkan no chōsaku no eikyō ni tsuite," *Indogaku bukkyōgaku kenkyū* 17/2. On Chengguan and his conception of Chan, see Peter Gregory, *Tsung-mi and the Sinification of Buddhism* (Princeton: Princeton University Press, 1991), pp. 63–68, 147–148; and Yoshizu Yoshihide, *Kegonzen no shisōshiteki kenkyū* (Tokyo: Daitō shuppansha, 1985).

42. T. 48.960b27–c2.

43. The Dharma-heirs of Tiantai Deshao are acknowledged in fascicle 27, but Yanshou is not mentioned.

44. This is the subject of Welter, *Monks, Rulers, and Literati: The Political Ascendancy of Chan Buddhism*.

45. T. 51.762c14.

46. *Linjian lu* (XZJ 148.294b).

47. XZJ 137.239–341, and *Lingyin sizhi* 6A.11–16.

48. See the previously mentioned study by Daniel Getz, "T'ien-t'ai Pure Land Societies and the Creation of the Pure Land Patriarchate."

49. Takao Giken, *Sōdai bukkyōshi no kenkyū* (Kyoto: Hyakkaen, 1975), p. 169.

50. Fascicle 25 of the *Lotus sūtra* (T. 9–262), and the *Sukhāvatāvyūha sūtra* (T. 12–360).

51. My account here is adapted from Welter, *The Meaning of Myriad Good Deeds*, pp. 80–81.

52. XZJ 148.71a–c.

53. XZJ 148.71a–c.

54. T. 49.264b–265a and XZJ 130.449–450.

55. See Welter, *The Meaning of Myriad Good Deeds*, esp. pp. 121–127.

56. The following discussion is adapted from Welter, *The Meaning of Myriad Good Deeds*, pp. 149–154.

57. T. 48.963b–964a. The four kinds of samadhi in the Tiantai school are: 1) sitting in mediation for a period of ninety days without engaging in any other religious exercise; 2) invoking the name of Amitābha for ninety days; 3) practicing seated and ambulatory meditation for a specified period to remove bad karma; and 4) practicing meditation based on the three contemplations in which one views phenomena from three standpoints (as specified in Tiantai teaching): as empty and ultimately devoid of reality, as existing temporarily and provisionally, and as the mean (i.e., the true state of suchness).

58. T. 48.964a.

59. T. 48.968b.

60. T. 48.962a.

61. Textbooks accounts of Yanshou include: John C. H. Wu, *The Golden Age of Zen* (Bloomington, Ind.: World Wisdom, 2004; originally published by Yangmingshan, Taipei: National War College in cooperation with the Committee on the Compilation of the Chinese Library, 1967), pp. 180–181; Kenneth Ch'an, *Buddhism in China: A Historical Survey* (Princeton: Princeton University Press, 1963), pp. 404–405; Heinrich Dumoulin, *Zen Buddhism: A History, India and China* (New York: Macmillan, 1988), pp. 235 and 285–286; and D. T. Suzuki, *Essays in Zen Buddhism*, second series (New York: Simon Weiser, 1933 and numerous reprints), pp. 150–151, and *Essays in Zen Buddhism*, third series (York Beach, Maine: Simon Weiser, 1934 and numerous reprints), p. 20. A perusal of current Japanese texts on Chinese Buddhism confirms the same impression.

62. The image of Yanshou as Chan–Pure Land syncretist has been given lengthy treatment by Shih, "The Ch'an–Pure Land Synthesis in China"; With Special

Reference to Yung-ming Yanshou (Ph.D. diss., University of Wisconsin, 1984), subsequently published as *The Syncretism of Ch'an and Pure Land Buddhism* (New York: Peter Lang, 1992).

63. T. 48.966c6–8.

64. T. 48.958c13–17.

65. ZZ–1088.365b–368b.

66. On the *Shou pusa jiefa bingxu*, see the comments by Tajima Tokuon, in Ono Gemmyō, ed., *Bukkyō kaisatsu daijiten* (Tokyo: Daitō shuppansha, 1932–1936), vol. 5, p. 103b. Many questions surround the compilation of the text, its title, and content. The title given at the end of the preface, *Fanwang pusa jieyi*, for example, is different from that given in either the table of contents or at the beginning of the preface.

67. T. 51.422a10–11.

68. Literally, "entering the gate of sweet dew." My translation follows the explanation of Nakamura Hajime, ed., *Bukkyōgo daijiten* (Tokyo: Tokyo shoseki, 1975), p. 186a.

69. The citation from the *Fanwang jing* is found in a line in a gatha (T. 24.1004a20).

70. ZZ–1088.365b9–15.

71. For this line, see T. 24.1004a19.

72. This is commonly attributed to Mazu Daoyi.

73. Literally, "the Buddha-nature precepts," referring to the precepts as restricting agents that prevent one from errors, thus allowing one to manifest the inherent purity of one's nature (i.e., Buddha-nature); see Nakamura, ed., *Bukkyōgo daijiten*, p. 1194a.

74. ZZ–1088.365c5–11.

75. ZZ–1088.367c–368a.

76. Chinese Buddhist doctrine determined three ascending levels of rebirth in the Pure Land, with each level composed of three stages or ranks, comprising nine stages in total. The lowest ranks refer to the three stages of the lowest level.

4

Dahui Zonggao (1089–1163): The Image Created by His Stories about Himself and by His Teaching Style

Miriam L. Levering

In 1101, at age thirteen by Chinese reckoning, the future Dahui Zonggao (1089–1163) started and abandoned a classical education and decided to become a Buddhist monk.[1] Three years later he was ordained. By the time he died in 1163, he had become one of the two or three preeminent Chan abbots and teachers of the empire, and the one of his generation who had the greatest impact on future generations. He had attracted many patrons and students from the educated elite, including Zhang Jiucheng (1092–1159), a scholar and official; Fu Zhirou (?–1156); Zhang Xiaoxiang (c. 1129–1170); Tang Situi (?–1164); Liu Zuhui (1107–1147); Lu Benzhong (1084–1145); Zhang Jun (1096–1164), a military governor of Shu (present-day Szechwan) who became chief minister and prosecuted the war against the Jin; and Wang Yingchen (1118–1176).[2] He had found a new method for making Linji Chan teaching and practice more effective, and thereby changed the way teaching and practice were done in the Linji house. Within the Song dynasty Chan Buddhist school, Dahui Zonggao formulated and popularized the form of *gongan* study called "looking into and observing a saying," the saying being a word, sentence, or phrase that crystallizes a specifically chosen *gongan* problem. This method of *gongan* study is sometimes called "inspecting the critical phrase," or in Chinese, *kan huatou*. This method of *gongan* study remained at the heart of most Chinese Chan training not only for the rest of the Song dynasty but also for all the succeeding centuries in China, Korea, and Japan. His Dharma-heirs and others from the Linji house who were inspired by him occupied many of the abbacies at major Song dynasty Chan temples. At the end of his life he presided over two of the empire's most prominent monasteries, Mount Ashoka (Ayuwangshan) and Mount Jing (Jingshan). He enjoyed the patronage of the Emperor Xiaozong (r. 1163–1190), who gave him the name Dahui, meaning Great Wisdom.[3]

In the generations of Chan teachers in China after Dahui Zonggao, most used a version of his method. Influential Song dynasty monks who owe a debt to Dahui include Wumen Huikai (1183–1260), the author of the *gongan* commentary collection called "The Gateless Gate." In the Yuan dynasty, Gaofeng Yuanmiao (1238–1295) and Zhongfeng Mingben (1263–1323) wrote important essays on *huatou* practice that closely followed Dahui's understanding. Ming dynasty and later Buddhist masters took Dahui Zonggao's Chan as a model, including Yunqi Zhuhong (1535–1615), Hanshan Deqing (1546–1623), and Miyun Yuanwu (1566–1642).

In the modern era, the importance of Dahui Zonggao and the meditation method he clarified and popularized has continued. Master Hsu Yun (1840–1959) led meditation retreats in China in which he lectured to the participants on the *huatou* method.[4] Garma C. C. Chang (Chang Chen Chi; 1920–1988)—who in the 1950s wrote what was until recent times the best introduction to Chan Buddhism for the West, *The Practice of Zen*—translated into English excerpts from *Dahui's Letters* so that Western students could learn properly how to do *huatou* practice.[5] The Venerable Sheng Yen, an outstanding contemporary Chinese writer about Chan in English, taught the *huatou* method to his students in Taiwan, the United States, and elsewhere by lecturing on excerpts from Dahui's letters and individual Dharma-instructions *(fayu)*.[6]

In Japan and Korea, important teachers who particularly valued and taught Dahui's approach to practice include Chinul (1158–1210), Musō Soseki (1275–1351), and Hakuin Ekaku (1686–1769), the founder of today's Rinzai Zen. Chinul, the founder of Korean Sŏn Buddhism, commissioned a text of *Dahui's Letters* to be brought to Korea from China. Reading it enabled him to awaken. *Dahui's Letters* has been a very important part of almost all Korean Buddhist monastic education since Chinul and remains so today. Japanese Rinzai Zen Buddhists such as Hakuin adopted Dahui's *kan huatou* teaching method and lectured on *Dahui's Letters* in monasteries. Hakuin also cited Dahui's emphasis on integrating Chan practice with secular activity when he addressed his lay community. In his *Orategama I*, for example, Hakuin writes that "The Zen Master Dahui has said that meditation in the midst of activity is immeasurably superior to the quietistic approach."[7]

There is no question that in his own time and for many generations up to the present, Dahui has gained a mostly positive, but in some instances sharply negative, image. In future studies scholars may examine in more detail the image that his contemporaries and later masters had of him as reflected in Song dynasty Chan and secular anecdote collections, as well as in later sources. Here we will undertake a more fundamental inquiry: what image of Dahui is offered in the *yulu* collections that present his own sermons and writings, and in the chronological or "annalistic" (year-by-year) biography (*nianpu*) for Dahui that was compiled shortly after his death?

Because Dahui's image has many dimensions, his *yulu* collections are vast, and his chronological biography is long and detailed, not every aspect of his image can be touched on here. We will focus only on some of the more important dimensions of Dahui's image.

The main sources for this chapter are the *Recorded Sayings (Yulu) of Chan Master Dahui Pujue* (*Dahui Pujue chanshi yulu*) in thirty fascicles,[8] and the *General Sermons (Pushuo) of Chan Master Dahui Pujue* (*Dahui Pujue chanshi pushuo*) in five fascicles.[9] These two will be the texts that will govern the topics selected in relation to Dahui's image. I will often refer to the first as "Dahui's *yulu* collection."[10] There are no critical editions of these texts; I have selected the closest to the original, most readily available and most widely used, as the sources for this essay. *Dahui's Letters* (*Dahui Pujue chanshi shu*), to which I will occasionally refer, circulated separately in the Song dynasty and thereafter, but now is most easily found in the *Recorded Sayings (Yulu) of Chan Master Dahui Pujue*, which is based on an early text. In addition, I will draw on the *Chronological Biography of Chan Master Dahui Pujue* (*Dahui Pujue chanshi nianpu*) completed in 1183, twenty years after Dahui's death, and revised in 1205.[11] The *Chronological Biography* (*nianpu*) is largely based on information from Dahui himself from extant and nonextant sources. A full study of Dahui's image as presented in that text and in the *Chan Arsenal of Master Dahui Pujue* (*Dahui Pujue chanshi zongmen wuku*), on which I will occasionally draw, must be deferred to another occasion.[12]

Dahui as Autobiographer

Dahui's image as found in these texts is primarily created by his own words about himself, as well as by his other words and deeds. The whole is edited, no doubt, by his followers and in some cases by himself. One would expect a Chan master's image to be conveyed in his teachings and his teaching style; it is, indeed, standard for a reader in early modern China or elsewhere to derive the image of a master from his or her words and actions as he interacts with those he would enlighten. His contemporaries and later readers certainly formed an image of Dahui Zonggao through his recorded teachings and actions. But Dahui's image was to an even greater extent created by his own stories about himself as found in his *yulu* collections and his *Chronological Biography*. Dahui tells stories about himself in his scheduled, formal sermons (*shangtang, xiaocan,* etc.) and in his unscheduled, informal sermons (*pushuo*) to the assembly of monks, nuns and their lay guests, as well as in his written Dharma instructions (*fayu*) and his letters (*shu*) addressed to individuals. These stories provide a very distinct image of the man as Chan student and teacher, one that no reader of his works can ignore.

Whether this is unusual for a Song dynasty Chan master, we cannot know. Most other masters of the Song left much shorter *yulu*; or there were *yulu* compilations in which, perhaps, stories about themselves were left out by editors. At the very least, it is highly unusual to find such stories in the edited *yulu* compilations of Song Chan masters. Let us begin with those stories, and then turn to Dahui's teachings and his teaching style. From Dahui's point of view, his stories about himself were part of his teachings, thus both can be called his "Chan." Taken together, they form Dahui's image.

Dahui's Image as Seen in Stories about Himself

Dahui was not a fully educated literatus, although he received a literary education through the age of thirteen. In his extant discourse records Dahui tells his listeners and readers virtually nothing about his secular background. Dahui was born to the Xi family in Xuanzhou in Ningguo district (present-day Xuancheng county), in present-day Anhui province. His family does not appear to have been a prominent one. Neither Dahui himself nor his *Annalistic Biography* tells us anything about family or recent ancestors who served in government positions. I have searched the extant lists of exam graduates in gazetteers for his unusual surname, Xi, in his family's home region and found only one name. That name could not have fit Dahui's family.

Dahui's autobiographical stories do make it clear that he was not a full member of the literati class by education, if by literati we mean the class of people who had a literati education and either served or did not serve in government. We can draw no conclusions about his family.

Dahui's *Annalistic Biography* (*nianpu*) gives an account of his youth that combines a few facts with hagiographic tales. Two elements of that account are worth mentioning here. First, a no longer extant source quotes Dahui as saying that from his birth the family's financial fortunes steadily declined, even more so after a devastating fire when he was ten.¹³ Second, the *Nianpu* describes Dahui being forced to pay a fine and leave the local school at the age of thirteen after only thirteen days because he threw an inkwell that accidentally hit the teacher's hat.¹⁴ An extant sermon confirms at least part of this. In it Dahui says, "I started school at thirteen, and had only thirteen days of school."¹⁵

According to the *Nianpu*, Dahui turned down an opportunity to study for the civil service examinations. Under the heading for his sixteenth year, the *Nianpu* says that although his family rented space for him to study for the government examinations, Dahui did not like the project and soon left, taking in that same year his first religious vows with a Buddhist teacher.¹⁶ The *Nianpu*'s entries convey an impression that Dahui as a young man neither received nor wanted to receive a secular classical and literary education. Later in life Dahui was befriended by poets and scholars, and formed teaching relationships with distinguished literati; this fact forms another important part of his image. However, he was not trained in the classical tradition himself.

One might think that a Song dynasty hagiographer would see it as an advantage in a future monk that he had no interest in secular education. However, Song dynasty hagiographers typically included secular educational achievements in the biographies of eminent monks, seeing those as a mark of eminence. Likewise, contemporary historians might suppose that without more secular education a monk would be ill prepared for a career at the highest levels of Song Chan. The Buddhist world of the Song dynasty was very much dependent on and a part of literati culture.¹⁷ But Dahui makes clear in his *yulu* collection that it is awakening that opens the door to success in all aspects of Chan, in his own case as in others. Awakening itself results in the command of expression in words that a Chan master needs, whether or not he has literary training.

AFTER ORDINATION DAHUI SHOWED AN EARLY AND CONSISTENT INTEREST IN CHAN, STUDYING GONGAN AND COMMENTARIES ON GONGAN WITH TEACHERS AND THROUGH BOOKS. In a general sermon, Dahui says, "From the time I left home at age nineteen I sought out teachers, asked for instruction, and looked at Chan stories (*kan huatou*)."¹⁸ Dahui tells many stories of his early teachers and Chan studies. From these, one can see that Dahui was a talented young man who had an interest in and a gift for Chan, and also see what Chan study consisted of in his day. At eighteen, he began formally studying Chan in his native Xuanzhou with a teacher in the Yunmen lineage. Prior to this, he obtained a copy of and fell in love with Yunmen's *yulu* collection. In a general sermon (*pushuo*) Dahui tells the story:

Soon after my head was shaved I knew that there was This Matter. Although I was in a village temple, I often wanted to buy the discourse records of various masters. Even though I did not yet understand them I loved the conversations of Yunmen and Muzhou [Yunmen's teacher].[19] [Muzhou said,] "All of you! Those who do not yet have insight into Chan [literally, "who have not yet reached an entry"][20] must attain entry. Those who have already attained an entry should not be ungrateful to your old teacher afterward."[21]

At the age of nineteen, Dahui left Xuanzhou and went to Taipingzhou, where he studied with Ruizhu Shaocheng, also called Baoyin Dashi, a teacher of the Linji school.[22] A story that Dahui tells from this period gives his listeners a good idea of the kind of study he was doing and its results. He attained "a place of joy" and thought he understood Chan when reading in Xuansha Shibei's (835–908) discourse record the story of Ruiyan Shiyan (dates unknown; his teacher Yantou died in 887), who every day sat in his abbot's quarters calling out "Master of the house!" and then answering himself, "Yes." He would then call out, "Are you wide awake?" and answer, "Yes." He would call out again, "Later on don't let yourself be fooled by anyone." And again answer, "Yes, yes."[23]

Dahui says that he sought out Shaocheng to ask about his understanding.[24] He told Shaocheng that had he been there in the monk's place, he would have said "Yes" to Xuansha's last question. When Xuansha replied, as Dahui thought he must, "See if you can call out," Dahui would have repeated the whole of Ruiyan's calling and answering. "After all, everyone has a 'master of the house.' There is no reason why he could call out but I cannot call out." Dahui says that when he understood this he was considerably freed and enlivened, and Shaocheng approved his understanding (*kenke*). Dahui says, "At the time I also thought I was right. I was happy for a long time."[25]

According to Dahui's *Arsenal* (*Wuku*), Dahui asked Shaocheng for instruction on Xuedou Mingjue's (980–1052) *Niangu* and *Songgu*.[26] According to Dahui's account in one sermon Shaocheng had personally studied with Xuedou.[27] When Shaocheng turned the request around and asked Dahui to explicate these texts, he was so impressed with Dahui's understanding that he suggested that Dahui was the reincarnation of Xuedou.[28] Perhaps this story shows a young Dahui who believed, in keeping with the literati-influenced nature of Song dynasty Chan, that Chan was best approached through stories about Tang and Five Dynasties masters as mediated through Song dynasty poetic commentaries. Dahui tells his audience that he served as an attendant to Shaocheng for two years, discussing *gongan* with him every day.[29]

DAHUI STUDIED FROM TEACHERS AND TEXTS OF ALL CHAN LINEAGES, INCLUDING ESPECIALLY LINJI AND CAODONG LINEAGES. Dahui often emphasizes in his sermons and mentions in his letters that he studied with teachers of all of the various schools of Chan before his final awakening under Yuanwu Keqin (1063–1135) in 1125: "I went forth and traveled everywhere visiting teachers. Yunmen, Caodong, Guiyang, Linji, even 'The three worlds are only mind, the ten thousand dharmas are only consciousness'—I mastered all of these various schools of Chan. When I got to a place, I only had to enter the interview room of the teacher twice before I understood the teaching. But always in the end my feeling of doubt was not broken through."

This broad experience is an important part of the image of himself Dahui wants to create: someone who has worked with all of the different teaching methods of the various Chan schools, and who is thus able to evaluate them from firsthand experience. Dahui especially emphasized this point after he began his long campaign of criticizing some forms of practice encouraged by Caodong teachers.

The key to his creation of this image is the emphasis that he places on his studies at the Taiyang Monastery in Hubei, a major center for the Caodong lineage. As Morten Schlütter and Ishii Shūdō have demonstrated, the Caodong lineage was at that time in the midst of a major revival with new teachings and modes of expression.[30] The chief Song dynasty reviver of the Caodong tradition, Furong Daokai (1043–1118), had spent thirteen years as abbot at Taiyang Monastery before leaving in 1095.[31] Here, in 1108–1109, Dahui studied with the current abbot, a Caodong teacher named Dongshan Daowei (n.d.), whom Dahui identifies as an eminent disciple of Furong Daokai.[32] Dahui also mentions having studied with two of his assistants, "First Seat" Yuan and "First Seat" Jian.[33] Dahui says, "Within two years [at Taiyang Monastery] I mastered the cardinal instructions of the Caodong house."[34] Dahui does say that Daowei did teach awakening, unlike some teachers of whom Dahui was critical.[35]

From Dahui's autobiographical stories it is clear that thereafter most of his teachers and associates until the beginning of his study with Yuanwu belonged to the Huanglong branch of the Linji lineage. Dahui tells many stories of his time studying with Zhantang Wenjun (1061–1115) at Jewel Peak Monastery (Baofeng si) in the Stone Gate Mountains in the northern part of present-day Jiangxi Province.[36] Some of Dahui's stories mention an unexpected benefit of studying with Zhantang at Jewel Peak, namely, that a second opportunity to learn Caodong teachings presented itself.[37] In the assembly was a relative of Zhantang's whom Dahui refers to as Attendant Jian. Dahui tells his hearers that Jian had been an attendant of Furong Daokai for more than ten years, and obtained Daokai's Way, including all of the important instructions of the Caodong house. Perhaps this is the same Jian as the First Seat Jian mentioned above. Dahui relates that he took this opportunity of being with Attendant Jian to understand these teachings more thoroughly.[38]

DAHUI WAS NOT AN ICONOCLAST OR A NONCONFORMIST. Stories about his time with Zhantang serve the creation of Dahui's image in one particularly interesting way. Instead of describing himself as a free spirit, an iconoclast, a spontaneous inventor of startling actions and striking modes of communication during this time of maturing practice, Dahui described himself as the "parfait knight," the perfect Chan monk.

Through a close study of the various versions of the records of Tang master Linji and the developing versions of the *Linji lu* in which these records were brought together in the Song dynasty, Albert Welter has shown that from the late Five Dynasties through the early Song dynasty the changes made are in the direction of making Linji's language and gestures in his interactions with students more dramatic and action-filled. The later versions of the stories about Linji represent him as a dynamic, enigmatic, and iconoclastic action figure, rather than a conventional Buddhist abbot who gives sermons to audiences of monks and lay people.[39] Welter suggests that the implausible, even grotesque physical descriptions of figures such as Mazu and Huangbo, and the novel behavior that Chan masters such as Linji exhibited in the later texts, with such antics as shouting, slapping, hitting, nose-tweaking and the like, are deployed by Song dynasty writers as caricatures. These images imply that Chan masters are "new kinds of champions who expose the boundaries of previous limitations and suggest ways to break through to a new kind of existence, a new way of living."[40] Such images of new champions were responding to cultural needs brought on by the breakdown of the Tang order, as well as the political need of the new Song dynasty to establish a new order. The visual representations of some Chan masters have the same convention-breaking aspect; the artist plays with physical proportions and depicts bulging eyes and mirthful dispositions, "to exhibit [through expressive representations of Chan figures] the unique style of Chan through an unconventional appearance."[41]

All of this vanishes, Welter argues, when Song masters themselves are described or depicted. Little time passes between the lifetime of a well-known master and the public circulation of his *yulu*, a circumstance that promotes a more fact-based representation. Song dynasty masters are generally described as possessing the refined manner and sophistication to which their literati contemporaries aspired.

Certainly his *yulu* collections and his *Nianpu* do not represent Dahui as a dynamic action hero of grotesque appearance who breaks the bounds of convention. Nor does Dahui in his autobiographical stories describe himself in that manner; quite the opposite. How does Dahui depict himself as the perfect Chan monk? He says in a sermon, "Everything that the Buddha praised—precepts, samadhi, wisdom, liberation, correct views—each one I did according to what he said, right down to the three thousand rules of deportment and the eighty thousand small karmic acts, every one I was perfectly clear and precise about. And everything the Buddha forbade I did not do, I did not dare disobey."[42] Dahui never describes himself as a nonconformist, one who uses the freedom produced by his training to startle or surprise anyone. The exception, and this is an important exception, is the way he describes his attacks on teachers who teach "quiet sitting" or "silent illumination Chan."

Zhantang also thought Dahui was perfect in his performance of all aspects of his teaching role as First Seat. As Dahui tells it, Zhantang called the younger monk to him and made the following comment:

> "Senior monk Gao [i.e., Dahui], you understood my Chan at once. When I ask you to explain it, you explain it well. When I ask you to hold up stories of the ancients (*niangu*), or make up poems praising the masters of old (*songgu*), to give instructions to the monks, or to give general sermons (*pushuo*), you also do all these things well.[43] There is only one thing that is not right. Do you know what it is?"
>
> Dahui replied, "What is it that I do not know?"
>
> Zhantang said, "Ho! You lack this one liberation."[44]

IT IS NOT SITTING, IT IS PRACTICING UNINTERRUPTEDLY AND DOUBTING, THAT BRINGS AWAKENING. Later in his life, when telling of events during this period of study with many teachers, Dahui says that he was not as enthusiastic about the practice of sitting meditation as some others. When others wanted to do sitting meditation all night, Dahui wanted to stretch out his legs and sleep. Dahui tells this story about himself to make a positive point: it was not special devotion to sitting meditation that eventually got him to awakening, but never letting his doubt-filled investigation drop.[45] Dahui makes the same point when he says in another sermon, "I studied Chan for seventeen years. In my tea, in my rice, when I was happy, when I was angry, when I was still and quiet, when I was disturbed (*luan*), I never once let myself be interrupted."[46]

THE IMPACT OF ZHANG SHANGYING ON DAHUI'S IMAGE. In 1115, when Dahui was twenty-seven years old by Chinese reckoning, Zhantang died, and Dahui, still without the full certification he needed to be an abbot and an independent teacher, was left without a mentor. Zhantang's death resulted in Dahui's seeking out the prominent lay Buddhist scholar Zhang Shangying (T. Tianjue) (1043–1122), also called in Buddhist circles "the Inexhaustible Layman" (Wujin), to ask him to write a biographical epitaph (taming, literally, "stupa inscription") for his teacher. When Dahui met Zhang at his home in Jingzhou in 1115, and visited him again five years later, Zhang was a former chief minister, a Dharma-heir of the Linji Huanglong branch Chan master Doushuai Congyue (1044–1091), a scholar of Huayan Buddhism, and a prominent defender of Buddhism against its critics and political enemies. In 1120, in his thirty-second year by Chinese reckoning, Dahui visited Zhang Shangying again and stayed with him for eight months. It was on this second visit that Zhang Shangying recommended to Dahui that he study with Yuanwu Keqin. In the former Chief Minister Zhang Jun's stupa inscription for Dahui he mentions that Zhang Shangying offered to give Dahui money to travel to study with Yuanwu.

Why and in what contexts does Dahui bring up the special attention given to him by Zhang Shangying? One illuminating fact is that Dahui describes his visits to and conversations with Zhang Shangying in a sermon with particular significance.[47]

Although the image that Southern Song dynasty Chan masters present of themselves and their successful students is that they are as free from all worldly concerns, it is probable that they were also aware of the desirability of sustaining claims to authority and transformative power. Chan had been strongly supported by the court in the Northern Song period, but found itself under somewhat serious restriction in the early Southern Song. As the Southern Song court left more regional affairs to local gentry and officials, Chan needed support from local literati and their families more than before. Chan was still well supported and popular among parts of the elite, but had been coming under intellectual and cultural attack since the Confucian (or Classical) revival of the Northern Song. Chan masters no doubt were aware of this need to mount successful claims to authority on behalf of their tradition of teaching and training. In addition, Chan masters may have felt this need for their own lineages and for themselves individually.[48]

The sermon in the *Pushuo*[49] in which Dahui tells of his friendship with Zhang Shangying and about Zhang's recommendation of Yuanwu took place in a heightened social and institutional context. It was given in the evening of the day of his formal installation as abbot of the large, public, imperially supported monastery at Mount Ashoka. This was a gathering at which many monastic and lay Buddhists as well as more than a few literati and officials would have been present. It occurred on the twenty-third day of the twelfth month of the Chinese lunar calendar of 1157.[50]

At that time Dahui was returning to monastic life near the capital after a long period spent in exile among the "southern barbarians." In 1137 he had been given the abbacy of the major temple on Mount Jing, which he then expanded into a major center. There he taught two thousand monks in residence, more during summer retreats, and received visits from laywomen, nuns, and literati as well as monks. Four years later he had been accused of the unmonkly behavior of talking politics with Zhang Jiucheng (1092–1159), a scholar, imperial teacher, and high official whose faction opposed the policies of the current chief minister, Qin Gui (1090–1155).[51] He had been defrocked, his ordination taken away, and like Zhang sent into exile. A few years later a court document reviewing Dahui's exile alleged that Dahui's scurrilous political behavior had only gotten worse, and he was banished deeper into the hinterlands of the malarial south. In 1156, following Qin Gui's death in 1155, he had been given his freedom to return and allowed to become a monk again.

Career patterns among Song dynasty Chan monks culminated in abbacies; it was as abbot that a master taught and produced Dharma-heirs. For the imperially regulated temples, which included of course all of the wealthy ones that could accommodate many students, abbots were chosen by the court on the recommendation of local officials. The local officials in turn usually took the recommendation of the other abbots in the surrounding area.[52] Dahui had been highly esteemed in the capital region seventeen years previously, but while he had been in exile his lineage brothers and cousins seem to have been in retreat. Qin Gui favored Tiantai Buddhism over Chan. Major Chan centers such as Dahui's old Dharma seat at Mount Jing were occupied by Caodong Chan teachers, not by members of Dahui's Linji lineage.

Even though his ordination had been rescinded, during his exile Dahui had not cut off all contact with Chan students and literati. On returning from exile, he was given the abbacy at Mount Ashoka at the recommendation of his age-mate, the Caodong school abbot Hongzhi Zhengjue of the large monastery on Mount Tiantong, also in present-day Zhejiang province, whose teachings he had verbally attacked, although mostly indirectly. Mount Ashoka was both a Chan training center and a major pilgrimage center, for it housed the most sacred Buddhist relic in China, the Buddha's finger bone. As one of the most prominent imperially sanctioned Chan monasteries, it merited the leadership of a first-rate abbot.

On the evening of his installation as abbot, Dahui needed to reintroduce himself and his philosophy, as well as set forth his claim to suitability for high monastic office. His association with Zhang, the late Northern Sung high official who was briefly chief minister and was much admired in Buddhist circles as a distinguished scholar of Buddhism and as a prominent defender of Buddhism, could only help polish his reputation for excellence, scholarship, and Chan insight.

DAHUI'S AWAKENING: ONE OR MANY? Over many centuries in Asia and in the West, no one who has written about Dahui has been unaware of the story of his great awakening under Yuanwu. Dahui himself told the story in shorter and longer versions many times in his sermons and letters. Not least because Dahui was an untiring proponent of the necessity of an awakening if one wanted to break through samsara to Buddhahood, as well as a relentless critic of those who he said thought it unnecessary, Dahui's account of his awakening is a very large contributor to his image as a truly awakened teacher.[53]

Dahui's accounts of his own awakening shatter an image of accomplished Tang and Five Dynasties Chan adepts that Song dynasty genealogical lamp histories and edited discourse records (*yulu*) encourage: the image of the attainment of enlightenment as a sudden, once-and-for-all thing. Dahui's account of his first real, authentic, thoroughgoing awakening is not a description of an enlightenment that took place on one day through one encounter with one teacher on one occasion. Instead, it involved three awakenings: one upon hearing words in a sermon by Yuanwu Keqin; one after working on a different *gongan* with Yuanwu for six months; and the third two years later when reading the *Huayan* sutra.

The Context of Dahui's Awakening

According to Dahui, his teacher Zhantang did not give Dahui a certification of awakening. There ensued a ten-year period during which, according to his own account, Dahui was plagued by doubt. He doubted himself and he doubted Chan. He doubted his own attainment, as he seemed to be an awakened person in the daytime, but had frightful dreams at night. And after so many years of study without attaining what the ancients had attained, that is, becoming a person of seamless awakening, he doubted that Chan had been successfully transmitted to his own day. Zhang Shangying had shared with him his own view that the Huanglong branch of the Linji school, in which Dahui had spent many years, had had but two recent teachers of high quality; both were dead now. Perhaps he did not urgently pursue a teacher-student relationship with Yuanwu because he did not sufficiently believe that studying with Yuanwu would be different. He says that in fact he actually doubted Yuanwu more than the other available teachers.[54] In a sermon he says:

If it turned out [with Yuanwu Keqin] as it had with all those previous teachers who gave me approval (*yinke*, J. *inka*), I was going to write an essay saying that there was no Chan—I would not believe that there was a Chan school [anymore]. I thought it would be better to teach scriptures and commentaries so as not to lose out on being a person of the Buddhadharma [in my next life].[55]

Dahui's account of his awakening under Yuanwu is well known. Dahui narrated his awakening story from this point several times in sermons in various degrees of detail. Through connections he enrolled in Yuanwu's assembly at the Tianning Monastery in the capital. One day, when Yuanwu had "ascended the hall" to give a sermon to a large assembly at the invitation of a female lay donor, Dahui heard Yuanwu raise for the assembly's inspection the *gongan*. "A monk asked Yunmen: 'what is the place where all the Buddhas are emancipated?'[56] Yunmen replied, '[Where] the East Mountains walk on the river.'" Yuanwu continued: "If someone were to ask me today what the place is like where all the Buddhas are emancipated, I would reply, 'The *shun* wind comes from the south, and produces a slight coolness in the palace.'"[57]

Dahui suddenly felt that "before and behind were cut off. It was like bringing a ball of tangled silk up against a knife—in one stroke it was sliced through. At that moment perspiration covered my whole body. Although no moving images arose, yet I was sitting in a place of total nakedness."[58] In another sermon, Dahui describes his experience differently:

Suddenly at this point I broke through the lacquer bucket. All of my various views and bits of knowledge from the past [years of study] melted like snow in hot soup—they vanished without a trace. I was so lively.... When the following year [Yuanwu] elevated me to First Seat, I made a great vow to take this Matter that is our original allotment and give it to monks and nuns so they would understand.[59]

He continues:

One day I went to enter Yuanwu's chamber. Yuanwu said, "For you to reach this state was not easy, it is a pity that you have died and cannot come to life. Not doubting words is a great malady. Don't you know that it is said, 'You must let go your hands while hanging from a cliff, then you become master of your own fate. When afterwards you return to life again, no one can deceive you.'[60] You must believe that there is this principle." I said to myself, based on what I attained today I am already very lively. I cannot understand [what he is talking about?].[61]

Yuanwu assigned me to the "Selecting Leaders Hut" as an attendant without duties.[62] Every day I entered Yuanwu's chamber several times with literati for individual instruction. Yuanwu raised only, "The word 'being' and the word 'nonbeing' are like a wisteria vine clinging to a tree." As soon as someone opened his mouth, Yuanwu would say, "Wrong!" It was like that for half a year. I just concentrated on investigating [this one *gongan*].

One day when I was in the abbot's quarters with some officials partaking of the evening meal, I just held the chopsticks in my hand and completely forgot to eat. Yuanwu said "This fellow is investigating 'boxwood Chan.'"[63] I offered an analogy. I said, "Teacher, it is the same principle as a dog staring at a pot of hot oil; he cannot lick it, but he cannot leave it alone, either." Yuanwu said, "You have hit on a wonderful analogy. This is what is called the diamond cage [so hard you cannot get out of it], the prickly chestnut ball [that cannot be swallowed]."[64]

Finally, Dahui asked Yuanwu what his teacher Wuzu Fayan had said when Yuanwu asked him about this same statement (*hua*). Yuanwu was not willing to talk about it. Dahui said:

"When you asked [Wuzu], you were not just by yourself. You asked in front of the whole assembly. What could prevent you from telling about it now?" Yuanwu said, "Once I asked him, 'What about "being" words and "nonbeing" words which are like a wisteria vine clinging to a tree?' Wuzu said, 'You cannot describe it, you cannot depict it.' I asked further, 'Suppose the tree falls and the vines die—what then?' Wuzu said, 'How important their companionship is to them.'"[65] The minute I heard him raise this, I understood. I said, "I got it!" Yuanwu said, "I am only afraid that you have not yet become able to pass through the *gongans*." I said, "Please raise them." Yuanwu then raised a series of *gongans*. I cut through them in two or three revolutions. It was like setting out on a trip in a time of great peace—when you get on the road you encounter nothing to stop you. Yuanwu said, "Now you know that I have not deceived you."[66]

Multiple Awakenings

The Ming dynasty Buddhist teacher Yunqi Zhuhong (1535–1615) had great respect for Dahui. In his *Zhuchuang ribi* (Jottings at the Bamboo Window, second series) published in the mid-seventeenth century, Zhuhong told a story about Dahui to illustrate his own comments on "great awakening" and "small awakening." "According to the lore, the venerable Dahui [Zong]gao [underwent] great awakening eighteen times, [his] small awakenings being countless."[67] Hakuin Ekaku, who revived Rinzai Zen in Japan, quoted Yunqi Zhuhong's report many times, writing that this was his own experience as well.[68] At least from Zhuhong's time this transmitted tradition became part of Dahui's image. Do Dahui's *yulu* collections and the *Nianpu* support the idea that Dahui experienced eighteen major awakenings?

First, in these collections, does Dahui say anything of the sort? It is possible to go through Dahui's autobiographical stories and find stories about moments prior to his large enlightenment under Yuanwu in which he reports glimpses, moments of happiness, and the like. For example, Dahui summarizes his experience prior to meeting Yuanwu as follows: "I started studying Chan when I was seventeen, and I was thirty-four years old when I shattered the lacquer cask [of deluded mind].[69] Before that I had passed *gongans*. I had understood when confronted with 'a blow, a shout' [the teaching technique associated with the Linji school]. I had gone [up against] 'flint-struck sparks and lightning flashes' and understood."[70] Dahui actually tells us of several of these moments in which he understood, seemed to understand, or received approval from his teacher. For example, in one sermon Dahui tells that he himself, before he met Yuanwu, had already been challenged with the "East Mountain walks on the water" *gongan* by a First Seat named Fang.[71] After working on it constantly for a couple of weeks, when the First Seat brought it up to him again, he understood part of it. After that he made up hundreds of turning words for it, but he could not get one that fit definitively. Finally, when he was reading the "Record of Words (*yulu*)" from when Donglin Zhaojue had been living at Letan [that is, Jewel Peak] in Jiangsi, he came upon an exchange (*wenda*, J. *mondo*) in which the answer was "his heels do not touch the ground." He was overjoyed, and went to the First Seat to say that he had understood.[72] When the First Seat asked once more the meaning of "The East Mountain walks on water," Dahui replied, "His heels have not touched the ground." Dahui then reports that not only did he think that he had passed the *gongan* this time, but he wrote a eulogy (*song*) about the *gongan*, and also raised it as an instruction topic.[73]

Several meanings of "awakening" or "enlightenment" were accepted in Chan by the time of Dahui. As Kenneth Kraft writes, the concept of enlightenment was flexible enough to embrace specific insight experiences and advanced states of awareness. Awakening could refer to the full range of awakening experiences, from a tip-of-the-tongue taste to a profound realization, as well as to a full awakening or full buddhahood.[74] Certainly in considering the accuracy of

Zhuhong's report it would be appropriate to count all the insight experiences Dahui recounts. But in his *yulu* collections and the stories of his quoted in the *Nianpu*, Dahui usually dismisses the importance of these glimpses and moments of joy as compared with his awakening under Yuanwu. Looking back on this period of his study of Chan prior to meeting Yuanwu, he said: "I studied for seventeen years. I did have fragmentary awakenings. Under Yunmen house teachers I understood some things. Under Caodong teachers I understood some things. The only thing was that I could not attain front and rear being cut off."[75] Furthermore, he creates the impression that sometimes what seemed to be understandings were only episodes of verbal facility or mental cleverness. Reflecting Dahui's own perspective, the Japanese Rinzai monk Musō Soseki writes:

> Dahui was a wandering monk in his youth, and he learned "lip-Zen." He flattered himself that he had attained complete satori, but he realized at last that that was not true. He visited Yuanwu, and finally had his lumps of illusion smashed to pieces. After that he always spoke of his mistake as a way of warning his disciples. Today's students, too, must keep this teaching in mind.[76]

Since Dahui tends in his *yulu* collections to downplay these earlier partial glimpses as based on mistaken ways of investigating *gongan*, stories about them do not strongly support the image of Dahui created by Zhuhong. Dahui's lack of investment in these small awakenings after his great one is particularly striking if one compares Hakuin's reports about his many large and small awakenings with Dahui's self-reports in his *yulu* collections and *Nianpu*. Here is one of Hakuin's accounts:

> Alone in the hut, I thrust my spine up stiff and straight and sat through the night until dawn. . . . After a month of this life, I still hadn't experienced a single pang of hunger. On the contrary, my body and mind were fired with a great surge of spirit and resolve. My nights were zazen. My days were sutra-recitation. I never let up. During this period, I experienced small satoris and large satoris in numbers beyond count. How many times did I jump up and jubilantly dance around, oblivious to all else! I no longer had any doubts at all about Dahui's talk of eighteen great satoris and countless small ones. How grievously sad that people today have discarded this way of kensho as if it were dirt!
>
> As for sitting, sitting is something that should include fits of ecstatic laughter—brayings that make you slump to the ground

clutching your belly. And when you struggle to your feet after the first spasm passes, it should send you kneeling to earth in yet further contortions of joy.[77]

Although Dahui sometimes says that he had a moment of joy, or a happiness that lasted a long time, his reader gets no encouragement to imagine Dahui dancing around jubilantly or experiencing contortions of joy or fits of ecstatic laughter. Ecstasy is not a part of the image of Dahui.

On the other hand, after his initial awakening with Yuanwu, there were at least two more large awakenings. As we have seen above, Dahui's enlightenment process did not end on the first day on which the bottom of the lacquer bucket fell out and he rushed to Yuanwu's chamber. Six months later, now as an attendant of Yuanwu, he was still working on the next *gongan*. His insight triggered by that *gongan* was perhaps his first large awakening. It enabled him to pass a long series of *gongans*, and presumably Yuanwu sanctioned his attainment.

But Dahui was still to have another large experience of awakening. In the sermon given at Mount Ashoka after his return from exile, Dahui continued his narration of the story of his awakening beyond the moment of his successful answering of *gongans* at Tianning Monastery in the capital. He relates a conversation that took place a few days later about someone else's Chan verse (*song*) in which he told Yuanwu that he wanted to compose an excellent Chan verse of his own. He had the idea for it, but he could not think of the words. Just then he heard the words of a servant boy walking past outside the window, Dahui turned to Yuanwu and said, "Just this is the song I wanted to offer to you." Yuanwu was very pleased.

From that point on, Dahui said, he talked fluently about a lot of things, and had no doubts about the words of the various Chan teachers in the empire: "But I still had not attained the great freedom. [This occurred] later [in the summer of 1128][78] when I was at [Cloud-cliff Chan Temple] on Tiger Hill [near the town of Suzhou in present-day Jiangsu Province] and read the *Avatamsaka Sutra* [the *Huayan sutra*], and got to the passage about the Bodhisattva's entering into the eighth *bhumi* or stage, called 'Immovable.'"[79]

The scripture says that when a bodhisattva attains complete acceptance of the nonorigination of things, the attainment appropriate to stage seven, one obtains entry into this eighth stage, where one is a bodhisattva of profound conduct, difficult to know and without any distinctions. The bodhisattva's conduct leaves behind all forms, all thoughts, all attachments, and is measureless. This profound conduct is impossible for the followers of the Buddha who have not chosen to be bodhisattvas (that is, the sravakas and the pratyeka buddhas) to attain. He or she leaves behind all noisy striving, and complete stillness [nirvana] appears.[80]

> The scriptural passage in question says that in that stage the bodhisattva abandons all effortful, active practices (*gongyong xing*) and obtains the effortless dharmas (*wu gongyong fa*). Thoughts of the karma of body, speech, and mind all cease, and he dwells in reward-conduct.[81] Take the example of a person who in a dream sees his body fall into a great river. Because he wants to cross the river, he puts forth a courageous determination and uses great skill-in-means. Because of his great courage and his employing great skill-in-means, he wakes up. As soon as he wakes up, everything that he is doing ceases. The bodhisattva is also like this: he or she sees that the bodies of sentient beings are in the four currents [that carry the unthinking along].[82] In order to save them, he or she gives rise to a great courage and vigorous effort to advance. Therefore he or she attains the Immovable Stage. On attaining it, all activities (*gongyong*) cease.[83] When I reached this point [in the text], for the first time nirvana appeared, and I attained the Great Freedom. . . . My being able to trust my mouth to preach began at this time.[84]

In a second sermon, Dahui ends the story with a different comment; he says:

> At this, I suddenly lost the cloth bag and I entered the realm of realization (*jingjie*) of the Flower Garland (*Huayan, Avatamsaka*). From this point on my words flowed; I could talk up, down and sideways without having to rely on a single word of text. When students came into my presence I did not wait for them to reveal themselves, I knew immediately whether or not they were correct.[85]

Clearly this experience was significant for Dahui in giving him perfect nirvana and great freedom, including especially freedom in the employment of words.

This is the last "large awakening" of which Dahui speaks in his sermons or writes in his letters and Dharma-instructions contained in his *yulu* collections or recorded in his *Nianpu*. If Dahui did in fact experience eighteen great awakenings in his lifetime, that exact number does not form part of his image in his public, published, and widely circulated records.

Teachings and Teaching Style

Dahui's teachings and teaching style are the source of the most positive dimensions of his image, particularly among those who attained awakening in Linji, Rinzai or Sŏn contexts. Dahui's teachings and teaching style center on *huatou* practice and the central importance of awakening. Dahui's teachings about *huatou* practice and successful experiences with using *huatou* with his own students have been thoroughly explored by scholars.[86] Here we are interested in the effect of Dahui's teaching style and teaching emphases, as represented in his own words and records, on his image. As a teacher, Dahui presents himself and his methods as lively, effective, intimately concerned, and what the Chan tradition calls "steep," while at the same time making a path forward abundantly clear. The image Dahui presents is of a man intent on, and succeeding in, defining and establishing an orthodoxy and orthopraxy within Chan.

Ishii Shūdō suggested and Morten Schlütter has made a brilliant case for the argument that Dahui's development and promotion of the *huatou* method was a result of his deep desire to counter the interest literati were taking in "silent illumination practice."[87] In tandem with his promotion of *huatou* practice, particularly among lay people, Dahui attacked what he called "heretical teachers" with "false teachings" who were ruining the chances of sincere Chan practitioners to attain awakening. These attacks, which have attracted the attention of scholars, were harsh and derogatory. Not only that, his campaign continued throughout Dahui's career. All of this is pervasively reflected in Dahui's *yulu* collections and the *Nianpu*: these are indeed almost the only sources from which scholars study this dimension of Dahui's teachings.

Although previous Linji school teachers, beginning with Linji himself in the *Linji lu*, are depicted as scolding heretics and deluded practitioners, as well as repeatedly defining true or orthodox Chan teachings and practice, nothing can be found in Song Chan literature to compare with Dahui's unrelenting attacks on "silent illumination." The texts that present these attacks also present Dahui as well aware of what he is doing: he says, "I am called [Zong]gao who scolds (*ma*) Heaven."

According to his *yulu* compilation and the *Nianpu*, Dahui began criticizing "silent illumination Chan" in 1134. In 1137, he was appointed to the abbacy of the Nengren Monastery on Mount Jing, where his attacks continued with great regularity. He had accomplished a lot at Mount Jing by the time he was fifty-three, including raising money and building a dormitory for an additional thousand monks. In 1141 the official Li Hanlao, a longtime friend, wrote about the impression Dahui made on those who knew him in an inscription *(ji)* for Mount Jing to commemorate the opening of the new dormitory:

> The master is the twentieth generation grandson of Linji. His Way is broad, and those whom it attracts are myriad. His gate is steep, and those who climb it find it difficult [to live up to his strict standards]. His instructions hit the mark, and those who are enlightened under him feel close to him. His discussions are lofty, and those who listen are amazed. But, there are also people who become frightened and disconcerted by his lofty talk. Among his contemporaries, those who doubt him criticize and slander him. I know that there is gossip, defamation, and suspicion circulating about the master and cannot but feel enraged by this.[88]

From within Dahui's corpus we cannot know how his contemporaries perceived him in light of his ongoing campaign of attacks. The gossip, defamation, and suspicion circulating about Dahui may well have been because of his polemical rhetoric.

Conclusion

Contemporary scholars are now getting a sense of the full extent to which the handed-down image of Tang Chan masters was crafted by later hands. One would expect that images of Song dynasty Chan masters might have been equally crafted by the editors of the records of their words in *yulu* compilations. The interval between the death of Dahui and the publication of his *yulu* was short; in fact, one of his *yulu* circulated fifteen years before his death. Freedom to shape Dahui's image was thus more limited.

As compared with the teachings of Linji presented in the much shorter *Linji lu*, it is striking how derivative and repetitive Dahui's teachings seem to be. Dahui is involved in very few stories that become *gongan*, much less *huatou*, in the later tradition.[89] Dahui's language is rarely inventive of new images; rather, it is filled with quotations from sutras and the words of earlier Chan teachers. The highly imagistic discourse of the Linji tradition as familiar to us from Yuanwu's *Blue Cliff Record* permeates Dahui's teachings as well. Dahui repeats himself from letter to letter and sermon to sermon as he returns again to certain themes. It seems that what the market, which was composed of literati and monks who produced and had access to printed texts, demanded was more and more of Dahui's words.

When one thinks of Dahui's records in this way and forgets how crafted the words of the Tang masters as presented to us are, it is not hard to conclude, as earlier generations of scholars have done, that Chan declined in the Song, that it lacked the freshness and originality of Tang Chan. When one reads Dahui's letters, on the other hand, a different picture emerges. Dahui comes across as a brilliant, clear, inspiring teacher with a deep grasp of Chan practice as lived every day and an extraordinary gift for relating Buddhist philosophy and psychology to ordinary mental and emotional experiences.

NOTES

1. Chinese customarily refer to Dahui Zonggao by his ordination name, Zonggao, and not by Dahui, one of three names given to Zonggao by emperors to honor him. Japanese authors customarily refer to him by one of the honorific names, Dahui, followed by his ordination name, or simply Dahui.

2. On these laymen and their relationship to Dahui, see Miriam Levering, "Ch'an Enlightenment for Laymen: Ta-hui Tsung-kao (1089–1163) and the New Religious Culture of the Sung," Ph.D. dissertation, Harvard University, 1978.

3. For a general account of Dahui's life and teachings, see Miriam Levering, "Ch'an Enlightenment for Laymen," and Chun-fang Yu, "Ta-hui Tsung-kao and Koan Ch'an," *Journal of Chinese Philosophy* 6 (1979): 211–235.

4. Master Hsu Yun, *Ch'an and Zen Teachings*, series two, translated by Lu K'uan Yu (Charles Luk) (London: Rider, 1961).

5. Garma C. C. Chang, *The Practice of Zen* (New York: Harper and Brothers, 1959).

6. Master Sheng Yen's disciple Jimmy Yu told me that in the United States Master Sheng Yen lectured on *huatou* practice using J. C. Cleary's translation, *Swampland Flowers* (New York: Grove, 1977).

7. Philip Yampolsky, *The Zen Master Hakuin: Selected Writings* (New York: Columbia University Press, 1971), p. 33. Note that this statement by Hakuin paraphrases a statement in a letter in *Dahui's Letters* [*Dahui shu*], T. 47.918c.

8. T. 47.1998A.881–943. Hereafter I will cite this text as DY (*Dahui yulu*). This text was included in the Song dynasty canons, and the Taishō version is very close to extant Song dynasty editions.

9. Hereafter I will cite this as the DP (*Dahui Pushuo*). I have used the edition in *Nihon kotei daizōkyō* 1.31.5.395a–480d in five fascicles.

10. Here I follow Morten Schlütter's suggestion in "The Record of Hongzhi and the Recorded Sayings Literature of Song Dynasty Chan" in Dale Wright and Steven Heine, eds., *The Zen Canon: Understanding the Classic Texts* (New York: Oxford University Press, 2004), pp. 181–205. Schlütter suggests that the term "*yulu* proper" be used for a collection of sermons and talks given by a master, sometimes including encounters and dialogues he had with others, which purport to have been written down by someone who was present at the occasion. He suggests that the term "*yulu* collections" be used for compilations that always include one or more *yulu* proper but also include other types of texts, including some that were composed and written down by the master himself. *Dahui Pujue Chanshi yulu* includes texts composed and written down by the master himself, and thus is a "*yulu* collection."

11. *Dainihon kotei daizōkyō*.8.1a–16a. This text is of some dubiety. It was published in the Ming dynasty canon together with the Recorded Sayings of Chan Master Dahui Pujue. Ishii Shūdō has published a critical edition of the *Dahui Nianpu*.

12. This text is in T. 47.1998B. I will cite it as *Wuku*.

13. Ishii Shūdō, "Daie Fukaku zenji no nenpu no kenkyu," *jō, chū*, and *ge*, *Komazawa daigaku bukkyō gakubu kenkyū kiyō* 37 (1979): 110–143; 38 (1980): 97–133; 40 (1982): 129–175. Hereafter, I will give short references. Here the reference is Ishii, "Nenpu (*jō*)," pp. 112–113. All ages given for Dahui will be according to Chinese reckoning by which a person is one year old at birth and becomes two years old at the next New Year holiday. I will leave the ages in Chinese reckoning in Dahui's narratives.

14. Ishii, "Nenpu (*jō*)," p. 113.

15. DP, p. 418c.

16. Ishii, "Nenpu (*jō*)," p. 113.

17. Among several important studies, Albert Welter, *Monks, Rulers and Literati: The Political Ascendency of Chan Buddhism* (New York: Oxford University Press, 2006) is particularly useful in understanding the close relation of Chan monks, rulers, and literati in the Northern Song dynasty. So are the chapters by Schlütter, Huang, Borrell, Welter, and Levering in Peter N. Gregory and Daniel A. Getz, eds., *Buddhism in the Sung* (Honolulu: University of Hawaii Press, 1999).

18. DP, p. 396a.

19. Yunmen's first teacher was Muzhou Daozong. This is in *Muzhou yulu*, 35b.

20. Urs Erwin App, "Facets of the Life and Teaching of Ch'an Master Yunmen Wenyan (864–949)," Ph.D. dissertation, Temple University, 1989), p. 329.

21. Chang Chung-yuan, trans., *Original Teachings of Ch'an Buddhism* (New York: Random House, 1969), p. 107.

22. DP, p. 396a; *Wuku*, T. 47.953ab. According to Dahui, Shaocheng was in the lineage of Langya Huijue through his disciple Xingjiao Tan. Cf. Ishii Shūdō, *Daijō butten* (Chūgoku, Nihon hen), vol. 12, *Zen goroku* (Tokyo: Chuo Koronsha, 1992), p. 458; and Ishii, "Nenpu (*ge*)," p. 132b.

23. This story is included as case twelve in the *Wumenguan*, and in the *Wudeng huiyuan, juan 7*. Cf. Hirata Takashi, *Mumonkan, Zen no Goroku*, vol. 18 (Tokyo: Chikuma Shobō, 1969), pp. 55–58.

24. Dahui says in another general sermon that he served as Shaocheng's attendant for two years, discussing *gongan* with him every day. DP, p. 430c.

25. DP, p. 446a. The same story is told in DP, p. 424bc and DP, p. 446a. What text Dahui referred to as the *Xuansha Heshang yulu* is unclear.

26. A *songgu*, "eulogy of the ancient," is a *gongan* commentary in which a story about an ancient Chan master is told, followed by a poetic commentary in the free-form *zi* style in which the meaning of the story is somewhat cryptically restated. A *niangu*, "picking up the ancient," is a *gongan* commentary in which a story about an ancient Chan master is told, followed by a prose commentary. On these two genres and on Xuedou's collections, see M. Schlütter, "*The Record of Hongzhi*."

27. DP, p. 446a.

28. T. 47.953ab.

29. DP, p. 430c.

30. Morten Schlütter, *How Zen Became Zen: The Dispute over Enlightenment and the Formation of Chan Buddhism in Song-Dynasty China* (Honolulu: University of Hawaii Press, 2008); and Ishii Shūdō, *Sōdai Zenshūshi no kenkyū: Chūgoku Sōtōshū to Dōgen Zen* (Tokyo: Daitō Shuppansha, 1987).

31. Ishii, *Daijō butten*, pp. 458–459.

32. T. 47.953b; DP, p. 428b. See Schlütter, *How Zen Became Zen*, p. 166. Schlütter believes that Daowei during his lifetime was a prominent disciple of Furong Daokai.

33. *Wuku*, T. 47.953b. These two are unknown in other sources.

34. DP, p. 425d.

35. DP, p. 428b.

36. Ishii, "Nenpu (ge)," p. 133a. This monastery is also known as Letan after a local lake.

37. *Wuku*, p. 953b; DP, pp. 425d and 428d.

38. DP, p. 425d.

39. Albert Welter, *The Linji lu and the Creation of Chan Orthodoxy* (New York: Oxford University Press, 2008), p. 137.

40. Welter, *Linji lu*, p. 138.

41. Welter, *Linji lu*, p. 139.

42. DP, p. 426b.

43. An abbreviated version of this is in DP, p. 426b.

44. T. 47.953b.

45. DP, p. 418.

46. DP, p. 421a.

47. See Miriam Levering, "Dahui Zonggao and Zhang Shangying: The Importance of a Scholar in the Education of a Song Chan Master," *Journal of Sung-Yuan Studies* 30 (2000): 115–139. DP, p. 418d. Zhang Shangying, like Yuanwu, was from Szechwan.

48. Janet Gyatso discusses the need to establish one's own lineage as distinct from others as an important factor in the popularity of autobiographical writing by Buddhist monks in Tibet in her *Apparitions of the Self* (Princeton: Princeton University Press, 1998). Morten Schlütter pursues this theme in *How Zen Became Zen*, where he connects Dahui Zonggao's unrelenting verbal attack on the practice and teaching of "silent illumination Chan" to the challenge posed to Linji Chan lineages by the sudden and successful revival of the Caodong Chan lineage during Dahui's time. See also Schlütter, "Silent Illumination, Kung-an Introspection, and the Competition for Lay Patronage in Sung-Dynasty Ch'an," in Gregory and Getz, eds, *Buddhism in the Sung*, pp. 109–147.

49. DP, p. 418.

50. This and other biographical detail and historical context discussed in this section are discussed at greater length in Miriam Levering, "Ch'an Enlightenment for Laymen." See also Ishii Shūdō, *Daijō butten*, pp. 403–499, for a discussion of Song Chan and a biography of Dahui.

51. On Zhang Jiucheng, see Ari Borrell, "*Ko-wu* or *Kung-an*? Practice, Realization and Teaching in the Thought of Chang Chiu-ch'eng," in Gregory and Getz, eds., *Buddhism in the Sung*, pp. 62–108.

52. See Morten Schlütter, "Vinaya Monasteries, Public Abbacies, and State Control of Buddhism under the Northern Song (960–1127)," in William Bodiford, ed., *Going Forth: Visions of Buddhist Vinaya* (Honolulu: University of Hawaii Press, 2005), pp. 136–160.

53. A good account in English is in Chun-fang Yu's "Ta-hui Tsung-kao and Kung-an Ch'an," *Journal of Chinese Philosophy* 6 (1979): 221–235. For a more detailed account, see Miriam Levering, "Was There Religious Autobiography in China?" *Journal of Chinese Religions* 30 (2002): 97–122. Many of the quotations from Dahui's *yulu* collections in this section of this essay are also used in a different context and to support a different argument in Levering, "Autobiography."

54. DP, p. 399c.

55. DP, p. 418d.

56. Urs App has: "What is the place from whence all the Buddhas come?" See *Zengojiten*, p. 205b on the meaning of *qushen*, which is more like "come out of bondage"; and App, *Master Yunmen* (New York: Kodansha, 1994), p. 94.

57. This couplet is found in the following story given in the *Tang shi jishi*, juan 40, in the section on the Tang poet Liu Gongquan. "On a summer day the emperor Wenzong was making up linked verses (*lianzhu*) with various scholars. He offered, 'Others all suffer from the heat, but I like the long summer days.' Liu Gongquan continued the verse, saying: 'The *hsun* wind comes from the south, and produces a slight coolness in the palace.'"

58. Cf. *Blue Cliff Record*, case 6, which has "Though you be clean and naked, bare and purified, totally without fault or worry, this is still not the ultimate" (Cleary, trans. Shambala Publications, 1992, p. 44.)

59. DP, pp. 410b–412b.

60. These words appear in the *Jingde chuandeng lu*, juan 20, and also in the *Blue Cliff Record*, case 41, in the commentary on the original case.

61. This is also told at DP, p. 421a.

62. *Zhemu* is an allusion to a sentence: "good birds select the trees on which they roost—one selects the leader whom he would follow."

63. The *huangyang* plant is a plant in the box or boxwood family that allegedly grows only an inch a year. Here it is an image for being stuck in a partial awakening with nothing at work in you to move you further along.

64. *Zengaku daijiten*, p. 145b; *Zengojiten*, p. 473a. Alternately: seat of thorns (Yu).

65. The following two sentences appear in *Zongrong lu*, 87: "Being words and nonbeing words are like wisteria vines climbing on a tree. Suddenly the tree falls and the wisteria dies—where do the words go then?" Cf. T. Cleary, *Book of Serenity: One Hundred Zen Dialogues* (Hudson, N.Y.: Lindisfarne, 1990), p. 372.

66. T. 47.883ab. This story is also told at DP, p. 421a. In T. 47.883b–c Dahui tells about further postawakening conversations with Yuanwu.

67. *Jottings under the Bamboo Window* text is in the *Yunqi fahui* (Collected Works of Master Yunqi), ci 25. (Nanjing: Jingling kejing chu, 1897).

68. See Hakuin Ekaku, *Wild Ivy: The Spiritual Autobiography of Zen Master Hakuin*, translated by Norman Waddell (Boston: Shambhala, 1999), p. 63; also p. 109.

69. Actually, if we follow the *Nianpu*, he was thirty-seven.

70. In the *Blue Cliff Record*, Yuanwu says, "You must realize that what is at stake here does not reside in words and phrases: it is like sparks from struck flint, like the brilliance of flashing lightning. However you manage to deal with this, you cannot get around losing your body and life." T. 48.177c8–10. Translated by App, *Master Yunmen*, p. 79.

71. DP, pp. 410b–412b. In one sermon Dahui says that he passed this *gongan* in a Yunmen school context; DP, p. 396a.

72. Donglin Zhaojue refers to Donglin Changzong, known as Zhaojue Chanshi (1025–1091). Cf. T. 51.573c.

73. *Nianti*; similar to *niangu*?

74. Kenneth Kraft, *Eloquent Zen: Daito and Early Japanese Zen* (Honolulu: University of Hawaii Press, 1992), pp. 90–91.

75. T. 47.883a.

76. Musō Soseki, trans., "West Mountain Evening Talk," in W. S. Merwin and Soiku Shigematsu, *The Sun at Midnight* (San Francisco: North Point Press, 1989), p. 161.

77. Waddell, trans., *Wild Ivy*, pp. 63 and 65. See also p. 109 and p. 122.

78. According to the *Nianpu*, it was 1128.

79. DP, p. 421b. The eighth stage is one in which the bodhisattva has completed all cultivation of the path to Nirvana.

80. I cannot find in any of my dictionaries the compound that I tentatively translate "noisy striving." This passage, lines 10 to 17 of T. 10.199a, is quoted by Dahui in his telling of the story in a sermon in T. 875bc. In the other two tellings of it he begins quoting with line 17, with which I begin my quotation in the next paragraph. This would lead one to conclude that what struck him in the passage was contained in lines 17 to 24.

81. The version of Dahui's telling of the story found at p. 459c omits this last phrase.

82. These are views, desires, existence, and ignorance.

83. T. 10.199a, lines 17–24. The quotation in the versions at DP, pp. 459c and 421b end here at line 24 of the sutra text. The quotation in the version at T. 47.875c goes on to line 28 of the sutra text.

84. DP, p. 421b.

85. DP, p. 459c.

86. Foremost among these scholars are Yanagida Seizan, Ishii Shūdō, Robert Buswell, and Morten Schlütter. Important articles and books are: Robert E. Buswell, Jr., The 'Short-cut' Approach of K'an-hua Meditation: The Evolution of a Practical Subitism in Chinese Ch'an Buddhism," in Peter N. Gregory, ed., *Sudden and Gradual Approaches to Enlightenment in Chinese Thought* (Honolulu: University of Hawaii Press, 1987), pp. 321–377; Miriam Levering, "Miao-tao and Her Teacher Ta-hui," in Gregory and Getz, eds., *Buddhism in the Sung*, pp. 188–219; and Morten Schlütter, "Silent Illumination, Kung-an Introspection, and the Competition for Lay Patronage in Sung Dynasty Ch'an," in Gregory and Getz, eds., *Buddhism in the Sung*, pp. 109–147.

87. Morten Schlütter, "Silent Illumination, Kung-an Introspection," and Schlütter, *How Zen Became Zen*, p. 213 n.2. (where Schlütter credits Ishii).

88. *Nianpu* under Shaoxing 11th year, pp. 39b–40a. This translation combines my own with that of Chun-fang Yu in "Ta-hui Zonggao," p. 216.

89. For a positive example, see Ari Borrell's chapter in *Buddhism in the Sung;* for another example, see Hakuin's investigation of a verse by Dahui as a kōan as reported in his autobiography, *Itsumadegusa*.

5

Dōgen, Zen Master, Zen Disciple: Transmitter or Transgressor?

Steven Heine

East Asian training methods generally emphasize that in order to succeed as an appropriator of a particular line of teaching, a disciple should be able to equal or to surpass his mentor, who must be magnanimous enough to acknowledge and encourage the value of the comeuppance that is often demonstrated in a dramatic or even combative way.[1] Chan/Zen Buddhism is a tradition particularly known for transmitting lineages whereby an advanced current disciple, who is an imminent or soon-to-be-realized master, at once pays obeisance to and severely criticizes the patriarch, often through an exchange of ironic insults or physical blows, and receives disingenuously faint praise in response. The locus classicus for this trope is found in the legends of successive generations of Tang dynasty Hongzhou school leaders, including the transmission from the patriarch Mazu to his foremost disciple Baizhang, whose ears are screamed in and nose tweaked by the teacher; from Baizhang to Huangbo, who slaps his mentor and is called a "red-bearded barbarian," thus evoking Bodhidharma, as a form of admiration; and finally from Huangbo to Linji, the founder of the Linji (J. Rinzai) school who is both the striker and the one being struck in their complex, dynamic set of edifying interactions.[2]

Although the formative stage of Chan puts an emphasis on demonstrative displays and rather outrageous histrionics, in other examples of training traditions in East Asia as well as later stages of Zen, the act of going beyond one's mentor is demonstrated in a subtle, purely rhetorical fashion. For example, in the early medieval Japanese poetic technique of *honkadori* (allusive variation), a junior poet makes a seemingly minor but very significant alteration in alluding to the verse of his mentor or another senior author.[3] This technique does not involve a mere passing reference to an older poem but extensively quotes passages from the precedent piece to the point of what might be considered plagiarism in the West for several reasons: it features the poet's knowledge and skill in citing the corpus; evokes the atmosphere of the earlier example while infusing it with contemporary meaning; and helps move the imaginative interaction between creative minds to a higher stage of understanding with a minimum of revision.[4]

A sense of the power of rhetoric based on purposeful understatement in highlighting yet somehow distancing from or breaking with a predecessor also is prevalent in Chan discourse. This is evident in an anecdote cited in Dōgen's "Gyōji" fascicle, which is a transmission of the lamp-style essay recounting the patriarchs of the Chan lineage. According to this passage, Yuanzhi delivers an unconventional eulogy by casually summing up his relationship with his senior colleague, Guishan, a disciple of Baizhang who helped Yuanzhi oversee a temple, "I lived on Guishan's mountain for thirty years, eating Guishan meals and shitting Guishan shit. But I did not learn the way of Guishan. All I did was take care of a castrated water buffalo."[5] Of these remarks featuring the mentor's disingenuous self-deprecation filled with ironic praise for the senior partner, Dōgen comments that the junior's training was characterized by "twenty years of sustained practice (*gyōji*)."

The rest of this chapter examines the various ways Dōgen's image and sense of self-identity are formed by his twofold approach to his predecessors, particularly Rujing, which epitomizes the tradition by transgressing it in encompassing attitudes of either admiration/emulation or rejection/ridicule. I situate Dōgen's citations of Caodong school patriarchs Hongzhi and Rujing in the context of the full range of Chan masters he also deals with in his works, and focus on how he cites as well as why he praises or refutes their teachings in terms of what this indicates about his view of transmission. The seemingly contradictory nature of Dōgen's discourse appears to indicate that his view toward sectarian issues was complex and perhaps not fully resolved as he tried to find his way in establishing a new movement in Japan by transmitting Chinese Chan amid the ever-shifting and highly competitive religious environment of the early Kamakura era.

Caodong School and Early Chan Masters

Table 5.1 shows that Dōgen cites his Chinese mentor Rujing (J. Nyojō) and Hongzhi (J. Wanshi), the eminent patriarch at Mount Tiantong (J. Tendō), who was the two-generation predecessor or "grandfather of Rujing," far more extensively than other Chan figures; he did this in order to establish a sense of lineal affiliation with a particular Chinese stream for the sake of expanding his movement in Japan. However, the citations of the Song Caodong (J. Sōtō) school masters must be seen in the context of his extensive citing of Linji school masters primarily from the Tang dynasty. The next main figure dealt with by Dōgen is Zhaozhou, who is featured in innumerable kōan cases, and this referencing occurs with greater frequency than citations of Dongshan. This highlights one of the important aspects of Dōgen's writing: the major role it played in introducing and disseminating Chan literary sources to Japanese monks without bias.

The key point is that Linji school citations, which are cast in a positive, pansectarian vein, are primarily from the period before Dōgen's move to Echizen and the founding of Eiheiji Temple. During this early phase of his career, he does not deal very much with either Rujing or Hongzhi, surprisingly enough, but during the transitional stage he becomes at times excessively negative regarding the Linji school as be begins to develop a sectarian focus on Caodong patriarchs. Beginning with the Echizen period, especially in the *Eihei kōroku*, a pattern emerges whereby Dōgen cites eminent masters from both the Linji and Caodong schools in his vernacular and Chinese-style sermons, yet is also willing to challenge, revise, and rewrite their sayings to express his own understanding and appropriation of Buddhist teaching. Dōgen clearly relishes his role as a critical commentator and revisionist of leading Chinese masters. A common refrain in many of the sermons is, "Other patriarchs have said it that

TABLE 5.1. Dōgen's Most Frequently Cited Chinese Chan Masters

Master	No. citations	Master	No. citations	Master	No. citations
Rujing	74*	Xuansha	12	Yueshan	10
Hongzhi	45	Dongshan	12	Fayan	9
Zhaozhou	33	Yuanwu	12	Huanglong	9
Sakyamuni**	17	Mazu	11	Huangbo	9
Baizhang	13	Xuefeng	10	Bodhidharma	8
Yunmen	13	Guishan	10	Linji	8
Huineng	12	Nanchuan	10		

Source: Kagamishima Genryū, *Dōgen zenji to in'yō kyōten-goroku no kenkyū* (Tokyo: Mokujisha, 1985).

*Excludes allusions only, memorials, and *Hōkyōki*
**Indian Buddha

way, but I [Eihei] say it this way. . . ." Part of his theme is that with the possible exception of Rujing, nearly all the teachers and followers he met during his travels in China were disappointing in that they lacked some essential element of authenticity in the pursuit of the Dharma.

Once the move to Echizen is completed and he is fully ensconced in Eiheiji, Dōgen turns increasingly to Hongzhi and Rujing as models for Chinese (or, more accurately, Sino-Japanese, since it is a hybrid grammatical form) *kanbun* sermons contained in the *Eihei kōroku*, while continuing his criticism of the Linji school and also remaining willing to critique the Caodong patriarchs, when appropriate, in what can be referred to as a "trans-sectarian" fashion. This means that his approach cuts across lines of sectarian division as part of an ongoing quest for personal integrity, authenticity, and autonomy. In accord with the style of transmission-as-transgression, for Dōgen individuality is more highly prized than blind devotion or loyalty to the lineage.

Rather than relying on physical slaps or blasphemous taunts, Dōgen's literary works epitomize the process of using language indirectly yet forcefully in vernacular sermons as an effective rhetorical means for challenging and going beyond his illustrious predecessors, whom he also admires and praises for their positive influence on developing his thought and practice. Throughout his writings, especially in the Japanese vernacular (*kana*) sermons of the *Shōbōgenzō* that was primarily composed in the late 1230s and early 1240s, Dōgen dutifully cites several dozen Chinese Chan masters whose works he had first studied while visiting China and training at Mount Tiantong (J. Tendō) a decade before. While dependent on their insight and creativity, he almost always deviates from their interpretations in order to establish his individual perspective, and often quite adamantly criticizes their views or attitudes. He is even so scathing in some of his comments that, according to one theory of interpretation, a different version of the *Shōbōgenzō* was created in order to eliminate some of the fascicles that contained offensive language. From the standpoint of this theory, either Dōgen himself or one of his early followers was aware of the partisan, sectarian tone of some of his criticisms and decided to delete passages from the standard 75-fascicle *Shōbōgenzō* by creating an alternative 60-fascicle text.

The existence of the 60-fascicle version, which was strongly supported by the Tokugawa-era Sōtō scholastic Tenkei Denson, may indicate that there was awareness early in the tradition of Dōgen's sometimes excessive rhetoric and harsh polemical elements, as well as the need to evaluate the founder's real intentions about the formation of the *Shōbōgenzō*. Although the origins of the 60-fascicle edition remain obscure, perhaps the act of deletion was done deliberately by Dōgen's collaboration with Ejō in order to create a perfected text during his lifetime, or by later generations of interpreters who retrospectively sought to sanitize his writings, such as Giun, a fourteenth-century Sōtō patriarch and fifth-generation abbot of Eiheiji.[6]

According to table 5.2, eleven fascicles from the 75-fascicle *Shōbōgenzō* that are not included in the 60-fascicle edition contain sharp criticism of rival streams, especially those stemming from the Linji school.[7] Most of the fascicles deleted from the 60-fascicle *Shōbōgenzō* were composed in the early 1240s, when Dōgen was in the process of making a transition from Kōshōji Temple in Kyoto to Eiheiji Temple in the Echizen Mountains. He was trying to establish his sectarian identity in light of pressures from the Japanese government and contests or conflicts with the Tendai sect and other emerging religious movements, in connection with the teachings of Rujing and the Caodong school more generally.

Of the eleven deleted fascicles, nine were composed during the first three-quarters of a year after Dōgen's move to Echizen province in the summer of 1243. Just before this phase, as he was struggling to move his monastery and to hold together and possibly expand a small but intense band of followers, he received a copy in 1242 of the recorded sayings (C. *yulu*, J. *goroku*) of Rujing that was sent from China, and also began to focus on delivering sermons in *kanbun* rather than the vernacular sermons of the *Shōbōgenzō*. While supporting the axis of Caodong masters, including founder Dongshan and Hongzhi as

TABLE 5.2. Eleven Fascicles Not Included in the 60-*Shōbōgenzō*

Fascicle	Target of Criticism (or Praise)
Shinfukatoku	Deshan
Sansuikyō	Yunmen
*Sesshin sesshō	Linji and Dahui (praises Dongshan)
*Shohō jissō	Three Teachings are One, Laozi and Zhuangzi (praises Rujing and also Yuanwu)
*Butsudō	Five Schools of Zen Sect, Linji, Deshan, Chizong and *Rentien yanmu* (praises Shitou, Dongshan and Rujing)
*Mitsugo	Linji and Deshan (praises Xuetou, Rujing's predecessor)
*Bukkyō (Buddhist Sutras)	Linji and Yunmen, Dongshan (four thoughts and four relations, three phrases, three paths and five relative positions, Confucius and Laozi briefly) (praises Sakyamuni and Rujing)
*Menju	Yunmen lineage; in an appendix, two lesser-known monks, Chengge and Fuguo Weibai (praises Dongshan and Rujing)
*Sanjōshichihon bodaibunpō	Zaike (Lay) and Shukke (Monk) are One, "Zen sect"
*Daishugyō	Linji and Deshan
*Jishō zanmai	Dahui

Note: These fascicles contain direct fundamental criticism of Zen masters, schools, texts, and theories.

*Fascicles composed in 1243–1244 in Echizen province

representatives of authentic lineal transmission, Dōgen sharply attacks Hongzhi's Linji school rival, Dahui.[8] However, just half a decade earlier, in *Shōbōgenzō zuimonki* 6.19, he said he admired Dahui's commitment to continuous, diligent practice of *zazen* while having hemorrhoids (the same scatological passage in which Dōgen notes that diarrhea prevented him from entering China when the ship first docked).[9] Yet now he harshly criticizes the Song master, particularly in "Jishō zanmai," one of the fascicles excluded from the 60-fascicle *Shōbōgenzō* that was written in Echizen in the winter of 1244.

Dōgen goes so far as to challenge the authenticity of the enlightenment experience of Dahui, which Miriam Levering shows in her chapter is a controversial and contested part of the biography of the Song dynasty Chan master who, he says, could not recognize the Dharma even in a dream. This was in large part because one of Dahui's lineage was associated with the monks who legitimated the transmission to Dainichi Nōnin, the founder of the controversial, proscribed Daruma school of early Japanese Zen who never traveled to the mainland but sent his disciples to be sanctioned by one of Dahui's followers, Deguang. Dōgen received several Daruma school monks into his community, including such prominent figures as Ejō, Gikai, and Giun, the second, third, and fifth patriarchs of Eiheiji, respectively. He further asserts that only those in the Dongshan lineage, including Rujing and Hongzhi, can have a genuine spiritual experience.

Table 5.3 indicates the masters associated with the Linji school who are severely criticized in the controversial fascicles, including Tang dynasty monks Linji, Yunmen, Deshan, and Guishan, in addition to Dahui's teacher, Yuanwu, author of the *Blue Cliff Record* (C. *Biyanlu*, J. *Hekiganroku*) kōan collection. At the same time, Dōgen's approach was not altogether one-sided, and there are many examples of his writings during this period when he evokes the life and teachings of a wide variety of Chan masters without regard to their lineal status and contrasts them with the deficiency of practitioners in Japan. For example, "Keiseisanshoku," which is included in the 60-fascicle *Shōbōgenzō*, cites numerous Chinese masters from various streams who were notable for dwelling in mountain forests. Yet, even here, there is a sectarian edge to the writing. Dōgen describes how those who seek fame and fortune were labeled "pitiful" by Rujing, who probably borrowed this phrase from the *Suramgama Sutra*. He goes on to comment, "In this country of Japan, a remote corner of the ocean, people's minds are extremely dense. Since ancient times, no saint has ever been born here, nor anyone wise by nature."[10] This fascicle also emphasizes the need for repentance as a means for overcoming spiritual deficiency. This may have been intended to send a message about the powerful impact of karmic retribution to monks converting to Dōgen's

TABLE 5.3. Fascicles with Criticism of Linji School

Linji	Deshan
Sokushin zebutsu	Sokushin zebutsu
Daigo	Shinfukatoku
Bukkōjōji	
Gyōji	Bukkōjōji
*Sesshin sesshō	Kattō
*Butsudō	*Butsudō
*Bukkyō S	*Mitsugo
*Mitsugo	*Mujō seppō
*Mujō seppō	*Daishugyō (12-SH)
*Kenbutsu	
*Daishugyō (12-SH) Kattō	Yuanwu
	Bukkōjōji
Yunmen	
Sansuikyō	*Shunjū
Kattō	
	Guishan

*Not included in 60-Shōbōgenzō

new movement from the Daruma school, which apparently disdained the precepts and monastic rules in the belief that all beings are originally endowed with the Buddha-nature.[11]

In the sermons contained in the *Eihei kōroku*, Dōgen incorporates praise with criticism of Chan masters. He is especially critical of Zhaozhou, one of the patriarchs along with Hongzhi, to whom he refers as an "ancient master" (*kobutsu*), as in record nos. 1.140, 2. 154, 4.331, and 4.339. In the second of these examples, Dōgen appears to be defending the Chinese master in citing a passage from his recorded sayings against a critique proffered by a disciple, but concludes by overturning Zhaozhou's standpoint:

> Consider this: A monk asked Zhaozhou, "What is the path without mistakes?" Zhaozhou said, "Clarifying mind and seeing one's own nature is the path without mistakes." Later it was said, "Zhaozhou only expressed eighty or ninety percent. I am not like this. If someone asks, 'What is the path without mistakes?' I would tell him, 'The inner gate of every house extends to Chang'an [the capital, literally, "long peace"].'"
>
> The teacher [Dōgen] said: Although it was said thus, this is not worth considering. The old buddha Zhaozhou's expression is correct. Do you want to know the clear mind of which Zhaozhou spoke? [Dōgen] cleared his throat, and then said, Just this is it. Do you want to know about the seeing into one's own nature that Zhaozhou

mentioned? [Dōgen] laughed, then said, Just this is it. Although this is so, the old buddha Zhaozhou's eyes could behold east and west, and his mind abided south and north. If someone asked me [Daibutsu], "What is the path without mistakes?" I would say to him, Do not go anywhere else. Suppose someone asks, "Master, isn't this tuning the string by gluing the fret?" I would say to him, Do you fully understand tuning the string by gluing the fret?[12]

The phrase, "Do not go anywhere else" refers to appropriating enlightenment through concrete manifestations of phenomenal reality rather than conceptual abstractions, and "gluing the fret" suggests a misunderstanding of the function of spiritual experience decried by Dōgen.

In *Eihei kōroku* 3.207, Dōgen criticizes Yunmen and the whole notion of the autonomy of a "Zen school," which should not take priority over the universality of the Buddha Dharma:

[Dōgen] said: Practitioners of Zen should know wrong from right. It is said that after [the Ancestor] Upagupta, there were five sects of Buddha Dharma during its decline in India. After Qingyuan and Nanyue, people took it upon themselves to establish the various styles of the five houses, which was an error made in China. Moreover, in the time of the ancient buddhas and founding ancestors, it was not possible to see or hear the Buddha Dharma designated as the "Zen school," which has never actually existed. What is presently called the Zen school is not truly the Buddha Dharma.

I remember that a monk once asked Yunmen, "I heard an ancient said that although the [patriarch of the Ox Head School] expounded horizontally and vertically, he did not know the key to the workings of going beyond. What is that key to the workings of going beyond?" Yunmen said, "The eastern mountain and the western peak are green." If someone were to ask Eihei [Dōgen], "What is that key to the workings of going beyond?" I would simply reply to him, "Indra's nose is three feet long."[13]

Note that in Dōgen's rewriting of Yunmen's response, neither of their expressions directly addresses the question, although each has its merits as a reflection of Zen insight. Yet Dōgen seems to suggest that Yunmen's phrasing is deficient and that his own saying is on the mark, perhaps because it is at once more indirect and absurd yet concrete and down-to-earth.

It may seem that Dōgen is driven primarily by sectarian concerns to use a high-pitched and in some cases vituperative rhetoric against rival schools. Once again, however, at times he is pansectarian in citing masters from all Chan schools, as well as nonsectarian in that he also denies the existence of an independent "Chan sect" altogether. In "Bukkyō" [Buddhist Sutras] he attacks "stupid, ignoramus skinbags" who either highlight Chan at the expense of basic Buddhism more generally or blur Buddhist doctrine as one of the "three teachings" along with Daoism and Confucianism.

Dōgen's supposed sectarian-based outlook is tempered by an element of his approach which is particularly interesting, that is, the way he shows no reluctance in revising or even rejecting the Caodong school leaders. In some cases, Dōgen cites the source text nearly verbatim as a sign of reverence, but is quick to critique the Caodong sages, whom he feels have misread or misinterpreted a key notion or citation from the Chan classics. For example, in *Eihei kōroku* 4.296 delivered on the occasion of the winter solstice in 1248, Dōgen cites Hongzhi, as he had on several of these seasonal occasions, including nos. 2.135 and 3.206. Dōgen says, "'My measuring cup is full and the balance scale is level,' but in the marketplace I buy what is precious and sell it for a low price," thereby reversing the statement in Hongzhi's sermon, "Even if your measuring cup is full and the balance scale is level, in transactions I sell at a high price and buy when the price is low."[14] Perhaps Dōgen is demonstrating a bodhisattva-like generosity or showing the nondual nature of all phenomena that only appear to have different values.

Furthermore, Dōgen's mentor Rujing is not immune to this revisionist treatment, as in *Eihei kōroku* 3.194:

> [Dōgen] said, I remember a monk asked an ancient worthy, "Is there Buddha Dharma or not on a steep cliff in the deep mountains?" The worthy responded, "A large rock is large; a small one is small." My late teacher Tiantong [Rujing] said, "The question about the steep cliff in the deep mountains was answered in terms of large and small rocks. The cliff collapsed, the rocks split, and the empty sky filled with a noisy clamor."
>
> The teacher [Dōgen] said, Although these two venerable masters said it this way, I [Eihei] have another utterance to convey. If someone were to ask, "Is there Buddha Dharma or not on a steep cliff in the deep mountains?" I would simply say to him, "The lifeless rocks nod their heads again and again. The empty sky vanishes completely. This is something that exists within the realm of the buddhas and patriarchs. What is this thing on a steep cliff in the deep mountains?" [Dōgen] pounded his staff one time, and descended from his seat.[15]

The phrase, "The lifeless rocks nod their heads again and again," is a reference to Daosheng, Kumarajiva's great disciple and early Chinese Buddhist scholar, who, on the basis of a passage in the *Mahaparinirvana Sutra* that all beings can become buddha, went to the mountain and preached the Dharma to the rocks, which nodded in response.[16]

The Influence Yet Critique of Hongzhi

A close look at volumes 2–4 of the *Eihei kōroku*, which contains *kanbun* sermons from the early years at Eiheiji delivered in the mid- to late-1240s as edited by Ejō, shows that Dōgen asserts the primacy of the discursive style of the recorded sayings of Song predecessors, especially Hongzhi.[17] He wages a campaign to identify himself with the Hongzhi-Rujing axis that occupied the abbacy in the twelfth and early thirteenth centuries during the glory days of Mount Tiantong, one of the pillars of the Chan Five Mountains monastic institution, which was also directed intermittently by Linji school masters. This enables Dōgen to distinguish his lineage from rival Zen movements in Japan, and to support the rejection of Dahui because his lineage in China gave sanction to the fledgling Daruma school that was led by Dainichi Nōnin.

Unlike Rujing, who remained obscure in Chan/Zen discourse generally except for his connection to Dōgen, Hongzhi was widely recognized as one of the premier sermonizers and poets during the peak of the Caodong school, which had undergone a period of revival inspired by Furong Daokai (J. Fuyū Dōkai) two generations before. Whereas Rujing appears with great frequency in the *Shōbōgenzō*, as tables 5.4 and 5.5 show, Hongzhi's role is quite prominent

TABLE 5.4. Classical Chan Texts Cited in the "Eihei kōroku"

Text	No. citations
1. Jingde chuandeng lu (J. Keitoku dentōroku)	68
2. Hongzhi lu (J. Wanshi roku)	43
3. Zongmen tongyao ji (J. Shūmon tōyōshū)	25
4. Zongmen liantong huiyao (J. Shūmon rentōeyō)	24
5. Rujing lu (J. Nyojo roku)	10
6. Jiatai pudeng lu (J. Katai futōroku)	7
7. Yuanwu lu/song gu (J. Engo roku/juko)	9
8. Tiansheng guangdeng lu (J. Tenshō kōtōroku)	9
9. Dahui lu (J. Daie roku)	2
10. Huangbo lu (J. Ōbaku roku)	2
11. Xu chuandeng lu (J. Zoku dentōroku)	2
Total	211

TABLE 5.5. Dōgen's Citations or Allusions to Hongzhi

Eihei Kōroku Citations	Other Examples	
Winter Solstice	EK 3.203, 1246 (full)	EK 5.418, 1250
EK 2.135, 1245	EK 3.246, 1247 (full)	EK 7.481, 1252
EK 3.206, 1246	EK 4.269, 1248 (full)	EK 7.494, 1252
EK 4.296, 1248	EK 7.498, 1252 (full)	EK 7.514, 1252
New Year		EK 8.s.13, 1240s
EK 2.142, 1246		EK 8.s.20, 1240s
EK 3.216, 1247	*Allusions Only*	EK 9.25, 1236
EK 4.303, 1249	EK 2.180, 1246	EK 9.88, 1236
5.5 Day	EK 3.186, 1246	
EK 3.242, 1247	EK 3.187, 1246	*Shōbōgenzō*
EK 4.261, 1248	EK 3.222, 1247	Gyōbutsuigi, 1241
EK 4.326, 1249	EK 3.223, 1237	Zazenshin, 1242
Bathing Buddha	EK 3.227, 1247	Gyōji, p. 1, 1242
EK 3.236, 1247	EK 4.264, 1248	Kobusshin, 1243
EK 3.256, 1248	EK 4.285, 1248	Shunjū, 1244
EK 4.320, 1249	EK 4.329, 1249	Ōsakusendaba, 1245
Summer Retreat	EK 4.337, 1249	Jinshin inga, 1253?
EK 3.257, 1248	EK 4.340, 1249	
EK 4.322, 1249	EK 4.341, 1249	*SBGZ Zuimonki*
EK 4.341, 1249	EK 4.344, 1249	
Mid-Autumn	EK 4.397, 1250	3.10, 1237
EK 4.344, 1249	EK 5.400, 1250	
	EK 5.403, 1250	*Bendōwa* (1231)

only in the *Eihei kōroku*.[18] While Dōgen sees Rujing as a charismatic and inspirational teacher who deeply touched his life as well as that of other disciples, he admires Hongzhi, whom he never had a chance to meet, mainly for his ceremonial role. Particularly during 1245–1246, Dōgen frequently turns to Hongzhi as a model for ritual occasions at a time when he also begins to rely heavily on the standard Chan monastic rules text, the *Chanyuan Qinggui* (J. *Zen'en shingi*) of 1103. Dōgen cites Hongzhi three or four times on the occasion of the Buddha's birthday between 1246 and 1249. He also evokes Hongzhi on other occasions such as new year, opening the summer retreat, Boys' Festival, and other seasonal ceremonies. A major consequence of overlooking the *Eihei kōroku* in comparison to the *Shōbōgenzō*, as some scholars have done, is to neglect the importance of Hongzhi's influence, as he is cited over forty times. In *Eihei kōroku* 2.135 Dōgen cites Hongzhi in creating his sermon for the winter solstice, and in no. 2.142 he cites the Song master for the new year's sermon, while no. 2.148 alludes to the *Book of Serenity* case 5 (C. *Congronglu*, J. *Shōyōroku*) (also *Blue Cliff Record* case 30) and no. 2.170 alludes to the *Book of Serenity* case 69, among other examples.

It is clear that references to Hongzhi, which are primarily concerned with ritual occasions when the master's words serve as a model Dōgen emulates, yet sometimes revises reach a peak in the late 1240s and seem to fade just as those to Rujing begin picking up again in the early 1250s. The reliance on Hongzhi for the most part does not continue in the later sections (volumes 5–7) of the *Eihei kōroku* recorded by Gien, a former Daruma school monk who ten years after Dōgen's death took the text to China to have it certified at Mount Tiantong and returned with a controversial abbreviated version, the *Eihei goroku*. In fact, noted Dōgen scholar Ishii Shūdō finds that the main change in the *kanbun* sermons edited by Gien, which cover the final years at Eiheiji, is that Dōgen is no longer as heavily influenced by Hongzhi's recorded sayings. There also seems to be a greater emphasis on karmic causality based largely on the citation of early Buddhist scriptures rather than Mahayana sutras or conventional Chan sources, but there is no significant alteration in ideology regarding *zazen* or kōan interpretation that is supposedly based on the teachings of Rujing.[19]

As mentioned, Dōgen's reverence does not prohibit Zen-style criticism of the masters he favors, although generally this criticism falls short of blasphemy. In citing Hongzhi, Dōgen rarely loses the opportunity to critique or one-up him. A main example is *Eihei kōroku* 2.135, delivered in the first year in Echizen when the temple later named Eiheiji in 1246 was still known as Daibutsuji:

> When the old buddha Hongzhi was residing at Mount Tiantong, during a winter solstice sermon he said, "Yin reaches its fullness and yang arises, as their power is exhausted conditions change. A green dragon runs away when his bones are exposed. A black panther looks different when it is covered in mist. Take the skulls of all the buddhas of the triple world and thread them onto a single rosary. Do not speak of bright heads and dark heads, as truly they are sun face, moon face. Even if your measuring cup is full and the balance scale is level, in transactions I sell at a high price and buy when the price is low. Zen worthies, do you understand this? In a bowl, the bright pearl rolls on its own without being pushed."
>
> "Here is a story," [Hongzhi continued]. "Xuefeng asked a monk, 'Where are you going?' The monk said, 'I'm going to do my communal labor.' Xuefeng said, 'Go ahead.' Yunmen said [of this dialogue], 'Xuefeng judges people based on their words.'" Hongzhi said, "Do not make a move. If you move I'll give you thirty blows. Why is this so? Take a luminous jewel without any flaw, and if you carve a pattern on it its virtue is lost."

The teacher [Dōgen] then said: "Although these three venerable ones [Hongzhi, Xuefeng, Yunmen] spoke this way, I, old man Daibutsu, do not agree. Great assembly, listen carefully and consider this well. For a luminous jewel without flaw, if polished, its glow increases." With his fly-whisk [Dōgen] drew a circle and said: "Look!" After a pause [Dōgen] said, "Although the plum blossoms are colorful in the freshly fallen snow, you must look into it further to understand the first arrival of yang [with the solstice]."[20]

Here, Dōgen is indebted to Hongzhi's original passage, which cites Mazu's famous saying, "Sun face [or eternal] buddha, moon face [or temporal] Buddha," as culled from the *Book of Serenity* case 36, and he also includes a saying about the bright pearl that appears in the fourth line of Hongzhi's verse comment on this case. But Dōgen challenges all the masters. After making a dramatic, well-timed demonstration with the ceremonial fly-whisk as a symbol of authority, he evokes the image of plum blossoms in the snow to highlight the need for continually practicing *zazen* meditation. This is reinforced by his rewriting of the jewel metaphor to put an emphasis on the process of polishing.

To give another example, in *Eihei kōroku* 3.236 for "Bathing [the Baby] Buddha," a celebration of the Buddha's birthday in 1247, Dōgen tells that in a sermon delivered on the same occasion when Hongzhi was abbot at Mount Tiantong, he had cited an anecdote in which Yunmen performed the bathing ritual and had apologized to the Buddha for using "impure water." However, Dōgen criticizes Hongzhi's interpretation by suggesting:

Although the ancient buddha Hongzhi said it like this, how should I [Eihei] speak of the true meaning of the Buddha's birthday? Casting off the body within the ten thousand forms, the conditions for his birth naturally arose. In a single form after manifesting as a human body, he discovered anew the path to enlightenment. What is the true meaning of our bathing the Buddha? After a pause [Dōgen] said, "Holding in our own hands the broken wooden ladle, we pour water on his head to bathe the body of the Tathagata."[21]

Rujing as Chan Model

Although it serves as the centerpiece of the Sōtō sect's transmission mythology, modern scholars have questioned Dōgen's eulogizing of Rujing, who was generally not well known or highly regarded in the setting of Chinese monastic life, especially compared to Hongzhi's illustrious reputation as a highly accomplished literary figure.[22] But Dōgen considers his mentor an ideal Chan teacher, not so much for his feats as one of the literati as for combining spontaneous sermonizing at all times of the day, rather than only during regularly planned ritual occasions, with a deep sense of integrity in terms of adhering to codes of discipline and maintaining a rigorous disdain for any form of corruption. Rujing was committed to the sustained practice of *zazen* as the premier form of Buddhist training, and was also willing to acknowledge and support the dedication of young Dōgen, an outsider to the Chinese Buddhist system who had been poorly treated by the previous abbot at Mount Tiantong.[23]

In *Dōgen's Manuals of Zen Meditation*, which overturns conventional theories about the dating of the *Fukanzazengi*, an important meditation manual long considered one of Dōgen's earliest writings composed in the year of his return to China in 1227, Carl Bielefeldt points out:

> Not until the 1240s, well over a decade after his return from China and at the midpoint of his career as a teacher and author, does Dōgen begin to emphasize the uniqueness of Ju-ching [Rujing] and to attribute to him the attitudes and doctrines that set him apart from his contemporaries. Prior to this time, during the period when one would expect Dōgen to have been most under the influence of his Chinese mentor, we see but little of Ju-ching or, indeed, of some of those teachings now thought most characteristic of Dōgen's Zen.[24]

This comment indicates that the emphasis on Rujing became intensified and reached fruition fully fifteen years after the trip to China, at the time of Dōgen's move to Echizen and the challenge of accepting erstwhile Daruma school followers.[25]

In numerous *Shōbōgenzō* fascicles from the first several months after the move, when he and a small band of dedicated followers were holed up over the long first winter in a couple of temporary hermitages, Kippōji and Yoshiminedera, before settling into permanent quarters, Dōgen provides his followers with a strong sense of lineal affiliation by identifying with Rujing's branch. He claims this was the only authentic Chan school. The high estimation of Rujing expressed during the "midpoint of his career" was not apparent in Dōgen's writings before this juncture. While praising and elevating the status of his mentor, Dōgen also embarks on a devastating critique of rival schools, which he referred to as "filthy rags" and "dirty dogs" that defame the Buddha Dharma.

Dōgen notes receiving Rujing's recorded sayings (C. *Rujing yulu*, J. *Nyojō goroku*) on 8.6.1242 in *Eihei kōroku* 1.105.[26] But the first indication of renewed interest was in *Shōbōgenzō* "Gyōji" (part 2), which was written several months earlier and contains four citations as part of a lengthy discussion of Rujing, which comes at the end of a survey of the biographies of monks who represent the pinnacle of Chan practice.[27] Although there were some references to Rujing in writings dating back to the early 1230s, the full acknowledgment and celebration—or possibly idealization and exaggeration—of the mentor come at this time. The citation of Rujing's attack on Dahui follower Deguang seems to highlight the contrast between Rujing's brand of rigorous monasticism and the antinomianism that typified the Daruma school's rejection of the precepts. The list in table 5.6 shows that, apart from "Gyōji" (part 2), which was a year or so earlier, all the *Shōbōgenzō* fascicles containing multiple references to Rujing stem from the period of the move to Echizen.

As seen in table 5.7, reliance on allusions to Rujing expressed in *Shōbōgenzō* fascicles from the 1240s continued to proliferate throughout the later stages of Dōgen's career in *Eihei kōroku* sermons from the 1250s. Note that memorials for Rujing were not begun until 1246, but were then continued for seven years until the end of Dōgen's career, when illness forced him to stop preaching. Generally, these are brief and cryptic.[28] In *Eihei kōroku* 2.184 from 1246, for example, Dōgen expresses self-deprecation in celebrating Rujing's wisdom: "When I entered China, I studied walking like someone from Handan. I worked very hard carrying water and hauling firewood. Do not say that my late teacher deceived his disciple. Rather, Tiantong [Rujing] was deceived by Dōgen."[29]

The abundance of citations of Rujing at certain periods—and their lack at other times—suggests a delayed reaction and retrospective quality. As demonstrated by recent Japanese scholarship, Dōgen's citations and evocations of Rujing are at times at variance with the recorded sayings, even though Tokugawa-era Sōtō scholar/monks heavily edited this text precisely in order to prove such a consistency.[30] This raises basic questions about Dōgen's portrayal of his mentor and use of other Chan sources, as well as why his approach seemed to have changed despite claims of unwavering continuity by the sectarian tradition. On the other hand, more frequently than one might suppose,

TABLE 5.6. *Shōbōgenzō* Fascicles Citing Rujing Multiple Times

Date	Fascicle	Place	No. Citations
1243.9.16	Butsudō	Kippōji	2
1243.9	Bukkyō	Kippōji	2
1243.9	Shohō jissō	Kippōji	2
1243.11.6	Baika	Kippōji	8
1243.12.17	Ganzei	Yamashibudera	7
1243.12.17	Kajō	Yamashibudera	5
1244.2.12	Udonge	Kippōji	2

132   ZEN MASTERS

TABLE 5.7. Dōgen's Citations or Allusions to Rujing

Shōbōgenzō	Shōbōgenzō zuimonki, 1236	EK 3.194, 1246
	Senmen, 1239	EK 4.318, 1249
Makahannyaharamitsu, 1233-1	Busso, 1241	*EK 4.319, 1249
Senjō, 1239-1	Busshō, 1241	EK 5.379, 1250
Shisho, 1241-1	Zazenshin, 1242	*EK 5.390, 1250
Kankin, 1241-1	Darani, 1243	*EK 5.406, 1250
Gyōji 2, 1242-4	Menju, 1243	EK 6.424, 1251
Gabyō, 1242-1	Jippō, 1243	EK 6.432, 1251
Kobusshin, 1243-1	Zanmai ōzanmai, 1244	EK 6.437, 1951
Kattō, 1243-1	**Others**	EK 6.438, 1951
After Move to Echizen	Tenzokyōkun, 1234-2	EK 6. 469, 1951
*Butsudō, 1243-2	Chiji shingi, 1246-1	EK 9.86, 1235
*Shohō jissō, 1243-2	*Shuryō shingi, 1249-1	EK 7.502, 1252
*Bukkyō (S), 1243-2		*EK 7.503, 1252
*Mujō seppō, 1243-1		*EK 7.522, 1252
*Kenbutsu, 1243-1	*Eihei Kōroku*	EK 7. 530, 1252
Baika, 1243-8	**Memorials**	EK 10.80 (3)
Hensan, 1243-1	EK 2.184, 1246	EK 10.84
Ganzei, 1243-7	EK 3.249, 1247	**References**
Kajō, 1243-5	EK 4.274, 1248	EK 1.48, 1236
Udonge, 1244-2	EK 4.342, 1249	EK 1.105, 1241
Tenbōrin, 1244-1	EK 5.384, 1250	EK 1.118, 1241
Ho-u, 1245-1	EK 4.276, 1251	EK 2.128, 1245
Ango, 1245-1	EK 7.515, 1252	EK 2.148, 1245
Ōsaku sendaba, 1245-2	**Citations**	
Kokū, 1245-1	EK 2. 147, 1246	
References/Allusions Only	EK 2.179, 1246	
Bendōwa, 1231		

*Passage not in Rujing's record, C. *Rujing yulu*, J. *Nyojō goroku*

an evocation of Rujing's authority is not far removed from critique and revision of the master.

Rujing the Master and Dōgen the Transmitter

There are several main aspects of Rujing's influence on Dōgen. Perhaps the best known example of master-disciple interaction is the transformational experience of *shinjin datsuraku,* or casting off body-mind, as depicted in the sect's two main biographies, the *Kenzeiki* and the *Denkōroku*. Dōgen's enlightenment was triggered by the strict manner of training, whereby Rujing insisted on the total commitment and dedication of disciples to the practice of meditation. The moment of *shinjin datsuraku* occurred when the monk sitting next to Dōgen was scolded by Rujing for dozing off while doing *zazen* during a *sesshin* held as part of the summer retreat, although according to a theory it may have transpired earlier than this as a kind of "satori at first sight" when the master and disciple first met.

The importance of the doctrine of *shinjin datsuraku* is referred to in a passage that appears in *Hōkyōki* as well as other texts (with minor variations), including *Bendōwa*, "Gyōji," and several passages in the *Eihei kōroku*. According to Rujing, who confirmed Dōgen's personal insight during a private meeting in his quarters, "To study Zen under a master is to cast off body-mind through single-minded sitting meditation, without the need for burning incense, worshiping, reciting the *nembutsu*, practicing repentance, or reading sutras.... To cast off body-mind is to practice sitting meditation (*zazen*). When practicing single-minded sitting meditation, the five desires will be set aside and the five defilements will be removed."[31]

There has long been a debate about whether Dōgen heard Rujing correctly or modified his phrasing deliberately. Rujing and other Chan masters of the time were not known to utter the words "casting off body-mind" but did occasionally use a similar locution, "casting off the dust from the mind," or "casting off mental objects or impression," which might imply a subject-object dualism in that the pure mind is defiled and must be freed from contaminated objects. The two expressions sound alike (they are identical in Japanese pronunciation, *shinjin*, and have a slight variance in Chinese, in which "body-mind" is *shenxin* and "dust from the mind" is *xinchen*), but may have a subtly different connotation that depends on the meaning of body in this context as something either separate from or integrated with mind. In other words, does "body" essentially refer to the same as "dust," or is there a different implication, perhaps influenced by Kūkai or other Japanese notions of affirming this-worldly reality as the locus for realizing enlightenment? To Dōgen's ear as a nonnative speaker of Chinese, it may have been easy for him to get the phrases confused. It is also plausible that he had what can be called a creative misunderstanding or sought deliberately to modify and revise Rujing's utterance in order to free it from dualistic overtones. This could well be a part of Dōgen's tendency to evoke and rely on the authority of Rujing and also to distance himself and proclaim his autonomy.

Perhaps an even more important influence than the specific occasion of his personal breakthrough in shaping Dōgen's overall religiosity is his sense of awe at Rujing's teaching style. Of the compositions from the early 1240s, the "Baika" and "Ganzei" fascicles consist almost entirely of commentary on Rujing's teachings. "Baika," a sermon delivered on 11.6.1243 during the year of Dōgen's move to Echizen when he was still struggling with the transition, evokes lyrical imagery as a symbol for enlightenment. It is dedicated to remembrances and citations of the sayings of the mentor, who apparently spoke frequently about the symbolism of the plum tree, whose fragrant blossoms appearing at the end of the winter season are a harbinger of spring, and, thus, spiritual renewal. According to the colophon, three feet of snow fell that day, and we can only imagine that Dōgen was perhaps a bit despondent and seeking out sources of inspiration.[32] In addition to reflecting on the natural image, Dōgen recalls his feelings during the time of his studies in China when he realized how fortunate he was as a foreign novice, since not many native Chinese had the ability or opportunity to take advantage of their contact with such an eminent teacher:

> In sending the [monks] away, [Rujing] said, "If they are lacking in the essentials, what can they do? Dogs like that only disturb others and cannot be permitted to stay in the monastery." Having seen this with my own eyes and heard it with my own ears, I thought to myself: Being natives of this country, what sin or crime must they have committed in a past life that prevents them from staying among us? What lucky star was I born under that, although a native of a remote foreign country, I was not only accepted in the monastery, but allowed to come and go freely in the abbot's room, to bow down before the living master and hear his discourse on the Dharma? Although I was foolish and ignorant, I did not take this superb opportunity in vain. When my late teacher was holding forth in Song China, there were those who had the chance to study with him and those who did not. Now that my late teacher, the old master, is gone, it is gloomier than a moonless night in Song China. Why? Because never before or since has there been an old master like my late teacher was an old master.[33]

Dōgen appreciates the qualities of openness and flexibility that afforded him a unique avenue for accessibility to the abbot. In *Hōkyōki*, a record of Dōgen's conversations with Rujing that was discovered posthumously and whose authenticity has since been questioned by modern scholars, he reports that Rujing invited him to come to the abbot's quarters on demand and without reservation, which would have been a rare privilege, indeed. According to a passage in the *Shōbōgenzō zuimonki*, Rujing offered Dōgen the slot of head monk, but he declined in deference to native seekers.

Part of the image of Rujing that emerges in the writings of the transitional period is that of a master who breaks out of the mold of a formal monastic setting to deliver dynamic, spontaneous sermons. Dōgen considers Rujing's approach uniquely compelling for the charismatic appeal and sincere authenticity he projected. Unlike many Chan masters who stuck to regulations and schedules, even for informal sermons, Rujing was inspired to preach in different places of the temple compound at odd times of the day, including late hours. He gave lectures not only in the Dharma Hall on a fixed schedule but also at any time of day or night when the inspiration struck.

Shōbōgenzō "Shohō jissō" was presented by Dōgen in 1243, after "eighteen years had swiftly passed" since a remarkable occasion of mystical exaltation during the fourth watch of the night in the third month of 1226.[34] At that time, Rujing gave a midnight sermon in the abbot's quarters, when Dōgen heard the drum beating, with signs hung around the temple announcing the event. Monks were burning incense and waiting anxiously to hear, "You may enter [the abbot's room]." The sermon concluded with the saying, "A cuckoo sings, and a mountain-bamboo splits in two."[35] Dōgen says that this was a unique method of intense, personal training not practiced in other temple districts. In several other passages in the Shōbōgenzō and Eihei kōroku, Dōgen describes the excitement and thrill of studying with someone of Rujing's stature who attracted followers from all over China. In addition to Dōgen, Rujing invited other disciples to approach his quarters at various times when he or they felt the need for instruction. Therefore, Rujing demonstrated supreme discipline along with ingenious innovation. It is interesting to note that the Shōbōgenzō fascicle "Kōmyō" from the sixth month of 1242 was delivered at two o'clock in the morning, as Dōgen proudly declares in the colophon, while the monks listened attentively as a heavy storm poured down during the rainy season.[36]

There are several important passages in the Eihei kōroku that express Dōgen's view of the powerful and popular method of delivering kanbun sermons based on Rujing's model. A prominent example is the second passage in the second volume, Eihei kōroku 2.128 from 1245, which reveals Dōgen working through the complex stages of transition from informal vernacular to formal Chinese lectures and thus provides a good indication of why the kana style of the Shōbōgenzō was being phased out.[37] The passage is especially interesting, not because it repudiates kana in favor of kanbun sermons, but because it highlights the significance of lecturing in general as the key function of a monastic community. It explains Dōgen's admiration for Rujing, who was skillful at delivering several styles of informal lectures, including evening sermons (bansan), general discourses (fusetsu), and lectures for small groups (shōsan). Technically, no. 2.128, although in kanbun, is different from the customary style of Chinese sermon because it was delivered in the evening, the typical time for informal lectures; it is one of a handful of evening sermons that appear at the beginning of the second volume of the Eihei kōroku, that is, in the earliest phase of the Echizen period.

Dōgen begins no. 2.128 by recalling how master Ciming Quyuan, in discussing the meaning of the size of monasteries, cautioned his followers not to equate quantity of followers or the number of monks in attendance with the magnitude of the temple. According to Ciming, a temple with many monks who lack determination is actually considered small, while a temple with a few monks of great dedication is quite large. This part of the passage could be seen as reflecting a defensive posture; perhaps Dōgen was explaining why he was not attracting many followers. However, that suspicion is undercut by the preface to the second volume as well as the excerpt from the sermon, which makes it clear that this is a statement about the need for selectively identifying quality disciples.

Dōgen next contrasts several Tang masters, all of Linji lineages, it turns out, who preached worthy evening sermons to fewer than twenty monks, with unnamed contemporary leaders who preach meaningless words before hundreds of followers. He then expresses regret that "for many years [in China] there were no evening sermons." Since the golden age of Zen in the Tang, no one was capable of delivering a lecture with the same vigor until "Rujing came to the fore," which represented "an opportunity that occurs once in a thousand years." Recalling passages in *Shōbōgenzō zuimonki* 3.30 and *Shōbōgenzō* "Shohō jissō" about Rujing's charismatic style of delivery, Dōgen praises his mentor as he had since *Bendōwa* from 1231. Here, Dōgen does not set himself up in opposition to other lineages, but displays a multibranched, pansectarian approach to Zen genealogy so that any trace of mean-spiritedness or bitterness, if it was ever there, is now faded.[38]

Once again, the main feature of Rujing's leadership that Dōgen admires is his ability to offer numerous spontaneous, off-the-cuff lectures at any time of day that the inspiration struck for an eager band of followers who must have shared in the excitement and charisma of the occasion:

> Regardless of what the regulations in monastic rules manuals actually prescribed, at midnight, during the early evenings or at any time after the noonday meal, and generally without regard to the time, Rujing convened a talk. He either had someone beat the drum for entering the abbot's quarters (*nyūshitsu*) to give an general discourse (*fusetsu*) or he had someone beat the drum for small group meetings (*shōsan*) and then for entering the abbot's quarters. Or sometimes he himself hit the wooden clapper in the Monks Hall (*sōdō*) three times and gave an open talk in the Illuminated Hall (*shōdō*). After the open talk, the monks entered the Abbot's Quarters (*hōjō*). At other times, he hit the wooden block hanging in front of the

head monk's quarters (*shuso*) and gave an open talk in that room. Again, following the open talk the monks entered the abbot's quarters. These were extraordinary, truly exceptional experiences!

Dōgen then declares, "As a disciple of Rujing, I [Daibutsu] am also conducting evening meetings that are taking place for the very first time in our country."[39] Dōgen describes the excitement that was so special in his Chan teacher's approach and also sets the standard for introducing various styles of sermons to Zen temples in Japan.

Dōgen goes on to cite a story in which Danxia from the Caodong lineage notes that Linji master Deshan, from whom the Yunmen and Fayan lineages were descended, said to his assembly, "There are no words or phrases in my school, and also not a single Dharma to give to people." He further comments, "He was endowed with only one single eye. . . . In my school there are words and phrases (*goku*). . . . The mysterious, profound, wondrous meaning is that the jade woman becomes pregnant in the night." According to Dōgen, however, "Although Danxia could say it like this. . . . In my school *there are only words and phrases (yui goku)*" (emphasis added), echoing the view of the unity of Zen and language that is expressed with a more sustained though partisan argumentation in the "Sansuikyō" fascicle. While Dōgen's statement certainly goes beyond Danxia's, it does not necessarily represent criticism and, indeed, Danxia's student Hongzhi is frequently quoted by Dōgen in the ensuing volumes of the *Eihei kōroku*. In fact, this phase marks the beginning of Dōgen's extensive reliance, which lasts for about three or four years, on Hongzhi's recorded sayings as well as the *Book of Serenity*, the kōan collection he helped to create. As we have seen, the pattern is to emulate Hongzhi's sermon almost to the point of plagiarism, yet conclude with a devastating albeit respectful critique—in a kind of pious irreverence—of him as well as Rujing and other predecessors.

Dōgen as Transgressor

The reverent tone of a dutiful follower that is so apparent in the *Hōkyōki*, which deals with Dōgen's days as a disciple sitting at the feet of the Chinese mentor, is not necessarily duplicated in the *Eihei kōroku*, where he subjects Rujing's interpretations of Chan kōans and other sayings to a process of revision and rewriting. In *Eihei kōroku* 2.179, Dōgen critiques five prominent figures, Sakyamuni and four Chinese Chan masters including Rujing, who respond to a statement of the Buddha in the *Surangama Sutra*, chapter nine, as also cited and discussed with the same conclusion in *Shōbōgenzō* "Tenbōrin":

[Dōgen] said, The World-Honored One said, "When one person opens up reality and returns to the source, all space in the ten directions disappears." Teacher Wuzu of Mount Fayan said, "When one person opens up reality and returns to the source, all space in the ten directions crashes together resounding everywhere." Zen Master Yuanwu of Mount Jiashan said, "When one person opens up reality and returns to the source, all space throughout the ten directions flowers are added on to a brocade." Teacher Foxing Fatai said, "When one person opens up reality and returns to the source, all space in the ten directions is nothing other than all space in the ten directions."

My late teacher Tiantong [Rujing] said, "Although the World-Honored One made the statement, 'When one person opens up reality and returns to the source, all space in the ten directions disappears,' this utterance cannot avoid becoming an extraordinary assessment. Tiantong is not like this. When one person opens up reality and returns to the source, a mendicant breaks his rice bowl."

The teacher [Dōgen] said, The previous five venerable teachers said it like this, but I, Eihei, have a saying that is not like theirs. When one person opens up reality and returns to the source, all space in the ten directions opens up reality and returns to the source.[40]

Another key example of Dōgen's creative rewriting of Rujing's words is *Eihei kōroku* 2.147, which displays some of the qualities of the *honkadori* poetic technique in terms of how revisions are made based on extensive quoting of the original passage:

Dōgen held up his monk's staff, pounded it once on the floor, and said: This is the staff of Daibutsu. Buddhas and lands as numerous as the sands of the Ganges River are all swallowed up in one gulp by this staff. All the living beings in these lands do not know and are not aware of it. All you people, where are your noses, eyes, spirits, and headtops? If you know where they are, within emptiness you can place the staff vertically or hold it horizontally. If you do not know, there is rice and gruel for you on the sitting platforms [in the meditation hall].

I remember that a monk asked Zen Master Baizhang Dazhi, "What is the most remarkable thing [in the world]?"[41] Baizhang said, "It is sitting [or practicing *zazen*] alone atop Great Hero Peak [of

Mount Baizhang]."[42] Moreover, my late teacher Tiantong [Rujing] said, "If someone asks the venerable monk Rujing, 'What is the most remarkable thing [in the world]?' I would simply reply to him, 'What remarkable thing is there? Ultimately, what is it? I moved my bowls from Jingci temple to Tiantong and ate rice.'"[43]

The source record evoked by the sermon, *Blue Cliff Record* case 26,[44] seems a bit surprising in its emphasis on meditation, as Baizhang is known primarily for his emphasis on rules expressed in the first (and probably apocryphal) Zen monastic code, the *Chanmen guishi* (J. *Zenmon kishiki*). This text stresses the role of the charismatic abbot's sermons that are supposed to be held two times a day, before and after the midday meal, far more than the practice of *zazen*, which is left up to discretion of the disciple rather than being strictly confined by a uniform schedule.[45] When Rujing rewrites the response as, "It is just eating rice in a bowl at Jingci Temple on Mount Tiantong,"[46] he shifts the focus from *zazen* to everyday praxis and from Mount Baizhang to his own mountain temple.

Dōgen reflects on this case at least five times in his works. He cites Rujing's revision approvingly in "Kajō" (1243), but in *Eihei kōroku* 2.147 from the same year as "Ho-u" (1245), he rewrites the concluding statement. In the context of discussing the value of wielding the Zen staff (*shujō*),[47] which metaphorically encompasses all aspects of reality, Dōgen cites Rujing's response, but this time he says, "I would answer by raising high my staff at Daibutsuji temple in Japan," and he then puts the staff down and steps off the dais.[48] Dōgen shows both a willingness to challenge his mentor and a ritual use of the staff as a means of proclaiming the legitimacy of his approach. Similarly, in *Eihei kōroku* 2.145, Dōgen refers to his lineage as "a diverse amalgamation . . . horns grow on the head, dragons and snakes mix together, and there are many horses and cows . . . they all discern the monk's staff and complete the matter of a lifetime." To mention a few of the many other instances, in no. 2.150 he holds up the staff and pounds it on the floor saying, "Just this is it," and in no. 2.168 he asks rhetorically, "Is there a dragon or elephant here who can come forth and meet with Daibutsu's staff?"

An additional example of Dōgen's approach to appropriating Rujing is found in *Eihei kōroku* 5.379, which is a sermon in supplication for clear skies delivered toward the end of his life on 6.10.1250.[49] In this sermon, Dōgen states that his intention is to invoke a clear sky, and says that "last year rain fell ceaselessly but now I wish for fine weather like my master at Mount Qingliang Temple [a temple where Rujing was abbot before serving at Mount Tiantong], who went to the Dharma Hall to wish for fine weather. When he did not go to the

Dharma Hall, the Buddhas and patriarchs did not go either. Today, I am in the Dharma Hall, just like my former teacher."

Despite citing Rujing in this supernatural context, Dōgen concludes with an ironic, iconoclastic commentary by pausing, sneezing, and saying, "Once I sneeze, clouds break and the sun appears." Then, he raises the fly-whisk and remarks, "Monks! Look at this. The cloudless sky swallows the eight directions." Many other sermons express the power of the fly-whisk, a ceremonial object that symbolizes the authority of the Zen master derived from pre-Buddhist shamanistic purification devices as well as imperial scepters, to beat up a pack of wild foxes, turn into a dragon or snake, or perform other miraculous functions. An emphasis on ritualism in Dōgen's late discourse is also seen in *Eihei kōroku* 5.388, which tells a story of repentance involving demons and celestial spirits.[50]

Questioning Dōgen's Portrayal of Rujing

I conclude by reflecting on various questions and areas of skeptical doubt that have been raised by modern scholarship regarding the accuracy of Dōgen's portrayal of Rujing, which seems to be used primarily for sectarian purposes. Dōgen's portrayal of Rujing is suspect in terms of accuracy and is problematic because of its connections to partisan rhetoric, and these factors perhaps form the roots of the 60-fascicle *Shōbōgenzō* edition, which seems to represent an attempt to weed out of the text whole fascicles that may be considered unreliable or untenable. The image of Rujing presented by Dōgen as an idealistic, charismatic religious leader is somewhat contradicted by the fact that he is generally not regarded as one of the luminaries of the Song Chan school and was, in fact, given rather short shrift according to annals of the period.

It appears that the biggest and perhaps only real supporter of his illustrious status was Dōgen, and ironically, Mount Tiantong is best known today not so much for Rujing as for Dōgen's admiration of him.[51] Furthermore, it is questionable whether Dōgen's enthusiasm for Rujing's sermon style is warranted. Perhaps his emphasis on the extraordinary informal method of Rujing's sermonizing is due to his acknowledgment that his mentor's recorded discourse was rather pedestrian and not as stellar as that of better-known Chinese masters, and so he wants to stress that the unrecorded pedagogy was what made Rujing sensational.

Another dubious aspect of the Dōgen-Rujing relationship is that there are numerous examples of Rujing's sayings not found in the recorded sayings of the mentor. Since nearly a dozen of his citations cannot be tracked to the *Nyojō goroku*, itself a problematic source, it is possible that Dōgen exaggerated or invented at least some aspects of the image of his mentor and his teachings in a way that was exacerbated by subsequent editors. According to the analysis by He Yansheng, this text was no doubt drastically reconstructed, or even fabricated, by Tokugawa-era Sōtō editors precisely to create a match-up, which is missing in some glaring cases. The fascicles in which Dōgen cites passages not found in the *Nyojō goroku* deal to a large extent with a sectarian agenda of criticizing the Dahui lineage in "Shohō jissō" and other streams of Chan in "Butsudō" and "Bukkyō" [Buddhist Sutras].

In these sources which Dōgen may have misquoted or invented, Rujing sounds considerably more polemical and combative in tone than in passages that can be traced to the *Nyojō goroku*.[52] Dōgen depicts his mentor as a divisive and partisan figure who was hypercritical and who vehemently attacked Chan monks. All of these fascicles are excluded from the 60-*Shōbōgenzō*. In another excluded fascicle, "Menju," delivered just two weeks prior to "Baika," Dōgen stresses that he gained face-to-face transmission, which was "transmitted only to my monastery; others have not dreamed of it." There is a rather belligerent tone attributed to Rujing, who is said to refer to incompetent monks as "dogs," evoked as part of Dōgen's claim for the authentic status of his own temple. Once again, the implication is that he evokes the authority of Rujing as a vehicle for self-expression and the advocacy of sectarian identity.

Although Dōgen's portrayal of Rujing is consistent throughout his writings, there are numerous inconsistencies between Dōgen's presentation of his mentor and what is known about Rujing's approach from his recorded sayings. Nakaseko Shōdō suggests that by analyzing differences in the teachings of master and disciple we can see contradictions in Dōgen's appropriation of Rujing.[53] According to Nakaseko, there are two sets of doctrines—one is how Rujing is portrayed in Dōgen's writings, and the other is how he is expressed in the *Nyojō goroku* (assuming its authenticity). As seen in the works of Dōgen, Rujing is a strict advocate of intensive *zazen* training, which was the only form of religious practice he consistently followed after he began training at the age of nineteen, according to "Gyōji" (part 2). Rujing is also portrayed as a severe critic both of reliance on kōans as well as the corrupt lifestyle of many of his contemporary monks. According to Dōgen, Rujing criticized a variety of doctrines that found currency in Chinese Chan. The objects of his criticism include:[54]

1. the unity of the three teachings (according to *Shōbōgenzō* "Shohō jissō");
2. the *kikan* or developmental, intellectual approach in the notions of the three phrases of Yunmen (*Shōbōgenzō* "Bukkyō" [Buddhist Sutras]);

3. the four relations of Linji, the five ranks of Dongshan, and numerous other doctrinal formulas (*Shōbōgenzō* "Butsudō");
4. the sectarian divisiveness of the five houses of Chan that defeats the unity of all forms of Buddhism (*Hōkyōki*);
5. the autonomy of the Zen sect (*Hōkyōki*);
6. a view that advocates the separation of Chan from the sutras (*Hōkyōki*);
7. the "naturalist fallacy" that affirms reality without transforming it (*Hōkyōki*);
8. the tendency in some forms of Chan thought toward the negation of causality and karmic retribution (*Hōkyōki*).

As Nakaseko points out, much of this stands in contrast with the thought that is evident in the *Nyojō goroku*, which is for the most part a conventional recorded sayings text reflecting the doctrines and literary styles of the Song period.[55] In this text, there is not so much emphasis on *zazen* or the rejection of kōans, or on criticism of the laxity in the lifestyle of monks. Furthermore, Rujing does not dismiss Confucius or indicate that the other teachings were inferior to the Buddha Dharma, and he does not express concern with the five houses or the autonomy of Chan, or the view that separates Chan from the sutras. He does not criticize the *kikan* formulas or the naturalist heresy. Nor does he stress causality or emphasize lyrical imagery in a way that varies from what was typical for Song Chan masters appealing to an audience of literati.

It is in this context that the *Hōkyōki* is seen to be of questionable authenticity and is subject to being redated as a constructed text from the end of Dōgen's career rather than a fresh, hands-on sense of the conversations held in China a quarter of a century earlier. According to Takeuchi Michio's analysis of the contents of *Hōkyōki*, as indicated in table 5.8 below, a third of the dialogues in the text focuses on doctrine, a third on *zazen*, and the rest on rituals, precepts, ceremonies, people, and texts.[56] Of the more than twenty items dealing with doctrine, there is a sharp criticism of *kyōge betsuden* (special transmission outside the scriptures) theory in nos. 2 and 21, of *kanna-zen* (Dahui's kōan-introspection) in no. 3, and of original enlightenment in no. 4, which are views that do not seem consistent with what is known of Rujing. Several passages (nos. 10 and 22) emphasize the doctrine of *kannō dōkō* (reciprocal spiritual communion defining the transmission between master and disciple) that is also featured in "Hotsubodaishin" from the 12-fascicle edition of the *Shōbōgenzō*, another late text. In addition, the attack on lax behavior and the wearing of long hair by monks in no. 9, as well as the affirmation of the bodhisattva precepts in no. 5, seem to reflect Dōgen-oriented views rather than the priorities of Rujing (who

TABLE 5.8. List of *Hōkyōki* Topics

Topic	No. Entries
Doctrine	17
Rituals or Precepts	13
Zazen	17
Doctrine and People	3
Doctrine and Practice	2
Total	52

would have emphasized the full precepts) that are echoed in "Jukai" of the 12-fascicle *Shōbōgenzō*.

To summarize, almost all we know about Rujing is through the lens of Dōgen's writings and the perspectives they express, so that we may be learning more about the Japanese founder of the Sōtō sect than his Caodong school Chinese mentor. Much of Dōgen's eulogizing of Rujing can be accounted for as a way of using Chan as a rhetorical device for creating a sectarian identity in Japan grounded exclusively in Caodong/Sōtō teachings. However, this is not necessarily problematic. It is very much in accord with the tradition of transgressing while transmitting, as Dōgen navigates his path through positions that are alternately:

sectarian, or supporting the Sōtō sect exclusively;
pansectarian, in generously citing early Chan masters;
nonsectarian, in opposing the designation of a "Zen school" in China and/or Japan;
and trans-sectarian, in seeking the universality of Buddha-nature,

in establishing his movement in early Kamakura Japan. In this sense, there may be a different sort of transgression, which deliberately violates historicality and is used for the sake of legitimating and constructing hagiography in support of lineal transmission.

NOTES

1. Some of the material in this chapter was adopted from Steven Heine, *Did Dōgen Go to China? What He Wrote and When He Wrote It* (New York: Oxford University Press, 2006).

2. A collection of the records of the four masters, the *Sijia yulu* (J. *Shike goroku*), is a Song text with materials culled from various transmission of the lamp records.

3. Robert H. Brower and Earl Miner, *Japanese Court Poetry* (Stanford: Stanford University Press, 1961), pp. 14–15.

4. For an interesting Western parallel, see Harold Bloom, *The Anxiety of Influence* (New York: Oxford University Press, 1973).

5. DZZ I: 53.

6. It was long believed that the 60-*Shōbōgenzō* was compiled by Giun, who wrote a preface and verse commentary in 1329 that was handed down in his lineage through the fifteenth century. However, a recent theory proffered by Kawamura Kōdō maintains that this version consists of Dōgen's first-draft arrangements of the fascicles included in the 75-*Shōbōgenzō*, whose order and wording were later revised. According to Kawamura, there are interlinear notes in manuscripts of the 60-fascicle version that disclose how at least some of these fascicles were altered for inclusion in the 75-fascicle version. Kawamura maintains that Ejō edited this edition years later on the basis of Dōgen's own selection of fascicles before he died. This theory suggests that the 60-*Shōbōgenzō* is the "real" text and the 75-fascicle edition is secondary, but it is not clear whether this claim is also meant to imply that Dōgen himself excised the controversial fascicles. See Kawamura Kōdō, *Shōbōgenzō no seiritsu-shiteki no kenkyū* (Tokyo: Shunjūsha, 1986).

7. Four fascicles from the 12-fascicle *Shōbōgenzō* were also included in the 60-fascicle text.

8. Dōgen referred to Rujing as "former teacher" (*senshi*) and Hongzhi as "old buddha" (*kobutsu*).

9. Ikeda Rōsan, *Gendaigoyaku Shōbōgenzō zuimonki* (Tokyo: Daizō shuppan, 1993), pp. 330–331.

10. DZZ I: 270–280.

11. However, this fascicle was composed on 4.20.1240, a few months before the Daruma school conversion.

12. DZZ III: 98; Taigen Dan Leighton and Shohaku Okumura, trans., *Dōgen's Extensive Record: A Translation of the Eihei Kōroku* (Boston: Wisdom, 2004), pp. 180–181. Note that in quoting the translation, the wording is sometimes slightly altered.

13. DZZ III: 140; Leighton and Okumura, *Dōgen's Extensive Record*, pp. 219–220.

14. DZZ III: 194; Leighton and Okumura, *Dōgen's Extensive Record*, p. 278.

15. DZZ III: 132; Leighton and Okumura, *Dōgen's Extensive Record*, pp. 210–211.

16. Leighton and Okumura, trans., *Dōgen's Extensive Record*, p. 211.

17. For example, the *Hongzhi guanglu* (J. *Wanshi kōroku*, T. 48:1–121) consists of nine volumes: 1. *jōdō* and *shōsan*; 2. *juko* and *nenko*; 3. *nenko*; 4. *jōdō* and *jishu*; 5. *shōsan*; 6. *hōgo*; 7–9. poetry; see Sakai Tokugen, "Eihei kōroku," in *Dōgen no chosaku*, edited by Genryū Kagamishima and Tamaki Kōshirō (Tokyo: Shunjūsha, 1980), pp. 75–118.

18. With the prominent exception of the "Zazenshin" and "Jinshin inga" fascicles, where Dōgen critiques and rewrites his views of meditation and causality.

19. See Ishii Shūdō, "Saigo no Dōgen-Jūnikanbon *Shōbōgenzō* to *Hōkyō-ki*," in *Jūnikanbon "Shōbōgenzō" no shomondai*, edited by Genryū Kagamishima and Kakuzen Suzuki (Tokyo: Daizō shuppan, 1991), pp. 319–374.

20. DZZ III: 80–82; Leighton and Okumura, *Dōgen's Extensive Record*, pp. 162–164.

21. DZZ III: 158; Leighton and Okumura, *Dōgen's Extensive Record*, p. 237.

22. Genryū Kagamishima, *Tendō nyojō zenji no kenkyū* (Tokyo: Shunjūsha, 1983).

23. Kawamura Kōdō, *Shohon taikō Eihei kaizan Dōgen zenji gyōjō: Kenzeki* (Tokyo: Taishūkan shoten, 1975).

24. Carl Bielefeldt, *Dōgen's Manuals of Zen Meditation* (Berkeley: University of California Press, 1988), p. 28.

25. At the time of the move, Dōgen began citing Rujing with great frequency, but some of the passages are not found in the Chinese master's recorded sayings.

26. DZZ III: 69; Senne, the compiler of this volume of the *Eihei kōroku*, notes in this passage, "Many words were not recorded." Presumably, Dōgen spoke more, but Senne only wrote down what is included here. This sermon is also notable for Dōgen's emphasis on the role of language in relation to silence in communicating the Dharma.

27. DZZ I: 196–202.

28. For example, no 4.274 (DZZ III: 183; Leighton and Okumura, *Dōgen's Extensive Record*, p. 263) says, "On this day Tiantong [Rujing] mistakenly made a pilgrimage. He did not travel to Mount Tiantai or Mount Wutai. How sad that for ten thousand miles there is not an inch of grass. The old master Guishan became a water buffalo and came here." The phrase "inch of grass" and the mention of Guishan as water buffalo are obscure references to old Chan sayings that highlight Dōgen's veneration of Rujing.

29. DZZ III: 122–124; Leighton and Okumura, *Dōgen's Extensive Record*, p. 203. "Walking like someone from Handan" refers to a story by Zhuangzi in the chapter on "Autumn Water," in which someone from the countryside went to the city of Handan and imitated the fashionable walking of the townspeople, but before mastering this he lost his native ability and had to crawl home on hands and knees; see Burton Watson, trans., *The Complete Works of Chuang Tzu* (New York: Columbia University Press, 1968), p. 187. Memorial day for Rujing was 7.17; Other memorial sermons are nos. 3.249, 4.274, 4.276 (out of sequence), 5.342, 5.384, and 7.515.

30. See He Yansheng, *Dōgen to Chūgoku Zen shisō* (Kyoto: Hōzōkan, 2000); Kagamishima, *Genryo Tendō Nyojō zenji no kenkyū* (Tokyo: Shunjūsha, 1983); and Nakaseko Shōdō, *Dōgen zenji den kenkyū-Sei* (Tokyo: Kokusho kankōkai, 1997).

31. *Hōkyōki* nos. 16–17, in DZZ VII: 20–22.

32. In a *waka* verse composed on September 25, 1244, Dōgen writes, "Crimson leaves/Whitened by the season's first snow—/Is there anyone/Who would not be moved/To celebrate this in song?," in DZZ VII: 154.

33. DZZ II: 71–72 (emphasis added, redundancy in original).

34. DZZ I: 457–470.

35. DZZ I: 467–468.

36. DZZ I: 144.

37. DZZ III: 72–74.

38. In *Eihei kōroku* 4.290, for example, Dōgen says, "In recent years there have not been masters such as Linji and Deshan anywhere, however much we may look to find them."

39. DZZ III: 72; Leighton and Okumura, *Dōgen's Extensive Record*, pp. 153–154.

40. DZZ III: 118; Leighton and Okumura, *Dōgen's Extensive Record*, pp. 198–199.

41. Dazhi, literally "Great Wisdom," was an honorific posthumous name given to Baizhang by the emperor.

42. "Great Hero" Peak (Daxiong) was the name of the summit above Baizhang's monastery where the master and other monks would hold special meditation retreats withdrawn from the monastery.

43. Jingci Temple, where Rujing resided as abbot before Mount Tiantong, was the fourth-ranked of the five mountains, or major temples of the country. Tiantong was ranked third among the five mountains, so Rujing's move was an elevation in status.

44. This saying, "It is sitting [or practicing *zazen*] alone atop Great Hero Peak [of Mount Baizhang]," can be taken to mean that Baizhang went on retreat to one of the main mountain peaks located behind the temple to practice *zazen*, or that he is characteristically identifying himself with the name of the mountain and thus saying, in effect, "I sit alone." In the kōan cited in *Biyanlu* no. 26, the disciple claims to understand the comment, and Baizhang slaps him.

45. T. 51.250c–251b.

46. DZZ IV: 280.

47. Baizhang was particularly known for carrying a ceremonial fly-whisk (*hossu*), which also figures prominently in the gestures and demonstrations Dōgen uses in his sermons.

48. DZZ III: 92–94; Leighton and Okumura, *Dōgen's Extensive Record*, p. 175.

49. DZZ III: 242.

50. DZZ III: 258–260.

51. In 1998, a shrine to Dōgen was constructed on the grounds of Mount Tiantong, including a stele and portrait as part of a campaign to attract Japanese tourists.

52. For example, in *Shōbōgenzō*, "Butsudō" Rujing says, "In recent years the truth of the patriarchs has degenerated into bands of demons and animals" (DZZ I: 481).

53. See Nakaseko, *Dōgen zenji den kenkyū—Sei*.

54. Nakaseko, *Dōgen zenji den kenkyū—Sei*, pp. 206–209.

55. See Kagamishima, *Genryo Tendō Nyojō zenji no kenkyū*.

56. Michio Takeuchi, *Dōgen* (Tokyo: Yoshikawa kōbunkan, 1992), p. 136.

6

The Zen of Books and Practice: The Life of Menzan Zuihō and His Reformation of Sōtō Zen

David Riggs

Menzan Zuihō (1683–1769) was one of the most illustrious writers and reformers of the Tokugawa period. During this era, there were major changes in Zen practice as well as a wide-ranging reevaluation of Buddhist doctrine. Menzan was probably the most creative and prolific of all the Sōtō Zen writers of the time.[1] His approach to learning and his emphasis on historical sources continue to this day to be characteristic of the Sōtō school, and his writings about doctrine and details of monastic practice are the foundation of the contemporary school. At the same time, Menzan was a popular teacher of Buddhism to lay men and women, and a revered Zen master who led strict training sessions for many years. He succeeded in training so many disciples that he gave dharma transmission to twenty-seven of them, many times the norm and more than all except one other Sōtō teacher. Menzan took a strikingly moderate attitude toward practice by, for example, adapting a more humane and more mainstream Buddhist outlook toward precepts. He was very critical of an excess of zeal, whether through use of the stick in the meditation hall or through excessive effort leading to the risk of mental illness. Many of these more moderate positions were not ultimately accepted in the Sōtō mainstream, so in spite of influence on the later school, some of his positions were rejected.

Despite his accomplishments, Menzan is not remembered in Sōtō Zen circles as an innovative figure, and the Tokugawa period was for many years dismissed as a backward embarrassment. In the Sōtō Zen community, Dōgen is taken as the source of all authority, and today, as if to emphasize that attitude, the school often refers to itself as "Dōgen Zen." Menzan's writings, although highly respected, are regarded as merely helpful notes and background information with which to gain access to the great insight and awakening of the founder. Menzan certainly wished to be seen that way, but in many regards he was as much a revolutionary as a conservator. Not only did Menzan read Dōgen with the greatest attention to textual detail and painstakingly research Dōgen's sources but he also attempted to put into daily practice what he saw as the way that Dōgen would have done things. In this campaign Menzan was willing to go against both the practices of the established powers and the ways of his own teachers, whom he held in the greatest respect. Menzan's detailed command of the works of Dōgen is widely noted, but his efforts did not stop there. Perhaps even more impressive was his willingness to fill in areas that Dōgen left blank and to decide ambiguities in Dōgen's work by interpreting the texts to which Dōgen would have had access. Menzan used ancient materials that would have been available to Dōgen, but the selection and interpretation were very much his own.

To understand the importance of Menzan as well as his role in the development of Dōgen Zen, a word about Dōgen is in order. Dōgen is present in almost any study of Sōtō Zen, but why is it that he occupies such a dominant position? From the perspective of the modern Sōtō school, it is not surprising that Menzan should have devoted his life to the study of Dōgen. Indeed, in the last century, the vast majority of Sōtō-related studies, both in Japan and in the West, have been focused on some aspect of Dōgen.[2] Dōgen was certainly responsible for the introduction of the Sōtō Zen lineage to Japan, and his writings have become the font of orthodoxy for contemporary Sōtō Zen. It is all too easy to assume that this should obviously be the case, and that he has always been regarded in this way. Before the Tokugawa reforms championed by Menzan, however, his role was much more limited. His writings, especially the collection of essays that is now called the *Shōbōgenzō*, were treated as secret treasures, but there was no commonly accepted version and no commentaries were written from about 1300 until the seventeenth century.[3] Although Sōtō monks traced their lineage to Dōgen, the content of Sōtō practice and doctrine was determined by what was passed down from teacher to disciple. In the medieval era, religious authority (and indeed authority in general) relied on the relationship of master and student. Texts and other paraphernalia were used to certify this transmission of authority. In the case of Sōtō Zen, the possession of a

Dōgen text, rather than the understanding of the contents of that text, authenticated the religious practices and teachings of the possessor.

In the seventeenth century, the *Shōbōgenzō* and Dōgen's writings about monastic practice became more widely circulated in manuscript form and were printed for the first time. It gradually became apparent that there was a discrepancy between the contents of the *Shōbōgenzō* and contemporary Sōtō customs. Even before Menzan's time, there had been attempts to reform customary practices to bring them more into line with the texts of Dōgen. These attempts used the slogan of *fukko*, which means to return to the old (ways), but with the implication that the old ways were the only correct ways. The most prominent attempt was led by Manzan Dōhaku (1636–1741), who succeeded in his attempt to reform dharma transmission, the ceremonial authentication of the status of a Zen teacher.[4] Dōhaku, as I will refer to him henceforth to avoid confusion with Menzan, made a creative leap by reinterpreting a 1615 government decree which specified that the house rules of Eiheiji, the temple founded by Dōgen, should also be the rules for all temples of the lineage. Dōhaku made the startling claim that this rather specific legalistic decree meant that any writings by Dōgen (not just the current Eiheiji house rules), as the founder of Eiheiji, should be the source of authority for the entire Sōtō school. He then used this claim to make use of one chapter of the *Shōbōgenzō* (which is certainly nothing like a set of house rules) to justify his campaign to reform Sōtō practices of dharma transmission. His case for a sweeping transformation was thus based on a text by Dōgen that had been ignored for hundreds of years. Whether or not it was the intent of the 1615 government ruling, Dōhaku's interpretation carried the day and resulted in an enormous expansion of interest in the writings of Dōgen. He succeeded in publishing his own version of the *Shōbōgenzō* in 1686, but because of the problems arising from disputes about the *Shōbōgenzō*, in 1722 the Sōtō hierarchy requested that the government prohibit its publication, a prohibition that was not lifted until 1796, though manuscript copies continued to be available.[5] Thus Menzan's entire research project on the *Shōbōgenzō* was carried out under the constraint of this prohibition.

From Dōhaku's beginning, Menzan worked to push the reform movement far beyond the original topic of dharma transmission and its focus on just one chapter of the *Shōbōgenzō*. Menzan sought out different manuscript versions of the chapters of the *Shōbōgenzō* and investigated the various traditions of organizing these chapters into a single collection. He also worked on Dōgen's other writings, such as his separate essays (in Chinese) about monastic regulations and a variety of independent pieces. He used these texts as his basis for authority, but he also read very widely into the sources that Dōgen himself relied upon and used these to fill in questions that Dōgen had not addressed. On this broader basis, he advocated a much more radical overhaul of Sōtō affairs, including the rollback of some of Dōhaku's reforms that were not sufficiently close to Dōgen. For example, Dōhaku had also created a set of monastic regulations that he claimed were based on Dōgen and earlier Chinese ways. Menzan exposed this rule as being based on contemporary Chinese practices as seen in the Ōbaku temples that had become very popular in Japan.

These temples traced their lineage to a series of Chinese masters who came to Japan starting in the seventeenth century. As trade with China grew in the early part of the seventeenth century, Chinese traders in the port city of Nagasaki established temples and brought in Chinese monks to run them. Although the temples were set up for the Chinese merchant community, many Japanese monks came to Nagasaki to see for themselves this contemporary Chinese Buddhism, which came to be referred to as Ōbaku, after the mountain name of the main temple, Manpukuji.[6] Menzan's position was that the only true sources of authority were the writings of Dōgen and the texts on which he drew, and he strenuously objected to taking contemporary practice (either Chinese or Japanese) as a model. Menzan emphasized that the old texts were to be read directly, making use only of texts that were contemporaneous or, of course, prior texts for contextualization. He did not rely on the views of living teachers and avoided commentaries. Menzan studied with a variety of teachers, of course, and revered his own lineage master Sonnō Shūeki (1649–1705). Nonetheless, when Menzan attempted to establish authority he relied neither on customary practice nor on orally transmitted knowledge. Although they insisted that they were merely transmitting the teachings of Dōgen, Menzan and the other reformers can be seen as the founders of a new tradition that derived its authority from textual commentary and scholarship, not from long-established customs and rituals. Although tradition can be thought of as a gradual accumulation of teachings or an organically developing system of practices, it can also be a deliberate construct used to bring about change to long-established customary practices.[7] Thanks in great part to the textual work of Menzan, the Edo reform of Sōtō Zen is an example of a crafted tradition, that is to say a tradition that presents a surface of great authority and antiquity yet skillfully conceals the seams and supports used to construct that surface.

Menzan was profoundly influenced by the works of Dōgen, but he was also very much a man of his times, in that he used the textual tools and promoted the value of the contemporary trend of returning to the earliest texts, discarding centuries of oral and written secret commentary.[8] For example, in the Ancient Learning (Kogaku) school of Confucian studies, contemporary teachers and their Neo-Confucianism were rejected in favor of reading the texts of Confucius directly.[9] Of course, secret lineages and practices continued for many trades and skills, but one of the most important intellectual developments in Japan at the time was this emphasis on open discussion (within prescribed boundaries of permissible topics) and increased reliance on textual analysis and commentary rather than on esoteric initiations.

Sōtō reforms of this period have been depicted in sectarian histories as simply a purging of impurities acquired during centuries of degenerate practice, yet they can also be seen as a creative application of the new trend in Japanese thought toward emphasizing original texts. Menzan is not alone in his enthusiasm for Dōgen and reforms, but his output is much larger and more comprehensive than anyone else's. Menzan argued his case for what he characterized as authentic Dōgen Zen with such a painstaking attention to textual detail and comprehensive use of materials that his influence is seen throughout the practices and teaching of the school to this day.

Early Years in Kyushu

The outline of Menzan's life can be found in the year-by-year list of events of his life, the *Chronology of the Life of Teacher Menzan, Founder of Eifuku [Temple]* (*Eifuku Menzan Oshō Nenpyō*), which constitutes fascicle twenty-six of his *Extended Record*.[10] It was compiled by Kōda Soryō (1702–1779), one of his most important disciples, and as is usual for this genre, it mainly consists of a list of bare facts of where Menzan was, whom he met, what ceremonies he participated in, and what he wrote. Unless another text is explicitly cited for details of Menzan's life, the *Chronology* is the source in the following narrative. To the dry details of the *Chronology*, I have added the more lively stories found scattered in prefaces to Menzan's works, and occasional asides in the texts wherever I have happened upon them.[11] Since much of Menzan's life is occupied with the texts he was writing, selected works are briefly described to give an overview of how his interests developed, and a few pieces will be discussed in some detail. When Menzan's age is mentioned, it is given in Japanese style: he was two years old after the first New Year's day following his birth.

Menzan was born in 1683 in the southern island of Kyushu, in what is now Kumamoto prefecture, Kamoto County, Ueki City. In the *Chronology*, Menzan is depicted as having the precocity expected of one who would become such an illustrious writer. He read the Chinese classics and basic Buddhist texts before his teens, and by his twelfth year his father recruited him to read the petitions that he was required to take care of as government station master (*ekichō*). When he was fifteen, his mother died. The following year, on the memorial day of her death, Menzan went to her grave site and shaved his head, expressing his desire to become a monk. His father was furious that his son did not first seek permission, especially when Menzan's support was most needed by the family. His father soon relented, however, and in 1698 Menzan was ordained by Ryōun Kohō (n.d.), the abbot of a local temple, the Ryūchōin. Menzan was given the Buddhist ordination name of Zuihō, which he kept throughout his career.

Menzan's home town of Ueki is on the plain to the west of the large bay (Ariake Sea) that is behind the peninsula of Nagasaki, and is therefore not far from very active areas of foreign influence. Commerce, both Western and Chinese, was tightly controlled and confined to Nagasaki, and there was a steady stream of Japanese visitors to the area. It was not possible to travel to China, but the Chinese community set up its own temples in Nagasaki, and many Japanese monks came to see Chinese Buddhism at first hand. Although it was far from the political and cultural capitals, this area was at the forefront of the changes in Buddhist thinking. Menzan's youth occurred at a time of changes in other aspects of Japanese culture. He grew up during the Genroku era (1688–1704), when Japanese society was at peace and had settled into the strict rules of the now established military government. This period is known for the flourishing of the popular arts. The illustrious poet Bashō was developing new styles, and Saikaku had created a new kind of comic writing that described the pleasure quarters and lampooned figures of the establishment, including Buddhist monks.

As mentioned above, this was also the period of the flowering of the study of Chinese thought and a new interest in philological studies, which Menzan drew upon in his work. Along with this explosion of literary and scholarly activity came the transformation of book manufacturing and trade into an efficient system that could quickly and inexpensively bring out woodblock-printed copies of a work in the same year it was written.[12] Japan had experimented with moveable type, but woodblocks were quicker to produce because of the enormous number of type faces for different characters and the desire for Japanese-style reading marks (*kunten*) in the margins of Chinese texts. Unlike expensive type, which was taken out of the printing frames and reused for other texts, the woodblocks could simply be stored. If and when the initial print run sold out, more copies could be produced with very little additional expense. Buddhist books were a major part of this trade in earlier parts of the Tokugawa period; judging from colophons to Menzan's works, it was a simple matter for a lay disciple who had the money to take a short text to Kyoto and have it published almost immediately. This new availability of print was probably one of the most important factors in Menzan's long-term success. I know of no survey of how many copies of his works were actually distributed, but I have found that when I visit temples, even small country temples, upon learning that I am interested in Menzan, the abbot frequently produces well-worn copies of Menzan woodblock texts that have been in the temple's possession for generations. Menzan was not part of the power structure of Sōtō, and it was only after his death that his most important reforms were implemented. The key to his success was his texts, not his personality or his connections. Without easily available printing, his reforms would probably not have met with the success they did.

After his ordination, Menzan practiced under the direction of Ryōun and also studied with other teachers. For example, he read the *Record of Linji* with a teacher of the Myōshinji line of Rinzai Zen. He also read the *Brahma's Net Sutra*, one source of the precepts most commonly taken in Japan, with a teacher specializing in Vinaya. These two texts appear repeatedly as lecture topics later in his life. Neither his ordination teacher nor the temple is well known, and Ryōun seldom appears in Menzan's writings, but there are a few paragraphs about him in Menzan's *Tribute to the Life of Zen Master Tōsui (Tōsui Oshō densan)*.[13] This work is a biographical sketch consisting largely of popular stories about the eccentric monk Tōsui (d. 1683), with a preface by Menzan explaining why he came to compose such a piece. Menzan relates in his preface that his teacher Ryōun was the blood nephew of the famous Tōsui, and was also connected to him through ordination: Ryōun's ordination teacher was Sengan (n.d.), who had been ordained by the same teacher as Tōsui. Menzan relates that he had often heard how important Tōsui had been to Ryōun, and that Ryōun had always wanted to prepare an account of the life of Tōsui so that others could benefit from his teaching. Nearly fifty years later, Menzan took up the task and composed this account as a token of his gratitude to his ordination teacher Ryōun. Of greater interest here than the story of Tōsui is what we can gather about Menzan and his early relationship to the Ōbaku Zen lineage.

Menzan tells us in his introduction to the *Tribute* that Ryōun and another student had been sent by their teacher to Manpukuji, the main training temple of Ōbaku, and had spent ten years there. The other student stayed on and eventually became abbot of an Ōbaku temple, but Ryōun returned to Kyushu to take care of Zenjōji, and later became the next abbot of Ryūchōin, his teacher's temple. Tōsui himself was not sent to Manpukuji, but he sent his most promising students there and they stayed and became Ōbaku abbots in their own right. So Menzan's own ordination master had trained as an Ōbaku monk, and he was surrounded by teachers who had sent their best students off to study with the Ōbaku lineage masters. He mentioned this in passing, without further comment, yet throughout his other writings Menzan displayed an implacable opposition to the influence of the Manpukuji training on Sōtō monks. He sought to bring the school back to the writings of Dōgen, which for him included getting rid of later influences, both from the Chinese Zen teachers of Manpukuji and from medieval Japanese customs. Perhaps this early experience of seeing Sōtō monks go to Manpukuji for Ōbaku training and never return to their roots was part of the reason that Menzan was especially critical of Ōbaku teachings and practices.

Just before his twentieth year, Menzan was informed by Ryōun that he was soon going to retire, and Menzan went to Kinpōsan, the local mountain overlooking the bay, for a week-long solitary retreat to contemplate his future course of practice. Before he went up the mountain he slipped a piece of paper with a prayer for guidance written on it into the enclosed altar of a Shintō shrine at the foot of the mountain. When he returned from his retreat, during which he stayed up each night reciting the *Diamond Sutra*, a snake appeared from the same opening where he had placed the paper. Menzan interpreted this as an auspicious omen for travel, and Ryōun encouraged him to go immediately, rather than wait for his formal retirement.

Finding a Teacher in Edo

Menzan went to Edo that spring (1703), and met several of the major figures of the Sōtō world, including Dōhaku, who had just completed his successful bid to force a reform of dharma transmission practice. Toward the end of the year he met the relatively unknown teacher Sonnō Sōeki, and soon after, he left the famous teachers of Edo behind and followed Sonnō back to Taishin'in, his small temple in Sendai. Sonnō was a native of Yomezawa, some fifty miles to the southwest of Sendai in the central mountains of present-day Yamagata prefecture. He had received transmission from an obscure abbot in the Ketsudō Nōsho faction (one of the Sōjiji factions, the pillar of the sect), and had been abbot since 1697.

Sonnō is of interest here due to his influence on Menzan's thought, but Sonnō's own life is worthy of a separate study, as he was one of the earliest teachers to emphasize strictly following Dōgen. Sonnō's emphasis on strict practice, and especially his respect for Dōgen, were lasting influences on Menzan, in stark contrast to the influence of his ordination teacher, who was heavily involved in the Ōbaku movement. Sonnō once expelled a student for the casual mistake of placing an ordinary text on top of one of Dōgen's texts on a bookshelf. The student underwent seventeen days of repentance before Sonnō relented and readmitted him. Menzan received a set of precepts (*daikai*) from Sonnō during his first winter retreat. Presumably this set was some form of the bodhisattva precepts, and giving them to a new student was an indication of the importance of precepts for Sonnō, but no further discussion is given in the *Chronology*. Sonnō was known for accepting all requests to give talks, whether at famous temples or lay gatherings. Menzan went everywhere with him, and described this as a far better way to learn than just going to hear various famous teachers lecture.

In early 1705, Sonnō decided it was time to send Menzan out to visit other Zen teachers of all lineages throughout eastern Japan. Despite his youth, he was asked to lecture at villages during his travels. He spent an entire week lecturing on Dōgen's *Advice on Studying the Way* (*Bendōwa*). Menzan lectured on this text repeatedly over the next sixty years, but it was not until just before his death that his commentary on the text was printed. He spent three evenings teaching about the precepts of the *Brahma's Net Sutra*, and he lectured on a *kōan* from the *Checkpoint of Wumen* (*Wumen Guan*). When Menzan returned from his lecture tour, Sonnō gave Menzan his approval.

In the privacy of the abbot's room, they had the following exchange. Sonnō said, "If a person asks you, 'What is this?' how will you reply?" Menzan replied, "What is this?" Sonnō continued, "Silver mountain, iron wall." Menzan responded, "Iron mountain, silver wall." Sonnō bowed and Menzan did obeisance. Sonnō then urged Menzan to preserve what was most important: to look upon the face of Dōgen, and not the face of others. Sonnō regarded this as his greatest legacy to Menzan. Although Menzan does not comment, this was presumably a direct order not to follow the lineage of the Ōbaku teachers who had been influential in his life just three years earlier. After this exchange, Sonnō revealed that he was ill and unlikely to recover.

The phrase "silver mountain, iron wall" is a stock metaphor for something that cannot be grasped, as the truth of Zen cannot be grasped by the intellect. Dōgen used it once, in his *Extensive Record* (*Eihei Kōroku*), and it occurs several times in the *Blue Cliff Record* collection, including once at the end of case fifty-six, where it appears with the same inversion that Menzan used in his reply.[14] Menzan's study and use of the classic *kōan* cases continued throughout his life, and *kōan* also played a crucial role in his own Zen practice. As is discussed below, this is a quite different matter from *kanna*, the single-minded concentration on a phrase taken out of context.

Despite his illness, Sonnō presided over the summer retreat, and out of respect for a monk of the Rinzai lineage in attendance, he devoted his lectures to the *Record of Linji* (*Linji lu*). Sonnō insisted on the primacy of Dōgen's teaching, but it is clear that he was not interested in using that view to exclude anyone from his assembly, nor to overlook a text like the *Record of Linji* just because it was very important to Ōbaku teachings. Before the retreat was over, Sonnō completed the series of ceremonies for dharma transmission to Menzan. He passed away shortly thereafter. Menzan had known Sonnō for barely two years, but the latter's influence shaped the remainder of Menzan's life. With the dharma transmission ceremonies and written certificates from Sonnō, Menzan now had the status to ordain his own students and become the abbot of his own temple. The abbacy of Sonnō's temple was not offered to him, but Menzan stayed for two months of mourning. It was 1705, and at the age of twenty-three Menzan had received dharma transmission, but he had no position, not even a place to reside.

Years of Wandering and Long Retreats

Menzan made his way to Edo, where he was allowed to stop over at the residence of Ōtomo Inaba no kami Yoshisata, who belonged to the family of the Lord of Bungo (in Kyushu). Judging from the frequency of Menzan's subsequent visits, Ōtomo became something of a patron for Menzan during these early years. As was his usual habit, Menzan went to see well-known monks of various lineages, and he also raised funds to have a portrait of Dōgen printed and distributed, presaging his later work on a popular Dōgen biography. On his deathbed, Sonnō had charged Menzan to do a one-thousand-day retreat reading Dōgen's *Shōbōgenzō* and sitting in meditation. Menzan had made a copy of the *Shōbōgenzō*, but it is not clear which of the various versions of the *Shōbōgenzō* this was.

In the village of Hashima southwest of Edo (present day Kanagawa prefecture), Menzan found the situation to fulfill his promise to Sonnō. He lectured for a week on the *Lotus Sutra* and then presided over a precept assembly wherein people received the three refuges. By using this universal set of precepts combined with lectures on the popular *Lotus Sutra*, Menzan could draw villagers closer to Buddhism and to his own teaching without disturbing the rigidly enforced affiliation to a particular temple and its teaching lineage. This was the first of many precept assemblies Menzan presided over throughout his life, though his later assemblies were for precepts specific to his Sōtō Zen lineage. At the end of this particular assembly, he announced that the village elder and ten people in his household had promised to support Menzan and to bring him food every day in his three-year retreat in the local temple of Rōbaian. Before beginning the retreat, he returned to Edo to discuss his plans with his circle of acquaintances, including Ōtomo. During this trip he went to see teachers who specialized in Buddhist regulations or Vinaya, and he also took the *samaya* esoteric precepts from a Shingon teacher who went by the name of Kisan Biku. By way of reciprocating, Menzan taught him the meaning of seated meditation as practiced in Sōtō Zen. The *samaya* precepts (*sanmayakai* in Japanese reading) are taken in the initial ceremony of the *abhisheka* ritual of esoteric Buddhism. These precepts emphasize compassion and the promotion of awakening for all beings, and were to be taken in addition to the usual full precepts of the lineage.[15] Apparently Menzan took only these precepts without going on to the later sections of the *abhisheka* ritual.

In the fourth month of 1706, Menzan returned to Rōbaian and began his three-year retreat. He read and and reread the *Shōbōgenzō* in alternation with meditation. He later regarded this period as the beginning of his lifelong study of the *Shōbōgenzō*, a task that some fifty years later led to the publication of his ten-fascicle work on the sources used by Dōgen, the *Source Texts Cited in the Shōbōgenzō* (*Shōbōgenzō shōten roku*). Menzan was not isolated during this time. Someone came six times a month to shave his head, and he performed ordination ceremonies (*tokudo*) for several people. He had visitors who came to discuss Buddhism, including a novice monk who wanted to talk to Menzan about the precepts used in his Tendai lineage. Halfway through the retreat, a monk came from Edo to be his assistant, and began doing a daily round of begging for food.

After completing his retreat in the first month of 1709, Menzan gave talks in a variety of places and continued writing and reading in many temple libraries. He began his lifelong project of reading the one-hundred-volume *Mahaprajnaparamita sutra*.[16] This massive text is often used in Japan for ceremonies to make spiritual merit, and a special chest containing these volumes can still be seen today in the main hall of Zen temples. In this ritualized reading, a few words from each volume are recited while turning the remainder of the pages from the volume (*tendoku*). Each volume is "read" in this way, often with several priests chanting and turning simultaneously. Menzan, however, actually studied the entire text, and late in his life he finished his commentary in which he summarized the gist of each of the six hundred chapters with a Chinese verse. He saw Dōhaku several times, and at Dōhaku's urging Menzan wrote his first work of scholarship, the *Record of the Activities of the Founder of Eihei* (*Eihei Kaisan Oshō jitsu roku*). This spare text is a compendium of the events of Dōgen's life based primarily on what can be gleaned from Dōgen's own writings. Material from other sources is also considered, but Menzan attempted to check everything against Dōgen's own words. The *Record* was printed in 1710 with a long colophon by Dōhaku, and remains to this day a useful and reliable guide to Dōgen's own words about his life. Menzan's commitment to emphasizing original sources, not to mention his early command of Dōgen's writings, shows clearly in this first work. Thus he began his publishing career at age twenty-seven in his characteristic style, and continued to write and publish for the next fifty-nine years.

In 1711 Menzan spent the summer retreat at Kūinji, in the town of Obama in present-day Fukui prefecture, north of Kyoto on the Japan Sea. Later in life, Kūinji became his main temple, but this time he was merely the assistant to the preceptor for the retreat. After this he made his first visit to Eiheiji and then returned to his retreat site of Rōbaian to begin his study of the *Eihei kōroku*, the Chinese-language collection that records Dōgen's formal talks. He returned to Kyushu to take care of his sick father, and after his father's death, he returned to the Kansai region and was an officiant at the funeral of Dōhaku in 1715. In obedience to his father's dying wish, Menzan made another retreat at Rōbaian. During this one-year retreat he made a stupa of rocks, each rock representing one character of the *Lotus Sutra*. He finished the stupa in the first few months and spent the remainder of the retreat reading other sutras and meditating. Menzan's early experience of solitary meditation combined with textual study may seem a little surprising. Apparently the Zen practice of meditation in the monks' hall (where reading was strictly prohibited) was not a norm of training when Menzan was young. The sources do not mention what Menzan's contemporaries thought of his retreat practices, and it is not clear whether or not this kind of solitary retreat combined with textual study was an unusual event for a Zen monk.

Abbot of Zenjōji and Kūinji

In late 1717, at age thirty-five, Menzan received letters of invitation to become the next abbot of Zenjōji (where his ordination teacher had been abbot). Even though Zenjōji was a small temple, it must have been a welcome offer. After raising the necessary funds, Menzan went to Eiheiji for the required honorary abbot ceremony (*zuise*), and then he made his way to Kyoto for the ceremony at the imperial court. I refer to "raising the necessary funds," although I have not been able to determine the exact amount or how he managed to raise it. However, recent scholarship utilizing ledgers and other materials has made it possible to estimate just how enormous this expense would have been. For the *zuise* ceremony at the head temple (Eiheiji) for an ordinary abbot required about forty *ryō*, of which five *ryō* went to the head temple and the rest was spent in Kyoto.[17] The imperial house in Kyoto was the preeminent source for awarding religious titles and the right to wear colored robes, especially the purple robe of an imperially recognized abbot. The monks gained greater prestige, and the imperial house and its various agents collected large sums. It is clear that becoming an abbot, even of an obscure temple, was something that involved the larger community and required a very serious level of commitment from them.

Menzan arrived at his first post of abbot with these very expensive credentials from Eiheiji and the Kyoto Court, but this was apparently not enough to ensure his acceptance. Due to some problem that is not further described, he was obliged to spend the winter in a nearby temple, apparently without any duties, waiting for some resolution to the impasse. In the spring, he returned to the Kyoto area, and was persuaded to come back to Kyushu only when an assistant arrived with letters of support from the current abbot and the two prior abbots of Zenjōji. This time he took up the post without incident, an indication that local support and local politics were as important as the incredibly expensive special robes and certificates from Eiheiji and the Court.

Menzan was abbot for twelve years, teaching and restoring temples throughout the region. During this period, he lectured on a wide variety of topics and texts, including the *Record of Linji* and the *Platform Sutra of the Sixth Patriarch*. In a number of cases, the lectures and drafts he constructed during this time were used in his later publications, though some texts recorded in the *Chronology* have been lost. Menzan drew audiences from across the spectrum of Buddhist lineages, not just Sōtō followers. In 1720, for example, he lectured for six weeks on the *Record of Linji* to monks of the Rinzai and Ōbaku lineages as well as Sōtō. The contemporary interest in the *Record of Linji* reflects the influence of the Ōbaku lineage, which was responsible for a new emphasis on the text. Despite these lectures, Menzan never committed a commentary to paper. That same year, he gave lectures on the *Lotus Sutra* to Pure Land lineage devotees. He also presided over lay precept ceremonies and wrote (but did not publish) several works on precepts and basic monastic procedure, including a piece on the chants at mealtime. He also finished his first major research project, which concerned the meaning and history of the ordination precepts. This detailed work in three volumes was not published until twenty years later. During this time, he wrote the *Buddha Samādhi*, a relatively informal piece in praise of Dōgen's way of meditation. According to the colophon, a lay follower found this text years later when Menzan was a well-established teacher, and received permission to have it printed in Kyoto and distributed. This work has been popular ever since, and copies in original woodblock form of this and several of Menzan's other short works can still be purchased at the Baiyō bookstore in Kyoto.

The *Buddha Samādhi* also contains two disparaging comments about *kanna* practice, which is one of the characteristic features of modern Rinzai Zen and is typically opposed by contemporary mainstream Sōtō Zen teachers.[18] This practice focuses great effort on breaking through to the understanding of a single phrase culled from the *kōan*, which is referred to as observing the critical phrase of the *kōan* (*kanna*). Menzan recognizes that *kanna* has its roots in China, but he regards it as an unorthodox offshoot and writes that *kanna* practice is a misguided attempt to force the attainment of a dramatic breakthrough. His comments consist of just a few sentences, yet the entry on the *Buddha Samādhi* in the encyclopedia *Zengaku daijiten* claims that Menzan's text is an attack on the Rinzai Zen practice of *kanna*.[19] In fact, Menzan never mentions Rinzai here, and it seems much more likely that he was criticizing monks in his own school for their unruly behavior, which is what Menzan saw as the outcome of *kanna* practice. The *Zengaku daijiten* is a publication of Komazawa University, which is both the main university attended by Sōtō priests and a center for textual Buddhist scholarship, especially of Zen texts. This small example highlights the strong tendency to read back the contemporary linkage of *kanna* and Rinzai Zen into earlier texts, and to assume that the Rinzai and Sōtō lineages were as strictly separated in the past as they are now.

Menzan's temple was close to Nagasaki and the Chinese enclave, and it is not surprising that Menzan had considerable contact with the Ōbaku Zen community, apparently continuing the friendly relations he inherited from his ordination teacher, whose circle contained many clerics who became full members of the Ōbaku community. In 1725, he made a trip of several months to Nagasaki for the explicit purpose of learning more about the customs of the Chinese monks. In 1728, Menzan was in his forty-sixth year and despite all his manuscripts, he had actually published nothing of his own since the work on the life of Dōgen eighteen years earlier. Much of his time in Kyushu had been spent raising funds and managing the restoration of temples. That year representatives came to invite Menzan to become abbot of Kūinji, the temple where he had spent one retreat some seventeen years before. Although Menzan had two years earlier refused an offer to be abbot of a temple not far away on the southern tip on Honshu, he accepted the offer from Kūinji, which was to be his home base until his death.

Kūinji enjoyed a more active retreat schedule and was geographically much closer to Eiheiji and to Kyoto, the traditional capital and printing center. Apparently his audience at Kūinji was to include people with ties to the Kyoto printing establishment, which issued a flood of works by Menzan during the following decades. After his installation ceremony as abbot of Kūinji, which was attended by representatives of some forty temples of the region, he presented himself to the temple sponsors and began the summer retreat. Apparently for the first time, Menzan lectured on a fascicle of Dōgen's *Shōbōgenzō*, the "Ango" fascicle, which is concerned with the meaning of the training session. After his early work on Dōgen's life, it is surprising that Dōgen was not a topic of his formal lectures until now, though this may have simply been because the new emphasis on Dōgen had not reached Kyushu. In the fall, Menzan held another precepts assembly and made the trip to Eiheiji to receive his robe of advancement in rank and to meet the new abbot, Taikyo Katsugen (d. 1736), who was to be Menzan's major supporter during the next few years. Menzan recorded this meeting in the preface to his comprehensive work about the pure rules, published many years later:

> Katsugen said, "At Kūinji you have your ordination platform, office, and monastic supervision to deal with, so you certainly have no leisure. Still, I hear that you are zealous in honoring our Founder. I have two great wishes. The first is to apply to the government to return to the Founder's ordination procedures. The second wish is to build a monks' hall at this monastery, and to implement therein the monastic rule of the Founder. I hope you will be in accord with these wishes. Does this not accord with the deep wishes of the Founder?"[20]

Menzan apparently took this to heart, since his efforts for the following years were directed to his work on monastic rules and, of course, to his teaching during the retreats at Kūinji. Katsugen praised his research and brought Menzan to Eiheiji for a three-week visit to look at the manuscripts there and to edit Katsugen's own work on the precepts. Menzan continued to travel in order to find manuscripts of Dōgen as well as of other Sōtō authors. Beginning in 1736, he served a one-year term as abbot in rotation (*rinjū*) for Ryūkeiin in present-day Nagoya. He knew that this temple had a monks' hall still standing, though it was being used as a meditation hall, and he had hoped to try out his new rules.

Menzan advocated implementing the monks' hall practice (as opposed to the meditation hall practice followed by Ōbaku monks), which he called "returning to Dōgen's way." In this system, which Dōgen had observed during his visit to Song China and which Katsugen had referred to when Menzan met him at Eiheiji, the monks ate, slept, and meditated in the monks' hall. The practice of contemporary Ming China was to use separate buildings for different activities, and Ōbaku temples followed that system, as described in the rule composed for their use in Japan, the *Ōbaku shingi*. Menzan wrote that, of all the important urban temples, only Tōfukuji still had the old style monks' hall, and even the rural temples that still had the building were using them in the new style, for which they were not really suited.[21]

He was not able to put into effect his vision of the original Song rules during his one-year stay at Ryūkeiin, but during that time he traveled to find examples of old monks' halls in the area to study their construction. Upon the completion of his one-year term, he returned to Kūinji and immediately set about converting its hall to the monks' hall style. In 1737, he held the retreat using the old style of practice, which Menzan continued to emphasize was the way that Dōgen had done the practice. The popular view within Sōtō communities accepts that assertion, but it needs to be emphasized that Menzan had himself reconstructed the practice, on the basis of his own reading of Dōgen, creatively imagining Dōgen's intent where necessary, by drawing on texts that Dōgen was familiar with. Menzan was not following the style of monastic practice that his teachers had taught him, and Dōgen's writings do not provide a systematic and detailed description of the full range of monastic routine. Menzan had high hopes of implementing the same reforms at Eiheiji, but Katsugen died before he could do anything, and his successor at Eiheiji did not seem interested in monastic reform. Menzan's dream of changing Eiheiji practice, which would have been a major step toward reforming the standard for Sōtō practice generally, was not realized during his lifetime. It took years of discussion, culminating in a bitter dispute that nearly paralyzed major monastic centers, before Menzan's vision of the reformed rules became the official standard in 1804.[22]

Menzan turned down offers to be abbot of Kasuisai and of Kōshōji, which were major temples with powerful political connections, and instead began arrangements to build a small retirement place. Up to this point, his work was largely concerned with monastic rules, and in 1741 he finished the writing of his research, entitled *Selections for Ceremonial Procedures from the Pure Rules for the Monks Hall of Sōtō* (*Tōjō sōdō shingi gyōhō shō*), and its companion, the *Additional Record of Historical Research Concerning the Pure Rules for the Monks Hall of Sōtō* (*Tōjō sōdō shingi kōtei betsuroku*). This work was not to be published for another twelve years, but he published other texts about monastic practice, including two smaller pieces about seated and walking meditation, the *Buddha Samadhi* mentioned earlier and the *Standards for Walking Meditation* (*Kinhinki*), both of which have been very widely read guides right up to the present.[23]

Some of his most important work during this time was to defend the earlier reforms of Dōhaku and others. Tenkei Denson (1648–1753) continued his attacks on the reforms even though they had become official government-approved Sōtō policy, and arguments about dharma transmission continued through the end of the Tokugawa period; it is still a sensitive topic.[24] Because it is both the certification of awakening and the documentation required before becoming abbot of a temple, dharma transmission is the pivotal event in the life of a Zen figure. Dōhaku had pressed for a new system whereby a single dharma lineage would be held for life, rather than requiring a new lineage be taken on with new temple responsibilities. Menzan was picking up the torch for the deceased Dōhaku, fighting a rear-guard action against Tenkei's attempt to turn back the reforms and return to the old system of temple transmission.

For example, in his *Fireside Chat on a Snowy Eve* (*Setsuya rodan*), Menzan defended Dōhaku's reforms, using his exegetical skills to justify his reading of an admittedly obscure and difficult passage in Dōgen.[25] As is frequently seen in his writings, much of Menzan's argument here turned on narrow questions of philology. Menzan launched into a detailed analysis of the passage in question from the "Menju" chapter of the *Shōbōgenzō*, which he and Dōhaku read as allowing one and only one face-to-face dharma transmission. He showed how Dōgen is actually setting up an absurd example expressed as a contrary-to-fact conditional, which Tenkei had taken literally. In this way Menzan defended Dōhaku's reading as one that follows the meaning, even though it was the opposite of the literal reading. Menzan brings into the argument examples of similar usage and provides definitions of key terms. He is also at pains to base his reading on a full and accurate text, something that his opponents were not doing. Even in such an intimate ceremony that is at the core of the school's self-understanding, Menzan argued not from the position of authority of the awakened teacher, but from careful textual exegesis.

Another key part of the old style of dharma transmission was the genre of secret documents, called *kirikami*, that described the ceremonial details and claimed to come directly from the earliest days of the school, often attributed to Dōgen himself. To Menzan, these were obviously forgeries that were being used to justify the customs he was trying to eliminate. To expose these documents for what they were, Menzan wrote the *Personal Record of the Rejection of the Kirikami of the Sōtō Abbot's Room* (*Tōjō shitsunai danshi kenpi shiki*), in which he revealed their anachronisms and other egregious mistakes.[26] Neither this nor the other works he wrote on the same theme were published until the modern collections, but they were circulated in manuscript form and led to a general discrediting of this kind of secret document. Menzan followed this approach in all his areas of research and in publications in which he attempted to demonstrate the authenticity of his proposed reforms. As is discussed below, in other areas he demonstrated his ability to write for a wider audience and also a willingness to be more free with textual details.

The two pieces discussed above are rather technical in nature in comparison to what is perhaps the best window into his teaching style: *Sermons of [the Abbot of the Temple of Mount] Kenkō* (*Kenkō fusetsu*).[27] In the preface to this Chinese language work, he writes that it was discovered at Kūinji (whose mountain name was Kenkō, hence the title) in a worm-eaten state, left over from his teaching there thirty years prior to its 1765 printing. Some lay followers had asked permission to publish them, in part as a commemoration for his years of public teaching. In one place in the text, Menzan mentions that he was being repeatedly invited to come from Kyushu to teach at Kūinji, so one can infer that at least some of these lectures were given in the late 1720s, before he began his position as abbot of Kūinji. The talks were presumably attended by both laymen and monks, in keeping with the title, which means sermons of a public nature.

I have selected two topics from this text for translation below, in order to give an idea of Menzan's colorful and popular style, and as a window into Zen practice of the times. As already mentioned when discussing the *Buddha Samādhi*, Menzan had a low opinion of *kanna* practice, and references to what he calls the degenerate *kōan* practices of the Song or of "these days" are common, often with comments about shouts and blows or sweating blood. After some opening remarks in chapter 3 about the transmission of the practice of sitting from India, Menzan launches a sustained attack against those who concentrate on the critical phrase, calling them merely:

> narrow-minded zealots who hold up the flower, blink, smile, laugh, stare at walls, do bows from their place, and mistakenly rely on the wordless teaching. This is a deluded understanding of the mind-to-mind transmission. When I see this it seems like the vulgar arguing over a puzzle: when they solve it they are satisfied with their accomplishment.
>
> This evil has continued so long that they cannot return to the old ways. From the end of the Song to the Yuan and Ming, many masters affirm this to be the secret essence of the separate transmission outside the teachings. They sweep away the sutra and the commentaries like old fashioned calendars that they will never use again. This evil has overflowed [China] and entered Japan, piling evil upon evil. It continues and gets worse and worse.
>
> Recently one sees so-called "people of good mind" who have taken up a practice of Zen that entails being given just one word (*watō*) from an old [*kōan*] case. These tyros are urged on by being told: "Make it your constant theme: walking, standing, sitting, lying down. Awake now! Wake up now! If you can't achieve awakening, kill yourself. Just stick your neck out and come forward: hear one word and [there are] a thousand awakenings."
>
> I have no space for the rest [of that kind of talk], but concerning the ways of physically driving on students [I can mention that] they bind hands or feet, they force people to sit for long periods, and there is painful sleepiness. The students are hit with the fist, slapped, stepped on and kicked, even whipped. Really this is nothing but corporal punishment, in some places done by the teachers and in some places by the students to each other.

Later, in chapter 5, Menzan develops a complex textual argument attempting to show that the way the later Chinese tradition attributes the practice to early masters will not stand up to careful historical scrutiny. After this he gives some examples of various odd occurrences that happened when people were putting extreme pressure on themselves to concentrate on their *wato*. Then he says:

> This is just abnormal psychology, not something to be honored. When I was in Okushū [practicing under Sonnō] I heard this story. There was a widow who was taking instruction with a teacher of the Rinzai school. She worked for a long time on the True Man of No Rank *kōan*, and a ten-foot-tall monk appeared before her. He was utterly black, like lacquer, without mouth, ear, or nose, and he appeared every time she did zazen. She lived in constant fear, and came to enquire of this to my former teacher. He said "It is merely something made up in meditation. You should drop the *wato*, and this thing will not appear again." This kind of thing happened countless times. How can anyone think this sort of thing is the true and properly transmitted teaching of the Buddhas and Patriarchs?[28]

In this case the practice is clearly linked to a Rinzai teacher, and the problem is not just unseemly behavior. The problem is that it causes this nice lady to have terrifying psychological problems, and the solution is quite clear: stop doing the practice. In all these cases, Menzan is not denying that *kanna* practice does have results, but claims that the results are at a low level and come with undesirable side effects.

From a later perspective, it may be possible to interpret passages like these from Menzan as invectives against Rinzai Zen or Hakuin (1686–1769), who is seen by the contemporary members of that lineage as the reviver of their school and as the champion of the practice of observing the phrase. Hakuin, however is not mentioned by name, and there is no evidence of which I am aware that these two figures knew of each other in any way. Of course, they could have met at some point in their long and nearly contemporaneous lives, but apparently they never resided in the same area at the same time. Menzan has no use for *kanna* practice, but in most cases his disapproval is of monks identified only by their unruly behavior or their participation in the practice of regarding the phrase, not as Rinzai monks.

Chapter 4 of the *Sermons* echoes some very modern concerns about the use of the *kyōsaku* (also read *keisaku*), a heavy, hard, stiff stick used during group meditation. The often frightening use of the *kyōsaku* to keep people awake or just to "encourage" them is a fixture of Japanese monastic practice that was not always appreciated by Zen practitioners in the West, and was regarded by some as little more than hazing. As can be seen below, Menzan had exactly the same opinion nearly three hundred years earlier. Unlike so many Zen monastic details, this particular item does not appear in the standard rules from China, and Dōgen does not say anything about its use, either. Thus there is no textual authority to keep the practice from becoming excessive, a problem that is not a modern development, as we shall shortly see. In this as in so many other particulars, Menzan is arguing for a more humane and mainstream style of Zen Buddhism, relying on ancient Vinaya texts whenever he can, attempting to curb what he sees as overzealous excesses.

In this chapter, Menzan promotes the innovation of going back to the very old "meditation stick" (*zenjō*), instead of the current *kyōsaku*, which has no textual justification. The meditation stick is a piece of equipment for the meditation hall which is mentioned in the Vinaya, though not in the rules of the Zen schools, and the term is not generally used in Zen texts. The "zen" of the word refers to meditation, not to the Zen school, hence my translation as meditation stick.

> In the Vinaya the Buddha explained the way to use the meditation stick.[29] It is made of bamboo or reed and one end is wrapped in something soft, so it will not hurt when used. The meditation stick does not appear in the old meditation rules because it was not necessary: everyone did *zazen* on the long platform, and if someone was sleepy, they quietly took off their robe and slipped away to do walking meditation alone in the corridor. However today we do *zazen* as a group and walking meditation as a group. . . . The *kyōsaku* was made for when sleepiness cannot be avoided. Although its usage is based on the usage of the meditation stick, is not orthodox. It is used like a whip for inflicting a punishment or like using a whip on a horse. Nonetheless, nowadays because there is no rule for the use of the stick in the Pure Rules, the people who are guiding *zazen* often use it with abandon as much as they want. Once this abuse has arisen, it tends to run wild.
>
> I have gone to various practice places to see how the *kyōsaku* is used, and . . . sometimes when a person puts up with the pain of the stick, they get sicker and sicker, until they die of it. This terrible situation arises when monks are beaten up and bloody even around the head, eye, ear, and nose. Many of the assembly have wounds filled with puss on their shoulders. . . . In this country and time, *kyōsaku* usage is so violent that I have heard of tens of *kyōsaku* being broken. This is told of throughout the population of monks. . . .

In the teaching of our founder Dōgen, for *zazen* there is a rule, and for walking meditation there is a method. . . . So I took a piece of bamboo and made a meditation stick for myself. The proper way to use the stick is as follows. If you see someone sleeping, formally pick up the stick and quietly walk over to the sleeping one's place. With the tip of the stick, stroke the top of his shoulder. In this way wake him up, and bow with the stick to display apology. If he again is sleepy, again with the tip gently push up his shoulder, and when he wakes up, bow with the stick to display apology. If he is sleepy a third time, lightly tap him on the shoulder. The stick should not be more than a foot in length. When he wakes up, bow with the stick to display apology. . . .

If you do it properly, then giving and receiving [the stick] cannot be separated, like milk and water. The way of *zazen* has been properly transmitted by Buddhas and Patriarchs. The main purpose of the stick is only to wake up sleepers. If someone is soundly sleeping, snoring and talking, we call out to him to wake him up. If someone is sleeping a bit in meditation, is it necessary to hit him strongly, to violently startle him? If a person lets go of things and his mind is quiet, then his sleep is light. If someone clings to many things and his mind is flustered, his sleep is heavy.[30]

Stepping Down to His Study Retreat

In 1741, at age fifty-nine, Menzan turned over Kūinji to Katsudō Fukan (n.d.) and moved to the nearby small retreat temple of Eifukuan, devoting himself in earnest to writing. He had been abbot for twelve years, but apparently Menzan did not have the political connections to place his own dharma heir at Kūinji, just as he had not been able to at his former temple Zenjōji in Kyushu. These temple lineages did come back to his line, however, and now these temples have abbots that trace themselves to Menzan. They host an annual memorial for Menzan at Eifukuan, which attracts a score or more of Menzan's heirs from around the country (and at least one foreign visitor from time to time). At this point in his life, Menzan was largely finished with his work of defending Dōhaku's dharma transmission reforms that had been approved back in 1703, and he had completed his major works on monastic practice rules that very year. He did continue to write shorter works about specific aspects of monastic life, but he gave up on the effort to bring his ideas into practice at Eiheiji and in Sōtō monasteries more widely.

He returned to his earlier project about the life of Dōgen, which culminated in the 1754 publication of the *Revised and Expanded Record of Kenzei*, his popular rendition of the life of Dōgen.[31] Menzan used the *Kenzeiki*, written by Kenzei (1415–1474) the fourteenth abbot of Eiheiji, as his basic text, but in fact his revisions and additions are quite substantial, something which was overlooked until the 1970s. Menzan's new biography gave the Sōtō community an accessible story of the life of its founder for the first time. Menzan's earlier publication had cleared away the almost complete darkness about basic details of Dōgen's life with a dry collection of key facts, but this new work of hagiography was to receive a very wide readership. The *Revised and Expanded Record of Kenzei* (*Teiho Kenzeiki*) was frequently reprinted, including an 1806 printing with illustrations that was part of the official celebration of the Dōgen memorial year. The foreword to this edition describes how a series of fundraising efforts throughout the country made it possible to have illustrations made for the new edition and for copies to be distributed throughout Japan. Thus the *Revised and Expanded Record of Kenzei* became the main source of popular knowledge of Dōgen and, until recently, was accepted in the scholarly community as well. Because it quickly became the standard, texts that Menzan used as sources were no longer copied and were nearly lost.

In 1975, Kawamura Kōdō published a comparative edition of newly discovered manuscripts of the *Kenzeiki*, and the extent of Menzan's changes have become apparent, throwing into doubt some long-accepted ideas about Dōgen, including most of the well-known and dramatic elements in his life. For example, Menzan inserts a paragraph about Dōgen's activities at age fifteen.[32] In all of the oldest manuscripts of the *Kenzeiki* for this year there is the simple statement that Dōgen entered the room of the founder of Kenninji and first heard of the way of the Rinzai school. Kenninji was founded in 1202 by Eisai, after his return from China with certification as a fully qualified Zen teacher, but by the time Dōgen was fifteen Eisai had already died. In Menzan's expanded version, Dōgen is depicted as assiduously studying the sutras and commentaries, and having doubts about the doctrine of intrinsic awakening, a key teaching of Japanese Buddhism, especially in the Tendai lineage that Dōgen first followed. After first seeking local guidance, Dōgen was sent to Eisai of Kenninji for a solution to this difficult problem. All of this is lacking in the manuscripts, and yet this is the core of the popular image of Dōgen's youthful doubts, and his dissatisfaction with Tendai teaching. Menzan's version then adds a long note about the contents of the interview between Dōgen and Eisai, a mysterious *kōan* dialogue about original nature for which Menzan gives no source, and for which no source has ever been found.

The 1806 version, which was distributed throughout the country, has illustrations that show this meeting and the prior event when Dōgen was being sent to Kenninji for guidance. Thus the popular illustrated text highlighted events that are absent or unclear in the original *Kenzeiki*. These problems have caused some diminution of Menzan's reputation as a careful scholar, but it should be pointed out that this was not one of Menzan's works of philological scholarship (like his first biography of Dōgen), but a text explicitly written for a popular audience and crafted to paint a portrait of the founder whom Menzan was promoting as an inspiration to all. He makes this purpose clear in the preface, yet such was Menzan's reputation that for many years his story was taken as the definitive biography, rather than inspirational hagiography.

During this period, Menzan also wrote the *Record of the Activities of Zen Teacher Tiantong Rujing* (*Tendō Nyojō Zenji anroku*), a biography of Dōgen's teacher Rujing, and published an edition of the *Record of the Hōkyō Era* (*Hōkyōki*), which purports to be Dōgen's record of his time in China with Rujing (1163–1228). Menzan continued his major research efforts on the *Shōbōgenzō* and began to publish commentaries on Dōgen's shorter independent pieces. Due to internal squabbles about the proper text of the *Shōbōgenzō*, the government had agreed to a ban on printing of the *Shōbōgenzō* itself starting in 1722, so Menzan did not have the opportunity to publish his own edition. He printed his *Fukan zazengi monge* and *Zazenshin monge*, commentaries on Dōgen's texts about seated meditation. The word *monge* in these titles is appended to the name of the text to which it is a commentary. Menzan used *monge* to mean an explanation in response to a question, and it became a standard tag phrase used for his Japanese-language commentaries.

Despite his many earlier lectures on the precepts in general, he had not published anything on the particular precepts appropriate to Dōgen's lineage. His major work on this topic, *The Teaching of the Correctly Transmitted Great Precepts of the Buddhas and Ancestors* (*Busso shōden daikai ketsu*), had been finished in 1724 but was published in 1748. During the following fifteen years, he published four more pieces on precepts. The research materials contained in these works are the foundation of Sōtō understanding of Dōgen's views on precepts. Some of Menzan's own ideas, however, which tended to emphasize a more mainstream interpretation of precepts, were not well received by most Sōtō abbots. Menzan took the position that as important as it was to receive the precepts, the taking was a confirmation of practice, not its completion. Menzan's general attitudes are plainly laid out in his *Precepts [Assembly] Sermons* (*Jakushū Eifuku Oshō sekkai*), which are his lectures delivered in 1752 during a seven-day precepts assembly attended by six hundred people, including both clerics and male and female laity. He emphasizes that for all their importance, the precepts are only one of the three main parts of the triad of precepts, meditation, and wisdom, likening them to the three legs of a pot.³³ Eventually Menzan's position lost out to the more radical interpretation of Banjin Dōtan (1698–1775), who stressed the uniqueness of precepts in Zen and their radical power to transform the recipient at the moment they are received.

In addition to all these projects, he managed to find time to finish his *Verses for the Chapters of the Mahaprajnaparamita sutra* (*Daihannyakyō chikukan keisan*). He had written verses on each of the first fifty chapters when he was twenty-six, but in the preface he says that work on monastic rules had kept him from returning to the text. Now, at the age of seventy-three, he completed the task for the remaining five hundred and fifty chapters and had it printed in 1756. This work is not collected in the Sōtō compendiums (*Sōtōshū zensho* and *Zoku Sōtōshū zensho*), but it is included in the Wisdom Sūtra section of the *Nihon daizōkyō*.³⁴ Only three other commentaries on this sutra are included in this comprehensive collection, and Menzan's commentary is as long as the other three combined. Nonetheless, this seems to have been a minor sideline for Menzan during moments away from his major effort, which was tracking down and commenting on the texts which Dōgen quoted in his *Shōbōgenzō*, a project which he says began in 1706 at the start of his three-year retreat and continued for some fifty years. By 1758, the writing was finished and the printing of his massive *Source Texts Cited in the Shōbōgenzō* began the next year. This work has remained the essential companion to the reading of the *Shōbōgenzō*.

New Topics in His Ninth Decade

The completion of this project marked a turning point for Menzan. He had entered the seventy-seventh year of his life, and he had finished the work on Dōgen that had been his goal ever since he was a young monk. His work on monastic regulations had been well received at first at Eiheiji, but had later been effectively shelved, and his interpretations of proper precepts for Sōtō Zen were not accepted. Although his work on the *Shōbōgenzō* eventually came to be highly regarded, it was scarcely a popular work, and its usefulness was limited until the prohibition against printing the *Shōbōgenzō* itself was lifted in 1796. Despite the volume of his printed output, at this point he must have been quite uncertain about the extent of his influence and about how long it would last.

From the late 1750s on, Menzan spent much of his time as a guest at various places in Kyoto, most often in subtemples of the great Rinzai Zen temple Kenninji. He continued to publish short pieces about the Zen precepts and ordinations, now in rejoinder to attacks on his previously published pieces, and commentaries on independent works by Dōgen like the *Gakudō yōjinshū monge*, and the *Tenzo kyōkun monge*. He presided over precept assemblies nearly every year in either Edo or Kyoto, giving precepts to several hundred people at a time, including the 1752 assembly mentioned above, in which six hundred people received the precepts.

It is unclear whether he felt he was finished with his work on Dōgen and the rules and procedures specific to Sōtō, or he felt he had failed to achieve proper recognition and wanted to turn to something different, but at this time a new focus appears in his research. He began to work on the classic Chinese Zen texts, and especially on the great collections of *kōan* commentary. In 1758 he composed and put into print his *Explanations of the Old Cases Presented by the Old Buddha of Xi Province* (*Shisshū kobutsu juko shōtei*), a commentary on the great classic collection of one hundred old cases by Hongzhi Zhengjue (1091–1157), which is excerpted from Hongzhi's record.[35] Hongzhi was the teacher of the Sōtō (C. Caoding) lineage in China who was crucial for the revival of the lineage and has been held in the highest regard by the lineage in Japan. These cases of Hongzhi form the core of the famous compendium of *kōan* cases and commentary, the *Book of Serenity* (*Congrong lu*), published in 1224.[36] There are a number of commentaries on this work, but Menzan's is apparently the only one to be printed in premodern times.

He wrote other pieces in connection with Hongzhi at about the same time, and in 1763, at age eighty-one, he was invited to come from Kyoto to the major Edo temple of Seishōji to give a six-week series of lectures about Hongzhi and this *kōan* collection. According to the entry in his *Chronology*, it was attended by six hundred people, including fifty abbots of Edo area temples. This was apparently the only time that Menzan was in the spotlight of the Sōtō institution in Edo. He was the guest of more than one abbot of Eiheiji, and he often lectured in Kyoto, but the center of power was in Edo, and this is the only time that he was the speaker at such an illustrious event. Considering that he had already printed some forty-five works (including the multivolume works on pure rules and on the *Shōbōgenzō*), it is probably significant that he was not more often invited to give lectures in this kind of setting. His work on pure rules and on matters more directly related to Dōgen were still controversial for such a setting, and perhaps he wanted to avoid controversy that would threaten the unity of Sōtō Zen. He implied this when he wrote in his 1755 preface to the *Additional Record of Historical Research Concerning the Pure Rules for the Monks Hall of Sōtō*, "These rules for the head temple are also in effect rules for all the Sōtō temples of the entire country. There may be some opposition, and if there is, then a widespread debate between me and other Sōtō monks cannot be avoided."[37] In contrast, Hongzhi was a much safer topic. He was a universally respected figure, and his *kōan* were far removed from contentious details of ceremony or the specifics of monastic life.

Despite the prestigious setting for these lectures, the *Explanations of the Old Cases* is not included in the modern Sōtō collections. The following year, Menzan wrote a similar commentary on the one hundred *kōan* cases of Xuedou Chongxian (980–1052), which became the basic text for the *Blue Cliff Record* (*Biyan lu*) commentary printed in 1128.[38] Xuedou was one of the most celebrated poets of Chinese Zen, and the *Blue Cliff Record* is regarded as perhaps the greatest of the elaborate works of literary *kōan* commentaries. This work was the model for Hongzhi's later work that Menzan had just written about. The *Blue Cliff Record* has tended, in Japan at least, to be identified more closely with the Rinzai lineage of its authors. Nevertheless, he composed the *Explanations of the One Hundred Old Cases of Zen Teacher Xuedou Hsien* (*Shisshū kobutsu juko shōtei*), which was printed in 1788 and reprinted in 1833, 1859, and several times in the late nineteenth century by the Baiyō bookstore in Kyoto. This text is not in the Sōtō collections, either, and due to the obscurity of the references in both Menzan's *Chronology* and the *Zengaku daijiten*, it is very easy to overlook the fact that this text exists at all. Nonetheless, it seems to be the most often reprinted commentary on the *kōan* of Xuedou. This kind of work was clearly much in demand, and apparently there was no expectation that Menzan would confine himself to Dōgen or even to the *kōan* collection more closely linked to Sōtō. The modern editors who decided not to include these major works in their collections of Sōtō writings may have been influenced by contemporary sectarian thinking that makes a much sharper divide between Rinzai and Sōtō Zen than was seen in the Tokugawa era even by Menzan, the champion of Dōgen.

Menzan continued to write and publish until the end of his life. Just a few months before his death he wrote *On the Donations of the Faithful* (*Shinse ron*), a brief work about the importance of the monk's appreciation of the gifts offered by the laity. He continued to spend most of his time in Kyoto, sometimes at illustrious Rinzai temples like Nanzenji, and sometimes at more obscure Sōtō temples. Menzan's health began to fail in the ninth month of his eighty-seventh year (1769), while staying in Kyoto at Seiraiin, a subtemple of Kenninji where he had resided many times before when giving lectures and leading precept assemblies. His last public activity was to preach a sermon on causation, not to his monks or to the laity, but to the animals which were being used in the ceremony of *hōjōe* in which fish and birds are released from captivity. He wrote out his final testament, and when his students realized that death was near, they asked him for his final words, but he refused to say more. He was cremated in Kyoto, and his ashes were interred at Eifukuan, with portions going to nearby Kūinji and Zenjōji in Kyushu.

He had completed formal recognition of dharma transmission for twenty-seven of his students, enabling them to ordain their own students and advance to the position of abbot. About half of these heirs predeceased him, a comment perhaps on Menzan's stamina and long life. Judging from the standard lineage charts, only Dōhaku had more recognized heirs, and only a handful of other Sōtō teachers recognized even half as many heirs.[39] None of his direct heirs wrote anything of note, but Fuzan Gentotsu (d. 1789), a dharma heir to Kōda Soryō, one of Menzan's main disciples, is credited with nine titles. Despite the lineage order, when one considers the dates of their lives, it is clear that Fuzan must have studied directly with Menzan.

One striking omission in Menzan's works is a comprehensive commentary on the *Shōbōgenzō*. A set of commentaries exists, each chapter of which ends with his tag line *monge*. These became a popular introduction to reading the *Shōbōgenzō*, and were thought to be by Menzan. They are not. This mistaken attribution dates to 1891, when the collection was first published, and the pieces were attributed to Menzan by the editors. They were later incorporated into the standard collection of commentaries, and Menzan came to be identified with the rather pedestrian quality of these pieces. Nagakuta Taira has examined the manuscripts upon which he determined the first printed version was based, and concluded that only three of the ninety-five essays are by Menzan.[40] Nagakuta concludes that that the remaining essays are probably from talks given during 1775 and 1776 by Fuzan. Apparently they were attributed to Menzan simply on the strength of the word *monge* in the title. Partly because of the rather simple but kindly and detailed quality of these lectures (which were in fact not by him), Menzan came to be called "Baba Menzan," which can be translated as "Grandma Menzan." Fuzan's commentaries were clearly based on Menzan's teaching, rather than being from his own research, and it seems that none of his close disciples followed Menzan's habits of original research and publishing.

At the end of the *Chronology*, amid the usual laudatory formulas, the writer comments that in spite of the number of pieces Menzan published during his lifetime, it was only a drop compared to the ocean of what he had written, and which his students were just beginning to assemble. The editors assembled his twenty-six volume *Extended Record* (*Eifuku Menzan Oshō kōroku*) and had it printed beginning in 1773, four years after his death.

Menzan Compared to His Peers

Menzan was an innovative and humane teacher for people from many walks of life and a demanding trainer of a large number of Zen teachers. He is remembered, however, primarily for the quality of his writing and his meticulous attention to textual research, not to mention the quantity and range of his output: Menzan did fundamental work on nearly every aspect of Sōtō Zen teaching and practice. I have found 103 titles, and if we include the six major edited works (for example his own unpublished version of the *Shōbōgenzō*), there are 109 titles in 281 traditional volumes (*maki*). Fifty-five titles were printed during his lifetime, and four more within a few years of his death. In modern collected editions, he has a total of over 3,100 pages, and this does not include his large commentaries on major *kōan* collections from his late period. Aside from Dōgen and Keizan, no one comes close to Menzan in the Sōtō school. Indeed, he has more titles to his name in the collections than the next six most prolific Sōtō authors put together. Furthermore, his works touch on almost every aspect of Sōtō Zen, and there are other areas of major work, such as the extended commentaries on the massive *kōan* collections, that are not even commonly acknowledged. No one wrote as much as Menzan, and in the Sōtō lineage there is no one who equaled Menzan's meticulous approach and breadth of coverage. As Kagamishima has noted, Menzan's work is the beginning of doctrinal studies (*shūgaku*) in Sōtō Zen, and it is his framework that has continued, for better or worse, to define the field.[41]

Menzan was unparalleled in the ranks of Sōtō Zen, but he was not the only Japanese Zen monk to work in such a comprehensive way. There is one other, perhaps even more accomplished, Zen scholar-monk in premodern Japan to whom he can be compared: Mujaku Dōchū (1653–1745).[42] This Rinzai lineage writer, based in Kyoto, has some 374 works to his credit, including his editions of both Buddhist and secular Chinese texts. Mujaku's approach was to first establish a text on the basis of comparisons of the oldest copies available, and only then interpret difficult passages, using other examples of similar usage found in a wide range of texts. Menzan's count of 103 titles falls far short of Mujaku's, though the number of pages of original writing is harder to determine, due to the almost complete lack of modern printed editions of his work. Menzan's methods were very similar to Mujaku's, and it is unfortunate that there seems to be no evidence of direct contact between these two. However, Menzan often quotes Mujaku's own compendium of rules, the *Sōrin ryakushingi*, in his *Additional Record of Historical Research Concerning the Pure Rules for the Monks Hall of Sōtō*, so he clearly studied Mujaku. In the list of books Mujaku read is found Menzan's *Record of the Activities of the Founder of Eihei*, so at least they knew of each other's writings, although it is disappointing that Mujaku apparently only read this one early piece by Menzan.[43]

Despite the similarity of their methods, their publication record could hardly be in greater contrast. Mujaku published only one title during his lifetime, and even in the twentieth century only three more titles were typeset and a handful more were circulated in various forms of photographic reproduction. In sharp contrast, Menzan lived to see fifty-five of his titles published as woodblock prints, more than half of his total output. This quantity of printing of Menzan's very technical and lengthy works is all the more striking when we consider just what it meant to have something printed in eighteenth-century Japan.[44] Kyoto was the center of a thriving business in commercial publishing based on woodblock carving, which was preferred to movable type because of the greater flexibility for the intricate layers of punctuation of Japanese texts (especially Chinese written in Japan) and the ease of including illustrations. Books were an important part of life at all levels of society, but this was an era when a wild bestseller of a novel would have fewer than ten thousand copies printed. The cost of books is hard to grasp: an ordinary novel would cost as much as a month's worth of food, and even a cheap short story cost two weeks of food. Lending libraries were popular and would lend books for something like five days for 10 percent of the purchase price, still not a trivial amount. Buddhist books typically cost several times what secular works of similar size cost.

How many copies of Menzan's works were actually printed is altogether unclear, but woodblocks have to be recarved after only a few thousand copies at most. And the proprietor of the Baiyō bookstore (which owns the woodblocks of many of his works) claims that the blocks are the original carvings and laughs at the idea that anyone would have paid to have them recarved. He says this part of his business is sustained by a few professors who order copies for their classes. Menzan's works would perhaps have had an initial run of a few hundred copies, probably paid for in advance by subscription (as is implied by the prefaces). Perhaps it is not surprising that the woodblocks are not worn out after two hundred and fifty years: if we accept these rough estimates of prices, it seems that a copy of Menzan's *Source Texts* in ten volumes would have cost the equivalent of two to three years of food, at a time when food cost was a much greater part of living expenses.

Menzan's Impact

Menzan's influence came mostly from his published works, but in addition to his vast written output, he delivered a stream of public lectures, presided over sixteen major precept assemblies, counseled lay people who came to discuss Buddhist life with him, and led monastic retreats for decades. He was not an intimate of those in power, nor was he an attraction at countless public events, like Dōhaku, but he left an indelible mark on the school with his framework of Sōtō doctrinal studies and masterful textual research that is valuable even today. As the *Chronology* says in the concluding encomium, Menzan was a master of both exoteric and esoteric Buddhism and a great teacher of both Rinzai Zen and Sōtō Zen.

I suggested at the beginning that it is important to ask why it is that Dōgen is so important to Sōtō Zen. The reader might wonder if I am suggesting that the correct reply is "Because of Menzan." That, however, would be an unwarranted exaggeration, and indeed a disservice to Menzan himself. Dōgen's writings are themselves sufficient reason for Menzan's lifelong mission to understand them, beyond the fact that Dōgen was the first Japanese member of the lineage and useful to Menzan's agenda. Interest in what Dōgen wrote continues to grow stronger and more widespread year by year, even though it is over three hundred years since these reform efforts began. It is true, however, that Dōgen is not now, and probably never was, very approachable. His powers of language and his ability to inspire are not in question, but it is a daunting challenge to grasp what those inspiring words actually mean, much less put into practice the path he indicated. Menzan's work helped enormously to make it possible to understand Dōgen's writings, and his approach has set a tone for Sōtō Zen studies that has continued to the present.

Menzan brought learning and philological method to his study of Dōgen and presented his findings in print so that they were available to all lineages and all factions. With this flood of new material, the secret documents and rituals upon which rival Sōtō lineages based their power lost their luster, and in many cases were revealed by Menzan to be little more than unlearned forgeries completely lacking the pedigree of any connection to Dōgen. In this new light, the claim to authority based on Dōgen became something that could be tested against the scholarship of Menzan and others, not something that had to be accepted on trust. In other words, it was no longer enough to possess some precious chapters of the *Shōbōgenzō* and use that as a basis for claiming that one's own teaching and practice represented Dōgen's teachings. The learning that Menzan championed gave him the tools to construct a new tradition based upon old documents. He interpreted those texts in the light of contemporary values and adapted his readings to social conditions that were very different from those of Dōgen's time. With this interpretation, Dōgen became a powerful daily presence in Sōtō Zen, not just a revered but distant founder.

Menzan contributed to all aspects of the doctrinal discussion in Sōtō Zen, and even in an area such as precepts where his views did not prevail, his work brought together the resources and texts that defined the parameters of the arguments. It was probably his writing on monastic rules that had the greatest effect on the practical life of Sōtō monks in training. He demonstrated convincingly that Dōgen's monastic directions required a different building and a different routine than the rules widely in effect in early eighteenth-century Sōtō, which had been heavily influenced by Ōbaku Zen. His work led to procedures of monastic practice that were new to everyone, but which were clearly based on practices that could, in most cases at least, be dated to Dōgen's time. These practices are now a major component of the self-identity of the school, and Eiheiji is one of the best known of all Buddhist monasteries in the country. Dōgen and Eiheiji are so central to contemporary Sōtō Zen that it is hard to remember that in Menzan's time it was not even clear who Dōgen was or what he had really written, much less what his texts meant.

In the more popular arena, Menzan's most enduring legacy is his biography of Dōgen. The stories that Menzan presented, and the pictures that were soon attached to them, depicted a troubled young Dōgen who courageously overcame great obstacles in his quest for the dharma. It is now clear that this work is closer to a hagiography than was previously thought, but those images helped to hold together Sōtō Zen over the years and continue to inspire members of the community whether or not they read Dōgen's writings or engage in monastic practice. This life story, along with the more poetic and philosophical pieces from the *Shōbōgenzō*, contributed greatly to the popularity of Dōgen in Japan as well as in the West.

Despite his lifelong focus on Dōgen, Menzan studied and wrote about other Zen texts and spent much of his later life as an honored guest of major Rinzai Zen temples in Kyoto. Yet this aspect of his life is little noted, and it is striking that his major works of commentary on *kōan* collections are left out of the standard anthologies and generally overlooked, despite the fact that they enjoyed over a hundred years of reprintings in premodern times. In addition, he has been held up on very insufficient grounds as an early opponent of Rinzai *kanna* Zen, a position that is very important to the modern Sōtō school. Menzan is perhaps the beginning of the modern understanding of Dōgen, but it is not correct to attribute the opposition between Rinzai and Sōtō Zen schools to him, and a proper evaluation of his work must carefully bracket modern assumptions about this opposition.

But what of Menzan's failures? His quite mainstream ideas about precepts as the foundation for practice fell on deaf ears, and Sōtō Zen now treats precepts as little more than the topic for another esoteric ceremony with little moral emphasis. And his very compassionate idea that the thrashing of the hardwood *kyōsaku* should be replaced with gentle prods with a padded bamboo stick seems to have had no effect whatsoever. Unlike the modern strict separation from Rinzai, Menzan displayed little sectarian animosity, despite his rejection of the extremes of *kanna* practices. He respected many ways of dealing with *kōan* cases, from his own certification of awakening with a remark from a *kōan* to his commentaries on the great *kōan* collections. These, however, are just the kind of modern ideas and practices that have been emphasized in Zen communities in the West and perhaps will be followed some day.

The extent to which Sōtō Zen reflected and absorbed the values of Tokugawa society can hardly be exaggerated. Kagamishima expresses this very aptly when he asks himself whether or not we can accept the claim of Dōhaku and Menzan to have truly revived the old way of Dōgen. His answer is categorically no, because they were clearly men of their time, which was a very different time from the medieval period in which Dōgen lived.[45] Most important, Dōhaku and Menzan were willing to make compromises in order to keep the lineage going, to adapt to the stringent government controls and social demands. Furthermore, a return to Dōgen's way may not be possible because it may never have existed except as his own ideal. Dōgen died only ten years after moving away from Kyoto to begin building his own Zen monastery, properly constructed from the beginning according to his ideals. Eiheiji was not yet a fully functional monastery upon his early death. The spread of the lineage in the Middle Ages was possible because of the adaptation of Dōgen's message and introduction of new elements to fit the needs of the people.[45] In this sense, Menzan was not so much returning to the old ways as he was reading Dōgen for inspiration and for raw materials, and then writing for his own time.

Menzan needs to be seen in this light as both more creative and perhaps less literally accurate than has been previously thought. The Tokugawa reforms led to the present situation wherein Dōgen's preeminence is so central to the self-understanding of the school that contemporary writers usually speak of Dōgen Zen rather than Sōtō Zen. Such an exclusive focus on Dōgen constitutes nothing less than the creation of a new tradition of Zen within the old boundaries of the temples and people of the Sōtō lineage. As a better understanding of his accomplishments takes shape, Menzan may emerge from his chosen position in the shadow of Dōgen to take his rightful place as one of the major creative thinkers of Sōtō Zen.

NOTES

1. This chapter is revised and expanded from material that was first published as "The Life of Menzan Zuihō, Founder of Dōgen Zen," *Nichibunken Japan Review* 16 (2004): 67–100. My appreciation to the editor, James Baxter, and to the International Research Center for Japanese Studies for permission and for their support during the

work for that article. The beginnings of this research was carried out under the sponsorship of the Japan Foundation at Komazawa University, under Professor Kosaka Kiyū's patient tutelage. My thanks to all of these people and institutions for their generous support.

2. Carl Bielefeldt, "Recarving the Dragon: History and Dogma in the Study of Dōgen," in *Dōgen Studies*, edited by William R. LaFleur (Honolulu: University of Hawaii Press, 1985), pp. 21–24.

3. William M. Bodiford, *Sōtō Zen in Medieval Japan* (Honolulu: University of Hawaii Press, 1993), pp. 44–50.

4. William M. Bodiford, "Dharma Transmission in Sōtō Zen: Manzan Dōhaku's Reform Movement," *Monumenta Nipponica* 46/4 (1991): 423–451; and Lawrence William Gross, "Manzan Dōhaku and the Transmission of the Teaching," Ph.D. dissertation, Stanford University, 1998.

5. Kawamura Kōdō, *Shōbōgenzō no seiritsushiteki kenkyu* (Tokyo: Shunjūsha, 1987), pp. 396–397.

6. Helen J. Baroni, *Ōbaku Zen: The Emergence of the Third Sect of Zen in Tokugawa Japan* (Honolulu: University of Hawaii Press, 2000); and Jiang Wu, *Enlightenment in Dispute: The Reinvention of Chan Buddhism in Seventeenth-Century China* (New York: Oxford University Press, 2008).

7. Eric Hobsbawm, "Introduction: Inventing Traditions," in *The Invention of Tradition*, edited by Eric Hobsbawm and Terence Ranger (Cambridge: Cambridge University Press, 1983).

8. For a general discussion of the Sōtō reforms and the contemporary context, see David E. Riggs, "The Rekindling of a Tradition: Menzan Zuihō and the Reform of Japanese Sōtō Zen in the Tokugawa Era," Ph.D. dissertation, University of California, 2002.

9. Maruyama Masao, *Studies in the Intellectual History of Tokugawa Japan* (Princeton: Princeton University Press, 1974), pp. 39–51.

10. S-Goroku 3.

11. I have also consulted the compendium of details taken from the *Chronology* and other sources by Satō Hideko, a brief critical summary of his life by Kagamishima Genryū, and a more traditional presentation by Suzuki Kakuzen. For the two years he spent with his main teacher, Sonnō, the best source is Menzan's own record of Sonnō's life during that time, the *Record of the Teachings of the Hōei Era* (Kenmon hōei ki ZS-Hōgo). Kagamishima Genryū, *Manzan Menzan* (Tokyo: Kōdansha, 1988), pp. 47–59; Satō Hideko, "Eifukukaisan Menzan Zuihō Zenji nenpu," in *Menzan Zuihou Zenji nihyaku nijukai koenki kiyō*, edited by Eifukukai (Tokyo: Eifukukai, 1988); and Suzuki Kakuzen, "Menzan," in *Dōgen shisō no ayumi*, edited by Sōtōshū Shūgaku kenkyūjo (Tokyo: Yoshikawa kobunkan, 1993).

12. Peter Kornicki, *The Book in Japan: A Cultural History from the Beginnings to the Nineteenth Century* (Honolulu: University of Hawaii Press, 2001), pp. 136–158.

13. S-Shiden 328–329. For a complete translation see Peter Haskel, *Letting Go: The Story of Zen Master Tōsui* (Honolulu: University of Hawaii Press, 2001).

14. ZS-Hōgo 3:821. Ōkubo Dōshū, ed., *Dōgen Zenji zenshū* (Tokyo: Chikuma Shobō, 1969–1970), 2:189. T. 48.2003:190c27.

15. Ryūichi Abé, *Weaving of Mantra: Kūkai and the Construction of Esoteric Buddhist Discourse* (New York: Columbia University Press, 1999), pp. 43–44, 53–55.

16. T. 5–7.220.

17. Tamamuro Fumio, *Edo jidai to Sōtōshū no tenkai* (Tokyo: Sōtōshū shūmuchhō, 1999), p. 85; and Duncan Williams, "Representations of Zen: An Institutional and Social History of Sōtō Zen Buddhism in Edo Japan" (Ph.D. dissertation, Harvard University, 2000), p. 36. Forty *ryō* = 30,000 pounds of rice, which might today cost the same number of U.S. dollars. See Herman Ooms, *Tokugawa Village Practice: Class, Status, Power, Law* (Berkeley: University of California, 1996), p. 49; and Thomas C. Smith, *The Agrarian Origins of Modern Japan* (Stanford: Stanford University Press, 1959), pp. 6, 125.

18. ZS-Hōgo, pp. 463 and 465. For an annotated translation of the entire text, see David E. Riggs, "Meditation for Laymen and Laywomen: The *Jijuyūzanmai* of Menzan Zuihō," in *The Zen Canon*, edited by Steven Heine and Dale S. Wright (Oxford: Oxford University Press, 2004), pp. 247–269.

19. Komazawa Daigakunai Zengaku Dai Jiten Hensanjo, ed., *Zengaku daijiten* (Tokyo: Taishukan Shoten, 1985), p. 434.

20. S-Shingi, p. 208.

21. T. 82.2607:775–778. S-Shingi, p. 210.

22. Ōkubo Dōshū, *Dōgen Zenji shingi* (Tokyo: Iwanami Shoten, [1941] 1987), p. 284.

23. For an annotated translation of *Standards*, see David E. Riggs, "Meditation in Motion: Textual Exegesis in the Creation of Ritual," in *Zen Ritual*, edited by Steven Heine and Dale S. Wright (Oxford: Oxford University Press, 2006), pp. 223–259.

24. Kagamishima Genryū, "Edo jidai no tenkai: shūgi," in *Dōgen Zen no rekishi*, edited by Kagamishima Genryū and Tamaki Kōjirō (Tokyo: Shunjūsha, 1980); and Shibe Ken'ichi, "Tenkei," in *Dōgen shisō no ayumi*, edited by Sōtōshū Shūgaku kenkyūjo (Tokyo: Yoshikawa kobunkan, 1993).

25. ZS-Shitchū 669–680. For an overview of these reforms, see Bodiford, "Dharma Transmission in Sōtō Zen."

26. S-Shitchū. This text is discussed and selections translated in Ishikawa Rikizan, "Transmission of *Kirigami* (Secret Initiation Documents): A Sōtō Practice in Medieval Japan," in *The Kōan: Texts and Contexts in Zen Buddhism*, edited by Steven Heine and Dale S. Wright (New York: Oxford University Press, 2000), pp. 235–236.

27. ZS-Goroku vol. 2, T. 82.2604. *Taishō* pagination is provided for reference, but the reading is from the woodblock edition. For an interpretive modern Japanese rendering of the first five chapters, see Kagamishima, *Manzan Menzan*.

28. T. 82.2604.0728b08–b18.

29. Menzan does not specify, but he is apparently quoting from the *Mohe sengqilu*, T. 22.1425–513a.

30. T. 82. 2604.0726c01-0727b16.

31. S-Shiden 2.

32. Kawamura Kōdō, *Shohon taikō Eihei Kaisan Dōgen Zenji gyōjō Kenzeiki* (Tokyo: Taishukan Shoten, 1975), p. 7.

33. *Jakushū Eifuku Oshō sekkai*, S-Zenkai, p. 143.

34. Naka Takkei et al., eds., *Nihon Daizōkyō* (Tokyo: Nihon Daizōkyō Hensankai, 1914–1919), pp. 10: 79–153.

35. T. 48.2001.

36. T. 48.2004.

37. S-Shingi 209b.

38. T. 8.2003.

39. Komazawa, *Zengaku daijiten*, pp. 26–36.

40. Jinbō Nyōten and Andō Bun'ei, eds., *Shōbōgenzō chūkai zensho* (Tokyo: Nihon Sussho Kankōkai, 1956–1957); and Dai Honzan Eiheijinai Eihei Shōbōgenzō Shūsō Taisei Kankōkai, ed., *Eihei shōbōgenzō shūsho taisei* (Tokyo: Taishūkan Shoten, 1974–1982), 17: 697–708.

41. Kagamishima, *Manzan Menzan*, p. 6.

42. Urs App, "Chan/Zen's Greatest Encyclopaedist Mujaku Dōchū (1653–1744)," *Cahiers d'Extrême-Asie* 3 (1987): 155–174; and Yanagida Seizan, "Mujaku Dōchū no gakumon," *Zengaku Kenkyū* 55 (1966): 14–55.

43. Kagamishima, *Manzan Menzan*, p. 70.

44. Katshuhisa Moriya, "Urban Networks and Information Networks," in *Tokugawa Japan: The Social and Economic Antecedents of Modern Japan*, edited by Chie Nakane and Shinzaburō Oishi (Tokyo: University of Tokyo Press, 1990), p. 119; and Kornicki, *The Book*, pp. 179, 271–73.

45. Kagamishima, *Manzan Menzan*, pp. 4–5.

46. Bodiford, *Sōtō Zen*, p. 219.

7

The Use of Traps and Snares: Shaku Sōen Revisited

Michel Mohr

Kōgaku Sōen (1860–1919),[1] known during his lifetime as Shaku Sōen, was a teacher in the Rinzai denomination of Zen, affiliated successively with its Myōshinji branch, then with its Engakuji branch. His renown comes from his participation in the 1893 World's Parliament of Religions as chief of the Japanese delegation[2] and from the notoriety gained by his disciple Suzuki Daisetsu Teitarō (1870–1966). In spite of significant advances in the study of Sōen and his lineage,[3] serious Japanese scholarship on this figure is almost nonexistent and resources are dominated by sectarian accounts.

In 1909, Sōen published a collection of talks entitled *Record of Traps and Snares* (*Senteiroku*), an allusion to chapter 26 of the *Zhuangzi* that emphasizes the provisional function of words. According to the *Zhuangzi*, in the same way fish traps and rabbit snares only serve to catch prey, words should be forgotten once their meaning has become clear.[4] This metaphor served to emphasize the modest character of Sōen's talks, but his book, unfortunately, does not discuss language and its function. Ironically, as this collection records Sōen's candid views on the Russo-Japanese War, the author fell, to a certain extent, into his own trap. We will return to this crucial issue below when we deal with Sōen's views on war.

This chapter challenges some received ideas about Sōen. After providing a sketch of his life, I will examine the construction of Sōen's image as a Zen master, while occasionally filling some of the copious blanks left in his biography. This will lead us to examine attempts to deconstruct the master's image, either by casting doubt on his morality or by highlighting his links with militarism. Finally, I suggest reflecting on how the reevaluation of Sōen's image could move us closer to recovering his distinctive voice.

Sōen's Early Profile

Sōen's childhood and the circumstances surrounding his entrance into the Buddhist clergy are depicted in an autobiographical account, which was probably written in his early forties.[5] Sōen was born in Takahama in the west of present Fukui prefecture. His father, Ichinose Goemon Nobusuke, was the descendant of a samurai family from the Aizu domain in the northeast, which had embraced agriculture after moving to Fukui in the seventeenth century. Sōen's mother Yasuko was from the Hirata family.[6] They had six children, two sons and four daughters. Their elder son was Chūtarō.[7] Sōen, who was the youngest of the six, was given the name Tsunejirō. Sōen succinctly states, "our family was not as rich as in the past, but the household including more than ten members was living comfortably," and mentions that they had at least one maid.[8] He also discloses the fact that since childhood he was hot-tempered[9] and had a weak constitution.

His elder brother Chūtarō played a crucial role in Sōen's decision to become a monk. Chūtarō had frequented Buddhist temples since an early age and occasionally stayed at Jōkōji in Obama (Fukui prefecture), a Rinzai temple. Chūtarō had wanted to become a monk, but was not allowed to do so because of his duties as the elder son of the family. Thus, the young Sōen was persuaded to accomplish his sibling's dream and recalled, "I just took the place of my elder brother." Yet, the decision was not taken against his will. Perhaps to make it sound casual, he mentions how his brother used to tell him that even emperors become disciples of the Dharma (that is, listened to monks preaching the Buddhist teachings), and how he resolved to choose this path "without a precise objective," but rather out of "juvenile curiosity."

Sōen was ten years old in 1870,[10] when Ekkei Shuken (1810–1884)—a widely respected priest from the Rinzai temple Myōshinji[11] who was also a relative[12]— came to visit his family in Takahama. Chūtarō managed to convince his parents to entrust their younger son to Ekkei, who conditionally agreed by telling Sōen, "if you intend to become a great monk I will consent to it." First, the boy was given the ordination name Sokō, meaning "the light of the patriarchs," but his name was changed to Sōen ("expression of the principle"), the name of another novice who had died from sickness.[13]

Crucial Years of Wandering Practice

After the usual years of apprenticeship as a novice under Ekkei, mostly at Tōkaian (the Myōshinji subtemple reserved for the chief abbot), Sōen was entrusted to a subtemple of Kenninji, in the heart of Kyoto, where he studied and practiced under the direction of Shungai Tōsen (1830–1875), the abbot of Ryōsokuin.[14] When he came at age fourteen, only a handful of disciples were living there, but as Shungai's reputation spread their number quickly reached forty. Because of this, they chose to form a group of dedicated young student-monks who lived in a semi-autonomous way.[15] They gave the name Forest of Gathered Jewels (*Gungyokurin*)[16] to their improvised school and lodged in the adjacent Gokokuin. Among Sōen's description of his adolescent years, his perception of the Kenninji's surroundings is particularly interesting:

> Kenninji is located in the midst of Kyoto's amusement quarter. Right outside the temple gate are the Gion and Miyagawa wards, famous breeding grounds for wasting money in drink and pleasures. In short, these are the demons' dwellings (*makutsu*). Younger codisciples and I thought that it was fascinating to be in such a place observing the strict monastic rules, a Zen monastery popping up at the very core of these demons' dwellings, and we were all studying hard.[17]

When Shungai died in 1875 at age forty-five, it was a shock to Sōen and his fellow monks. They decided to engage in a mourning retreat period of forty-nine days in memory of their deceased teacher. This was to culminate with the *Rōhatsu sesshin*, the harshest week of meditation training held in December. Sōen was sitting with Mokurai Sōen (Takeda, 1854–1930),[18] a fellow monk of weak constitution, who later became the chief abbot of Kenninji;[19] Sōen reports having benefited immensely from this monk's encouragements. Although the expression is intentionally veiled out of modesty, it is during this *sesshin* that Sōen, who was now fifteen, reached a decisive awareness after having been sitting for days in the cold: "It is really at that time that I realized the existence of this One Great Matter right under my surplice (*yo ga kesaka ni kono ichidaiji aru o seishita*)."[20]

This marks the beginning of a precocious spiritual itinerary that led Sōen to consult several teachers, always recommended by his first spiritual mentor, Ekkei, who resided at Myōshinji but with whom he remained in close contact. Eventually, these early steps led Sōen to travel in and outside Japan, and to gain access to the highest rank in the Rinzai hierarchy. As described later, Sōen's monastic career culminated in 1883 with his certification by Kōsen Sōon (Imakita, 1816–1892) as Dharma heir.[21]

The Construction of Sōen's Image

Sōen's image as a Zen master and the construction of his portrayal for posterity includes four main layers: 1. autobiographical accounts, 2. biographies by disciples and admirers, 3. writings by apologists, and 4. the translation of his works.

Accounts by Sōen Himself

The first layer includes the autobiographical manuscript *Splits in a Monk's Robe* (*Koromo no hokorobi*), which ends with an account of the death of Gisan Zenrai in March 1878, as well as Sōen's voluminous correspondence and articles or books published while he was alive. Here, an important remark must be made concerning Sōen's so-called "Complete Works" (*Shaku Sōen zenshū*, published in 1929–1930). These ten volumes are by no means "complete." They mostly include minor textual commentaries, and comprise less than one-fifth of Sōen's published works.

The vast majority of Sōen's "writings" consists of oral teachings, written down by disciples or auditors, presumably with some accuracy. Stenography was commonly used since the Meiji period,[22] and some of Sōen's recorded talks include notes concerning reactions in the audience, such as laughter or applause,[23] and occasionally ellipses indicating that the transcriber was unable to catch a quote from the classics.[24] Texts published while Sōen was alive are likely to have been checked to some degree by the author, but the numerous anthologies of his teachings published after his death in 1919 may reflect his thoughts less faithfully.

The only publications actually written down by Sōen himself are letters, serials,[25] newspaper articles, and his various travel diaries written in classical Chinese. These diaries reveal the sequence of Sōen's major trips abroad and the publications following each of them:

(1) Trip to Ceylon (Sri Lanka) and Thailand from March 8, 1887 to October 12, 1889. He wrote *Buddhism in the Southwest* (*Seinan no bukkyō*),[26] published in January 1889—before his return—and *Chronicles of the Island of Ceylon* (*Seirontōshi*), published in April 1890. Parts of a draft entitled *Diary of a Journey to the West* (*Saiyū nikki*) were discovered in 1936 and published in facsimile edition in 1941 (a newly edited version was printed in 2001).

(2) Trip to Chicago from August 4 to October 29, 1893. He wrote *A Glance at the World's Parliament of Religion* (*Bankoku shūkyō taikai ichiran*), published in November 1893 (and reprinted several times), together with *Diary of a Trip*

to America (*Tobei nikki*).²⁷ This publication was based on notes taken by the interpreter, Nomura Yōzō, as Sōen acknowledges in his own explanatory notes.²⁸

(3) Trip to Manchuria. Shortly after the declaration of war against Russia (February 10, 1904), Sōen left Kamakura on March 12 (he spent some time in Hiroshima, departing from Hiroshima on April 21 and landing in Jinzhou on the Liaoning Peninsula on May 7). He went to the front in Manchuria, which he left on July 12, returning to Kamakura on July 25,²⁹ where he wrote *Journal on Defeating Demons* (*Gōma nisshi*), published in December 1904.

(4) Trip to the United States, Europe, and Asia. He left Kamakura on June 11, 1905, and arrived in San Francisco on June 27. He remained in the United States until April 23, 1906. With a gift received from the Russells (discussed below), he then visited England, arriving in London on April 30. After having been to Scotland, France, Germany, Austria, and Italy, he took the boat in Naples on July 4 and headed toward Asia via Egypt. He stopped in Ceylon between July 20 and 26, before continuing to India. He then returned to Colombo on August 8, and finally left Ceylon on August 17, reaching Kōbe on September 4, 1906. He wrote *Idle Conversations* (*Kankattō*), which was published in April 1907,³⁰ and *Diary of a Monk in Europe and America* (*Ōbei unsuiki*), published in October of the same year. Portions of these works were included in *Sermons of a Buddhist Abbot*, which carries the date 1906, but was printed in January 1907.³¹

(5) Trip to Korea and China at the invitation of the South Manchurian Railway. He left on October 8, 1912, from Shimonoseki and arrived in Pusan the following morning. He then left Changchun on October 31, earlier than expected, because of sickness; he was accompanied by Hōgaku Jikō (Seigo, 1875–1942)³² and Taibi Keishun (Shaku, 1882–1964), who took notes. A collection of talks he gave on various occasions during this trip was published as *A Guidebook to Practice* (*Shuyō no shiori*) in 1913, reprinted as *The Flower Held up and the Subtle Smile* (*Nenge mishō*) in 1915.

(6) Trip to Korea and China. He left on September 9, 1917, from Shimonoseki and arrived in Pusan on the evening of the same day; he returned to Nagasaki on November 15, 1917. He wrote *The Clouds of Yan [Hebei] and the Water of Chu [Hebei-Hunan]* (*En'un sosui*), published in May 1918.

Sōen's autobiographical pieces are mostly narrated from an almost impersonal perspective, as if he were describing someone else's deeds. These texts stand in sharp contrast to the "confession" genre that was more common among Chinese literati.³³ One Japanese author even characterizes Sōen's accounts as "masterpieces of reportage."³⁴ As we will see below, Sōen nevertheless occasionally revealed some of his own feelings.

Biographies by Disciples and Admirers

After Sōen's death in November 1919, Nagao Daigaku (also known as Nagao Sōshi, 1894–1965)[35] brought into print *Zen Master Sōen's Face* (*Sōen zenji no menmoku*, 1920), a first attempt to perpetuate his teacher's memory. He followed with *Those Who Surrounded Zen Master Sōen* (*Sōen zenji to sono shūi*, 1923), *A Selection of Zen Master Sōen's Exposition of Mu* (*Sōen zenji musetsushū*, 1925), and finally, the invaluable *Anthology of Zen Master Sōen's Letters* (*Sōen zenji shokanshū*, 1931). One of Sōen's former assistants, Taibi Keishun, also compiled his *Yearly Biography of Ryōgakutsu* (*Ryōgakutsu nenjiden*), which was not published until 1942. Ryōgakutsu (Lankā's Den) is Sōen's "chamber name" as a teacher, an allusion to his stay in Ceylon.

Writings by Apologists

The third layer includes works by apologists who did not directly know Sōen, such as Inoue Zenjō (1911–2006). In 1941, Inoue became the abbot of Tōkeiji—the temple where Sōen spent the later part of his life.[36] In the postwar period, Inoue held a near monopoly of all publications in Japanese related to Sōen, due to his position as the guardian of primary sources kept at the Matsugaoka treasure-house (*Matsugaoka hōzō*) within his temple.[37] Regardless of this priest's good intentions and his sometimes meticulous work, publications that saw the light of day under his supervision reflected a single purpose: to demonstrate how great a teacher Sōen was. Deploring the fact that most people ignored Sōen, but were familiar with the name of Natsume Sōseki (who briefly visited him at Tōkeiji), Inoue wrote: "My intention is to praise Sōen while using Sōseki as a pretext" (for attracting people).[38] Unsurprisingly, the October 1968 special issue of the journal *Zenbunka* in commemoration of the fiftieth death anniversary of Sōen (including an article by Inoue) contains contributions that all reflect the same hagiographic slant. Let us examine one example of how the sectarian bias informed Sōen's biography.

THE KEIŌ COLLEGE EPISODE. In his afterword to Sōen's *Diary of a Journey to the West*, Suzuki Daisetsu writes that "after having completed his three years at Keiō College he [Sōen] further wanted to spend three years abroad."[39] Using a similar shortcut, Nagao Daigaku also states, "In the spring of 1887 [Sōen] graduated from Keiō College."[40] The histories of Engakuji, of course, follow suit[41] and, as far as I know, Sōen's graduation from Keiō College has always been taken for granted.[42] Thus, the common assumption is that Sōen, exceptional in every task he undertook, swiftly completed his studies and then left for his first trip abroad. This contributed to the image of a Zen master who was open to modern forms of learning. The archives kept at Keiō University, however, tell us an altogether different story.

Admittedly, Sōen's choice to enter college can be described as a yearning for new approaches to learning. The way Sōen overcame the early opposition of his teacher Kōsen and eventually obtained his permission after the intercession of Torio Tokuan (Koyata, 1847–1905) constitutes one of the few relatively well-known episodes in Sōen's carrier.[43] Sōen's move—highly unusual for a Zen priest at this time—is attested by the name Shaku Sōen inscribed in the *Register of Entrances into the Keiō College Society* in Sōen's handwriting on September 1, 1885.[44]

At that time, Keiō College functioned with a system of several different sections that reflected the students' language proficiency, since instruction was largely given in English by foreign instructors. Fortunately, the archives of the Fukuzawa Research Institute contain the complete list of all students enrolled at Keiō, with the details of their grades. This allows us to see precisely when Shaku Sōen was affiliated with this institution, and the sections in which he studied, as well as the name of fellow students. The college records indicate that Sōen attended classes during a total of four trimesters, from the third trimester of 1885 to the third trimester of 1886, but never graduated. Details of his study pattern during this period of fifteen months is worth paying some attention to, because all sorts of legends about this abound, even in supposedly serious publications. During the first trimester, in September 1885, Sōen was enrolled in the section "Outside Curriculum" (*kagai*), and was "promoted to [the next] level (*tōkyū*)."[45]

During the next semester, his total grade was 394, with the best student in his class having a grade of 762, and Sōen's entry does not include "promoted to the next level."[46] He received a zero grade for the final examination in both foreign languages and mathematics, two tests he might simply have chosen not to take. This appears to confirm his limited command of English. He did very well in Chinese classics (100/100), but during his studies in the temples he had had little exposure to these newer branches of learning. Out of forty-eight students in this class, Sōen is listed as number thirty-three in the order of performance. The degree of effort Sōen invested in this exercise is unknown, but this ranking must have been a humiliating experience for someone who was already certified as a designated Rōshi.

For the following semester, in May 1886, we find Sōen listed in the Separate Curriculum (*bekka*), sixth grade. Here the requirements were slightly different, and he was the best of his small class of eight students where mathematics was not taught.[47] This was probably not a selective curriculum, so that he was automatically promoted to the next fifth grade, where we find him during the third trimester of 1886, again the best of his small class of ten students.[48] This constitutes the last recorded instance of Shaku Sōen's presence in the archives of Keiō College, and suggests that Sōen formally terminated his studies in December 1886. Had he intended to pursue his studies in this institution until graduation, he would have needed four additional trimesters to move from grade four to grade one. Unsurprisingly, Sōen's hagiographers pass rather quickly on this episode in Sōen's life as a student at Keiō College, which was undistinguished.

CURRICULUM AND MISSIONARIES. During Sōen's affiliation with Keiō College, he came into contact with Christian teachers. In his October 9, 1885, letter to Hasegawa Keitoku,[49] a friend who had just entered the Myōshinji monastery, Sōen mentions foreign mentors and the pressure he felt as a student:

> The tigers of physics and philosophy in front and the wolf of Christianity in the back are simultaneously coming [to me], each of them sharpening its claws and showing its teeth. For the time being, let us put aside the relative merits of Christianity. From the first they [the Christians] are experts in administrating the world's resources and are extremely good in using science. Concerning these two aspects, they are doubtlessly far better than the Buddhists (*naikyōsha*). Presently, in our college we have [two] hired lecturers called Lloyd[50] and Kitchin.[51] Both of them are missionaries of the non-Buddhist teachings (*gekyō*), but undeniably they are also great scholars who have graduated from universities in England and America, those countries claiming to be civilized.[52]

One may wonder what readings were given to the students. *The Mission Field* of July and October 1885 provides the list of classes taught by Arthur Lloyd (1852–1911). In history, students were assigned Parry's *World History*, and Quackenbos's *History of the United States, History of England*, and *Universal History*.[53] In law and philosophy, they read Fawcet's *Political Economy*; in elementary law, *Logic* by Mill;[54] and they had lectures on international law, as well as mental and moral philosophy. In the so-called literature classes they actually focused on history and political science, reading Guizot's *History of Civilization*,[55] Macauley's *Essays*, Mill's *On Liberty*, and Mill's *Representative Government*. Their classes in mathematics included arithmetic, algebra, geometry, bookkeeping, and trigonometry. In English, they had classes in grammar, reading, dictation, composition, conversation, and rhetoric.[56]

Such a curriculum appears rather dry, and it is understandable that Sōen was not thrilled by the prospect of having to spend another year and a half struggling with these textbooks. Nevertheless, the decision to quit this course of study must have been a difficult one, especially because of the support he had requested from Torio Tokuan. Unfortunately, there is no decisive piece of evidence allowing us to fathom Sōen's motivation for choosing to move on to a completely different approach and to focus for a while on the roots of the Buddhist tradition outside Japan. Some allusions are found in "The Career of Master Shaku Sōen" (*Shaku Sōen Zenji no keireki*), but this anonymous piece—likely to have been written by Nagao Daigaku[57]—appears to be based on hearsay. In any case, it strikes us as an unusual account for a text included in the "official" biography.

According to this source, while studying at Keiō, Sōen had gained a reputation for hanging out with friends and indulging in noisy drinking, embarrassing his fellow students with boisterous utterances. Yet at the same time, he appeared distressed (*hanmon*) at his own future in the clergy and was even considering the possibility of returning to secular life.[58] Apparently informed of these rumors, Kōsen discussed the issue with Fukuzawa, so that Fukuzawa was entrusted with the delicate task of using tact to convince Sōen to stay on the monastic track. Fukuzawa suggested: "Your determination is to find the Way, what about traveling to Ceylon and investigating the source [of your tradition]? You should not give up your original intention!"[59]

The above story indicates a sort of existential crisis experienced by Sōen when he completed his monastic training, after reaching the goal he set for himself since childhood. His experiment with Western approaches to learning obviously did not provide the sort of answer he was looking for, and he wanted to postpone institutional appointments in order to pursue his "long cultivation" (*chōyō*) outside the denomination's fold. Sōen eventually followed the advice of his teachers, setting out for an adventurous journey to South Asia. Another way to look at what happened would be to consider that Fukuzawa, who intended to improve morality within his institution, found an ingenious way to deflect the energy of his embarrassing Zen student, while giving him an opportunity to discover how strictly the precepts were observed in other Buddhist countries.

This might also be interpreted as an indication that Sōen, as gifted as he may have been in some areas, was pushed by a form of restlessness, and that although he had survived the monastic regimen, he hardly could endure academic constraints. Sōen's dislike for the academic approach can be seen in his publications, which reflect his wide repertoire in the classics and remarkable skills in oratory, but provide very little analysis and certainly do not display philosophical rigor. This inclination is even more visible when comparing the Japanese original of some of his discourses with their English translations.

192 ZEN MASTERS

Further Image-building through Translations

The role of Suzuki Daisetsu and other editors in "arranging" Sōen's writings for Western consumption was a crucial part of the process of building his image as a master. Here I will examine only three examples: the first address delivered at the 1893 World's Parliament of Religions; lectures given during his stay in the United States between June 1905 and April 1906; and a talk given after his return to Japan in September 1906.

ADDRESS AT THE 1893 WORLD'S PARLIAMENT OF RELIGIONS. In spite of a growing body of research dealing with the 1893 conference and the issues at stake, so far no researcher appears to have compared the Japanese original of Sōen's address with its English translation. There seems to be a good excuse for this neglect: the two texts are so different that at first glance they seem to have little in common.

Concerning the Japanese versions, at least four different editions of the same text are available, but they are almost identical except for added punctuation and minor stylistic changes.[60] Similarly, the two main English versions are almost identical.[61] What is striking is the great divergence of the English text from the original. The translators removed most technical terms and allusions to the sutras, and gratuitously invented almost poetical examples to illustrate Sōen's intent.[62] For instance, the beginning of Sōen's address in Japanese can be rendered thus:

> Ladies and Gentlemen, all the various things (*hinbutsu*)[63] succeed to each other in the unlimited [dimension of] time and are aligned in the endless [dimension of] space, but what are they made of? As far as I can tell, they emerge as the result of two mental causes (*shinteki gen'in*). And these two mental causes are [our] nature (*shō*) and [our] emotions (*jō*).

In the English version attributed to Suzuki Daisetsu this was expanded to:

> If we open our eyes and look at the universe, we observe the sun and moon, and the stars on the sky; mountains, rivers, plants, animals, fishes and birds on the earth. Cold and warmth come alternately; shine and rain change from time to time without ever reaching an end. Again, let us close our eyes and calmly reflect upon ourselves. From morning to evening, we are agitated by the feelings of pleasure and pain, love and hate; sometimes full of ambition and desire, sometimes called to the utmost excitement of reason and will. Thus the action of mind is like an endless issue of a spring of water. As the

phenomena of the external world are various and marvelous, so is the internal attitude of human mind. Shall we ask for the explanation of these marvelous phenomena? Why is the universe in a constant flux? Why do things change? Why is the mind subjected to constant agitation? For these Buddhism offers only one explanation, namely, the law of cause and effect.

This gives a general feeling of the contrast between Sōen's conciseness and the extended development of the English "translation," and a measure of the considerable liberties taken in interpreting Sōen's prose. In defense of the translator, it should be noted that some sections of the Japanese text as it stood would have remained extremely obscure to an unprepared American audience, because it required too much background knowledge, and its organization was rather chaotic, with a considerable amount of repetition.

LECTURES GIVEN IN THE UNITED STATES, 1905–1906. Publications in English by Suzuki Daisetsu, such as *Sermons of a Buddhist Abbot* (1907), constitute a special category in the construction of Sōen's image. When he published this anthology, Suzuki already felt confident of his command of English and his ability to adjust the teachings of Sōen to the tastes of Western readership. Thus he frankly wrote about the transcripts of Sōen's teachings entrusted to him: "In going over these documents critically, I found that I could not make use of all the material as it stood; for the talks during his stay on the Pacific coast were mostly of a very informal nature, and a copy of them prepared from shorthand notes needed a great deal of revision."[64]

After enumerating some of the choices made in the revision process, Suzuki further claimed, "In spite of these alterations and the liberties I have taken with the manuscripts of the Reverend Shaku, these lectures remain a faithful representation of the views as well as the style of preaching of my venerable teacher and friend."[65] In this instance, no Japanese original is left that would allow us to compare Suzuki's rendering with the discourses as they were given, but the *Sermons of a Buddhist Abbot* should be treated with caution, for they reflect Suzuki's own anticipation of what American readers might have expected.

"REFLECTIONS ON AN AMERICAN JOURNEY." Such editorial "improvement" based on Sōen's sayings did not end with the work of Suzuki Daisetsu. Another recent example is provided by Wayne S. Yokoyama and the way he translated the "Reflections on an American Journey" based on Sōen's account (1993). This piece is presented as "an adapted translation of *Tobei zakkan*" included in the first volume of Sōen's complete works.⁶⁶ Actually, this text was itself based on the presentation given by Sōen shortly after his return from the United States in September 1906, at the Eastern Association (*Tōhō kyōkai*), a piece included in *Record of Traps and Snares*. This first published version is much closer to the style of oral delivery; it contains salutations to the audience and verbose passages that have been cut in the complete works. This talk by Sōen and its successive incarnations, first in Japanese, then in English, provides us with a rare detailed example of how editorial choices were made and of what was left out in the process.

Aside from minor details eliminated to make the text more concise, the two successive filters applied to Sōen's prose reveal some of the criteria adopted by both the editor and the translator. First, in the version included in the complete works, the text was completely rewritten and the rather emotional account⁶⁷ of Sōen's acquaintance with Ida Evelyn Russell (1862–1917)⁶⁸ was reduced to a bare minimum. The first address recorded in *Senteiroku* included the following seven sections:

1. The Purpose of the Journey was My Own Benefit, the Benefit of Others, and Gratitude
2. The Motivation for Going to America: The Zen of Mrs. Russell
3. Activities as a Guest of the Russell Family
4. Tour to the Eastern Part of the United States
5. Trip to Europe as a Practice for My Own Benefit
6. The West Is Individualist: Piety Toward One's Wife
7. Pilgrimage to Buddhist Sites

It was recast in the following way for the collected works:⁶⁹

1. [How Americans] Were Inspired to Do Zazen
2. Sentient Beings Are All My Children⁷⁰
3. An Excellent Teaching [Found] in Japan
4. Prince Shōtoku Was a Great Hit

In the first version we see a much more personal account, where human relations and the encounter with the Russells is placed at the center of the story. Modesty being the rule, Sōen first diminishes the weight put on this trip, saying that it was planned "aimlessly" and was devoid of ambition and purpose. Then he frankly describes one of his reasons for going to the United States as being the wish to improve his health (*kenkō o yashinau ga tame*) and the additional incentive of the possibility that it might benefit others (*rita*).⁷¹ This was carefully excised from the version in the complete works and therefore is not visible in the English translation, either.

The English translation of the passage depicting Ida Russell's initial motivation for practicing meditation before coming to Japan includes the following seemingly innocuous passage: "In today's world of open scholarship, the scholarly investigations of religion made her realize that there are other religions in lands outside of Christiandom, religions beyond Christianity" (Yokoyama, p. 140).

What is remarkable here is that in the Japanese text Sōen said: "There are certainly religions *superior* to Christianity" (*kirisutokyō ijō no shūkyō*).[72] Sōen was here speculating about the reasons that led Mrs. Russell to such curiosity for non-Christian teachings, and he imagined how she thought that "there must be more to religion than Christianity." In this case we see the translator, consciously or not, editing Sōen's discourse to lessen the potential impact of his words on Western readership. It is often in those subtle emendations or in word choices that undisclosed intentions appear. There are other talks by Sōen that also convey the impression that he happened to speak frankly or even naively to his audience. One example is where he recalls that, despite having tried several times to quit smoking and drinking, he kept failing until he was invited to stay with the Russells.[73]

Overall, Sōen's original addresses were definitely more straightforward than subsequent versions. The alterations applied by editors and translators to his texts build an impersonal image transcending human emotions and worldly considerations. In other words, editorial work contributed to remove traces of weakness and the trivial dimensions of Sōen's character, and emphasized the solemn character of the master and his equanimity.

The Other Sides of Sōen and His Stance on War

Not many authors overtly challenged Sōen's authority or sincerity as a Zen master. Two of them, Inoue Shūten (1880–1945) and Brian Victoria, deserve closer examination. The first, Inoue Shūten, was a disgruntled former Sōtō priest who began advocating pacifism after returning from the Russo-Japanese War. Some of Inoue's favorite topics were social (in)justice, the consequences of Asian colonization, and the arrogance of Zen teachers who lacked proper understanding of Chinese sources.[74] In the 1910s, Inoue was one of the few Japanese intellectuals who had traveled to Theravada countries and to China, but unlike Sōen, he considered Buddhism abroad more authentic. Tensions between Inoue and Suzuki Daisetsu, fueled by Inoue's criticism of Sōen, resulted in the exchange of a series of virulent articles that came to a head in 1912, marking the definitive breakup between the two men.[75]

The real issues dividing Suzuki and Inoue seem to have been their respective positions toward the emperor. Yet Inoue resorted to a below-the-belt tactic, insinuating that Sōen was a depraved monk: "One hears it was common for the priest Sōen when he returned from a preaching travel to make his assistant go back to the temple first; he would then go alone and stay overnight in the pleasure quarters (*karyū no chimata*)."[76]

Whatever the veracity of such hearsay, this way of publicizing gossip did not serve Inoue well and seems to have undermined his credibility as a scholar. Yet the testimony of historian Haga Kōshirō (1908–1996), who engaged in a convoluted defense of Sōen, ironically reinforces the impression that these rumors were not entirely unfounded. He wrote,

"According to what I directly heard from Sōen's Dharma-heir Sōkatsu, Sōen was extremely strict in his observance of the precepts and in his behavior until 1898, when he gave his certification to Sōkatsu."[77]

Aside from his academic career, Haga was also a Zen practitioner in the lineage of Tatsuta Eisan (1893–1979), who had been certified by Sōkatsu. Such background suggests that Haga's conversation with Sōkatsu was more than an outsider's interview. Because this also evokes the above-mentioned story about Sōen's reputation at Keiō College, it might indicate some form of deep ambiguity in Sōen's character and demeanor. This dimension obviously was never publicly discussed and does not allow us to advance further hypothesis. Let us therefore examine aspects of Sōen's life that are better documented, if not necessarily less ambiguous.

Sōen's views on war deserve to be scrutinized, especially in the wake of Brian Victoria's publications, *Zen at War* (1997) and *Zen War Stories* (2003). Victoria forced the Japanese clergy to face their war responsibility, and he has thus helped to open the debate on a topic considered taboo in the postwar period. His discussion of Sōen, however, is limited to presenting him as a typical example of one of many who "promoted the idea of a close relationship between Buddhism and war."[78] Before we examine more closely the sources used to support this statement, two elements of background information should be taken into account: the way Sōen experienced the British presence in Asia, and the informed opinion of one of his colleagues with whom he had practiced in Kyoto.

Sōen's Views on Colonialism

We have already seen the circumstances surrounding Sōen's departure for Ceylon. Sōen wrote about his impressions abroad in a series of letters to Fukuzawa Yukichi, which were partially published in the *Jiji Shinpō*, the newspaper owned by

Fukuzawa.[79] They clearly reveal Sōen's indignation at the way the local population was treated by the British in Ceylon. For instance, in a letter published on July 5, 1887, he observed:

> Already 70 or 80 years have elapsed since this country began to be plundered (*ryakudatsu*) by England. From that time onward everyone well knows how the British government has been ill-treating (*gyakutai*) the natives (*domin*). Just to mention one extreme example, from age 15 to age 60 each single citizen is required to pay a tax [equivalent to] 25 *sen* every year, [indicating] that people are treated exactly in the same way merchandise (*shinamono dōyō*) would be handled.

Sōen's depictions of life under the colonial regime abound in details, such as taxes imposed on each coconut, one of the most important resources of the island. What is important for our purpose is to note that his descriptions are not purely factual; they reveal Sōen's acute perception that the colonial rule was profoundly unfair and in direct contradiction to ideals of universal justice proclaimed in the books he had studied at Keiō.

Aside from Sōen's direct experience of being treated almost like an animal on board the German ship that took him to Ceylon,[80] the above-mentioned outrage may have been furthered by contacts he had with the Theosophical Society during his stay. In a letter composed on his way back to Japan, on June 19, 1889, he wrote to fellow monks:

> I left Galle[81] two or three days ago and, presently, I am staying at the Theosophical Society in Colombo, waiting for a reliable ship. . . . The other day (June 16), Mr. Olcott (accompanied by three Japanese Shinshū priests) arrived here coming back from his trip to Japan. . . . At tonight's meeting Mr. Olcott spoke about the present situation in Japan and expressed his wish that in the future friendship between this country and ours would be further promoted.[82]

Given the anti-missionary agenda of Henry Steel Olcott (1832–1907),[83] it is not surprising that at that time the two men shared an aspiration to resist the Western presence in Asia. They were both witnesses to the geopolitical unbalance brought about by the Industrial Revolution and the rise of Western military power across the world. Later in Sōen's career, though, we see that he was much less critical of Japan's colonial role in Korea and, after having deplored the excessive presence of Christian missionaries there, he concluded "I think that we must bear the responsibility of transplanting Japanized Buddhism in that land to guide (*yūdō*) the Koreans."[84] Sōen's criticism of colonization appears thus to be limited to its Western manifestations, and reflects a lack of distance from his own context. It is therefore reasonable to wonder whether the frustration he experienced in Ceylon and the political awareness derived from this limited exposure to life abroad led him to justify violence and, if so, to what degree.

Mokurai's Understanding of the Word "Killing"

Before we further discuss Sōen's position, it is important to see how his friend Mokurai Sōen clarified the usage of a word crucial for our inquiry. Here is how he explained his understanding of the verb "to kill" (*korosu*), beginning with an anecdote:

> Quite a long time ago, the military officer Torio[85] came to me and, when our conversation moved to "killing" he said, "my profession precisely consists in killing people." Yet, when I use this word it doesn't mean to kill the physical body (*shintai*). To kill the mind (*kokoro*), to kill craving (*yokushin*), to kill the sixth consciousness [sic] and the eighth consciousness, to kill them all completely, this is what I mean.[86]

In case this could be interpreted as a rhetorical device to justify Japanese militarism, let us have a glimpse at the metaphor of "the sword that gives life versus the sword that kills people" as it is used in the classics. In the eleventh-century Chinese *Jingde chuandeng lu*, we find the following critique of Ciming Chuyuan (also known as Shishuang, 986–1039): "Although Shishuang has the blade killing people, he lacks the sword giving them life."[87]

Classical sources use "life" and "death" in the spiritual sense, with "death" or "killing" indicating the removal of bondage and delusion or the absorption in *samadhi*, while "life" refers to the "revival" coinciding with the reemergence of the true self. Either aspect can be emphasized, depending on the skills of the teacher, as indicated by a phrase in the *Anthology of Verses Used in Zen Monasteries* (*Zenrin kushū*):

> Manjusri holds aloft the sword that slays people.
> Vimalakirti draws the sword that gives people life.[88]

Such textual sources do not exclude the possibility that the metaphor's meaning could have been distorted by Zen teachers. Yet it is clear they were originally used in the context of meditation practice, where the primary concern is dying to one's small self and awakening. This should facilitate a serene discussion of Sōen's perspective, without, on the other hand, displaying any complacency toward his political leanings or toward atrocities perpetrated by the military.

Sōen's Writings about War

As discussed previously, English texts attributed to Sōen, such as *Sermons of a Buddhist Abbot*, should be taken with a grain of salt, because they reflect to a large extent Suzuki Daisetsu's own ideas and expressions. In addition, Suzuki and Sōen's tour of the United States should be understood in the context of Japan's victory in the Russo-Japanese War of 1905. This victory had attracted the attention of many Westerners, who were intrigued by what could have made this mysterious Far Eastern country powerful enough to beat the Russian empire. In the same year, Okakura Tenshin (1862–1913) wrote "The average Westerner... was wont to regard Japan as barbarous while she indulged in the gentle arts of peace: he calls her civilized since she began to commit wholesale slaughter on Manchurian battlefields."[89] Sōen and Suzuki Daisetsu no doubt capitalized on this fascination. In any case, the *Sermons of a Buddhist Abbot* cannot serve as the primary resource for discussing Sōen's stance on war; one must turn to his publications in Japanese.

Among several addresses where Sōen deals with this topic, his "Attainment of Peace of Mind for the Military," which appeared in the April 1904 issue of the magazine *Taiyō* (The Sun), discloses, quite frankly, some of his intentions for joining the army as chaplain *before* he moved to the battlefield:

> Because this war constitutes a brilliant feat (*kaiji*)[90] and a unique opportunity, I have chosen to follow the army anyway. As some among the soldiers are studying Zen and a lot of them appear to understand it to a certain extent, I thought it would really be fortunate if by going to the front I could provide some spiritual support. The Nishi Honganji has spared no effort in sending many priests to serve as war chaplains,[91] but I have not yet heard of priests being sent from the Higashi Honganji. From the Zen denominations, there is no other war chaplain besides me. Of course, I don't know where we will be sent, but I will go where the army goes, and to begin with I am planning to spend four or five months at the front.[92]

No reservations and no doubts are expressed concerning the legitimacy of the Japanese intervention in this conflict, and one can even discern Sōen's idealization of his role. Shortly after this declaration he landed near Jinzhou, jumping into the water in the night of May 7 like all other soldiers, and he quickly experienced his baptism of fire. He left a day-by-day account of his involvement with the troops in *Journal on Defeating Demons* (*Gōma nisshi*).

In the political arena, Sōen clearly identified the "enemy." He blamed in particular Konstantin Pobedonostsev (1827–1907)—the éminence grise of Tsar Alexander III—for being "the giant leader of the non-Buddhist evil spirits" (*akuma gedō no kyokai*), who "regards himself as the messenger of God" and "brings the Russian Tsar to his knees."[93] On the other hand, Sōen made clear in his Foreword to the diary that the "demons" he was planning to defeat during his trip were as much internal as external, writing "outside the mind there is no Buddha, how could one notice a demon with the eyes?"[94]

On the ground, however, the task proved much harder than Sōen had expected; rather than preaching, he ended up spending most of his time visiting field hospitals, where flocks of wounded soldiers received emergency treatment, and conducting funerals. Many soldiers did not survive and, in his journal entry for May 17, Sōen recalls being so overwhelmed in front of two dead bodies that he could not even chant the sutras.[95] He mentions that wounded Russian soldiers were admitted into the field hospital, adding "being also loyal to their country, even if they are enemies, how could one not feel deep pity for them?"[96] He also describes the plight of local peasants who came to beg for mercy, saying that they had to endure the worst from both Russian and Japanese troops, and that they had not eaten for three days. Sōen notes, "having finished speaking, they burst into tears, and I also was left wordless."[97] Sleep-deprived and starving, Sōen describes thirst and lack of water as the worst ordeals. After a month following the army, he still did not have the opportunity to wash himself, let alone do any laundry, and like all soldiers, he was infested by fleas.[98]

The two months spent in Manchuria took a toll on Sōen's body, and he started complaining of abdominal pain on July 8. When Prince Fushimi Sadanaru (1858–1923) was recalled to Japan, Sōen was allowed to follow him and left Dalian on July 12, 1904, earlier than he had originally planned. Reading Sōen's description of how, when the boat passed Okayama, he remembered his young days at Sōgenji and his handkerchief was drenched with tears,[99] one can easily imagine the physical and psychological wounds left by his war experience, which today might be labeled "post-traumatic stress disorder." He was so sick that he had to stay in bed for three days on his way to Kamakura.[100]

The overall significance of the Manchurian experience on Sōen's thought is difficult to measure, but it certainly turned out to be more than the "brilliant feat" he had expected. His ailments led him to resign his position of chief abbot, with the indirect effect of prompting him to accept the invitation of his friends the Russells to go to the United States. When, as we saw above, Sōen disclosed that one of the purposes of his trip was the wish to improve his health, it was not a figure of speech. After a month spent at the Nasu Hot Spring in September 1904,[101] he still had not recovered. The repercussions of the Russo-Japanese War on Sōen were, however, not limited to his own person; one of his dearest disciples never made it back to Japan.

THE IMPACT OF UEMURA SŌKŌ'S DEATH. Among Sōen's disciples, the presence of Uemura Sōkō (Teizō; 1875–1906) and the attention given to him deserve a special mention because of its connection to the war issue. After having graduated from the Department of Philosophy at Tokyo Imperial University in 1899, Uemura first spent a year as a volunteer in the army. He requested ordination by Sōen in January 1901 and received the new name Sōkō. Suzuki Daisetsu was already in Illinois at that time, and the expectations for the future of a monk with such intellectual background seem to have been high. Even Nishida Kitarō wrote that he felt humbled by Sōkō's determination.[102] A couple of years after his ordination, when the group led by Ida Russell stayed at Engakuji between July 1902 and March 1903, Sōkō was one of the interpreters, an indication of his proficiency in English.[103]

Shortly after Sōen's return to Japan, Sōkō was sent to the front in November 1904,[104] as second lieutenant (*shōi*). News that Sōkō had died in Manchuria first reached Sōen on January 14, 1906, while he was in San Francisco.[105] Suzuki Daisetsu, who was present at the side of his teacher, testified that "the dark sadness emanating from the Rōshi at that time was unforgettable."[106] For a while, he received conflicting reports that Sōkō had been captured and was still alive, but eventually hope vanished. When Sōen came back to Tōkeiji in September 1906, one of his first tasks was to perform a memorial service for Sōkō and to erect a five-story small stūpa, which he could see from his quarters, and which is still visible at Tōkeiji. It is only much later, in 1937, that the circumstances of Sōkō's death became clear and were reported in the press.[107] A former Japanese officer who was searching the area interviewed a Manchurian witness, who reported that he had seen Sōkō captured, and since he was an officer he had received preferential treatment, but that he chose to fast to death.

Sōen was deeply affected by the consequences of the Russo-Japanese War, physically and morally. The war also harmed his Dharma lineage, as he lost one of his most promising heirs. Sōen's views on war were informed by all these events and, although he kept viewing the conflict with Russia as legitimate, to a certain extent he seems to have ceased to romanticize war.

Thus, Sōen's perspective, like that of all thinkers examined in earnest, was not static but changed with time. We must therefore briefly direct our attention to the anthology of his talks published a few months before his death, *An Alert Person, A Swift Horse* (*Kaijin kaiba*, 1919).[108] This is the only Japanese text mentioned by Victoria, but the three passages he quotes mostly emphasize the relation between Zen and Bushidō during the Kamakura period, and the relevance of Zen for the modern period.[109] There are several other passages in the book that would have been much more pertinent to the discussion of militarism. One of them is the rather surreal chapter where Sōen discusses the fate of Wilhelm II, the exiled German emperor, and the involvement of Woodrow Wilson in the negotiations to put an end to World War I.[110] After having summarized the latest political developments, Sōen half-jokingly suggests that if Wilhelm lived in Japan he could become a monk to retire in an honorable manner, but reaches the conclusion that it is not entirely feasible. Nevertheless, Sōen's suggestion goes as follows:

> He could from the bottom of his heart enter the state of mind of a monk (*shukke no kibun*) and, based on what he deduced from his own experience, he could in a majestic and manful way proclaim the reasons that led him to realize (*satoru*) that whatever the factors [that lead to it], war is a tragedy (*hisan*) causing countless harms and not a single benefit. Defining his position [in favor of] disarmament (*heibi teppai*) and world peace (*bankoku heiwa*) he could try to travel to every nation, emphasizing the tragedy of war.[111]

Sōen focused on the misfortune of the deposed emperor and on the disastrous consequences of the ongoing world war, but through this fantasy he also projected some of his own hopes onto the international scene. This is not to say that Sōen became a pacifist; his loyalty to the imperial system clearly prevented him from condemning the Japanese military ambitions in Asia; he also resolutely opposed socialist ideas.[112] After the Manchurian experience, and toward the end of his life, he nonetheless appears to have become acutely aware of the futile and devastating effects of war.

This stands in stark contrast to the belligerent position he had advocated earlier in his *Record of Traps and Snares*, where he explicitly justified taking life for the sake of a "righteous war" to oppose the injustice committed by the Russian government toward its own people.[113] Whatever ensnarement Sōen had in mind, in this former text he endorsed "great killing" (*daisesshō*), supposedly coming out of compassion, which he opposed to the "small killing" (*shōsesshō*) committed by the Russian troops as a result of the greed of their rulers.[114] In the particular context of this war, and before going to the front, Sōen did not use the word "killing" in its metaphorical sense.

Conclusion

Even a cursory examination shows that many of Sōen's public addresses, if taken out of context, could serve either to justify or to condemn his attitude toward contemporary events. What Sōen's inconsistent positions primarily reveal is that, even in the case of someone as famous as he was, considerable work remains to be done to advance primary research through the publication of sources representative of the wide range of his opinions. The publication and translation of his prolific output as well as the work of contemporary figures is necessary to gain a more balanced and comprehensive appreciation of the Meiji and Taishō intellectual and religious history. The task admittedly is huge, marked by urgency (documents are being eaten by bugs and are turning into dust, and witnesses are passing away before their testimony can be recorded), and requires collaborative efforts.

Sectarian hagiographies have dominated the scene for almost a century, but now the time seems ripe to put this into perspective, and finally come to terms with the fact that Zen teachers are not beyond the reach of critical studies and historical scrutiny. Presently, Japanese Zen denominations are so preoccupied with their survival and with marketing a positive image that in this regard very little can be expected from their side.

Western scholars have engaged since the 1990s in a systematic dissection of how Suzuki Daisetsu, especially in his English writings, promoted a romanticized version of Zen while subscribing to schemes of cultural superiority. On the other hand, Janine Sawada's meticulous study on religious communities up to the late nineteenth century has contributed to highlight the permeability of sectarian boundaries and has suggested the breadth of the intellectual fermentation taking place in the Engakuji circle (2004). Sōen represents the articulation between these two worlds, as the recipient of Kōsen's Tokugawa legacy, and as the teacher of Suzuki Daisetsu, entrusting his disciple with the task of developing exchanges with the outside world. Through various factors illustrated in this chapter, Sōen became acutely aware that the clergy needed to counterbalance the proselytizing efforts of competing religious groups. In the wake of major sociohistorical transformations, Sōen cannot entirely escape the charge of having sometimes made opportunistic choices. Yet, his pivotal role deserves to be further examined, and an enormous amount of work remains to be done to account for the full range of positions he expressed, without suppressing their unpleasant components.

Successive alterations in Sōen's biography gradually developed the image of an exemplary master, which served to sell Rinzai Zen to the public. The investigation of some less-publicized aspects of his life conducted in this chapter indicates the extent to which Sōen's profile was embellished, and invites circumspection in the handling of biographical materials. Biographies of Zen teachers such as Sōen are still being used as devices to divert our attention from the vulnerability of these figures to their own times. The opposite strategy of indicting them for what they did or did not do to conform to undefined present ethical standards appears equally unprofitable, because a mere tarnishing of the image similarly blurs the contours. It is only by looking through the sectarian rhetoric and by a careful examination of each utterance in its own context that we may be able to hear the distinctive voices of these teachers.

NOTES

Part of the research conducted for this chapter was carried out with the support of the University of Hawaii Japan Studies Endowment. The author also wants to express his gratitude to the staff of the library at Keiō University Mita Campus, who granted permission to consult their archives and always kindly responded to numerous requests and questions.

1. Most publications still have Sōen's date of birth incorrect. He was born on the eighteenth day of the twelfth lunar month, in the year Ansei 6, which corresponds to January 10, 1860, in the solar calendar. See Inoue Zenjō, *Shaku Sōen den* (Kyoto: Zenbunka kenkyūjō, 2000) (cited hereafter as Inoue 2000), p. 4. For ordained people active after the Meiji period, during their lifetime their name would be composed of the family name (*zokusei*) followed by the ordination name (*hōki* or *imina*; example: Shaku Sōen). After their death, it was and still is considered disrespectful to use the family name. The full name is thus indicated by the surname (*dōgō* or *azana*) followed by the ordination name (example: Kōgaku Sōen). For famous people who were widely known by their family name, it is frequently used even after death, although formally this usage is considered "inappropriate." Because the ordination name Sōen sounds more familiar than Kōgaku, hereafter I will simply speak of "Sōen," even in the period when he had not yet received this name, and even if Kōgaku would have been more symmetrical to the name of his teacher Kōsen.

2. His first discourse at the parliament has been edited by Wayne S. Yokoyama, "Two Addresses by Shaku Sōen: 'The Law of Cause and Effect, as Taught by Buddha,' translated by D. T. Suzuki, 'Reflections on an American Journey,'" *Eastern Buddhist* 26/2 (1993): 131–148. Studies mentioning the role played by Sōen at this conference include James E. Ketelaar, *Of Heretics and Martyrs in Meiji Japan: Buddhism and Its Persecution* (Princeton: Princeton University Press, 1990); Judith Snodgrass, *Presenting Japanese Buddhism to the West: Orientalism, Occidentalism, and the Columbian Exposition* (Chapel Hill: University of North Carolina Press, 2003); and John S. Harding, *Mahāyāna Phoenix: Japan's Buddhists at the 1893 World's Parliament of Religions* (New York: Peter Lang, 2008). There will be more on this text in the next section of this chapter.

3. See in particular the invaluable contributions by Richard Jaffe, "Seeking Śākyamuni: Travel and the Reconstruction of Japanese Buddhism," *Journal of Japanese Studies* 30/1 (2004): 65–96, and "Buddhist Material Culture, 'Indianism,' and the Construction of Pan-Asian Buddhism in Prewar Japan," *Material Religion* 2/3 (2006): 266–293; also see Janine Sawada, "Religious Conflict in Bakumatsu Japan: Zen Master Imakita Kōsen and Confucian Scholar Higashi Takusha," *Japanese Journal of Religious Studies* 21/2–3 (1994): 211–30; "Political Waves in the Zen Sea: The Engaku-Ji Circle in Early Meiji Japan," *Japanese Journal of Religious Studies* 25/1–2 (1998): 117–50, and *Practical Pursuits: Religion, Politics, and Personal Cultivation in Nineteenth-Century Japan* (Honolulu: University of Hawaii Press. 2004).

4. See Burton Watson, *The Complete Works of Chuang Tzu* (New York: Columbia University Press, 1968), p. 302.

5. These autobiographical notes are included in a manuscript entitled *Splits in a Monk's Robe* (*Koromo no hokorobi*). First published by Nagao Sōshi (= Daigaku). *Sōen zenji no menmoku* (Tokyo: Ryūbunkan, 1920), pp. 181–199 (cited hereafter as Nagao 1920), then included in SZ, vol. 10, pp. 257–276. The version in Inoue 2000, pp. 3–27, is incomplete and contains unacknowledged cuts and changes. Yet these notes only extend up to the death of one of his teachers, Gisan Zenrai (1802–1878), in March 1878. For the remaining part of his life we must rely on his disciples' accounts, on his letters, or on external sources. Concerning the dating of this manuscript, Inoue gives the approximation of 1899, on the basis of a poem composed when Sōen returned to his hometown of Takahama. Sōen wrote in the autobiography that he "went to visit the grave five or six years ago" and quotes the poem that he composed on this occasion, lamenting the demise of most of his relatives. Yet Inoue's reasoning that the autobiography "must have been composed seven years after the death of his father" is unclear, especially since he gives the date 1891 for the father's death (Inoue 2000, p. 4).

6. Concerning the family name of Sōen's mother, the first version of the autobiography published by Nagao correctly lists the village name followed by her family name (Nagao 1920, p. 181). The version in SZ, vol. 10, p. 258, dropped the village name, so that her family name became Wada, but this has been corrected by Inoue 2000, p. 3. The correct family name is corroborated by Nagao Daigaku (= Sōshi), ed., *Sōen zenji shokanshū* (Tokyo: Nishōdō, 1931) (cited hereafter as Nagao, ed. 1931), p. 1. The information concerning her dates is based on the note provided by Inoue 2000, p. 27, where he gives the date for Yasuko's death as February 1876. Coupled with the traditional age of fifty-four given for her death, she was apparently born in 1823. Inoue can be trusted, because he certainly had the registry of the deceased (*kakochō*) at his disposal.

7. Little is known about Chūtarō, except that he was born in 1845 (Kōka 2) and that "he died at a young age without witnessing the success" of his younger brother Sōen (Nagao, ed. 1931, p. 454). Sōen mentions Chūtarō in a letter from Ceylon sent to his parents on November 11, 1888, but this seems to be the last mention of him (Nagao, ed. 1931, pp. 56–58).

8. SZ, vol. 10, p. 260; and Inoue 2000, p. 6. Sōen describes how his mother would give directions to the maid(s) (*kahi*) for preparing the meals of the following day. It could be singular or plural.

9. For "hot-tempered," the original text in both Nagao 1920, p. 182, and in SZ, vol. 10, p. 258, has a different compound read *kanrai*, whose meaning is unclear. Because the second character *rai* is also used for "leprosy," although it could also indicate "scabies," Inoue assumed that it was a misprint and corrected it into *kanteki* without warning (Inoue 2000, p. 4). If we assume the correct word is *kanteki*, it refers to *kanshaku*, which can mean "nervousness" in the weak sense or, more strongly, "irrepressible accesses of anger." One way to understand this feature of Sōen's biography and his apparent restlessness might be to follow the suggestion that gifted children may have greater psychomotor, sensual, imaginative, intellectual, and emotional "overexcitabilities." See Sal Mendaglio, "Dabrowski's Theory of Positive Disintegration: Some Implications for Teachers of Gifted Students," *Agate* 15/2 (2002): 14–22. Another indication of Sōen's vulnerability in certain psychological areas, even during his adult years, is given by the anecdote concerning his phobia of snakes. See Brian Daizen Victoria, *Zen War Stories* (London: Routledge Curzon, 2003), pp. 112–113.

10. For years of age, I followed the Western reckoning, unless explicitly using the adjective "traditional." According to this reckoning, Sōen had his first birthday on January 18, 1861, although he was born in the sixth year of the Ansei era (1859). It may seem confusing because the solar Gregorian calendar was introduced during his lifetime, in Meiji 5, when the third day of the twelfth lunar month was declared to be the first January of Meiji 6 (1873). This means that in most cases one has to subtract two years from the traditional ages mentioned by Sōen, Inoue, and other authors. Here, Sōen says that he left home (*shukke*) in Meiji 4 (1871), traditional age twelve, but the date has been corrected in Inoue 2000, p. 7.

11. Ekkei is especially famous for having established the present-day Myōshinji training monastery (*sōdō*) within the Tenjuin subtemple. The new monastery's inauguration ceremony (*kaitanshiki*) was finally performed in the spring of 1878. See Nōnin Kōdō, ed., *Kundoku Kinsei zenrin sōbōden* (Kyoto: Zenbunka kenkyūsho, 2002) (cited hereafter as Nōnin, ed., 2002), vol. 1, p. 184. The chronicle of the opposition and hardship encountered by Ekkei is included in Ekkei's *Kinmōkutsu nisshi*, partially transcribed in Kimura Shizuo (Jōyū), "Ekkei: Myōshinji sōdō kaitan no ki," in Zenbunka kenkyūsho, ed., *Meiji no zenshō* (Kyoto: Zenbunka kenkyūsho, 1981), pp. 25–45. See also Myōshinji sōdō, ed., *Kinmōkutsu ihō*, rev. ed. (Kyoto: Zenbunka kenkyūsho, 2002).

12. According to Kimura, Sōen was the nephew (*nikutetsu*) of Ekkei, who was therefore his uncle (Kimura, "Ekkei," p. 28). Ekkei, who was also born in Takahama, came to celebrate the birthday of his mother, who had reached the traditional age of eighty-two. The character used for "nephew" suggests they were related through Sōen's mother, who might thus have been Ekkei's sister. If Ekkei's family name could be identified as Hirata, then it would be confirmed, but so far I only found an indication that, like several contemporary monks, he adopted the family name Shaku (simply indicating a disciple of Sakyamuni) when family names became mandatory in 1875 (*heimin myōji hisshō gimu rei*). This is mentioned by Kishida Kinuo, *Kikutsu no tan: Kindai zensō no sei to shi* (Kyoto: Tankōsha, 1994), p. 10, who merely provides a journalistic treatment and does not quote his sources.

13. The explanation given by Sōen is that after the enforcement of the new census register law of 1872, the bureaucracy had become so heavy that his teacher thought it

was easier to recycle the name of a novice of the Jushōin (a subtemple of Myōshinji) who had died. No further clarification is given, and this choice is described as having been "for reasons related to the register" (*kosekimen no tsugō*) (SZ, vol. 10, p. 263; and Inoue 2000, p. 11).

14. The date for the death of Shungai Tōsen, October 10, 1875 is confirmed by the records of Ryōsokuin. The year of his birth is calculated by subtracting forty-five years, since his traditional age upon death is given as forty-six.

15. The word used by Sōen is *jichitaiteki*, an adjective indicating a self-governing group. He also explains that they subsisted on donations of rice collected from the neighborhood. Because of the prohibition of mendicant rounds between 1872 and 1881, they could not openly practice *takuhatsu*. Sōen speaks of "gathering offered rice (*kumai*) three or four times per month."

16. It actually comes from a phrase written on a plaque hanging in front of the monk's dormitory (*shuryō*) at Kenninji.

17. SZ, vol. 10, p. 269; and Inoue 2000, p. 18.

18. As stated above, while a member of the clergy is alive he is identified by his family name followed by the ordination name, whereas the family name is not used after death. For the purpose of easer identification, I provide the family name in parenthesis when it is available. Sōen's friend was known as Takeda Mokurai while alive.

19. Apparently, there was a lot of mutual respect between Mokurai and Sōen, who followed common teachers (Ekkei, Gisan, and Shungai). Sōen had recommended that Mokurai join them at Gungyokurin, because Mokurai had such a fragile body that he could not endure the hardships of practicing in a monastery; Itō Tōshin, "Kenninji no Mokurai zenji," in Zenbunka kenkyūsho, ed., *Meiji no zenshō* (Kyoto: Zenbunka kenkyūsho, 1981), p. 259.

20. SZ, vol. 10, p. 270; and Inoue 2000, p. 20. The decisiveness of this phase in Sōen's practice is confirmed by an external observer. In his memories of Sōen, Mokurai wrote "as far as I can tell, I think that Sōen's *kenshō* dates back to this period" (Nagao Sōshi, ed. 1923. *Sōen zenji to sono shūi*. Tokyo: Kokushi kōshūkai (reprint in 1993 by Ōzorasha), p. 99. The word translated here as "surplice" (*kesa*) indicates the rectangular piece of cloth put above the monk's robe, symbolizing the original Indian robe made from scraps of material (Skt. *kasaya*).

21. The original seal of approval (*inka shōmei*) is reproduced in Takahamachō kyōdo shiryōkan, *Shaku Sōen: Kyōdo no unda meiji no kōsō* (Takahama: Takahamachō kyōdo shiryōkan, 2003), p. 4, but it carries no date. According to Taibi, it was composed in fall of 1883; Shaku Keishun (Taibi), ed., *Ryōgakutsu nenjiden* (Kanaoka mura, Shizuoka: Daichūji, 1942), p. 7. Inoue places the first verse of recognition back "at the end of the year 1882," but remains silent concerning the certification (Inoue 2000, pp. 32–33). The reason why Kōsen may have chosen not to include the date is that Sōen was still officially affiliated with Myōshinji until the autumn of 1883, when they went together to Kyoto and asked Ekkei for official permission to "transfer" Sōen from the Myōshinji branch to the Engakuji branch.

22. One indication of the widespread popularity of shorthand (*sokki*) is found in the autobiography of Hiratsuka Raichō (1886–1971), where she mentions having learned this technique during her third year of college in 1905. See Raichō Hiratsuka, *In the*

Beginning, Woman Was the Sun: The Autobiography of a Japanese Feminist, translated by Teruko Craig (New York: Columbia University Press, 2006), p. 89. The technique was seriously introduced in Japan since 1882, through articles in the *Jiji Shinpō* newspaper.

23. For instance, following a passage in Sōen's talk where he explained that "filial piety in Japan corresponds to the importance given to the wife in the West," the transcriber inserted within brackets "laughter bursting out"; Shaku Sōen, *Senteiroku* (Tokyo: Kōdōkan, 1909), p. 64.

24. Example in Sōen, *Senteiroku*, p. 90.

25. Sōen's contributions can be found across many periodicals, but the two journals published by Engakuji obviously contain the most significant number of contributions. The journal *Zengaku* (Zen Study) appeared between 1895 and 1900, whereas *Zendō* (The Path of Zen) was published between 1910 and 1923. There is a gap of ten years between these two publications, which may be related to Suzuki Daisetsu's sojourn abroad between March 1897 and April 1909.

26. Note that "Southwest" in the title intentionally indicates the position of Ceylon from the Japanese perspective, as opposed to the "Southeast" it represents from a Eurocentric perspective. Sōen's manuscript is dated August 1889 and was sent by mail to a friend named Itō Naozō, who wrote the afterword.

27. Concerning *Tobei nikki* (Diary of a Trip to America), Inoue mentions the existence of a second unpublished section kept at Tōkeiji, which was written with Nomura Yōzō (Umetarō 1870–1965). The two texts *Tobei nikki* and *Tobei zakkan* should not be confused. The 1893 *Tobei nikki* is included in SZ, vol. 10, pp. 189–224, while the 1906 *Tobei zakkan* is included in vol. 1, pp. 85–98.

28. Shaku Sōen. *Bankoku shūkyō taikai ichiran* (Tokyo: Kōmeisha, 1893 [second edition in December]). Nomura served as interpreter for Sōen during this first trip (Inoue 2000, p. 74), and he also introduced the Russells to Sōen in 1902 (Inoue 2000, p. 115). Concerning the biography of Nomura Yōzō (Umetarō), see Mori Kiyoshi, *Daisetsu to Kitarō* (Tokyo: Asahi shinbun, 1991), pp. 75–84.

29. This means that he actually spent two months and five days near the front.

30. Translated from English into Japanese by Kawakami Tetsuta, an employee of the publisher Min'yūsha (Inoue 2000, p. 169).

31. Inoue 2000, p. 156. The dedication to Sōen written by Suzuki Daisetsu in La Salle has the date January 10, 1907.

32. The most reliable source for the dates of Jikō seems to be Rikugawa Taiun, *Shinzenron* (Tokyo: Ryūginsha, 1968), p. 526. Rikugawa Taiun (1886–1966) was the disciple of Jikō and received his seal of transmission in 1940 after having also received the inka from Sōkatsu in 1935. The reading "Sumikiri" for Jikō's last name seems to be a mistake.

33. See Pei-yi Wu, *The Confucian's Progress: Autobiographical Writings in Traditional China* (Princeton: Princeton University Press, 1990).

34. Konno Washichi, "Shaku Sōen no hito to shōgai: Shinshiryō, Shaku Sōen no Seiron tsūshin shōkai," *Kindai nihon kenkyū* 4 (1987): 195–218, p. 200. Konno praises the precision in Sōen's account of the addresses given at the World's Parliament of Religion, which were "going right to the essential." Unfortunately, Konno completely missed the fact that the author of these summaries was Nomura Yōzō.

35. Concerning Nagao, little was known except that he was born in 1894 in Aizuwakamatsu (Nagao, ed. 1931, p. 476) and was ordained in September 1909 by Sōen (Inoue 2000, p. 165). A picture dated 1918 with him is included in Inoue 2000, p. 270, and a list of his publications is appended to Nagao, ed. 1931, pp. 486–487. According to the same source, he was the abbot of Chōkōzan Eishōji, an impoverished temple in the Shizuoka prefecture, and was appointed proselytizing teacher (*fukyōshi*) at Engakuji in 1930. A lucky phone call to Eishōji connected me to his granddaughter, Nagao Mitsumi, who examined the funerary tablets to tell me the date of his death: March 4, 1965, at age seventy-one (seventy-two in the traditional count). Verbal communication dated August 5, 2008.

36. After having announced in January 1905 that he resigned his position of chief abbot of Engakuji and Kenchōji, Sōen moved to the nearby temple of Tōkeiji at the end of April. See Inoue 2000, p. 126. He thus became free to respond to the Russells' invitation to go to the United States. Concerning mostly the pre-Meiji history of Tōkeiji when it was a nunnery, see Sachiko Kaneko Morrell and Robert E. Morrell, *Zen Sanctuary of Purple Robes: Japan's Tōkeiji Convent since 1285* (Albany: State University of New York Press, 2006).

37. Distinct from the Matsugaoka Library (Matsugaoka bunko), which is located above Tōkeiji and is administrated by a foundation, with a residing director.

38. Inoue 2000, p. iii.

39. Original reproduced in Shaku Sōen, *Shin'yaku Shaku Sōen "Saiyū nikki"* (Tokyo: Daihōrinkaku, 2001), p. 274. Quoted in Inoue 2000, p. 46.

40. Nagao, ed. 1931, p. 5. Actually, Nagao is not entirely to blame (except for his lack of discernment in using sources), because in his introduction he reproduced the Sōen entry in the *Zenrin sōbōden* containing this mistake. See Nōnin, ed. 2002, vol. 2, p. 382. As Sōen's last direct disciple born in 1894, Nagao could not have witnessed any of these events and used this source, which in this case is totally unreliable.

41. Tamamura Takeji and Inoue Zenjō, *Engakuji shi* (Tokyo: Shunjūsha, 1964), p. 699; Daihonzan Engakuji, ed., *Zuirokuzan Engakuji* (Kamakura, Daihonzan Engakuji, 1985), p. 75.

42. The latest reiterations are: in Japanese, by Yasunaga Sodō, "Kindai no shōzō: Kiki o hiraku," in the September 14 issue of *Chūgai nippō* (2006), p. 7; in English, by Morrell and Morrell, *Zen Sanctuary*, p. 139.

43. See the clear summary by Sawada, *Practical Pursuits*, pp. 139–141.

44. Fukuzawa kenkyū sentā, ed., *Keiō gijuku nyūshachō*, facsimile edition (Tokyo: Keiō gijuku, 1986), vol. 3, p. 172. What is most interesting is that in the column indicating the guarantor (*shōnin*), who probably needed to be present with the student at the time of registration, we have the inscription "Kawai Kiyomaru, representative of Torio Koyata from the nobility." Kawai Kiyomaru (1848–1917) was a student of the retired general Torio, and while revolving in and around the Engakuji circle he became the advocate of an incredible amalgam of Shinto, Buddhism, and imperial ideology. Kawai later became active in the Society of the Great Way of the Great Japanese National Teaching as he "handled public relations for the group" (Sawada, *Practical Pursuits*, p. 233). Sectarian histories have "May" for the entrance at Keiō, which is incorrect. The same inaccurate information is found in Shaku, ed., *Ryōgakutsu*

nenjiden, p. 10; Tamamura and Inoue, *Engakuji shi*, p. 699; and Daihonzan, ed., *Zuirokuzan Engakuji*, p. 75.

45. *Fukuzawa Kankei Monjo* (hereafter abbreviated FKM) microfilm K4/A54 p. 24. Because of space constraints I cannot include all the details here, but these records give precise figures for attendance and grades. I would be happy to provide this information to those who are interested.

46. FKM microfilm K4/A55, p. 18.

47. FKM microfilm K4/A56, p. 24.

48. FKM microfilm K4/A57, p. 28.

49. Died in September 1899. Limited information about Keitoku is found in Nagao, ed. 1931, pp. 477–478. He was one of Ekkei's disciples and later obtained the certification of Kokan Sōho (1839–1903), the Myōshinji teacher with whom Nishida Kitarō practiced.

50. Arthur Lloyd (1852–1911). Lloyd was a British missionary sent to Japan in 1884 by the Society for the Propagation of the Gospel. He remained there for almost twenty-five years. See Shirai Takako, *Fukuzawa Yukichi to senkyōshi tachi: Shirarezaru Meijiki no Nichiei kankei* (Tokyo: Miraisha, 1999), pp. 163–175.

51. William C. Kitchin (1855–1920) taught English between October 7, 1885, and July 31, 1886, which corresponds to Sōen's period at Keiō. Kitchin, an American missionary of the Methodist Episcopal Church, arrived in Nagasaki on September 20, 1882. See Shirai, *Fukuzawa Yukichi to senkyōshi tachi*, pp. 181 and 184.

52. Letter dated October 9, 1885 (Nagao, ed. 1931, pp. 19–21; and Inoue 2000, pp. 40–41, excerpts).

53. Probably the series of textbooks by George Payn Quackenbos (1826–1881), including the *Elementary History of the United States*.

54. John Stuart Mill (1806–1873).

55. Probably the *General History of Civilization in Europe*, by François Pierre Guillaume Guizot (1787–1874).

56. *The Mission Field*, October 1885, pp. 308–310, reproduced in Shirai, *Fukuzawa Yukichi to senkyōshi tachi*, p. 178.

57. The name of the purported editor of the "Complete Works" is Matsuda Take no shimabito, obviously a pseudonym. The contents of most biographical elements contained in this anthology are identical to those authored by Nagao Daigaku (1894–1965), who was in his thirties in 1929–1930, and he is the most likely candidate for having composed this piece.

58. SZ, vol. 10, p. 283.

59. SZ, vol. 10, p. 283.

60. This text is contained in the first edition of *Bankoku shūkyō taikai ichiran* (A Glance at the World's Parliament of Religion) (Tokyo: Kōmeisha, November 1893), pp. 74–83. In the second, more concise, edition of the same text dated December 1893, it is included on pp. 39–44. The third version was published in the February 1894 article "Bukkyō no yōshi narabini ingahō" (The Essential Principle of Buddhism and the Law of Cause and Effect), in the journal *Aikoku* (Patriotism), in the February 25, 1894, issue, pp. 17–19. Finally, the fourth version was included in SZ, vol. 10, pp. 152–155.

61. See Walter R. Houghton, ed., *Neely's History of the Parliament of Religions and Religious Congresses at the World's Columbian Exposition*, third edition (Chicago: F. Tennyson Neely, 1893), pp. 378–380; and John Henry Barrows, ed., *The World's Parliament of Religions* (Chicago: Parliament Publishing, 1893), pp. 829–831. The version published by Yokoyama in "Two Addresses by Shaku Sōen" in *Eastern Buddhist* is based on the latter.

62. The translation of this piece is usually attributed to Suzuki Daisetsu, but he could not possibly have written the final draft alone, as he had not yet been to the United States and his command of English was still limited. A letter by Suzuki dated July 1, 1893, mentions his struggle with the text without the help of appropriate dictionaries containing Buddhist terms. He also writes that the Rōshi promised to ask Nanjō Bun'yū or someone else to correct the English. See Inoue Zenjō and Zenbunka kenkyūsho, eds., *Suzuki Daisetsu mikōkai shokan* (Kyoto: Zenbunka kenkyūjō, 1989), p. 147. The final address was thus edited by a native speaker, but the rumor that Natsume Sōseki could have contributed to this was unfounded and was dispelled by Inoue 2000, pp. 90–94; Inoue and Zenbunka, eds., *Suzuki Daisetsu mikōkai shokan*, p. 464. Sōseki's brief stay at Kigen'in (a subtemple of Engakuji where Sōkatsu was the abbot) took place between December 23, 1894, and January 7, 1895, more than a year after the parliament. The final revisions appear to have been made by a "Dr. E. L. Hamilton from New York" (Inoue and Zenbunka, eds., *Suzuki Daisetsu mikōkai shokan*, p. 464). Further research is needed for precise identification of this Hamilton.

63. This term is understood in the sense it takes in the *Book of Changes*, where the first hexagram is glossed in the Tuan commentary as "Great is the indication of Qian's origin! The ten thousand things owe to it their beginning and all belonging to heaven"; Jing-Nuan Wu, trans., *Yi Jin.* (Washington, D.C.: Taoist Center, 1991), p. 219.

64. Shaku Soyen (= Sōen), *Zen for Americans: Including the Sutra of Forty-Two Chapters* (New York: Barnes & Noble, 1993) mentions "This is an unabridged reprint of the 1913 edition entitled Sermons of a Buddhist," but faithfully reproduces the 1907 *Sermons of a Buddhist Abbot;* "Translator's Preface," p. iv.

65. Shaku, *Zen for Americans*, p. v.

66. Unnumbered footnote in *Eastern Buddhist* 26/2 (1993): 138. Yokoyama mentions the other account of this trip, *Ōbei unsuiki* (Diary of a Monk in Europe and America, published in October 1907), as containing a "more detailed account of his 1905–06 journey." This is true, but this diary is a text completely distinct from the piece he translated.

67. Ida Russell, often identified as "Mrs. Alexander Russell" was the first Western woman to practice Zen under the direction of a Japanese teacher. In the more extensive version of Sōen's talk, he emphasized the resolve of Ida and her three companions, in a way suggesting his strong admiration for the group. A genuine friendship seems to have developed as he also asked Ida to teach him how to read the Bible.

68. The dates for Ida Evelyn Russell are based on Susan Hill Lindley and Eleanor J. Stebner, eds., *The Westminster Handbook to Women in American Religious History* (Louisville, Ky.: Westminster John Knox Press, Lindley, ed. 2008), p. 189.

69. The translations are mine. Compare with Yokoyama's, pp. 138–148.

70. Allusion to verses in the *Lotus Sutra* attributed to the Buddha, "Now this threefold world is all my domain and the living beings in it are all my children"; T. 9.262.14c26–c27; Burton Watson, tr., *The Lotus Sutra* (New York: Columbia University Press, 1993), p. 69.

71. Sōen, *Senteiroku*, p. 38. Concern for his health was apparently not only a figure of style, because Sōen had become sick after his trip as chaplain in Manchuria.

72. SZ, vol. 1, p. 87.

73. Sōen, *Senteiroku*, chapter 3, is entitled "Experiments in Abstaining from Alcohol and Tobacco," pp. 68–76, and was first published in the magazine *Seinen no tomo* (Young People's Friend) 1/7. There are several magazines with the same title, but it is likely to have been the one published from November 1907 under the editorship of the journalist Hani Yoshikazu (1880–1955), who also founded the magazine *Fujin no tomo* (Ladies' Friend). I have not been able to procure this issue.

74. See Sahashi Hōryū, *Inoue Shūten* (Tokyo: Meicho Fukyūkai, 1982), pp. 101–111.

75. Moriya, Tomoe, "Social Ethics of 'New Buddhists' at the Turn of the Twentieth Century: A Comparative Study of Suzuki Daisetsu and Inoue Shūten," *Japanese Journal of Religious Studies* 32/2 (2005): 295.

76. Inoue Shūten, *Hekiganroku shinkōwa* (Tokyo: Kyōbunsha, 1931), Postface; quoted in Sahashi, *Inoue Shūten*, pp. 8 and 97.

77. Asahi Journal, ed., *Nihon no shisōka* (Tokyo: Asahi Shinbunsha, 1978), vol. 2, entry "Shaku Sōen." Quoted in Sahashi, *Inoue Shūten*, p. 98.

78. Brian Victoria, *Zen at War* (New York: Weatherhill, 1997), p. 26.

79. The articles were published in the July 5 and November 22 issues in 1887, then in the April 25 and April 29 issues in 1889 of the *Jiji Shinpō*. See Konno, "Shaku Sōen no hito to shōgai."

80. Details of how he was treated on the vessel *Werther* are found in Sōen's *Saiyū nikki* (Diary of a Journey to the West), pp. 57–58. As a passenger in third class, three times a day the "meal" was a bowl of half-cooked old rice, thrown to him like to a dog, without a single vegetable or even a pinch of salt.

81. Galle is a small town located on the southwestern tip of Sri Lanka.

82. Nagao, ed. 1931, p. 68.

83. See Stephen R. Prothero, *The White Buddhist: The Asian Odyssey of Henry Steel Olcott.* (Bloomington: Indiana University Press, 1996), pp. 85–115.

84. Shaku Sōen, *Sōen zenna* (Tokyo: Ōsakayagō shoten, 1916; reprinted in 1921 by Zenna sōsho kankōkai), p. 272. Contains a talk on "The Korean Situation" given to the Youth Group of an association called Enjōkai during its fall conference. Sōen shared his observations on the Korean society and family system, apparently based on his 1912 trip.

85. Torio Tokuan is mentioned above in relation to his sponsorship of Sōen's studies at Keiō.

86. Takeda Mokurai, *Mokurai zenna* (Kyoto: Kenninji senmon dōjō, 1979; contains the reprint of three books originally published in 1907 and 1923), p. 28 of the third section of the book entitled *Zenshitsu zenna*, originally published in 1923.

87. T. 51.2076.326c05–06.

88. Victor Sōgen Hori, *Zen Sand: The Book of Capping Phrases for Kōan Practice* (Honolulu: University of Hawaii Press, 2003), p. 586.

89. Kakuzō Okakura, *The Book of Tea* (New York: Kodansha America, 1990), p. 31. *The Book of Tea* was originally published in 1906.

90. The term *kaiji* is often used during the Meji period in a sense similar to *kaikyo*, indicating a splendid achievement, an admirable act, or praiseworthy action, such as military success, rather than "a pleasant event," as in modern Japanese. See, for instance, the letter dated February 15, 1892, sent by Inukai Tsuyoshi to Ōkuma Shigenobu, in Waseda daigaku shiryō sentā, ed., *Ōkuma Shigenobu kankei monjo 1* (Tokyo: Misuzu shobō, 2004), which rejoices in electoral victory. In another passage of Sōen's same work, he uses *kaikyo* in a similar context. See Sōen, *Senteiroku*, p. 160.

91. The names of Kawakami Teishin and Onojima Hōdō, who joined the army at the same time as Sōen, are provided in Shaku, ed., *Ryōgakutsu nenjiden*, p. 64.

92. Reproduced in Sōen, *Senteiroku*, p. 126.

93. Sōen, *Senteiroku*, p. 160.

94. Shaku Sōen, *Gōma nisshi* (Kamakura: Tōkeiji, 1904), Foreword, p. 1a. The choice of this title actually comes from a calligraphic character that combines two characters—*gōma* (defeat demons)—that Sōen requested from Prince Sadanaru while they were on board the ship returning to Japan (Shaku, ed., *Ryōgakutsu nenjiden*, p. 71).

95. Sōen, *Gōma nisshi*, chapter 2, p. 11b.

96. Sōen, *Gōma nisshi*, chapter 2, p. 11b.

97. Entry for May 20, Sōen, *Gōma nisshi*, chapter 2, p. 13b.

98. Entry for May 20, Sōen, *Gōma nisshi*, chapter 2,. p. 14b.

99. Entry for July 20, Sōen, *Gōma nisshi*, chapter 3, p. 35b.

100. Entry for July 21, Sōen, *Gōma nisshi*, chapter 3, p. 36a. Sōen first stayed at Buttsūji, near Hiroshima, with an old friend who called a physician. His diagnosis was that Sōen suffered from a form of chronic enteritis and needed rest; entry for July 19, Sōen, *Gōma nisshi*, chapter 3, p. 34b. It may have been caused by giardiasis, a parasite carried by contaminated water. The issue of Sōen's health is complicated, as in November 1901 he had already had to spend two months in hospital for an unspecified "chronic disease" (*shukua*), which may have been a form of Crohn's disease. See Shaku, ed., *Ryōgakutsu nenjiden*, p. 56, and Inoue 2000, p. 114.

101. Shaku, ed., *Ryōgakutsu nenjiden*, p. 72.

102. Diary entry of January 18, 1901, quoted in Inoue 2000, p. 111.

103. Shaku, ed., *Ryōgakutsu nenjiden*, p. 60. The other interpreter was Shigeta Yūsuke (Shinden Koji), who died in 1904. The group introduced to Sōen by Nomura Yōzō included other persons whose name in Katakana makes the identification difficult, mainly Mrs. Dreksler (?) and Mr. Haw (?). According to another source, the name of Mrs. Russell's friend was, rather, "Dressel" (Mori, *Daisetsu to Kitarō*, p. 173).

104. Inoue 2000, p. 125.

105. Inoue 2000, pp. 130–131.

106. Suzuki Daisetsu's Afterword to *Saiyū nikki* (Diary of a Journey to the West), reproduced in Sōen, *Saiyū nikki*, p. 276. Two letters from Sōkō addressed to Daisetu

are included in Inoue and Zenbunka, eds., *Suzuki Daisetsu mikōkai shokan*, pp. 467–468.

107. This news appeared in the daily *Asahi shinbun* of June 16, 1937. Mentioned in Inoue 2000, pp. 132–133.

108. The title of the anthology is an allusion to the metaphor of the four thoroughbred horses and four thoroughbred persons included in the Pāli Canon, *Anguttara-Nikāya* IV.12.113; Nyanaponika Thera and Bhikku Bodhi, transl. and eds. *Numerical Discourses of the Buddha: An Anthology of Suttas from the Aṅguttara Nikāya*. (Walnut Creek, Cal.: AltaMira Press, 1999), pp. 105–106; transposed into the Chinese Canon (*Za ahan jing* 922; T. 2.99.234a16–b20).

109. Quoted in Victoria, *Zen at War*, pp. 98–99. Concerning Sōen, nothing new appears in Victoria, *Zen War Stories*.

110. The chapter is entitled "I suggest the Kaiser to engage in a world pilgrimage" (*Kaizeru ni sekai angya o susumu*). Sōen, *Kaijin kaiba* (Tokyo: Nisshinkaku, 1919), pp. 131–139.

111. Sōen, *Kaijin kaiba*, p. 135.

112. Sōen, *Kaijin kaiba*, pp. 107–108.

113. Sōen, *Senteiroku*, pp. 160–164. No date is provided for this chapter, but it appears to be a discourse made before going to Manchuria. It is expressed in a tone similar to the discourse published in the aforementioned April 1904 issue of the *Taiyō* magazine and mentions the fact that the Russo-Japanese War had just started. I suspect it was an address given to soldiers while Sōen was staying in Hiroshima's military cantonment, where he spent a month giving lectures before embarking for the front. See Shaku, ed., *Ryōgakutsu nenjiden*, p. 64.

114. Sōen, *Senteiroku*, pp. 162–163. In this passage, Sōen mentions Nichiren and his expression "enemies of the Buddha" (*butteki*) while referring to the contrast between "gentle conversion" (*shōju*) and "forcing submission" (*shakubuku*).

PRIMARY SOURCES

A. MAIN WORKS BY SŌEN OR ATTRIBUTED TO HIM IN JAPANESE (BOOKS ONLY)

1889 January. *Seinan no bukkyō*. Tokyo: Hakubundō.
1890 April. *Seirontōshi*. Tokyo: Kōkyō shoin. (SZ)
1893 November. *Bankoku shūkyō taikai ichiran*. Tokyo: Kōmeisha. (Second edition in December)
1894 February 25. *Bukkyō no yōshi narabini ingahō*. *Aikoku* (Patriotism), pp. 17–19.
1894 April. *Sōryōkutsu nenpu*. Tokyo: Tsukiji kappan seizōsho.
1894 September. *Daikaku zenji zazenron* (original text by Rankei Dōryū). Tokyo: Keisei shoin.
1894 September. *Zazenron wage* (original text by Imakita Sōon). Tokyo: Keisei shoin.
1896 November. *Teishō jūgyūzu*. Tokyo: Keisei shoin. (Reprint in 1897)
1897 August. *Busso sankyō kōgi*. Kyoto: Baiyō shoin.
1897 September. *Hōkyōsanmai kōgi*. Summer courses (*kaki kōshūkai*), co-authored with Ōuchi, Emura, and Takada. Tokyo: Kōyūkan.

1900 March. *Kongōkyō kōgi*. Tokyo: Kōyūkan. (Reprints in 1903 and 1934) (SZ under the title *Kongōkyō kōwa*)
1900 June. *Seiza no susume*. Ed. by Suzuki Daisetsu, comments by Seigo Hōgaku. Tokyo: Kōyūkan. (Reprint in 1908)
1901. *Kaki kōshūkai kōenshū*. Tokyo: Kōmeisha.
1902 June. *Zenkai ichiran kōgi*. Tokyo: Shōkakukai. (Reprint in 1918 by Kōyūkan)
1904 December. *Gōma nisshi*. Kamakura: Tōkeiji.
1907 April. *Kankattō*. Trans. and ed. by Kawakami Tetsuta. Tokyo: Min'yūsha.
1907 July. *Shinjinmei kōwa*. Tokyo: Kōmeisha.
1907 October. *Ōbei unsuiki*. Tokyo: Kinkōdō.
1909 February. *Senteiroku*. Tokyo: Kōdōkan.
1909 March. *Ichiji fusetsu*. Tokyo: Kōyūkan.
1909 September. *Mumonkan kōgi*. Tokyo: Kōyūkan. (Reprint in 1915) (SZ under the title *Mumonkan kōwa*).
1910 December. *Yūmō shōjin*. Tokyo: Horiba Kinjirō.
1912 July. *Zazen wasan kōwa*. Tokyo: Kōyūkan.
1912 July. *Bukkyō katei kōwa*. Tokyo: Kōyūkan.
1913 January. *Jūgyūzu kōwa*. Tokyo: Kōyūkan. (Reprint in 1916)
1913 January. *Shuyō no shiori*. Collection of talks given in Korea and Manchuria in 1912. (Book not for sale, published by Minami Manshū tetsudō kabushiki gaisha shomuka. Later incorporated in *Nenge mishō*)
1915. *Nenge mishō*. Tokyo: Heigo shuppansha. (Reprint in 1977 by Kokusho kankōkai)
1915. *Hekiganroku kōwa*. Tokyo: Kōyūkan. (Reprint in 1917 and 1933) (SZ)
1916. *Yo no hoka*. Tokyo: Kōyūkan (Series *Zendō sōsho*).
1916 October. *Sōen zenna*. Tokyo: Ōsakayagō shoten. (Reprint in 1921 by Zenna sōsho kankōkai)
1917. *Rinki ōhen*. Tokyo: Bunshōdō. (Reprint in 1935 by Daikyōdōzō)
1918 May. *En'un sosui*. Kamakura: Tōkeiji. (Reprint in 1999 by Yumani shobō in the series *Taishō chūgoku kenmonroku shūsei*, ed. by Kojima Shinji, vol. 4; Also included in Vol. 9. of SZ under the new title *Shina junshakuki*)
1918. *Kannongyō kōwa*. Tokyo: Kōyūkan. (Reprint in 1924) (SZ)
1919 May. *Kaijin kaiba*. Tokyo: Nisshinkaku.
1919 May. *Wagan aigo*. Tokyo: Hakubunkan.
1919. *Tatakeyo hirakaren*. Tokyo: Konishi shoten. (Reprint in 1925 by Seizankaku shoten, in 1929 and 1938 by Kyōbunsha shoten, and in 1972 by Mizuho shobō)
1920. *Saigo no ikkatsu*. Tokyo: Teikoku shuppan kyōkai.
1920. *Kokoro no me o hirake*. Tokyo: Fumondō shoten.
1920. *Jōri chōrai*. Tokyo: Nihon tosho shuppan.
1920. *Ryōga manroku*. 5 vols. Kamakura: Ryōgae.
1921. *Gedatsu no seikatsu*. Ed. by Nobata Kazuo. Tokyo: Kyōbunsha.
1921. *Ryōgakutsu kashū*. Ed. by Sasaki Nobutsuna. Kamakura: Tōkeiji.
1923. *Saikontan kōwa*. Tokyo: Konishi shoten. (Reprint in 1929 and 1934 by Kyōbunsha shoten, then in 1960 by Bun'itsu shuppan)
1927 February. *Motomeyo ataeraren*. Tokyo: Chūō shuppansha.
1928. *Zen no shinzui: Shōji gedatsu shingen kaihatsu*. Tokyo: Chūō shuppansha.

1929–1930. *Shaku Sōen zenshū*. 10 vols. Ed. by Matsuda Take no shimabito. Tokyo: Heibonsha.
1931. *Daruma no ashiato: Ishin denshin kyōge betsuden*. Tokyo: Chūō shuppansha.
1931 February. *Zen no kaibō: Niku to chi to kawa*. Tokyo: Jōkōkan shuppanbu.
1932. *Mā suware*. Ed. by Wada Kenji. Tokyo: Kyōbunsha shoten.
1933. *Jinsei akarui yowatari*. Tokyo: Seikōkan shoten.
1939. *Shisei ichinyo: Zenna*. Ed. by Ōta Teizō. Tokyo: Daitō shuppansha.
1940 April. *Hyakumannin no zen*. Tokyo: Chōbunkaku.
1941. *Saiyū nikki*. Ed. by Inoue Zenjō. Kamakura: Tōkeiji (new edition in 2001).
1941. *Zen*. Tokyo: Bungaku shobō.
1941. *Hara o tsukure*. Tokyo: Chōbunkaku.
1941 May. *Daruma*. Zensōsho vol. 1. Tokyo: Bungaku shobō.
1957. *Zen no seizui*. Ed. by Nakaoka Hiroo. Tokyo: Seishin shobō.
2001. *Shin'yaku Shaku Sōen "Saiyū nikki."* Tokyo: Daihōrinkaku.

B. WORKS BY SŌEN OR ATTRIBUTED TO HIM IN ENGLISH (BOOKS ONLY)

Shaku Sōen. 1893. "The Law of Cause and Effect as Taught by Buddha." In Houghton, Walter R., ed. *Neely's History of the Parliament of Religions and Religious Congresses at the World's Columbian Exposition: Compiled from Original Manuscripts and Stenographic Reports.* 3rd ed. Chicago: F. Tennyson Neely, pp. 378–380.
Shaku Sōen. 1893. "The Law of Cause and Effect as Taught by Buddha." In Barrows, John Henry, ed. *The World's Parliament of Religions*. Chicago: Parliament Publishing, pp. 829–831.
Shaku Sōen. 1907 (1906). *Sermons of a Buddhist Abbot: Addresses on Religious Subjects, including the Sutra of Forty-two Chapters*. Trans. by Daisetz Teitaro Suzuki. Chicago: Open Court. (Reprint in Shaku 1993; also reprinted by Kessinger Publishing, 2006)
Shaku, Soyen (= Sōen). 1993. *Zen for Americans: Including the Sutra of Forty-Two Chapters*. New York: Barnes & Noble. (First published in 1907 as *Sermons of a Buddhist Abbot*)

C. MAIN BIOGRAPHIES OF SŌEN AND RELATED COLLECTIONS OF MATERIALS

Inoue Zenjō and Zenbunka kenkyūsho, ed. 1989. *Suzuki Daisetsu mikōkai shokan*. Kyoto: Zenbunka kenkyūsho.
Inoue Zenjō. 2000. *Shaku Sōen den*. Kyoto: Zenbunka kenkyūsho.
Nagao Daigaku (= Sōshi), ed. 1931. *Sōen zenji shokanshū*. Tokyo: Nishōdō.
Nagao Sōshi (= Daigaku). 1920. *Sōen zenji no menmoku*. Tokyo: Ryūbunkan.
Nagao Sōshi, ed. 1923. *Sōen zenji to sono shūi*. Tokyo: Kokushi kōshūkai (reprint in 1993 by Ōzorasha).
Nagao Sōshi, 1925. *Sōen zenji musetsushū*. Kamakura: Matsugaoka sanbō.
Shaku Keishun (Taibi), ed. 1942. *Ryōgakutsu nenjiden*. Kanaoka mura, Shizuoka: Daichūji.
Suzuki Daisetsu. 1992. *Imakita Kōsen: Gekidōki meiji no kōso*. Tokyo: Shunjūsha. (First edition 1944)

8

True Person, Formless Self: Lay Zen Master Hisamatsu Shin'ichi

Christopher Ives

In April of 1944, facing the destruction and death around them, Hisamatsu Shin'ichi (1889–1990) and several of his students at Kyoto University founded the Association for Self-Awakening.[1] Hisamatsu guided his students through intensive practice and study of Zen as they searched for answers to the existential and moral questions that were pressing upon them. By the time he died thirty-six years later, he had achieved renown as a charismatic lay master. With his exposition of Zen in relation to Western thought, reformulation of Zen practice, and skill at calligraphy and the tea ceremony, he occupies an important place in modern Zen history.

As a Zen philosopher, Hisamatsu reflected at length on the "ultimate antinomy" to which Zen responded and sketched how the Zen view of elements in that antinomy—sin and death, value and existence—diverges from Western perspectives. He also wrote on the chief characteristics of "Oriental Nothingness" and gave talks on an array of Buddhist texts. His legacy is evident in the distinguished careers of those who studied and practiced Zen under him, including Abe Masao (1915–2006), Zen thinker and representative of Zen in interfaith dialogue; Yanagida Seizan (1926–2006), a scholar of Zen texts; and Tokiwa Gishin (1926–), a Buddhologist at Hanazono University.

Hisamatsu was not, however, a typical apologist. Though he trained under a traditional Zen master and lived much of his adult life in Myōshinji, a prominent Rinzai Zen head temple in Kyoto, he criticized Zen for its focus on awakening (*satori*) at the expense of due consideration of social and political issues. This criticism informed the orientation of the Association for Self-Awakening, which in 1958 evolved into the F.A.S. Society.[2] The abbreviation F.A.S. encapsulates Hisamatsu's vision of a reformed, true Zen:

> Awakening to the *F*ormless Self,
> the dimension of depth, the Self as the ground of human existence;
> Standing on the standpoint of *A*ll Humankind,
> the dimension of width, human being in its entirety;
> Creating history *S*uprahistorically,
> the dimension of length, awakened human history.[3]

This three-dimensional standpoint finds further expression in the Society's "Vow of Humankind":

> Keeping calm and composed, let us awaken to our True Self, become fully compassionate humans, make full use of our gifts according to our respective missions in life, discern the agony both individual and social and its source, recognize the right direction in which history should proceed, and join hands without distinctions of race, nation, or class. Let us, with compassion, vow to bring to realization humankind's deep desire for Self-emancipation and construct a world in which everyone can truly and fully live.[4]

As the dynamic leader of the society, Hisamatsu drew from established Zen practice in emphasizing the importance of *zazen*, rigorous Zen retreats, and the cultivation of the "Great Doubt Block," yet he also crafted new forms of practice, foremost of which were his "fundamental kōan" in lieu of the roughly 1,700 cases in the traditional kōan curriculum and his notion of "mutual inquiry" (*sōgo-sankyū*) instead of formal kōan interviews (*sanzen*) with a Zen master.

In this chapter I will explore Hisamatsu's stature as a Zen master along the lines of F, A, and S, beginning with his analysis of the basic human problem, Awakening as the solution to that problem, Nothingness as that to which one awakens, and the forms of practice he formulated as a path to Awakening. I will then turn to his arguments about "all humankind," "creating history suprahistorically," and the "postmodern" world. In passing, I will touch upon Hisamatsu's artistic legacy, and then close by highlighting several issues in his standpoint.

Awakening to the Formless Self

Growing up in Gifu Prefecture in a Shin Buddhist family, Hisamatsu was a "steadfast young believer,"[5] with what he later called "a 'leave-it-up-to-the-Almighty' type of faith that avoided all doubts."[6] In middle school, while studying science, he started questioning his faith, until his "doubts only became deeper and more complex."[7] As Hisamatsu relates in the third person, "He reached an impasse, and his indestructible iron faith, of which he had been so proud, eventually crumbled at his feet."[8] He "underwent a conversion from the naïve, medieval form of religious life that avoids rational doubt, to the critical attitude of modern people that is based on autonomous rational judgment and empirical proof."[9] At the same time, "his rational awareness of sin further deepened and the desire to be rid of it became acute."[10]

Matriculating at Kyoto University in 1912 as a philosophy major did not help, for despite intensive studies over his first few years there, he "came to despair of the powerlessness of philosophy to solve his fundamental problem. He lost all interest in graduating from the University, though he had not yet defended the graduation thesis he had submitted. He spent days up in his room, lost in silent thought. His behavior at the time was so bizarre that an older student in the Department of Medicine from his hometown, assuming that he had developed some psychological abnormality, proceeded to telegraph his father."[11] In the midst of this crisis, at the suggestion of one of his professors, renowned philosopher Nishida Kitarō (1870–1945), Hisamatsu turned to Zen.

After learning how to sit *zazen* in the autumn of 1915, he went on his first Zen retreat, the grueling *rōhatsu sesshin* over the first seven days of December, under Ikegami Shōzan Rōshi at Myōshinji in Kyoto. "Deeply disillusioned with both theistic religion and rationalistic philosophy," Masao Abe writes, "he threw himself into that first *sesshin* with all the energy he could command to resolve the crisis occurring within him."[12] By the third day he had become "a single Great Doubt Block, in which the doubter and the doubted were one. This one block constituted his entire being. Like a mouse entering a bamboo tube only to find itself trapped there by a snake, or like being at the top of a hundred-foot pole and unable to go forward or backward, he had reached a total impasse and could no longer move."[13] He did not remain in that state, however: "Right at that moment . . . the Great Doubt Block crumbled apart and melted like ice from within. That imposing wall, Shōzan, also crumbled away without a trace, leaving not a hair's breadth between the student and the rōshi. Awakened to his formless, True Self, he gazed upon Shōzan's True Face for the first time."[14] Hisamatsu expressed this experience in a poem:

> With the breaking up
> Of rain and cloud,
> Even clearer,
> The moon in the great sky.
> The intimacy:
> The sound of a waterfall
> After the downpour
> Breaking the quiet night.[15]

In following his path, Hisamatsu had "cast off the religion of medieval belief, turned to philosophy grounded in modern reason, broke through the extreme limit of rational philosophy based on objective knowledge, and awakened to the free and unhindered True Self."[16] In this way he grasped the crux of Zen, which, to him, was "to awaken to the Formless Self of True Emptiness by virtue of great wisdom, to manifest all wondrous being by virtue of great compassion, and to give rise to great functioning spatially for all humankind and temporally for the history of all humankind."[17] And through the resolution of his moral and existential quandary, he also laid a foundation for his own religious standpoint: "It is the living experience of self-realization that constitutes the concrete base of my own religion and philosophy."[18]

Using philosophical language distinctive in the history of Zen, Hisamatsu later detailed what, exactly, happened to him on that December day: "With the awakening to the True Self, the rational self is cast off in negation. This results in autonomy of a deeper dimension, which has broken beyond and completely shaken off the limitations of rational autonomy. It is fundamental, absolute autonomy free of the fatalistic, absolute antinomy that characterizes rational autonomy."[19] Hisamatsu's critique of the "rational self" with its autonomy and antinomy derives from his view of the ordinary structure of human existence. In one of his most important essays, "Ultimate Crisis and Resurrection," he asks, "Where in people does one find the 'moment' whereby they need religion?"[20] As I have briefly outlined elsewhere,[21] Hisamatsu argues that the fundamental religious problems are sin and death, the two insurmountable facets of human existence. In making this argument, he expands the scope of "sin": "Even if we could get rid of sin in a moral sense, we could not be free from the contrast between ugliness and beauty in the world of art, or opposition between falsity and truth in the world of science."[22] From this perspective, sin comes down to the inseparability of the poles in these three dyads in the arenas of the will, feeling, and intellect.

Hisamatsu also argues that "sin ought to be extended to include the problem of reason per se."[23] That is to say, "The opposition of rational and irrational is basic to the structure of reason, so that to remove what is irrational and leave behind only what is rational is, one must say, impossible."[24] This inseparability characterizes death as well, for death cannot be separated from life, and "at the bottom of life there exists the antinomy of life-and-death."[25] Our core existential problem is thus not our mortality but "our sharing in the nature of life-and-death.... Therefore, the meaning of death ought to be deepened to the extent that not mere death but life-and-death is death."[26] Hisamatsu develops this thesis by further construing sin as the opposition of value and antivalue, and death as the opposition of existence and nonexistence (sonzai-hisonzai). And, ultimately, these dilemmas converge:

> In both value and existence the human harbors insolvable contradictions at the starting point or basis of life. And in the concrete human being, the two contradictions are found to exist in an indistinguishable, inseparable way. In that sense, they are nondual contradictions, an absolute, ultimate contradiction. That is to say, they are ultimate worries, the "moment" in humans that requires ultimate deliverance.[27]

Simply put, Hisamatsu construes sin not as the problem of evil but as the paradoxical inseparability of good and evil, or of value and antivalue, and death not as physical death but as the inseparability of life and death, or of existence and nonexistence. With this character, sin and death constitute the axiological and ontological dimensions of what Hisamatsu terms the "ultimate antinomy" at the core of human existence. In this respect, they are the reason humans turn to religion. As Hisamatsu puts it, "This ultimate antinomy's pressing upon us is the true moment of religion. Any death or sin that one can look at is an abstract one, a mere object of thought. We are confronted by ultimate death, ultimate sin. This ultimate antinomy is the very self-awareness in which existence and value are one; it is not anything to be known objectively. It is original to people; it is at once my way of being and that of all humans."[28]

In its most profound form, this "self-awareness" is the Great Doubt Block, which is "something total, in which emotional anguish and volitional dilemmas, as well as intellectual doubting, are one fundamental subject."[29] Reason, or the discriminating, dualistic ego, is unable to manage this predicament. Self-power (jiriki) is of no avail. There is only one way to solve it: "We must have every fetter cut off. We must die a Great Death and be born again."[30] That is to say, "The only way to break through it [the Doubt Block] is to be awakened to the True Self, the Self in which the Doubt Block is resolved. This entails a leap. The self caught in the ultimate antinomy cannot with continuity become the True Self. Only when that self breaks up does the Self or Oneness awaken to itself."[31] Expressed from another angle, "By our awakening to this Formless Self, we overcome the ultimately antinomic self and come to be saved from the ultimate antinomy. This is achieved not by the ultimately antinomic self overcoming that antinomy. Rather, from the bottom of ultimate antinomy, the Self by which the antinomy is overcome awakens."[32] Upon this awakening, we overcome the dilemmas, anguish, and contradictions of the will, emotion, and intellect, and we extricate ourselves from the antinomies of good-and-evil and life-and-death.[33]

This True, Formless Self that awakens through our pursuing a "thorough inquiry into life-and-death"[34] is not "some thing" that is objectifiable, nor a mere static ground or void apart from actuality. In more standard Buddhist terminology, "By the seeing of one's nature we do not mean any objective contemplation, objective awareness, or objective cognition of Self-Nature or Buddha-Nature; we mean the Awakening of the Self-Nature itself. Since there is no Buddha apart from this awakening, to 'become Buddha' means to come to the true Self-Awakening."[35] As this buddha or awakened one, "the True Self or the Formless Self is beyond the opposition of self and world, within and without. . . . The True Self, without having in itself the structure of being and non-being, at the same time forms the ground of being and non-being."[36] In this way, the True Formless Self "does not negate the world of birth and death, but transcends birth and death, being free from the bonds of birth and death. It is not in space and time, and yet, transcending space and time, embraces them within itself."[37] It is unconditionally free. Beyond all forms, or, better yet, *prior to all forms*, the True Self can function without getting caught by the assumed form or the functioning. It is this liberated, unhindered activity that Hisamatsu refers to as the Formless Self. Only this Self realizes absolute autonomy beyond theonomy and ego-based autonomy. It is the Self that dwells nowhere—in neither life nor death, good nor evil, male nor female, east nor west—yet can function freely in all of these forms.

Hisamatsu elaborates on the True Self in terms of the Buddhist construct of Nothingness. He writes that "if one awakens to the True Self, one realizes that the True Self is Nothingness, and only when we know the Self as Nothingness are we able to truly live and truly function freely."[38] In a 1939 essay, "The Characteristics of Oriental Nothingness," Hisamatsu argues that Nothingness is "the active contemplating Mind, . . . Subject-Nothingness in which active and passive are one, and in which the duality of mind and object is left behind."[39] And he expounds on the True Self as Nothingness in terms of six positive characteristics of Nothingness.

First, in terms of the "Not a Single Thing" characteristic, Hisamatsu argues that Nothingness is the "Nothingness-state of myself, that is, it is no other than myself being Nothingness."⁴⁰ The self here is the Formless Self, which is free from all definition and limitation. More exactly put, it is not that there is "an entity" called the Self that has no form, but rather that not having any form whatsoever, not standing as "something" opposed to other things, is precisely the dynamic way of being called the Formless Self. Hisamatsu argues along these lines that the normal self always stands in opposition to things: "It may be said that there is almost no time when one is not entertaining some internal or external object. The ordinary 'I,' therefore, is an 'I' that is always connected with an object. This is the reason that consciousness is said to have the character of noema-noesis."⁴¹ The True Self, however, does not stand opposed to objects, for it is their unobjectifiable ground (an *Ungrund* ground, as it were): "The 'I' that does not have an object, the 'I' that does not have a single thing, is the 'I' that is no longer dependent upon or attached to anything. It is the 'I' that is not of the nature of noema-noesis."⁴²

Second, concerning the "Like Empty Space" characteristic, Hisamatsu writes that the True Self as Nothingness is Non-Abiding Subjectivity, which "neither abides in something nor abides in no-thing."⁴³ This Self is beyond all delimitation, including being and nonbeing. Since it is without beginning or end, it is unborn and undying (*fushō-fushi*) and hence neither becomes nor decays. It clings neither to things nor to itself, and for this reason it is "completely without anything 'obtained.'"⁴⁴

With regard to the "Mind-in-Itself" facet of Nothingness, Hisamatsu argues that "The True Buddha (True Self) is not without mind, but possesses Mind that is 'without mind and without thought'; and it is not without self-awareness, but possesses Awareness that is 'without awareness.' An egoless ego is not without life, but possesses life that is ungenerated and unperishing."⁴⁵ In contrast to our usual mind, which is obstructed and attached, this Mind is beyond birth and death, beyond obstructions, limitation, form, defilement, and attachments. It is free from all of the divisions and barriers erected by ego-centered thought.

In discussing the "Self" aspect of Nothingness, Hisamatsu writes that the True Self is a "pure, absolute subject."⁴⁶ It is an active seeing, not a "mind" that is seen. That is to say, the True Self as "Mind does not obtain as object, but obtains as subject."⁴⁷ And describing the fifth characteristic, freedom, Hisamatsu maintains that "Oriental Nothingness as the subjective subject is, further, the completely free subject."⁴⁸ What is entailed here is neither the sensuous freedom of children nor the mature rational freedom of which Kant speaks. By transcending reason and attaining liberation from sin as the inseparability of good and evil and death as life-and-death, one realizes true religious freedom. Of course, such a transrational, transmoral realm is also opened up in Christianity with its notions of grace and unconditional love. But Hisamatsu sees Zen as going beyond the dichotomy of human and God or human and Buddha and opening up "the truly free state that is neither bound nor obstructed by either humans or Buddha."[49] Again, this freedom is attained by ridding oneself of the ego-self and awakening to the True Self, by seeing into one's True Nature beyond the antinomic polarity at the heart of human existence. This "'seeing into one's True Nature,' not being anything, is every-thing, and being everything, is not anything. It is in this sense that the true meaning of 'absolute negation is none other than absolute affirmation; and absolute affirmation is none other than negation' (J. *zettai hitei soku zettai kōtei, zettai kōtei soku zettai hitei*) is to be understood."[50] Here, the True Self as No-thingness, being absolutely no-thing, permeates everything, and being nowhere, is everywhere.

Sixth, Hisamatsu sketches the creative aspect of Nothingness. He takes the True Self as creative along the lines of Scotus Erigena, arguing that "only in and as that which creates but is not created can creativity be said to be primary and absolute."[51] This creative Mind differs from Kant's "consciousness in general," for whereas the objects of consciousness in general come from the outside, "in Buddhism, on the contrary, that which is reflected in the mirror [Mind] is not something that comes from outside the mirror, but something that is produced from within the mirror."[52] Hisamatsu elaborates on this with a metaphor:

> The creative nature of Oriental Nothingness is to be illustrated by the relation between the water and the wave, in which the water is forever and in every *way* the subject. If one were to make a subject of the wave, which is produced and disappears, this would be the ordinary human self. It is in such an ordinary subject's reverting back from wave to water—that is, returning to its source—and reemerging as the True Subject or True Self that the characteristics of Oriental Nothingness must be sought and are to be found.[53]

Along these lines, Hisamatsu writes in another essay, "The satori of Zen is like the phenomenal waves returning from waves to water, recognizing water as their original feature, that is, as their noumenon. It is the return of the phenomenal waves to noumenal water."[54] This return to the noumenal water is nothing passive. The water is not a negative nothingness, but creative, active Nothingness, functioning in and among the rising and falling waves.

Masao Abe argues in an essay on Hisamatsu's philosophy that by experiencing at a young age the crumbling of his own "naive religious belief that avoids rational doubt,"[55] and then despairing of reason's ability to solve his most pressing existential problem, Hisamatsu himself passed through medieval theocentric faith and modern, anthropocentric, rational autonomy.[56] He realized the contradiction of rationality and irrationality inherent in the structure of reason, and sought a standpoint beyond modern anthropocentrism, a standpoint that would not be a facile turning back to medieval theocentrism. By penetrating absolute sin and absolute death, Hisamatsu awakened to the Formless Self as the basis of absolute autonomy beyond theocentrism and anthropocentrism. He thereby established "a standpoint of absolute autonomy, which, though atheistic, is deeply religious, and though religious, is never contradictory to rational autonomy."[57] This standpoint is not mere transcendence as in theocentrism, nor immanence as in anthropocentrism, but rather a transcendent immanence in which ultimacy as the True Self, the "Way of Subjectivity" (*shutaidō*)[58] is realized through the death of the ego-self.

Though it was Zen that reportedly solved the core existential questions with which he had been grappling, Hisamatsu did not accept the tradition in the form he had inherited. From his perspective, Zen historically has given Mahayana compassion that ostensibly animates it too narrow of a focus:

> If, as has been the case with Zen, activity starts and ends only with the so-called practice of compassion involved in helping others to awaken, such activity will remain unrelated to the formation of the world or creation of history, isolated from the world and history, and in the end turn Zen into a forest Buddhism, temple Buddhism, at best, a Zen-monastery Buddhism. Ultimately this becomes "Zen within a ghostly cave."[59]

Hisamatsu admits that "Rinzai Zen decries stopping at the standpoint of emptiness and becoming entangled in oneness, describing this in such ways as 'Zen person in a demonic cave,' 'attached, degenerating in a dark cave,' and 'the evil Zen of silent illumination (*mokushō Zen*).'"[60] But he claims that this stopping is, in fact, what Zen has done, and "if Zen ends in mere self-awakening and the awakening of others (*jikaku-kakuta*), it is not perfect awakened functioning."[61] Zen in all of its forms in modern Japan needs to reflect on and respond to problems facing humanity, even though there are "people who feel that not having an interest in such problems is a condition for true Zen practice."[62]

Hisamatsu's criticism of Zen extends beyond its overemphasis on satori to practice itself. He claims that Zen monastics typically engage kōans "quantitatively" as they work on and pass kōans one by one in what he terms "ladder" (*hashigo*) Zen, gradually transforming themselves but not realizing a complete and decisive Awakening. Deploying the metaphor of a polygon and a circle, he sees such practitioners as adding sides to a polygon to make it increasingly resemble a circle but never reaching true circularity. To attain the circle, what is needed is a negation, a qualitative disjunction.

Cognizant of this "ladder" pitfall in traditional kōan practice, Hisamatsu advances what he calls the "fundamental kōan" (*kihonteki kōan*), which subsumes all other kōans and purportedly brings the practitioner to a total realization. He proclaims, "I would like to establish a method for 'Cornered, one passes through, passing through, one changes,' in the simple form, 'Right now, if nothing you do is of any avail, what will you do?' (*Dō shitemo ikenai to sureba, dō suru ka*). If all our ways of being and all our actions are of no avail, what do we do? The expression, 'all our actions,' refers to our total actuality, but the situation where nothing will do is an absolute predicament, the last extremity."[63] In effect asking, "When you can neither do nor be anything whatsoever, what do you do?," this kōan includes all other traditional kōans, and its resolution is none other than complete, immediate Awakening (*tongo*).

Hisamatsu also questions the need to work with a certified Zen master. In the F.A.S. approach, one does not go to a particular master and present one's understanding of the kōan. Rather, one engages in "mutual inquiry" (*sōgo sankyū*) with other committed practitioners, on the assumption that one is ultimately meeting and engaging with the True Self. The context of this mutual inquiry has been the retreats of the F.A.S. Society three times a year at Reiun'in, a Myōshinji subtemple, and more recently at other sites in and around Kyoto, including Shōkokuji. Hisamatsu termed the retreats *betsuji-gakudō*, "special time for studying the Way," and like traditional Zen *sesshin*, they lasted for seven days with rigorous *zazen*, walking meditation,[64] three-bowl *oryōki* meals, physical labor, and chanting (*gongyō*) of such texts as the *Heart Sutra* (*Hannya shingyō*), "Daitō Kokushi's Admonition" (*Daitō kokushi yuikai*), and the "Vow of Humankind."[65] At the retreats, Hisamatsu offered sermons on classical Zen texts, sutras,[66] and Buddhist treatises, although he called his talks *teikō* rather than using the customary Zen term, *teishō*, which he thought was a less dynamic approach to Zen discourse.

In recent years, the retreats of the F.A.S. Society have become less frequent, but members do continue meeting on most Saturday evenings, primarily at Rinkō'in, a subtemple at Shōkokuji. These gatherings, termed *heijō dōjō*, "ordinary place for [practicing] the Way," begin with *jikkyū*, several thirty-minute periods of *zazen* with some walking meditation in between, followed by the serving of tea and about an hour of *ronkyū*, or discussion of Hisamatsu's talks or writings. Although monks and nuns have participated in F.A.S. gatherings, the primary focus has been on the laity. In fact, Hisamatsu believed that one did not need to become a monk to awaken to the True Self. If one had Great Faith, Great Resolution, and a Great Doubting Spirit, one could wake up, regardless of whether one was living in a monastery. Hisamatsu thus rejected the Zen of a small coterie of monastics and in its stead advocated a "Zen for the masses" (*taishū Zen*).

While forging his novel approach to practice, Hisamatsu was well aware of the pitfalls of an overemphasis on practice, just as he criticized those who overemphasized Zen scholarship at the expense of practice. Cognizant of these possible shortcomings, he advocated the "unity of study and practice" (gakugyō-ichinyo). Since practice without study is blind and study without practice is powerless, one must negotiate the Way while pursuing both religious practice and academic study. Hisamatsu thus advocated that the Zen path go beyond narrow monastic discipline—zazen, kōans, physical work (samu)—and include study of social, political, and economic dimensions of history. He criticized scholars of Buddhism, claiming that "modern Buddhology, while taking in new Western ways of study, has tended to follow in the footsteps of traditional Chinese methods emphasizing the doctrinal study of the different schools. Practice has become an object of research. Living practice has been all but ignored."[67] For this reason, Buddhologists "have become strangers to practice, and because of that, to satori itself."[68] In this respect, "It is not the objective and impartial study of ethical, philosophical, or religious phenomena, but gaining knowledge of how to 'live' morality, philosophy, or religion, that must be the essential concern."[69] That is to say, our concern "must be that fundamental human subjectivity should come to be the totally and ultimately unified self."[70]

One fact that must be kept in mind in surveying his critique of Zen is that Hisamatsu did not speak from the detached standpoint of an external observer. Kitahara Ryūtarō, one of his senior students, once commented that "Hisamatsu made his criticism only after having gone through all the kōans at Myōshinji,"[71] and "a criticism of traditional Zen coming from the mouth of someone who doesn't know anything about it is likely to be an erroneous one."[72]

As we have seen, Hisamatsu concurs with Zen masters before him that Awakening is the crux of his tradition, but from his perspective that realization alone is not sufficient, for one must then, as what he calls the True or Formless Self, take the standpoint of all humankind and create history anew:

> The Formless Self, which is no-birth-and-death freed from birth-and-death, must function and give rise to all things in actuality. This is the True Self (F), which constitutes the source of A and S. It is Self-Awakening. In that it is spatially boundless (formless), it is the basis of All Humankind, and in that it transcends the three periods of past, present, and future, it is the basis of Suprahistorical history. Since this Self is no-thought (*mu-nen*), no-mind (*mu-shin*), and the true reality of no-boundary, one can stand in the standpoint of all humankind and create history while transcending history.[73]

Let us now turn to these second and third dimensions of Hisamatsu's schema of F, A, and S.

Standing in the Standpoint of All Humankind

Having experienced the carnage of the Second World War, Hisamatsu recognizes the danger of the modern nation-state. He writes, "The second point (A) lies in transcending the fatally deadlocked egoistic structure of the nation-state, and in creating a universal and unified sovereignty for all mankind."[74] In a "Postmodernist Manifesto," he declares that "we can no longer trust absolute sovereignty to nation states. . . . Because of egoism, in the realm of politics, world peace is impossible, in the realm of economics, the free circulation of material and spiritual wealth is obstructed, and in the realm of ethics, universality for all humans is lost."[75] To replace nation-states, he calls for "a world system, in which all of the world is one, not a state system or a nation system."[76] The first requisite for that system is for the Formless Self to take the stance of "all humankind."

Hisamatsu views the dimension of humankind in Mahāyāna fashion, for he construes the Awakening of one person as simultaneously the Awakening of all people, while recognizing that most people do not realize that they are originally or fundamentally awakened. For this reason, the compassion that wells up from the depths of Awakening—rather than from Amida or God—directs itself to helping people confirm that they are fundamentally awake. In this respect, "True religious life lies not in our receiving compassion but in our turning over that approach and practicing compassion ourselves."[77] Hisamatsu construes this compassion as "Objectless Great Compassion":

> In one's original condition . . . there is no salvation. That is to say, in one's original place there is no saving and no being saved. Saving and being saved, seen from the standpoint distinguishing Expedient Dharma and True Dharma, are Expedient Dharma. Clearly realizing that one is originally saved, that saving and being saved are originally nonexistent, and then saving those who do not realize this fact—this amounts to Objectless Great Compassion. Therefore, if one is unawakened to the True Self, one cannot understand this point and in ignorance is convinced one must be saved.[78]

This can also be termed Bodhisattva Functioning (*bosatsu-gyō*), in which the actor is no ordinary ego but a "transcendent Person or transcendent humanity,"[79] operating on the basis of "the whole of mankind as width and such transcendent humanity as depth."[80] And as indicated by the "Vow of Humankind," Hisamatsu argues that humans must transcend their differences and work together to solve not only the fundamental religious problems of sin and death, value and existence, but also the various other forms of suffering in the world.

Creating History Suprahistorically

Like the spatial dimension of all humankind, the temporal dimension of creating history suprahistorically derives from the depth dimension of Awakening:

> The casting off and self-dissolution of the ultimately contradictory subject of history, and its freeing of itself with the emergence of the unhindered, self-abiding, fundamental subject is not achieved in the movement of history, that is, through the historical dialectic. It is accomplished at the root-source of history, which is prior to the birth of history. In living in history itself there is an ultimate contradiction, and this ultimate contradiction cannot be resolved by means of living in history. It can only be resolved through the self-dissolution of history itself. Therefore, though the term "the casting off and self-dissolution of history" has been used, this means that history "casts itself off," and returns to what is prior to its own birth.[81]

In short, we must break beyond not only the inherent contradictions of human existence but also the contradictions at the base of history, and in the resultant awakening, Hisamatsu claims, the True Self, the true world, and true history converge.

From Hisamatsu's Buddhist perspective, time is beginningless and endless. In Awakening, the past and future "roll back" into the Eternal Now, the *nunc stans* that contains past, present, and future. In Awakening to the Absolute Present, one grasps the *eschaton*, the end of history, right now, not in the future. Of course, although history is cast off and one awakens to Absolute Present, there still remains an aspect of "not yet," in the sense that work still needs to be done to awaken others and create a historical world in which all people can live peacefully in fulfillment. Hisamatsu construes this activity as a "creating without parting from Awakening,"[82] with the True Self transcending history while working within it. The True, Formless Self retains its freedom—as the Zen expression puts it, is "solitarily emancipated and non-dependent" (*dokudatsu-mue*)—and "it is only when we are free from our very action of creation that we can really create history."[83] In this respect, Hisamatsu claims, only the True Self can create history "suprahistorically."

Operating in tandem with the nation-state as an obstruction to taking the stance of all humankind and creating a different kind of history is modernity:

> The modern age collapsed as a consequence of excessive "multiplication." Accordingly, the method for the resurrection of the modern world lies neither in a restoration of the medieval world, which is lacking in multiplicity, nor in a further intensification of the approach of the modern world, which is completely devoid of "unity." Rather, it must be realized in the thoroughgoing actualization of existence itself as the non-dualistic oneness of unity and multiplicity in which multiplicity is realized in unity and unity in multiplicity. Herein, unity is the root-source to which multiplicity must return, while multiplicity is the expression of unity. Thus unity and multiplicity do not consist of a mere static relation, but rather a dynamic and creative one.[84]

To "resurrect" the modern world in this way, Hisamatsu argues for the creation of a "postmodern world." This new world does not, however, lie on a line of extension from antiquity, the middle ages, and modernity, for there needs to be a fundamental break between the modern and postmodern ages, paralleling the break between the antinomic ego-self and the True Self. "The postmodern world does not signify something merely coming after modern humanity in the temporal sense, but rather, in an ontological sense, the creative realization of being itself in human history, whereby the two indispensable conditions for existence [unity and multiplicity] will be equally . . . fulfilled."[85] As Abe Masao puts it, "By postmodern, he did not refer to some future time in a chronological sense, but to a time in which the ultimate basis of the modern age and all past time as well is fundamentally overcome and in which Self, world, and history are completely fulfilled."[86]

In his criticism of modernity, Hisamatsu rejects the "idealistic humanism" through which modern humans apply their rationality to solve the myriad problems confronting them. With its faith in the rational ego, idealistic humanism cannot penetrate to the deepest source of problems. However successful it may be at solving certain problems and ameliorating certain forms of human suffering in history, it does not resolve the basic human problem that causes those problems in the first place, nor does it resolve the antinomy at the base of history itself. As Hisamatsu writes, "the solution of the branch problems alone will not bring about the solution of the root problem."[87] Lacking this resolution of the fundamental problem in the structure of the ego and history, "idealistic humanism is a false endlessness. Attached to existence, it never overcomes the issue of the inseparability of existence and nonexistence. It tries to take only the existence side of existence-nonexistence . . . This is the standpoint of the delusion that it can reach an eternally unreachable goal."[88] As Hisamatsu elaborates, "From what standpoint are we to approach actual problems, as the unsettled wave or the formless water?" We must, as another of Hisamatsu's metaphors would have it, function like a spider, which never gets stuck in its web, not like a silkworm, which gets bound by its creation.

Hisamatsu's insight found expression not only in his standpoint of F.A.S. but also in his poetry, unorthodox calligraphy, and accomplished performance of the tea ceremony. During his many years of teaching at universities in Kyoto[89] and living in Hōseki-an,[90] part of the Shunkō'in subtemple of Myōshinji, Hisamatsu devoted himself to the practice of these Japanese arts. "Calligraphy, painting, and poetry," as Abe relates, "all became vehicles of awakened self-expression. Hisamatsu was especially fond of the tea ceremony, which for him was also an expression of the same Awakening, transcending all tea schools and ceremonial forms."[91] Abe further comments, "He looked with disfavor on the modern tea ceremony, in the forms into which it has fallen in modern times. In departing from the true spirit of Zen, he felt it had developed strong tendencies to mannerism. His role as a reformer can be seen in the time and effort he devoted to the Shincha-kai (Mind-Tea Society), which he organized in 1941 in an effort to infuse the tea ceremony with new meaning based on the spirit of Zen."[92] Hisamatsu also wrote on Zen aesthetics, and his most important work in that area, *Zen to bijutsu*, was translated by Tokiwa Gishin in 1971 as *Zen and the Fine Arts*.

Critical Assessment

At a time when bookstores abound with "Zen and the Art of" titles and many people are content to practice Zen simply as a way to cultivate self-discipline, mindfulness, or concentration, Hisamatsu's sustained focus on fundamental issues in human existence merits attention. His ongoing concern was the committed engagement with existential predicaments that many traditional Zen Buddhists would claim makes Zen a path of liberation, of salvation, if you will, rather than simply a hip hobby or a self-help technique. The trade-off here is that in focusing so much on fundamental existential issues, the impasse of the Great Doubt Block, and Zen awakening,[93] Hisamatsu says little about possible interim fruits of Zen practice, the partial transformation of the vast majority of practitioners, who have not experienced the Great Death and Great Awakening of which Hisamatsu speaks. Though Hisamatsu is to be applauded for not dwelling on relative concerns and attainments, his focus on Great Death and

Great Awakening runs the risk of rendering his path distant to most of "all humankind," if not elitist.

Along these lines, Hisamatsu seems to be arguing that the standpoint of F, A, and S can be understood and actualized only by those who are awakened to the True Self. Indeed, about our ability to understand the aesthetic side of Zen he once wrote, "In order . . . to determine which calligraphic style or which style of painting or which music expresses a Zen style, one must have a thoroughly vivid Zen realization. If one lacks this realization, one probably will not be able to understand why a certain calligraphic style . . . expresses Zen meaning."[94] Needless to say, his overwhelming emphasis on full awakening impacts his institutional legacy insofar as no members of F.A.S. have emerged with the stature and charisma of Hisamatsu as an "awakened True Self."

Another issue that emerges in Hisamatsu's standpoint is his claim that Zen awakening lifts us above divisions of nationality, race, class, and gender and equips us with the ability to function in the midst of such distinctions without getting caught up in them. The historical record indicates that supposedly awakened Zen masters have been far from enlightened on issues surrounding those distinctions, as evidenced by "Imperial-Way Zen" during the Second World War[95] and recent sex scandals in Zen centers. In fact, traditional blind spots in the areas of nationality, race, class, and gender have led some modern Zen thinkers to deny that awakening has any significant impact on one's social and political savvy. After the Second World War, D. T. Suzuki argued that "by itself *satori* is unable to judge the right and wrong of war."[96] Zen master Bernie Glassman has suggested that "even while possessing great realization, we still have our conditioning, our own particular characteristics, our own particular paths. Little of that changes overnight."[97]

Hisamastu's focus on what he sees as the basic predicament and its resolution, though more penetrating than much of what goes by the name of Zen these days, also tends to imply that other religious paths are shallow, that is, are insufficient as resolutions of sin and death. His discourse implies that only those who experience the Great Death and awaken to the True Self are truly qualified to address social and political problems. Of course, most people working to transform the world would accept his diagnosis of how contemporary problems and suffering derive in large part from the nature of the human ego (or more proximately from the institutions and practices it generates), but partial solutions—as opposed to Hisamatsu's apparently "all or nothing" approach—are possible in an ego-based way of functioning, even if it harbors the "false endlessness" of which he spoke. And especially outside the monastery walls, in the lay world where Hisamatsu chose to build the F.A.S. Society, most people are compelled to respond to problems of actuality in whatever way they can and do not have the luxury of waiting until they can do so as the Formless Self.

Moreover, Jews, Christians, and Muslims committed to social justice would surely question whether what Hisamatsu terms the "postmodern world" can be established only by means of an absolute discontinuity, the absolute death of the antinomic ego and history itself. A Christian, for example, might argue that an experience of grace frees one from narrow, selfish concerns and prepares and motivates one to respond to the problems of the world and history just as much as a Zen-style death of the ego does. Even nonreligious people have made major contributions to overcoming the suffering caused by nationalism and modernity, the main objects of Hisamatsu's concern. In fact, in the 1920s and 1930s, while ostensibly awakened Zen masters were jumping on the imperialist bandwagon, fully entangled in history and seemingly unable to see it clearly much less transcend it or create it "suprahistorically," it was the Marxists who were criticizing the nation-state. Perhaps Hisamatsu would argue that those nationalist Zen masters were not fully awakened to the True Self, but one wonders why Hisamatsu, with all of his concern about self-interested nation-states and human entanglement in them, did not more explicitly address the issue of Zen war responsibility in the decades following 1945.

Even if we allow for the sake of the argument that Hisamatsu's approach is not elitist and that a large number of people could awaken to the Formless Self, we are still left with the question of what, exactly, the "dropping off" of history might entail. At the moment of his awakening in 1915, how was World War One affected? How did his teaching and other actions in the three decades after that affect the historical process that led to Hitler, Tōjō, and the bombing of Hiroshima and Nagasaki?

We also confront the question of the exact forms the suprahistorical creation of history might take. Hisamatsu rejects the modern nation-state and advocates going beyond it to a world system of all humankind, but what exact steps are necessary to get us there? Hisamatsu offered no specific, concrete proposals. And on what other areas might the creation of history focus? Economic injustice? Environmental degradation? And what features of Hisamatsu's approach, if put into action, would distinguish it from the actions being taken by non-Zen actors committed to social justice? Hisamatsu might argue that I am setting up a false dichotomy between transforming oneself and transforming history, for he argues that the death of egoism, the turning over of the ego in the One Great Death, is nothing other than the turning over and transformation of history. But Hisamatsu never elaborated on the creation of history with any degree of detail. Nor did he take public stances or protest while alive, even though many Japanese with similar criticisms of nationalism were highly active in opposing state support of the Yasukuni Shrine, the security treaty with the United States, the Vietnam War, and other developments that were directly related to the problem of the nation-state, ostensibly Hisamatsu's main ethical concern. This lack of specificity about concrete issues and actions leaves Hisamatsu's standpoint vulnerable to such criticisms as Bernard Faure's characterization of F.A.S. as "an idealistic and rather grandiloquent lay movement."[98]

Steven Antinoff, who practiced Zen ardently with the F.A.S. Society in the 1970s, has addressed the pitfall of Hisamatsu's dominant focus on how the ego taints history and how humans must transcend the nation-state and stand in the standpoint of all humankind. In his Ph.D. dissertation on Hisamatsu, Antinoff writes, "The setting forth of the trans-national ideal, taken in conjunction with the total repudiation of the efficacy of less 'exalted' forms of international social organization and cooperation, reveals a perfectionistic utopianism of the most sentimental type."[99] He further argues:

> The perfectionistic and sentimental nature of his concrete proposal to transfer sovereignty to all humankind, the utter neglect of the question of what means are permissible in seeking to gain his objective or retain it against the onslaught of a determined opposition, and the absence of any basis or strategy for discerning and supporting the relatively better policy or cause in a struggle between admittedly egoistic forces where the actualization of his program is not an immediate issue, all show his advance over traditional Zen to be far from adequate.[100]

Antinoff turns to theologian Reinhold Niebuhr's "Christian realism" to explore how Hisamatsu's standpoint might be augmented to allow for serious consideration of injustice and proximate steps that egos in history might take to ameliorate human suffering, all the while recognizing that such actions and their positive fruits are partial and need to be scrutinized in light of the transnational ideal Hisamatsu lifts up. Antinoff also makes a proposal: "What is mandatory . . . is a dual perspective which realistically seeks to do justice to both ultimate and relative dilemmas in human existence, that is, a perspective in which the religious criticism of both polarities of any duality not only does not entail the suppression of the moral (or socio-political) imperative for the actualization of the positive pole, but is sensitive to the ambiguous and tragic aspects of any meaningful attempt to effect that actualization."[101]

Despite the questions I raise here about his approach, Hisamatsu will in all likelihood continue to be recognized as an important modern Zen master. His path to Zen and his treatment of the tradition were both informed by his particular historical situation, and as Abe has argued, "The originality of his standpoint lies in the fact that he awakened . . . by overcoming both theistic religious belief and rational humanistic philosophy, grasping the Nothingness of the Zen tradition."[102] If, like his teacher Nishida Kitarō, Hisamatsu's religious thought is, as I have in effect argued here, more sophisticated than his political and historical analysis, Hisamatsu's legacy will rest less on his exposition of "A" and "S" than on his exposition of "F." Like other important masters across the history of Zen, Hisamatsu offered a distinctive representation of the core religious teaching of Zen, and it remains to be seen whether his exposition of what he sees as *the* problem in human existence and his F.A.S. version of the Zen path will in future decades continue to attract the interest of scholars and those who might pour themselves into practice with the commitment that he and his immediate followers exhibited sixty-five years ago in the middle of war.

NOTES

1. The Japanese name is Gakudō Dōjō, and though the group translated it into English as the Association for Self-Awakening and Abe Masao rendered it "The Seat of Awakening," the expression literally means "place for studying the Way."

2. By virtue of arrangements made by D. T. Suzuki, in the Fall 1957 semester Hisamatsu taught at Harvard Divinity School, where he engaged in dialogue with theologian Paul Tillich; and in early 1958 he traveled to Europe, where he had discussions with Carl Jung, Martin Buber, Martin Heidegger, and others. A record of his dialogue with Tillich was published as "Dialogues East and West: Paul Tillich and Hisamatsu Shin'ichi," *Eastern Buddhist* 4/2 (1971): 89–107; 5/2 (1972): 107–128; and 6/2 (1973): 87–114. Parts of Hisamatsu's conversation with Jung can be found in "On the Unconscious, the Self, and Therapy: A Dialogue—Carl G. Jung and Shin-ichi Hisamatsu," *Psychologia* 11 (1968): 80–87.

3. Masao Abe, "Hisamatsu Shin'ichi, 1889–1980," *Eastern Buddhist* 14/1 (1981): 143.

4. The Vow of Humankind was crafted in 1951.

5. Hisamatsu Shin'ichi, "Memories of My Academic Life" (*Gakkyū seikatsu no omoide*), translated by Christopher A. Ives, *Eastern Buddhist* 18/1 (1985): 10.

6. Hisamatsu, "Memories of My Academic Life," p. 11.

7. Hisamatsu, "Memories of My Academic Life," p. 10.

8. Ibid.

9. Hisamatsu, "Memories of My Academic Life," p. 11.

10. Ibid.

11. Hisamatsu, "Memories of My Academic Life," p. 18.

12. Abe, "Hisamatsu Shin'ichi, 1889–1980," p. 143.

13. Hisamatsu, "Memories of My Academic Life," p. 25.

14. Hisamatsu, "Memories of My Academic Life," p. 26.

15. Ibid.

16. Ibid.

17. Hisamatsu Shin'ichi, "Atarashiki sekai no Bukkyōteki kōsō" (A Buddhist Conception of a New World), in *Hisamatsu Shin'ichi chosakushū* (The Collected Writings of Hisamatsu Shin'ichi; hereafter *HSC*) 3 (Tokyo: Risōsha, 1976), p. 72.

18. Hisamatsu Shin'ichi, "The Characteristics of Oriental Nothingness," *Philosophical Studies of Japan* 3 (1959): 65.

19. Hisamatsu Shin'ichi, "Ultimate Crisis and Resurrection, part II," *Eastern Buddhist* 8/2 (1975): 50.

20. Hisamatsu Shin'ichi, "Ultimate Crisis and Resurrection, part I," *Eastern Buddhist* 8/1 (1975): 16.

21. Christopher Ives, *Zen Awakening and Society* (London: Macmillan; Honolulu: University of Hawaii Press, 1992), pp. 72–75. For an extensive discussion of Hisamatsu's analysis of human existence, see Steven Antinoff, "The Problem of the Human Person and the Resolution of that Problem in the Religio-Philosophical Thought of the Zen Master Shin'ichi Hisamatsu" (Ph.D. diss., Temple University, 1990).

22. Hisamatsu, "Ultimate Crisis and Resurrection, part I," p. 20.

23. Ibid.

24. Ibid.

25. Hisamatsu, "Ultimate Crisis and Resurrection, part I," p. 23.

26. Ibid.

27. Hisamatsu, "Ultimate Crisis and Resurrection, part II," p. 45 (translation partially adapted here).

28. Hisamatsu, "Ultimate Crisis and Resurrection, part I," p. 24.

29. Hisamatsu, "Ultimate Crisis and Resurrection, part I," p. 26.

30. Hisamatsu, "Ultimate Crisis and Resurrection, part II," p. 61.

31. Hisamatsu, "Ultimate Crisis and Resurrection, part I," p. 28 (partially adapted here).

32. Hisamatsu, "Ultimate Crisis and Resurrection, part II," p. 49.

33. As Hisamatsu argued in his conversation with Jung, "The cure in psychoanalysis is to . . . treat isolated diseases individually. But, in Zen, as indicated by the expressions *do-issai-kuyaku* (save everything from suffering) and *kyūkyō gedatsu* (ultimate extrication), it is to be awakened to the 'Self' not enmeshed by things, and to get rid of all diseases at once." Hisamatsu and Jung, "Unconsciousness and No Mind," p. 87.

34. Hisamatsu Shin'ichi, "*Mondō*: At the Death of a 'Great Death Man,'" *Eastern Buddhist* 2/1 (1967): 31.

35. Hisamatsu Shin'ichi, "Zen: Its Meaning for Modern Civilization," *Eastern Buddhist* 1/1 (1965): 32.

36. Association for Self-Awakening, *Nothingness* (Kyoto: Association for Self-Awakening, 1957), p. 16.

37. Ibid.

38. Hisamatsu, "Atarashiki sekai no Bukkyōteki kōsō," p. 129.

39. Hisamatsu, "The Characteristics of Oriental Nothingness," p. 71.

40. Hisamatsu, "The Characteristics of Oriental Nothingness," p. 76.

41. Hisamatsu, "The Characteristics of Oriental Nothingness," p. 77 (translation partially adapted here).

42. Ibid.
43. Hisamatsu, "The Characteristics of Oriental Nothingness," p. 85.
44. Ibid.
45. Hisamatsu, "The Characteristics of Oriental Nothingness," p. 87 (translation partially adapted here).
46. Hisamatsu, "The Characteristics of Oriental Nothingness," p. 89.
47. Hisamatsu, "The Characteristics of Oriental Nothingness," p. 88.
48. Hisamatsu, "The Characteristics of Oriental Nothingness," p. 91.
49. Hisamatsu, "The Characteristics of Oriental Nothingness," p. 93.
50. Ibid.
51. Hisamatsu, "The Characteristics of Oriental Nothingness," p. 95.
52. Hisamatsu, "The Characteristics of Oriental Nothingness," p. 96.
53. Hisamatsu, "The Characteristics of Oriental Nothingness," p. 97.
54. Hisamatsu Shin'ichi, "Zen and the Various Acts," *Chicago Review* 12/2 (1958): 28.
55. Hisamatsu, "Memories of My Student Life," p. 418; cited by Abe, "Hisamatsu's Philosophy of Awakening," *Eastern Buddhist* 14/1 (1981): 28.
56. Abe, "Hisamatsu's Philosophy of Awakening," p. 28.
57. Abe, "Hisamatsu Shin'ichi, 1889–1980," p. 145.
58. Hisamatsu Shin'ichi, "The Nature of *Sadō* Culture," *Eastern Buddhist* 3/2 (1970): 18.
59. Hisamatsu, "Ultimate Crisis and Resurrection, part II," p. 64.
60. Hisamatsu Shin'ichi, "Jinrui no chikai" (The Vow of Humankind), *HSC* 3, p. 232.
61. Hisamatsu, "Atarashiki sekai no Bukkyōteki kōsō," p. 73.
62. Hisamatsu Shin'ichi, "Dōjō no atarashii kihonsen to shite no F.A.S." (F.A.S. as the New Foundational Direction of the Place for Practicing the Way), *HSC* 3, p. 464.
63. Hisamatsu, "Jinrui no chikai," p. 247.
64. The F.A.S. term for walking meditation is *gyōdō*, "going along the Way," rather than the traditional expression, *kinhin*.
65. With Tokiwa, I have also translated and published a number of Hisamatsu's *teikō* on the "Vow of Humankind" in the *F.A.S. Society Journal*.
66. With Tokiwa Gishin, I have translated and published Hisamatsu's talks on *The Record of Linji* (Ch. *Linji lu*, J. *Rinzairoku*) in *Critical Sermons of the Zen Tradition: Hisamatsu's Talks on Linji* (Honolulu: University of Hawaii Press, 2002).
67. Ives and Tokiwa, eds., *Critical Sermons of the Zen Tradition*, pp. 9–10.
68. Ives and Tokiwa, eds., *Critical Sermons of the Zen Tradition*, p. 10.
69. Hisamatsu Shin'ichi, "Ordinary Mind," *Eastern Buddhist* 12/1 (1979): 8.
70. Hisamatsu, "Ordinary Mind," p. 11.
71. Kitahara Ryūtarō, "Interview," *F.A.S. Society Newsletter* (Spring 1979), p. 3.
72. Ibid.
73. Hisamatsu, "Dōjō no atarashii kihonsen to shite no F.A.S," p. 516.
74. Hisamatsu Shin'ichi "For the Postmodernist," *F.A.S. Society Newsletter* 2/1 (1977): 1.

75. "Postmodernist Manifesto," *F.A.S. Society Newsletter* 1/1 (1976): 4.

76. Hisamatsu Shin'ichi and Watanabe Ryoji, "Posutomodanisuto hōdan" (Conversations about the Postmodernist), *Budisuto* (Buddhist) 4/4 (1982): 7.

77. Hisamatsu, "Atarashiki sekai no Bukkyōteki kōsō," p. 154 (translation partially adapted).

78. Hisamatsu, "Jinrui no chikai," p. 266.

79. Hisamatsu, "Jinrui no chikai," p. 326.

80. Ibid.

81. Hisamatsu, "Ordinary Mind," p. 28.

82. This expression appears in the *Vimalakīrti-nirdeśa-sūtra*.

83. Association for Self-Awakening, *Nothingness*, p. 16.

84. "For the Postmodernist," p. 4.

85. Ibid.

86. Abe, "Hisamatsu Shin'ichi, 1889–1980," p. 144.

87. Hisamatsu, "Ultimate Crisis and Resurrection, part II," p. 51.

88. Hisamatsu, "Dōjō no atarashii kihonsen to shite no F.A.S.," p. 487.

89. Hisamatsu taught at Rinzai Gaukuin (later renamed Hanazono University) and Ryūkoku University from 1919 until 1932, then at Kyoto University (1932–1949), and finally at Kyoto Municipal University of the Fine Arts (1952–1963).

90. Hisamatsu's Zen name was Hōseki, "stone embracing," and the character *an* means "hermitage."

91. Abe, "Hisamatsu's Philosophy of Awakening," p. 26.

92. Abe, "Hisamatsu Shin'ichi, 1889–1980," p. 145.

93. For expediency's sake, I am bracketing the issue of how scholars might critique Hisamatsu's portrayal of satori and claims about what constitutes the crux of Zen.

94. Hisamatsu, "On Zen Art," *Eastern Buddhist*, 1/2 (1966): 31.

95. As Ichikawa Hakugen, Brian Victoria, and I have outlined, ostensibly enlightened Zen masters were often eager supporters of Japanese imperialism over the first half of the twentieth century. See Ichikawa Hakugen, *Bukkyō no sensō-sekinin* (Buddhism's Responsibility for the War), vol. 3 of *Ichikawa Hakugen chosaku-shū* (The Collected Works of Ichikawa Hakugen) (Kyoto: Hōzōkan, 1993); Brian Victoria, *Zen at War*, 2nd ed. (Lanham, Md.: Rowman and Littlefield, 2006); and Christopher Ives, *Imperial-Way Zen: Ichikawa Hakugen's Critique and Lingering Questions for Buddhist Ethics* (Honolulu: University of Hawai'i Press, 2009).

96. "Sasshin" (Renewal of the Zen World), in *Suzuki Daisetsu zenshū* 28, p. 413; quoted in Brian Victoria, *Zen at War*, p. 148.

97. "Bernie Glassman Responds," *Tricycle* 9/1 (Fall 1999): 72.

98. Bernard Faure, *Chan Insights and Oversights: An Epistemological Critique of the Chan Tradition* (Princeton: Princeton University Press, 1993), p. 86.

99. Antinoff, "The Problem of the Human Person," p. 223.

100. Antinoff, "The Problem of the Human Person," p. 253.

101. Antinoff, "The Problem of the Human Person," pp. 245–246.

102. Abe, "Hisamatsu Shin'ichi, 1889–1990," p. 145.

9

Humanizing the Image of a Zen Master: Taizan Maezumi Roshi

Dale S. Wright

Hakuyu Taizan Maezumi Roshi (1931–1995) was the founder of the Zen Center of Los Angeles and one of the seminal figures in the history of American Zen Buddhism. His charismatic image as a Zen master helped define Zen for American culture, and by virtue of his giving authorization to twelve dharma heirs, his legacy continues to shape the further development of Zen practice in the West. Although he was an impressive and ground-breaking Zen master by any standard, the story of Maezumi Roshi's life is not without ambiguity and controversy. Indeed, it is difficult not to sense some degree of tragedy in this story. This double-edged complexity in the life of the Zen master is the primary element that differentiates the account of Maezumi's life from the idealized narratives of classical Zen masters, and for that reason is one significant factor that defines both his personal image and the image of contemporary American Zen.

    The first part of this chapter is a biographical account of the life of Maezumi from his early training in Japanese Zen Buddhism through his formative work in the American Zen tradition to the difficulties that shook his career and to his death in 1995. The second part explores the image of Maezumi Roshi as a Zen master. It asks what this image is, how it has been formed, and to what extent Maezumi's Zen image aligns with the paradigmatic lives of the classical Zen tradition.[1]

The Life of Hakuyu Maezumi

Hakuyu Maezumi was born directly into the cultural world of Japanese Zen Buddhism on February 24, 1931, in Otawara City, Tochigi prefecture. His father, Hakujun Kuroda Roshi, was an important priest in the Sōtō lineage of Zen Buddhism, serving in a variety of important administrative positions, including head of the Sōtō sect's Supreme Court.[2] Partly as a consequence of his significant position within the Zen sect, all six of his surviving sons would later become Zen priests. Although Maezumi was one of six brothers in the Kuroda family, rather than adopt his father's surname, as would have been customary, he was given his mother's family name—Maezumi—in order to perpetuate that family name, since his mother had no brothers to extend their lineage.[3]

Shortly after the Japanese attack on Pearl Harbor and the beginning of the Pacific segment of the Second World War, Maezumi at age eleven was ordained a Sōtō Zen monk on March 25, 1942.[4] Given the ordination name Taizan, meaning Great Mountain, he began the discipline of Zen training at his father's temple, Koshinji.[5] Although simultaneously attending the local school, the young novice was focused on Zen training, which he already knew would be his lifelong vocation. Maezumi began to learn English in his teens through contact with American soldiers who were stationed in his home area after the war. During one period, American occupation soldiers employed his father's temple as their base, giving the young monk direct contact with American-English language and culture, a factor that would affect his entire life and career.[6]

At the age of sixteen, while continuing his training to become a Sōtō priest, Maezumi left home to go to Tokyo to begin study under Koryu Osaka Roshi, a lay Rinzai Zen master and friend of Maezumi's father.[7] Koryu Roshi focused on Zen training for the laity, an emphasis that would years later be of great significance to Maezumi. Maezumi's work with Koryu Roshi was also the first step in his hybrid Zen education, which blurred the traditional boundaries of separation between the two most prominent Zen institutions in Japan. Four years later, he began his university studies at Komazawa University, the primary center of Sōtō Zen education, graduating with degrees in East Asian philosophy and literature in 1954.[8] A year later, at twenty-four years of age, Maezumi was given dharma transmission (*shiho*) by his father[9] and completed his training at the two principle Sōtō monasteries, Eiheiji and Sōjiji, where he performed the "honorary abbot" or *zuise* ceremony that same year.

A Zen Priest in California

Probably because of his English-language skills, Maezumi was given the assignment by the Sōtō School of Zen to travel to the United States to serve Japanese immigrants as a priest in California. Traveling with an inexpensive one-way ticket on a freighter ship, Maezumi took up residence in Los Angeles in 1956, at the age of twenty-five.[10] His assignment was to perform priestly duties at Zenshuji Temple, the Sōtō headquarters in the United States, at that time under the leadership of Togan Sumi.[11] Although this work was often conducted in Japanese, there were numerous English-language dimensions to the task, including ministering to the second and third generations of Japanese immigrants, for whom English was becoming the dominant language. Maezumi studied English in Los Angeles at Pasadena City College and later at San Francisco State University, where in 1959 he would meet Shunryu Suzuki and other early pioneers in American Zen.[12]

Maezumi's responsibilities as a Sōtō Zen priest stationed in California included weekly services, funerals, memorials, weddings, and other ceremonies required by the immigrant population of California. These were difficult times economically, in Japan and in the United States, and Maezumi held a series of part-time jobs to make ends meet, working whenever he could as a gardener and a translator for Japanese businessmen in Los Angeles. At one point, Maezumi is reported to have composed fortunes for Chinese fortune cookies![13] Maezumi was married during this period, but the marriage was unsuccessful and ended in divorce.

In spite of the widespread lack of interest in rigorous Zen training in his new environment, Maezumi continued his own advancement in the study of Zen after arrival in the New World, engaging in meditation, *kōan* study, and textual study whenever he had the opportunity. He read Dōgen's *Shōbōgenzō* with Reirin Yamada Roshi, the bishop of the American Sōtō mission, and engaged in serious *kōan* study with Nyogen Senzaki, a Rinzai Zen teacher who was at that time teaching in Los Angeles. Senzaki was the first Zen teacher to reside in the United States and had already accepted several European-American students interested in Zen, among them Robert Aitken.[14] His influence on Maezumi includes the previously unimaginable idea that Zen practices might be of interest to people whose heritage was not originally Buddhist.

Indeed, by the late 1950s that interest was already developing in San Francisco among a handful of Beat poets and writers. What was particularly attractive about Zen, however, was not the rigorous *zazen* and *kōan* study that Maezumi and others would be teaching a decade later, but rather the unusual discourse and eccentric behaviors of the masters of the "golden age" of Chinese Chan described in the classic literature of Zen, which at that time was being translated and narrated by D. T. Suzuki. Given the character of postwar American culture, the discipline of Zen was not what would initially attract attention to this spiritual tradition. In spite of a lack of interest among his own parishioners at Zenshuji in Los Angeles, Maezumi held weekly *zazen* meditation sessions at the temple. It would not be long, however, before interest in Zen meditation would spread through the youth movement in American culture.

Perhaps most significant for the formation of his identity as a teacher of Zen, Maezumi met Hakuun Yasutani Roshi, becoming a disciple in the early sixties just as Maezumi was forming the Zen Center of Los Angeles and bringing his interest in *kōan* studies to fruition.[15] Yasutani and his teacher, Daiun Harada, were instrumental in the revitalization of Zen in Japan that was beginning to take place after the war. These teachers combined Rinzai and Sōtō styles of teaching in a way that ignored the traditional bifurcation between these two schools of Zen. They revised Rinzai *kōan* practice in the setting of Sōtō emphasis on *shikantaza*—"just sitting." Yasutani stressed rigorous discipline in Zen training and focused on the prospects of "sudden awakening" as the goal of Zen. Eventually this would be the formula for Zen that would attract non-Asian interest, and the success of a book by one of Yasutani's students—Phillip Kapleau—would lay the foundations for American Zen by describing rigorous Zen practice in a way that would attract a widespread following. Yasutani was the Zen master featured in Kapleau's *The Three Pillars of Zen*,[16] and his fame spread quickly in the United States and Japan. When Yasutani visited the United States for lectures and *sesshin* trainings, Maezumi served as translator and interpreter.[17] Their relationship was fundamental to the Zen identity that Maezumi was fashioning during that period of time.

In 1969, Maezumi returned to Japan to complete his *kōan* training under Yasutani Roshi, placing the newly formed Zen Center under the leadership of his foremost student and eventual heir, Bernie Glassman. Fourteen months later, in December of 1970, Maezumi Roshi received *inka* approval from Yasutani Roshi.[18] Meanwhile, in 1970 Koryu Osaka Roshi, the friend of Maezumi's father and the Rinzai Zen teacher with whom Maezumi had studied in the fifties while at Komazawa University, came to the Zen Center of Los Angeles, there renewing the teacher-student relationship that the two had cultivated years earlier. Over the next several years Maezumi completed his kōan training with Koryu Roshi and, in 1973, received *inka* authorization in his lineage as well.[19] This series of relationships put Maezumi in the unusual position of having received Zen authorization from three different Zen masters in three distinct lineages, Sōtō, Rinzai, and the Harada-Yasutani line.

Maezumi Roshi at the Zen Center of Los Angeles

Due primarily to the widely read literature of the Beat poets and the books of D. T. Suzuki, serious interest in Zen among European-Americans began to develop in the mid-sixties. Several non-Japanese Americans began to attend Maezumi's weekly *zazen* gatherings at Zenshuji in Los Angeles to experiment with these novel practices. Purportedly because some parishioners and the other priests were skeptical or critical of this outreach to those outside of the Japanese community, Maezumi soon moved his meditation group out of the temple, first into an apartment on Serrano Street in the Wilshire district and then, in 1967, into a house in the Korea-town section of central Los Angeles.[20] The house was named the Los Angeles Zendo and was incorporated under that name in 1968.[21] Soon thereafter the name would be changed to the Zen Center of Los Angeles. Maezumi's father, Baian Hakujun Kuroda, was named the honorary founder of the institution, which was registered as a Sōtō temple and given the name Busshinji—"Buddha Truth Temple."[22] There was a profound sense that something important was about to happen to the dharma in the United States. Maezumi attended the opening ceremony for the Tassajara Zen Mountain Center in July of 1967, joining Suzuki Roshi, Katagiri Roshi, and other important Zen teachers at this historic event. No doubt Suzuki's remarkable success in San Francisco impressed Maezumi deeply.[23] Yasutani Roshi began a series of visits to the Zen Center of Los Angeles in the late sixties both to work with Maezumi on his *kōan* practice and on occasion to conduct some of the earliest and most influential *sesshins*—meditation retreats—in American Zen history. At that time Maezumi was just completing his own studies with Yasutani, becoming a *roshi* of full standing in the Japanese Zen tradition. Receiving *inka* approval from Yasutani Roshi solidified Maezumi's authority as a Zen master in America just at the moment when attention to Zen in the West was about to boom.

And boom it did. The Zen Center of Los Angeles (ZCLA) grew exponentially in the early seventies, and by the end of that decade it was clearly one of the most vibrant and significant religious institutions in Los Angeles. Interest in Zen had continued to develop among non-Asian Americans, and Maezumi Roshi's persona captured the attention of hundreds of new converts to *zazen* meditation. Urban properties adjacent to the original Zendo in Los Angeles were purchased for residential and religious purposes. At its height in the early eighties, ZCLA occupied almost all of one full city block, including several multistoried apartment buildings. Among the youth of America, Zen symbolized what was new and exciting about the globalization that was transforming American culture, and the rapid growth of ZCLA embodied that symbolism brilliantly.

The regimen of practice at ZCLA was rigorous and for the most part orthodox. Traditional Sōtō ceremonial procedures were painstakingly learned, practiced, and maintained. Trainees and visitors spent long hours in *zazen*, including week-long *sesshins* at regular intervals. Woven into this meditation schedule was a traditional *kōan* curriculum. Maezumi and other senior teachers assigned *kōans*, taking the mental and spiritual disposition of each student into account. The psychological pressure behind *kōan* study was accentuated through the requirement of periodic *dokusan* practice—one-on-one private interviews between master and disciple with the intention of pushing the *kōan* through to its conclusion. Visiting teachers from elsewhere in the United States and Japan were regular guests at ZCLA, often giving *teishō* lectures and performing the traditional ceremonies of Zen. Although Maezumi would encourage his American dharma heirs to innovate and to build a truly American Zen tradition, at his own center he would maintain strict adherence to orthodox Sōtō practices, thereby offering a meticulous transmission of the dharma in a new setting.

In 1975, Maezumi married Martha Ekyo Maezumi, with whom he had three children, Kirsten Mitsuyo, Yuri Jundo, and Shira Yoshimi, who were raised at ZCLA and later in Idyllwild.[24] Their lives unfolded at the very center of this extraordinary development in American religion and added an element of domesticity to Maezumi's image that departed to some extent from the monastic environment that the Zen master was intent on cultivating. Although Maezumi was by all accounts a loving father, his attention was clearly focused on the historic Zen enterprise that he had founded.

Under the lens of this focus, the Zen Center prospered as no one could have imagined. Membership lists grew weekly. Dozens of new and curious visitors arrived at the center every weekend to be introduced to Zen practice. Hundreds of lay practitioners became regular members who would frequent the center for meditation and instruction. And through the early eighties, over a hundred full-time practitioners resided at ZCLA, doing *zazen* morning and night every day and engaging in regular week-long *sesshins*. Publications such as an early book entitled *The Way of Everyday Life* and a Zen periodical called *The Ten Directions* began to be disseminated and were being read all over the English speaking world, focusing more and more attention on Maezumi and ZCLA. New affiliate centers began to be formed. Maezumi and his principal students envisioned a network of interrelated Zen centers throughout the United States, North America, and Europe, and began to implement a plan. Land in the San Jacinto mountains near Idyllwild, California, was purchased, and a Zen Mountain Center for *sesshins* and intensive training was launched. In 1976, Maezumi founded the Kuroda Institute for the Study of Buddhism and Human Values as an educational arm of ZCLA to encourage scholarly attention to the Zen tradition.²⁵ The institute organized and funded conferences, colloquia, and publications.

Although initially a counterculture movement, as the Zen movement morphed into a mainstream cultural institution; Zen practice in Los Angeles became increasingly established across the full socioeconomic spectrum. Practitioners included physicians, attorneys, psychiatrists, and professors, along with carpenters, electricians, and professionals from all occupational fields. Maezumi Roshi gave the Buddhist precepts to over five hundred people, ordained sixty-eight priests, and gave dharma transmission to twelve of his closest students.²⁶ At its height in the early eighties, the Zen Center of Los Angeles was one of the most vibrant and exciting religious institutions in the country, and Maezumi Roshi was the most widely known and admired Zen master in the West. For many people, his image symbolized the spiritual brilliance of Zen.

Crisis at the Heart of Zen

In 1983, at the height of Maezumi's influence and the success of his innovative Zen organization, two crises brought an end to the upward surge of his Zen movement and began to undermine the Zen master's image. One of these was the disclosure that Maezumi had had sexual relationships with several of his female students, including one of the recipients of his dharma transmission. This disclosure immediately split the community, throwing it into turmoil and controversy. While the "free-love" atmosphere of the seventies certainly prevailed at the Zen Center as a widespread assumption, it nevertheless shocked practitioners that the Zen master had compromised his position of authority as a spiritual leader and had violated his marriage in this way. Simultaneously with that troublesome disclosure, a second revelation further damaged Maezumi's image as an authentic Zen master. Although his alcohol consumption practices were relatively well known at ZCLA and up to this point generally accepted, this was the moment when both Maezumi and the community realized that his drinking was out of control.²⁷ Under enormous pressure and in emotional turmoil, Maezumi openly discussed the difficulties his drinking had caused and voluntarily checked himself into an alcohol rehabilitation center to address the problem.

Meanwhile, in his absence, Zen Center practitioners attempted to reconcile themselves to these now widely perceived shortcomings in the Zen master whom they had previously considered invulnerable to worldly problems. Many practitioners left ZCLA in anger, disappointment, or disillusionment. One dharma heir, Charlotte Joko Beck, having already departed Los Angeles to form a new center in San Diego, renounced affiliation with ZCLA and with Maezumi.²⁸

Although Maezumi returned to the Zen Center in less than a month, now seemingly in control of his drinking, other problems related to these crises continued to compound. Membership roles at ZCLA shrank quickly and dramatically within months after these disclosures, and the once-thriving organization was struggling to maintain itself. As monthly bills began to pile up, properties adjacent to the Zendo were sold, and over the next several years ZCLA was scaled down to a considerably diminished level of operation. By the time Maezumi had worked through his remorse and gathered himself to the point that he could respond constructively to the situation, the damage had already been done. ZCLA was a shadow of its former prominent self. Maezumi's wife and children had left their home at the Zen Center and had moved to the mountain community of Idyllwild near the Zen Mountain Center, and only a handful of faithful practitioners remained in residence at ZCLA.[29]

Deeply apologetic and remorseful about the damage he had caused, Maezumi struggled to regain himself spiritually. Close associates recall that it was many years before Maezumi returned to anything like his former exuberance and confidence, the spirit of Zen that had so animated his teachings. Even then, the damage to the reputation and standing of ZCLA would not abate, and although the Center continued uninterrupted through Maezumi's life, it would not recover the powerful spiritual image that it once radiated. Maezumi continued his practice of teaching for over a decade beyond the crisis, gradually winning back former and new members, but the memories and effects of failure would never be entirely thrown off. One effect of the crisis, however, was that leading disciples of Maezumi took the occasion to disperse around North America, founding Zen centers in Maezumi's lineage elsewhere, while beginning the long process of experimenting with innovative formulas for a truly American Zen. Although Maezumi was himself tarnished by the diminishment of ZCLA and its reputation, his heirs would extend the tradition through the formation of Zen centers all over the continent.

Death of the Zen Master

Very late at night on May 15, 1995, Maezumi Roshi died suddenly and unexpectedly at the age of sixty-four while visiting his family and Sōtō Zen leaders in Japan. Controversy surrounds Maezumi's death, as it had the later part of his life. Receiving the news of Maezumi's death by telephone, and in a state of shock, ZCLA leaders flew to Tokyo to attend the Japanese funeral services and cremation. They were told by family members in Japan that their teacher had died of a heart attack in bed. This understanding of Maezumi's death still held sway three months later, when an elaborate memorial event was held at

ZCLA on August 27, 1995. Over the next few months, however, it was learned that in fact Maezumi had drowned in the bathtub of his brother's house while under the influence of alcohol. This fact had been concealed by Maezumi's Japanese family in order to maintain the dignity of his substantial legacy. Even Maezumi's wife and central circle of students had been unaware of the actual cause of his death.[30]

The truth about Maezumi's death came to light when Wendy Egyoku Nakao, Maezumi's eventual successor at ZCLA, obtained a copy of the death certificate from Japan so that the Zen master's family could qualify to benefit from the life insurance policy that had been taken out in his name. The death certificate specified the cause of death as drowning and noted the presence of alcohol in his blood.[31] When confronted with this discrepancy, Maezumi's brothers would disclose the full story. Maezumi had been at the family home and temple, dining and drinking with his brothers, but had planned to travel back to Tokyo that night to be with another of his brothers and to stay there. Although clearly exhausted and advised against this journey, Maezumi set out for Tokyo by train. Apparently asleep, he missed the appropriate train station, thus extending his journey even further. When he finally arrived at his brother's home late at night, Maezumi announced that he would bathe and then go to bed. The next morning, Maezumi's brother found him drowned in the bathtub.

Concerned that the alcohol-related circumstances of Maezumi's death would undermine the Zen master's international reputation, his brothers decided to withhold the truth. When asked for an English translation of the death certificate for insurance use in the United States, they did not comply. But when the Japanese-language certificate arrived in Los Angeles, it was translated, thus initiating what would still be a slow process of full disclosure.[32] It was decided at ZCLA not to make a general announcement of these death details, since what had been thought to be the cause of death had already been announced publically. Gradually, however, the truth leaked out and began to circulate as a rumor among ZCLA leaders until, finally, in 1997, the ZCLA Sangha was given a full and formal account of the Zen master's death.[33] From that point forward, Maezumi's death would be yet another element of controversy shaping the image of this important Zen master.

The Zen Image of Maezumi Roshi

How do the sources of our knowledge of the life of Maezumi Roshi differ from those through which we have come to understand the classical masters of Zen?

How do we know about the Zen masters of antiquity? The evidence available to us is limited and very specific in orientation. Images of classical Zen masters come to us through literature written by later participants within each master's Zen lineage and were composed with the intention of cultivating the mythos of these masters and the lineage as a whole. As we can see in many of the essays in this volume, narratives giving account of the lives and personas of Zen masters in earlier epochs of Zen history bear remarkable resemblance to one another, especially those written to narrate the early centuries of Zen's legendary history. These narratives follow a unified model and were edited over time to fit uniformly into the comprehensive documents that transmit the tradition as a whole—the *Transmission of the Lamp* literature.

One byproduct of this uniformity in the narrative accounts is a corresponding similarity in what is believed to be the lives and personas of the Zen masters they depict. Classical Zen masters are identifiable as Zen masters precisely because they say and do Zen-like things and lead lives that are recognizably "Zen" in identity. All of these stories begin, proceed, and end in much the same way. For example, accounts of the deaths of Zen masters bear remarkable similarity—Zen masters are presented in such a way that they die at a time and in a manner of their own choosing; the power of their Zen-disciplined will dominates from the moment of their awakening all the way through death. Some are imagined to die seated in the lotus posture while engaged in deep meditative concentration, having just composed a traditional death poem. Their Zen practice and Zen minds are understood to be flawless from beginning to end.

Tracing these narratives back to their probable compositions, historians have found over and over that these stories are much more the products of evolving traditions than they are of firsthand report. The lives of the most famous Zen masters are saturated with legend, and their historical foundations are often unrecoverable. Much of this literature was composed many decades or even centuries after the lives of the masters they depicted. The reason for pointing this out is that these traditional methods of historical representation will not be duplicated in the cases of contemporary Zen masters like Taizan Maezumi. Firsthand accounts by followers and detractors are now deposited in our archives, not as a well-edited, unified story about a contemporary master but as scattered representations from a variety of points of view. It is hard to imagine that these sources will ever disappear, contained as they are now in electronic form and available to anyone, anywhere. So although the importance of a Zen master will grow and evolve depending upon the later success of his or her legacy, as was true in earlier epochs, it is unlikely ever to be the case that the firsthand accounts of their lives will be drastically altered, deleted, or lost. This appears to be the case with Maezumi Roshi. Unlike earlier Zen masters, what we have available to document the life of Maezumi is a wide variety of historical materials composed both by Maezumi and by hundreds of individuals who knew him personally. Although some of these reports are permeated with admiration, they are quite unlike the legend-based accounts of classical Zen masters.

How does our image of Maezumi as a Zen master get constructed? If we are thorough and take the time to work through the evidence at our disposal, the sources are amazingly voluminous. We have recorded talks by Maezumi, essays and books written by him, books and essays written about Maezumi by those who knew him best, film footage of Maezumi both in formal dharma talks and informal circumstances. The list of resources goes further. We have films about Maezumi, photographs by the hundreds—probably thousands—as well as newspaper articles, journal articles, and magazine articles that have discussed Maezumi's life at one stage or another. And it is still possible to gather verbal accounts from the hundreds of people who knew him in one context or another, along with verbal accounts from his families in both Japan and the United States. The volume of evidence from which to construct a thorough account of the life of this Zen master is thus enormous. This chapter simply adds a further layer to this evolving tradition, based as it is on the archive of print, electronic, and verbal resources, and written by one who had limited but occasional contact with Maezumi during his life.

For classical Zen masters, we have one or sometimes several well-edited, tradition-sanctioned accounts. For Maezumi, we have a vast archive of firsthand images, most of which are "edited" only by the varying perspectives of those who have provided us with their story. In the former case, we get an image of the Zen master conceived as an ideal. In the latter, we get judgments of every conceivable kind. The accuracy, realism, and perspectival variation of the latter curtail the extent to which an ideal can be imposed on the historical narratives by a subsequent idealizing tradition. From this point on in the history of Zen, we have the opportunity to see not just what a Zen master is supposed to be like but also the extent to which particular masters actually lived up to that image.

The Teachings and Practices of Maezumi Roshi

Unlike most Zen masters from the classical period of Chinese Chan, Maezumi was an author from whom we now have a substantial written legacy. Five important books make his teachings accessible to the public. The earliest of these was published in 1976, just as the Zen Center of Los Angeles was beginning to attract international attention. *On Zen Practice* consists of dharma talks by Maezumi and commentaries on classical Zen texts, both meant to introduce readers to the basics of Zen practice—*zazen, sesshin*, precepts, *kōans*, and the teachings of renowned masters such as Dōgen.[34] A sequel to this book was published the next year, 1977, called *The Hazy Moon of Enlightenment*.[35] This book builds on the basic practices described in the first volume by taking up the philosophical topics of enlightenment and delusion, the difference between sudden and gradual enlightenment, and the goal of embodying enlightenment in everyday actions.

Shortly thereafter, in 1978, a third volume was published, thereby solidifying the image of Maezumi and ZCLA as vibrant sources of Zen teaching. *The Way of Everyday Life* was a commentary by Maezumi on the famous segment of Dōgen's *Shōbōgenzō* called *genjōkōan*.[36] This volume features the aesthetic dimension of Zen. The Dōgen text is done in calligraphy on dark parchment, and the remainder of the book displays the Zen-inspired photography of John Daido Loori, one of Maezumi's dharma heirs. Some years later, the textual dimension of Maezumi's legacy was extended through the posthumous publication of his dharma talks, in *Appreciate Your Life: The Essence of Zen Practice*.[37] Published in 2001, this volume makes available some of the many dharma talks that ZCLA had recorded over two decades of Maezumi's leadership, although dates are not provided for these talks. And finally, a collection of dharma talks given at various Zen Centers around the United States and Europe toward the end of Maezumi's career between 1987 and 1994 were published in 2001 under the title *Teachings of the Great Mountain: Zen Talks by Taizan Maezumi*.[38]

Maezumi's teachings are grounded in the practice of *zazen*. Very often, in fact, his dharma talks either begin or revert back to this most basic Zen topic. He takes great pains to go over the specifics of posture, of breathing, and of ways to comport and conceive of the human body. Maezumi's Zen had a strong physical emphasis, a style that accentuates the fact that meditation has at least as much to do with your body as with your mind. Maezumi's first book was very appropriately entitled *On Zen Practice: Body, Breath, and Mind*. From his perspective, Zen practice can be encapsulated in these three domains of body, respiration, and mental orientation. A great deal of Maezumi's reflections on meditation take place in the context of his discussions of Dōgen's emphasis on *shikantaza*, "just sitting." He stressed the progression of the mind through its various acts of clinging to the self toward the capacity to "forget the self," letting the mind open wide enough for the world to pervade the self and overcome its boundaries.

Each of these themes provided Maezumi reason to give ritual a prominent place in his teachings. Indeed, a significant number of his *teishō* talks that have come into print are really about ritual procedures. He explains in great detail, for example, how to bow. Beginning with the physical postures necessary to perform Zen prostrations, Maezumi subtly moves to the state of mind that is being cultivated in this process. He explains how to configure the hands in *zazen* and in *kinhin*—walking meditation—how to breathe when chanting, and what to do with the mind while all of these activities are underway.

Emphasizing ritual in Zen was a risky move. Many of the youthful Americans who had come to practice Zen would have regarded ritual as the least authentic dimension of any religion, especially Zen. Due to several factors, including the long-standing Protestant critique of Catholic ritual and the antinomian, antidisciplinary emphases of that time, they would have expected Zen to be more a revolt against ritual than training in it. Maezumi's second dharma heir, Dennis Genpo Merzel, tells how his earliest conflicts with Maezumi were over the role of ritualized behavior in Zen. In response to the Zen master's emphasis on tradition and ritual, on one occasion Merzel slammed his shovel into the ground, yelling adamantly, "This is not Zen!"[39] Zen, for Merzel and other spiritual romantics of that time, meant looking beyond the proprieties of custom and ceremony to the deeper resources of spiritual life. From the point of view of the first generation of American Zen practitioners, if Zen was anything at all, it was a spirituality of rebellion.

Part of the brilliance of Maezumi as a Zen master was that he understood and appreciated the spirit of this rebellion. Indeed, he hoped to harness its power. While sympathizing with the spirit of resistance, he understood that it lacked comprehensive vision and endurance, and that authentic Zen would require cultivating sensitivities that only the disciplines of mindful ritual could instill. So while teasing the young romantics through their rebellion, Maezumi continued to instruct in the ways of Zen ritual with great patience.

Patience was a primary virtue for Maezumi. From his many years of Zen practice, he understood that this is what it takes to make serious progress in the meditative arts. Part of this emphasis had to do with the fact that many of his students were young, impatient, and eager for immediate demonstrable effects. It was also true that most American practitioners in the 1960s and 1970s were steeped in the Rinzai "sudden enlightenment" literature of D. T. Suzuki, for whom "patience" was anything but "enlightened." Urgency was a more fitting metaphor for that orientation to Zen, and Maezumi stressed the extent to which such impatience would more likely lead to disappointment and despair. His teachings emphasized that to progress in Zen training, it would be necessary to practice calm, anxiety-free modes of mindfulness and to experiment patiently with these new modes of being without expectations about outcomes or rewards.

Two of Maezumi's frequently used slogans reiterated that point. Practitioners remember him saying over and over "just be patient," and on other occasions dipping into the Spanish language of ZCLA's neighborhood, *poco a poco*, "little by little."[40] He commonly used the single word "relax" in order to encourage the patient, open-minded mentality that "just sitting" required. Maezumi's reputation also included the ability to personalize his teachings, sculpting them to the specific strengths and weaknesses of particular students.[41] This required, of course, that he know his students very well, and it is indeed a significant part of his image that Maezumi spent a considerable amount of time with his students and knew a great deal about their lives and personas.

Although the Zen master did spend relaxed social time with students, his reputation includes the sense that he was *always* teaching. Students remark that it was very clear that Maezumi considered Zen a full-time, around-the-clock aspiration.[42] In the midst of easy-going activities he might switch moods unexpectedly from playful to serious and concerned, or from friendly to severe. Students clearly expected that in the midst of everyday activities, Maezumi would leap suddenly into the depths of Zen discourse. Occasionally, as we have come to expect from classical Zen masters, Maezumi would speak in paradox or in a form of spiritual irony.

Students recall other times in which Maezumi would use the language of encouragement, offering useful "sayings" to help generate strong practice. Among his regular Zen slogans were "practice thoroughly," "put your whole self into it," "feel it in the depths of your *hara*" (midsection/abdomen), or "adjust your posture from the base."[43] The seriousness and rigor of Maezumi's teaching practice were never in question. For Maezumi, to practice Zen was at all times to practice vibrant and powerful forms of mindfulness.

Mindfulness is also the best way to characterize what was probably Maezumi's most characteristic teaching—"appreciate your life." By putting this phrase as the title of one of his books, Maezumi's editors indicate its centrality to his Zen teachings. But the subtitle of that book—*The Essence of Zen Practice*—makes it even clearer how much power Maezumi attributed to this teaching. When elaborating on this saying, Maezumi's dharma talks sometimes direct us toward appreciating the simplicity of life and at other times to its complexity and nuance.[44] Both the simplicity and the complexity of life were matters worthy of deep appreciation. No matter in which direction his readers and hearers were encouraged to look, what he meant to recommend is that practitioners clear their minds of distraction and learn to look directly at their lives—to appreciate things for what they are. Is there anything more basic to an enlightened way of being in the world than the simple but ever-so-rare capacity to truly appreciate the life you are living? Maezumi's response is clear. This appreciation is "the essence of Zen practice." The awakened quality of life that Maezumi taught entails the appreciation rather than the depreciation of the varied existence each of us lives—"just as it is."

Maezumi's teachings are also directed toward helping others locate whatever it is that prevents the appreciation of life. Students comment that he would examine the words and movements of his students, always looking for what it was that stood in the way of more awakened forms of existence. Several of Maezumi's common sayings show this concern for the negative dimension of life. He would frequently inquire: "Where is the hindrance?" "What binds you?"[45] Inability to identify and understand these hindrances, to recognize what it is that stands in the way of greater capacity to live an imaginative and engaged life, means that human freedom is diminished and with it the range of vision available to human beings. Knowing that he would not always be able to see into the interior of other lives to find these blockages, his question—"what binds you?"—opens the realization that practitioners are themselves responsible for finding and eliminating hindrances. For Maezumi, *zazen*, *sesshin*, and *shikantaza* provide the grounds upon which these barriers can be located and overcome, and *kōan* study along with *dokusan* contact with a Zen master are the tools most effectively used in carrying that work through to completion.

Students report frequently that Maezumi wanted them to train themselves, that they should not expect to "be trained" as though all enlightened figures arise out of the same mold. One student reports, "He really tried to get a person to train themselves; he really wanted you to gain your own strength."[46] Although each of his students had the Zen master as a model and guide on the quest, Maezumi made it clear that each of them would need to do what he had done— set out a discipline of spiritual awareness that suited his or her own character and needs, and then gather the energy to follow it through to conclusion.

The Persona and Character of Maezumi's Enlightenment

We learn about the enlightened character of famous Zen masters from antiquity by reading texts that describe their "sayings and doings." These "discourse record" texts purport to be firsthand accounts of the many ways that the great masters of the past expressed their enlightenment in everyday situations. Stories giving expression to Maezumi Roshi's character—the way his enlightenment was manifested in actual life situations—are voluminous. We find them scattered throughout the literature of disciples discussing the life of their teacher, many of these now enshrined in text and on film. As often occurred in classical Zen, however, these scattered stories eventually come together into larger, more comprehensive accounts that hope to express a full and complete image of the master's enlightenment. Surprisingly, this coalescence of stories has already begun to occur for Taizan Maezumi.

In 1986, award-winning novelist, disciple, and dharma heir Peter Mattiessen published his journals from the years 1969–1982 under the title *Nine-Headed Dragon River*.[47] These journal entries tell numerous stories that express the character of Maezumi, incidents in their student-teacher relationship where we get an internal glimpse of the Zen master's mind and persona. Then in 1999, poet, writer, and filmmaker Philomene Long published a book entitled *American Zen Bones*.[48] Inspired by her long-time discipleship and friendship with Maezumi, Long gathered stories from the students of Maezumi and put them together into a text that is explicitly modeled on the classical Zen "discourse record" literature. Following this classical model, there is no chronology, no order of topics. As readers move from page to page, they get glimpses of Maezumi saying and doing unusual and interesting things. In this text, Maezumi's "discourse record" would fit seamlessly into the classic *Transmission of the Lamp* literature.

Then, several years later, Sean Murphy published a book taking something close to this same "discourse record" format. In *One Bird, One Stone: 108 American Zen Stories*,[49] we read a series of stories about Maezumi, but in this case juxtaposed and joined together with stories from the lives of other famous American Zen masters. This is extraordinary literature in that it adopts a genre from classical Zen history and weaves into it a very new segment of Zen history. For our purposes, these stories along with many others give a clear account of ways in which the character of Maezumi's Zen emerged in everyday life.

One feature of the persona of Maezumi that appears in many accounts of him is the way his physical presence made an impression on people. We have already seen how Maezumi's teachings highlighted the physicality of *zazen*, how he taught students to sense their "center" (*hara*) and to gather themselves into that central domain of poise. Followers of Maezumi describe him as maintaining that center at all times. As a result, Maezumi is frequently described as "charismatic in a calm way." Calm and charisma are often considered opposing traits, but Maezumi's "calm charisma" was something for which he was widely admired and which is often mentioned in the literature describing him. Student descriptions of Maezumi refer to his dharma name, Taizan, Great Mountain, as if that metaphor perfectly captured the solidity of his physical presence. He is described as a "small man with a huge presence," as projecting a "confident beauty."[50] Peter Matthiessen wrote that "he moved beautifully, leaving no trace, like a bird across the sky."[51] He loved gardening and took great pleasure in the rigors of physical labor. One student described him as having "black fire in his eyes," saying that Maezumi lived a kind of freedom that made him unpredictable and uncategorizable.[52]

Maezumi's quick wit and sense of humor are frequently mentioned by those who spent time with him, and are clearly demonstrated in many of the stories about him. His charisma included the capacity to see clearly into the situations directly in front of him and to respond with insight. Consider, for example, the following story:

Maezumi Roshi was sitting on the front porch of the Zen Center of Los Angeles one evening with one of his students when a disheveled, inebriated, and extremely depressed-looking man staggered up to them.

"Whaarsh it like," the man slurred, " . . . to be enlightened?"

Maezumi looked at the man quietly.

"Very depressing," he answered.[53]

Related to the physicality and strength of his presence is the temper that Maezumi was well known to exhibit on occasion. All close disciples tell and write stories about it. When he got angry, Maezumi would rage with passion and energy until the matter was settled. He would not hold back, one disciple explained, because he was very "comfortable with his anger."[54] "Being comfortable with anger" meant being able to trust that what was done in anger would not turn out later to be a source of deep regret. Although anger is often a state out of which monumental mistakes are made, wherever that is not the case anger is less to be feared because it is more an expression of honest vision than an immature, self-centered loss of perspective. In all of these accounts, the assumption is that Maezumi's Zen anger operated under the framework of his Zen vision, and that in some sense it was intended as one form that his teaching practice would take. Peter Matthiessen wrote that his teacher would "push all of my buttons, keeping me off balance."[55] By all accounts, when the occasion for anger had passed, so had the anger. It "left no residue," one student claimed.[56] When it was over there was nothing left to infect the next encounter with the person who had just incited his anger. In that sense, Maezumi's anger was something far more or far less than anger.

Juxtaposed to this side of Maezumi is another dimension of his character in which his Zen persona took a soft and sensitive form. One of his dharma heirs describes Maezumi as "grandmotherly" in relating to students.[57] Although some students needed vibrant energy or stern discipline, others needed sensitivity and care. One story in *American Zen Bones* is entitled "Just Cry": "Luli Jiren Madero had a daughter who was born a dwarf. Her family was very loving and close, but still the condition caused a great deal of hardship and pain, for the child had to undergo multiple surgeries for her condition. One day, Jiren went to a private interview with Maezumi to find comfort. After telling Roshi her story, he reached into the sleeve of his robe and produced two clean handkerchiefs. He handed one to her, kept the other for himself, and they both cried."[58]

Maezumi was one of the first to ordain women, including women with children. His personal character included the innovative sense and courage to break new ground in Buddhism. There was something inherently experimental about the cultural atmosphere in the United States when Maezumi taught Zen. The diversity of backgrounds and sense of freedom were extraordinary, and Maezumi reveled in this sense of the times. Pat O'Hara wrote that "Maezumi Roshi came to this country as a young man and just fell in love with the freedom and real thirst for the dharma here. He seemed very open to new traditions, and part of it was that he empowered a lot of women."[59]

Another dimension to Maezumi's character and persona was his dedication to the task of teaching. Everyone who knew Maezumi and worked closely with him called him a "workaholic"; some teased him about this obsession with the dharma.[60] He made himself available for teaching purposes every day of the week and around the clock. As Daido Loori claimed, "His life belonged to his students."[61] This dedication to others did not appear to prevent Maezumi from being a deeply introspective and self-aware Zen master. Although frequently in public view, he also maintained a strict meditation practice and valued opportunities for introspection and thoughtful reflection. As we know, however, different dimensions of our characters emerge in different sets of circumstance, and in Maezumi's case this is certainly true of his persona after the "scandals" that damaged his Zen Center in the mid-eighties. And it is to that transformation that we now turn.

Scandalous Images

As we have seen, in 1983 the vulnerability and humanity of Maezumi Roshi were brought to light in two interconnected instances of criticism. First, several sexual affairs with female students were disclosed, causing serious interpersonal turmoil at the Zen Center. As students began to see how these affairs represented mistakes in moral judgment, Maezumi's alcohol consumption quickly came to be seen as the source of the problem, now appearing in new light as alcoholism rather than as an innocent and unproblematic love of liquor. For some students, these revelations proved to be the end of their Zen careers. They were massively disillusioned, and when the illusions were gone there was nothing left to bolster their interest in Zen. For other students, these shortcomings could be gradually reconciled with the belief that Maezumi was an awakened Zen master. Although they too were disillusioned, these were illusions that they would gladly shed, illusions that had previously encouraged them to think that being a Zen master meant being invulnerable to all human frailty. Once the aura of magic was lifted from their understanding of Zen, what it meant to practice Zen and to seek awakening underwent a transformation.[62]

Maezumi's love of drinking was long-standing and never hidden. When he was in San Francisco visiting Shunryu Suzuki, Maezumi would sometimes take Suzuki's wife out drinking, since Suzuki himself took very little interest in these activities.[63] Maezumi often joined his students and colleagues on social occasions, both at ZCLA and out on the road. Students at ZCLA knew that one way to get Maezumi into a good conversation was to arrive with liquor as an offering. They often assumed, though, that these social practices constituted a "time-out" from their practice of Zen and from Maezumi's teaching. But there are no time-outs in life. Peter Matthiessen writes that when he attributed his own sluggishness in *zazen* one day to the *sake* that they had consumed the night before, Maezumi snapped back that "*sake* is one thing, and *zazen* is another. They have nothing to do with each other!"[64]

As a skillful, therapeutic response to a student's petty excuse for weak practice, Maezumi's strongly worded barb was no doubt effective. But in retrospect, it may be possible to see in that response a significant lacuna developing in Maezumi's own rationalizations about alcohol consumption. After all, Buddhist philosophy argues against thinking of any two activities as starkly separated. It dwells insightfully on the deep interconnection between all things. Nothing stands on its own; nothing is really separate from anything else. Liquor consumption and the practice of *zazen* are not unrelated. In fact, they are intimately bound up with each other; they both have a significant bearing on one's state of mind. Failure to admit that alcohol affects mental discipline, mindfulness, and many other aspects of life prevents one from looking directly at this important relationship and recognizing that serious problems may be concealed there.

It may be that over time liquor came to play a particular role in Maezumi's Zen personality. He was known to have a highly attuned sense of humor while drinking. Students recall quick-minded jokes and puns, even occasions when Maezumi would break into hilarious skits such as geisha impersonations.[65] It's not easy to be funny in a second language, and Maezumi may have been aided by the dampening of inhibition that alcohol provides. More to the point, though, there could have been a significant relationship developing over time between alcohol consumption and the spontaneous and unique verbal behaviors expected of an authentic Zen master. Improvised, unusual behavior is more easily initiated under the influence of alcohol, and accounts of Maezumi saying strongly worded and unusual things while drinking are clearly present in stories about him.

So one may wonder to what extent the expectations of spontaneous, Zen behaviors might have contributed to the desire for alcohol to help give rise to uninhibited, nonself-conscious behavior. Suzuki Roshi is an interesting contrast on this point. He reportedly did not drink much, and did not like the feelings of intoxication.[66] He was also not known for shocking, eccentric Zen-like actions or words. Suzuki's power as a Zen master derived from a subdued wisdom, a quiet reserve that seemed to exude compassion and insight. Although in some moods Maezumi displayed a similar power of reserve, in other moods or on other occasions there was an eccentric energy to his persona, and it may have been that during the late seventies and early eighties this dimension of the Zen master was frequently initiated by the influence of alcohol.

Several weeks spent at Scripps Alcohol Rehabilitation Center were enough to educate Maezumi on the dangers of alcoholism. He admitted that he had never given it much thought before. This casual attitude toward alcohol is widespread in Japan, where a "disease" called "alcoholism" is simply not recognized, at least not in that era. Having received that upbringing, Maezumi now saw what he could not see before; he understood how his actions and relations to other people were affected by his desire for and consumption of liquor. Both he and his students began to see how one problem—drinking—may have set the stage for the other problematic action that marred Maezumi's Zen image.

The historical records seem to show that there were no sex scandals in medieval Zen monasteries. There were also no women. The Zen Center of Los Angeles was born at the height of a global revolution in sexuality that was made possible by advancements in birth control. Social changes, especially the women's movement, made the isolation of genders seem archaic and pointless. ZCLA, without being aware of this, would have been a laboratory of social experiment in gender relations. It was not clear that the opening up of sexual relations that came to be assumed at that time would exclude one participant—the Zen master—but that turned out to be precisely the requirement. As one practitioner claimed in the Zen Center film, "I had no idea that in 1984 in Los Angeles matters of sexual conduct between consenting adults would be so uproarious."[67] Essentially, nothing in this experiment was clear, or it was not until Maezumi's sexual relations struck many practitioners as deeply inappropriate and scandalous.

Once out of rehabilitation and educated on issues related to alcohol, Maezumi himself considered it "scandalous." "It's true," he said on film, "being alcoholic you become loose about morals. I agree that this negative part should be closely observed to become aware of it. Being an alcoholic, I didn't see the immoral things I did. It's really outrageous."[68] Students say that Maezumi never made excuses, that he took full responsibility for his own failures. Never defending himself, he was the most severe critic of his behavior. Indeed, it was Maezumi himself who argued that the chaotic situation that he had caused at ZCLA should be openly and honestly discussed in a documentary film about the center that had been scheduled to be shot, even though the film crew arrived at the height of the turmoil and exodus from the center.[69]

Wendy Egyoku Nakao has said that Maezumi "spent the rest of his life trying to make up for his errors."[70] As his attendant during the early nineties, she claims that Maezumi faced serious levels of depression upon recognizing what his unmindful behaviors had wrought. Due to the exodus from ZCLA after the scandals, the busyness that had consumed Maezumi before 1983 receded to some extent. Now, just when he might have least wanted it, he had free time for introspection and reflection. Those close to Maezumi after 1983 report that there was a significant change in the Roshi's personality. An empty *zendō* on the occasion of a dharma talk was something Maezumi had not faced for years, and he understood very clearly what had caused the decline. Looking directly at that effect of his own actions was devastating, and Maezumi took it upon himself to shoulder the blame with unrelenting ferocity. His self-criticism did not abate, even when followers suggested to him in all candor that self-condemnation was no longer necessary.[71]

Other contemporary Zen masters have faced scandals in their careers. These other cases show us that the presence of some form of ethical failure may or may not come to invalidate or alter perceptions of the authenticity of a Zen master's enlightenment. Sometimes it does, and in these cases others conclude that ethical errors of judgment show that a Zen master had not attained what before he had appeared to have attained. In Maezumi's case, those who knew him throughout his life—both students and nonstudents—claim that the depth of Maezumi's enlightenment is indisputable, given the evidence that his life presented. Overwhelmingly, those who had spent substantial time with him remained convinced that the depth of Maezumi's "enlightenment" was authentic and beyond serious doubt. No one, they claim, could have demonstrated this level of personal presence and depth of character and not have ascended to remarkable levels of Zen insight; no one could have faked the level of clarity and compassion that Maezumi's life so clearly demonstrated.

Depictions of Death

It is a tragedy of some significance that alcohol consumption figured into the death of Maezumi Roshi. It is tragic because Maezumi had overcome his desire and need for alcohol. He had lived for twelve years without drinking, and liquor played no discernable role in his life during that period of time, except as a constant reminder of the mistakes that had partly undermined his lifelong ambition to serve the dharma. So why did Maezumi die a death that was tied to alcohol? Piecing evidence together and imagining the most likely explanation, I have come to believe that Maezumi's life was completely alcohol-free when in the United States and elsewhere, but that on the few occasions when he traveled to Japan it was not.

It is highly unlikely that Maezumi ever talked to his Japanese family or anyone in Japan about his problems with drinking, or that this issue ever came up. Liquor consumption plays a somewhat different role in Japanese culture from elsewhere, and the expectation that brothers or work colleagues drink when they get together is virtually unassailable. Drinking is a firmly embedded expectation, a social custom that cannot be set aside without breaking the bonds of tradition and sociability. Moreover, addiction to and abuse of alcohol are not conceived of in the same way that they are in the United States. Few, if any, Japanese would think of alcoholism as a medical problem, especially at that time in the eighties, or as a disease requiring professional attention. Although Maezumi came to understand his addiction in this way through his education at the Rehabilitation Clinic and then later through organizations such as Alcoholics Anonymous, this was far different from the ways he had conceived of drinking before that time and the way that it was typically conceived in Japan.

Given these cultural differences and the awkwardness of not drinking in Japan, it seems relatively clear that Maezumi came to regard the control he had over his drinking to be solid enough that when he traveled to Japan he would simply suspend his abstinence for a short period of time in order to participate in family gatherings and other social events without the seemingly unnecessary restriction of having to break with social custom. Just living abroad is custom-breaking enough without having to add other restraints upon those that already exist. Or at least, so I now imagine Maezumi's thoughts on this matter when he traveled to Japan. Although the scandal of Maezumi's sexual relations could have only happened in the United States, given the unique sexual mores there, it seems relatively clear that an alcohol-related death would only happen to Maezumi in his native land where, from his point of view, drinking was unavoidable.

It also seems clear to me that Maezumi had achieved sufficient control over his drinking that he could drink while in Japan and then simply stop when he returned to the United States. He had accomplished that before with success, and no doubt assumed he would this time, as well. It would be hard to overestimate the strength and stamina of character that Maezumi have achieved in his later life. For the last twelve years of his life, the moral and spiritual struggle within him was intense. He battled with levels of guilt and a profundity of disappointment that few of us will ever face, and he did this while continuing on with his practice of teaching Zen. He knew how devastating his errors had been to ZCLA and to the dharma in America more broadly conceived. He had disappointed everyone, and let the momentum of the dharma slip out of his hands. Although profoundly ashamed of his mistakes, he knew that he had to gather himself and his energies into a new effort of enormous proportions just at the moment in life when most of us begin to relax a little, to coast on the momentum of earlier achievements. This he did admirably, although always apologetically. No doubt the disciplinarian character of his lifelong Zen training served him well in this. It taught him how to let go of the past just enough to keep focused on the present moment of challenge. And although that present would always be shadowed by the weight of his past, Maezumi did manage to regroup his energies and purposes to the point that he would rebuild the Zen Center that he had mistakenly undermined.

At first glance, the circumstances of Maezumi's death would seem worlds apart from the idealized deaths of the great masters of the golden age of Zen. Images of their deaths are marked by perfect control of circumstances and timing. There are no tragedies in the narratives of classical Zen. These images, of course, come to us not from firsthand reports so much as through the editing powers of the evolving tradition. If you have a choice when writing the history of great founders of your group, how would you have them die, in ignominious circumstances or in mastery and triumph? In Maezumi's contemporary case, there appear to be few choices. The facts of the matter just are what they are, in spite of the initial efforts on the part of the Zen master's brothers to edit out the potentially demeaning details of drowning in a bathtub under the influence of alcohol.

Taking a second look at the timing and circumstances of Maezumi Roshi's death, however, something more comes into view. First, as to the issue of timing, although the classical masters of Zen appear to choose the time of their own death, Maezumi's death is obviously unchosen. Ironically, however, it would be hard to imagine better timing. Maezumi had just spent a dozen years working through the damage to his Zen Center that his own actions and choices had wrought, and all this with considerable success. There really was not much more to be done; the rest would be up to his successors, the one dozen dharma heirs who were already well on their way to distinguishing themselves for the quality and innovation of their Zen teachings.

Several students note that Maezumi had come to feel that rather than furthering the mission of Zen in America he was now "standing in its way."[72] By this he meant that the new era of Zen in the West that Maezumi had helped to initiate would not really get underway until the older generation of immigrant Zen masters from Asia were replaced by Americans and Europeans and Latin Americans and so on throughout the world. Maezumi referred to himself as a "stepping stone."[73] He knew very clearly that the traditions from Japan that he had taught would be gradually altered and improved under indigenous circumstances and that, as the Buddha had said, this impermanence was the true condition of the world. Although he certainly did not look forward to his retirement and death, he understood that these events would open up the dharma in the West to transformations that even he could not anticipate. Maezumi had lived sixty-four years, all in good health, and had maintained his strength, humility, and sense of humor throughout. Those who remember him at the end of his life recall a wizened, compassionate, and humble Zen master still fully within the power of his Zen mind. Leaving that image under those circumstances would be far from tragic.

Indeed, the unchosen but impeccable timing of Maezumi's death was even more interesting than that. He had just made his final trip to his homeland. He had gone there in part to participate in the memorial service for his mother, whom he loved and respected with great sincerity. Perhaps most important, he had gone to Japan to finalize his dharma transmission to Bernard Glassman, his foremost disciple. In Zen tradition this is the final and official act of turning a legacy over to a successor, and in classical Zen it often happened in the final days of a master's life. That the poem Maezumi inscribed on the official *inka* certificate would also be his Zen death poem is perhaps as beautifully choreographed a departure as anyone could imagine. Maezumi had paid his last respects to his mother, his brothers, and his homeland, had visited the leaders of the Sōtō sect with whom he had worked all of his life, and had undergone formal ceremonies of transmission to his successor. If that was not a magnificently timed death, it would only be considered such on behalf of the three children that he was leaving behind in America.

The other factor mentioned above—the circumstances of his death—provides another way to make sense of Maezumi's legacy. His death under the influence of alcohol was tragic in the same way that his earlier alcoholism and sexual misjudgments had been. In them we see a Zen master of obvious greatness brought down to humbling proportions. However much Maezumi Roshi may have dreaded this outcome, it could very well be that among his greatest contributions to the global Zen movement now in formation is that the story of his life has helped to humanize our concept and image of Zen masters. We can now see a great Zen master as human in all the ways we are. Maezumi was by all accounts an impressive Zen master—someone who it was impossible not to love and respect—but with weaknesses and vulnerabilities that derive from the simple fact that he was also finite and human. While living a truly profound and visionary Zen life, Maezumi Roshi was at the same time mortal and vulnerable to the tragedies of life.

By humanizing our understanding of what it means to be a Zen master, Maezumi shows us that mastery in Zen is not mastery of everything in life.

There are other dimensions to life that are not automatically cultivated or enlightened once a certain depth of Zen mind has been attained. These other dimensions—many of them, including the moral dimensions having to do with sexual relations and substance use—would have to be cultivated on their own even though Zen mindfulness may be the overarching skill that most effectively allows one to enlarge oneself in these other spheres. Reflecting on Maezumi's life and legacy helps us get beyond a "magical" understanding of Zen practice wherein everything in life is perfected at the moment when the results of Zen practice come to fruition. It helps bring contemporary Zen to a maturity that we typically evade when we look at classical images of Zen masters, a maturity that need not consider Zen masters as gods in order to hold them in admiration and deep respect. If this is part of Taizan Maezumi's legacy to the global Zen tradition, that could very well prove to be a monumental contribution.

NOTES

1. Work on this chapter began with a group of Occidental College students in a seminar on "Zen Masters." In appreciation for the great conversation, exchange of ideas, and research suggestions, I thank Nikhil Addleman, Joellen Anderson, James Case, Henning De May, Jeff Eamon, Theodora Forbes, Kate Hruby, Ian Lam, Christine Lew, Jackson Lewis, Brennen Lynch, Morgana Petrison, Rob Riccardi, Natalie Sandy, Jackie Steele, and Zoe Walsh.

2. White Plum Asanga, "The Venerable Hakuyu Taizan Maezumi Roshi, founder, White Plum Asanga"; http://www.whiteplum.org/Maezumi%20Biography.htm.

3. Peter Matthiessen, *Nine-Headed Dragon River: Zen Journals 1969–1982* (Boston: Shambhala, 1998), p. 239.

4. James Ishmael Ford, *Zen Master Who? A Guide to the People and Stories of Zen* (Boston: Wisdom, 2006), p. 168.

5. Matthiessen, *Nine-Headed Dragon River*, p. 237.

6. Nora Jones, "White Plums and Lizard Tails: The Story of Maezumi Roshi and His American Lineage," *Shambhala Sun*, March 2004, p. 2.

7. Matthiessen, *Nine-Headed Dragon River*, p. 238.

8. White Plum Asanga, "The Venerable Hakuyu Taizan Maezumi Roshi."

9. David L. Preston, *The Social Organization of Zen Practice: Constructing Transcultural Reality* (Cambridge: Cambridge University Press, 1988), p. 32.

10. Jones, "White Plums and Lizard Tails," p. 1.

11. Ibid.

12. Taizan Maezumi Roshi interviewed by David Chadwick, April 7, 1995. http://www.cuke.com/Cucumber%20Project/interviews/maezumi.html.

13. Sean Murphy, *One Bird, One Stone: 108 American Zen Stories* (New York: Renaissance Books, 2002).

14. Helen Tworkov, *Zen in America: Five Teachers and the Search for American Buddhism* (Tokyo: Kodansha, 1994), p. 8.

15. Matthiessen, *Nine-Headed Dragon River*, p. 239.

16. Philip Kapleau, *The Three Pillars of Zen: Teaching, Practice, and Enlightenment* (New York: Anchor Books, 1989).

17. David Chadwick, *Crooked Cucumber: The Life and Teachings of Shunryo Suzuki* (Louisville, Ky.: Broadway Press, 2000).

18. Matthiessen, *Nine-Headed Dragon River*, p. 238.

19. Ford, *Zen Master Who?*, p. 164; Jones, "White Plums and Lizard Tails," p. 2.

20. Rick Fields, *How the Swans Came to the Lake: A Narrative History of Buddhism in America* (Boston: Shambhala, 1992), p. 244.

21. Matthiessen, *Nine-Headed Dragon River*, p. 123.

22. Fields, *How the Swans Came to the Lake*, p. 244.

23. Fields, *How the Swans Came to the Lake*, p. 261.

24. Jones, "White Plums and Lizard Tails," p. 3.

25. White Plum Asanga, "The Venerable Hakuyu Taizan Maezumi Roshi."

26. Ford, *Zen Master Who?*, p. 164.

27. Interview with Wendy Egyoku Nakao, Occidental College, Los Angeles, April 4, 2008.

28. Jones, "White Plums and Lizard Tails," p. 4.

29. Ibid.

30. Interview with Wendy Egyoku Nakao, April 4, 2008.

31. Ibid.

32. Ibid.

33. Interview with Jan Chozen Bays, Occidental College, Los Angeles, March 7, 2008.

34. Hakuyu Taizan Maezumi, *On Zen Practice: Body, Breath, Mind* (Boston: Wisdom, 2002).

35. Hakuyu Taizan Maezumi and Bernard Tetsugen Glassman, *The Hazy Moon of Enlightenment* (Boston: Wisdom, 2007).

36. Hakuyu Taizan Maezumi, *The Way of Everyday Life* (Los Angeles: Center Publications, 1978).

37. Taizan Maezumi Roshi, *Appreciate Your Life: The Essence of Zen Practice* (Boston: Shambhala, 2001).

38. Taizan Maezumi, *Teachings of the Great Mountain* (Boston: Charles E. Tuttle, 2001).

39. Interview with Dennis Genpo Merzel, Occidental College, Los Angeles, February 11, 2008.

40. Interview with Charles Tenshin Fletcher, Occidental College, Los Angeles, March 26, 2008.

41. Philomene Long, *American Zen Bones: Maezumi Roshi Stories* (Los Angeles: Beyond Baroque Books, 1999).

42. Interview with Charles Tenshin Fletcher, March 26, 2008.

43. Interview with Dennis Genpo Merzel, February 11, 2008.

44. Maezumi, *Appreciate Your Life*, p. 7.
45. Interview with Wendy Egyoku Nakao, April 4, 2008.
46. Franz Aubrey Metcalf, "Why Do Americans Practice Zen Buddhism?" Ph.D. diss., University of Chicago Divinity School, p. 239.
47. Matthiessen, *Nine-Headed Dragon River*.
48. Long, *American Zen Bones*.
49. Sean Murphy, *One Bird, One Stone: 108 American Zen Stories* (Renaissance Books, 2002).
50. Interviews with Jan Chozen Bays, March 7, 2008, and Charles Tenshin Fletcher, March 26, 2008.
51. Long, *American Zen Bones*, pp. 3–4.
52. Interview with Charles Tenshin Fletcher, March 26, 2008.
53. Murphy, *One Bird, One Stone*, p. 73.
54. Interview with Charles Tenshin Fletcher, March 26, 2008.
55. Matthiessen, *Nine-Headed Dragon River*, p. 128.
56. Interview with Wendy Egyoku Nakao, April 4, 2008.
57. Interview with Jan Chozen Bays, March 7, 2008.
58. Long, *American Zen Bones*, p. 73.
59. *Shambhala Sun*, "Women's Liberation: on what it means to be a woman dharma teacher and how they'd like to see Buddhism in America evolve," interview with Sharon Salzberg, Barbara Rhodes, Judith Simmer-Brown. and Pat O'Hara; http://www.urbandharma.org/udharma3/womlib.html.
60. Interview with Wendy Egyoku Nakao, April 4, 2008.
61. Jones, "White Plums and Lizard Tails," p. 4.
62. Anne Cushman, "Under the Lens: An American Zen Community in Crisis," *Tricycle: The Buddhist Review*; http://www.tricycle.com/issues/from_archive/2000-1.html.
63. Taizan Maezumi Roshi interviewed by DC, April 7, 1995.
64. Matthiessen, *Nine-Headed Dragon River*, p. 240.
65. Interview with Jan Chozen Bays, March 7, 2008.
66. Taizan Maezumi Roshi interviewed by DC, April 7, 1995.
67. *Zen Center: Portrait of an American Zen Community* (Lou Hawthorne, written and produced by Ann Cushman, 1987. 53 min., Miracle Productions, Albuquerque, N.M.).
68. Cushman, *Zen Center*.
69. Ibid.
70. Interview with Wendy Egyoku Nakao, April 4, 2008.
71. Interview with Dennis Genpo Merzel, February 11, 2008.
72. Ibid.
73. Tracy Cochran, "Into the West," *Parabola* 32/4 (Winter 2007), quoting Bernie Glassman.

10

Seung Sahn: The Makeover of a Modern Zen Patriarch

Sor-Ching Low

Buddhism will appear. American Buddhism will appear. Polish Buddhism will appear. Each country has its own culture. I only teach the bone of Buddha's teachings, not just Asian Buddhist culture. Let local people become teachers, each country's Buddhism will appear by itself.
— Seung Sahn

How a Zen master will be remembered by posterity is a delicate matter that is often as much an exercise in heuristics as it is one in hermeneutics. Because of the stakes involved in the creation of such an image—sectarian, national, global, and historical—the passions it evokes are always intense. The documentation of Chan patriarchs in Chan lineage records such as the *Transmission of the Lamp* (*Jingde chuandeng lu*) (1004), the *Baolin chuan* (801), and the *Zutang ji* (K. *Chodang jip*) (952) attests to this undercurrent of competition in works written presumably by disciples with the intention of securing for their masters their good name and reputation within the lineage. Who is left in or out of these esteemed documents is an intriguing question in itself and has become an important entry point for modern scholarship where—literally—no stone has been left unturned to reconstruct an account of the image left behind in historical documents, cave drawings, iconography, temple steles, and memorial inscriptions.

Contemporary Zen masters who hope to secure a place within the lineage must thus enter into the same process that others before them had similarly done; that is, write books, build a community of followers and temples, and then entrust that image to their disciples to protect and even defend for posterity. Modernity, however, presents to modern Zen masters challenges unforeseen and unimagined by their ancient predecessors. Modern Zen masters, in order to make a name for themselves, must travel the globe, teach Dharma in a language that is not familiar to them, attend television talk shows, enter the World Wide Web, and see their Dharma talks and discussions with their disciples turn into instant YouTube picture shows.

Such a contemporary Zen master was Seung Sahn Sunim (1927–2004). When he died in 2004, he had left behind a community of followers, more than a hundred schools in America and Europe, a temple in Korea, and an image of Zen in the West that is other than that shaped by the Japanese. When Seung Sahn first arrived in America in 1972, he confronted challenges that were more than linguistic or technological. America in 1972 was, to borrow Dale Wright's formulation, "already immersed in a prior understanding [of Zen] that is articulated in terms of Japanese Zen."[1] The entry into the English language of the Japanese word "Zen" to represent all branches of the school attests to Japan's dominance. It is perhaps all the more remarkable that despite this, Seung Sahn managed to impress upon his American audience a new image of Zen, one touted to be in contradistinction to Japanese Zen. Certainly, such a claim to the "new" is bound to raise not just a few eyebrows, especially if we bear in mind Wright's insight that "the new ways" are "never totally new" and that "they are always hammered out on the anvil of the preceding discursive practice and mediated through the culture's grasp of its new situation."[2] That granted, it still remains to be asked, what is "new" in Seung Sahn's image of Zen? It is the contention of this chapter that the image of Zen presented by the Korean Zen master to the West operates on two levels: a rhetorical one that masterfully weaves his own image and narrative with that of the Korean Sŏn lineage, and a practical level that skillfully adapts Korean Zen style to its new environment, even as it reappropriates the prevailing discursive practice defined by the Japanese. In other words, the image of Korean Zen was developed as a combination of old and new, so that what emerged appeared familiar yet fresh.

More than a practical and expedient strategy to penetrate the Buddhist Western market is at stake here, however. It will become apparent in this chapter that the contestation of Japanese Zen dominance in America has a subtext of protest derived from cultural and national pride. This protest, to be sure, is a muted one, especially in comparison with the more vociferous ones raised during the Japanese occupation of Korea (1910–1945), and further back in 1592, when Japan first invaded Korea. As this chapter contends, what Seung Sahn's image of Zen attempts to do is to protest the hegemony of Japanese Zen in the West and its presumption to speak for all the branches of the school. This intertwining of nationalism and religion is neither unusual nor a recent phenomenon, as scholars of Korean Buddhism have pointed out.

As Robert Buswell noted, we recognize that in premodern Korea Buddhist identity formation extended far beyond the confines and rhetoric of nationhood, and that many monks to this day are still apt to consider themselves members of a larger ordination line and monastic lineage.[3] Nevertheless, it is difficult by the early twentieth century to separate Korean Buddhist identity from the nascent emergence of Korean nationalism—forged particularly by its long periods of resistance to Japanese invasion and influence. Narratives of the lives of several prominent Korean Zen masters note not only their meditation prowess, reclusive habits, and mind-blowing moments of enlightenment but also their leadership in resisting the Japanese.[4] For example, Master Yongsong (1864–1937) led in the struggle for the independence of Korean Buddhism from the Japanese and represented Korean Buddhism in a nationwide demonstration against Japanese occupation.[5] Similarly, Seung Sahn's own grandmaster, Man'gong (1872–1946) was remembered for his "deafening Zen shout" at a Japanese governor and declaring, "For what reason should Korean Buddhism follow Japanese Buddhism? The person who stresses such an idea must be in hell."[6]

Bernard Faure, however, reminds us that these "nationalistic" tensions predate Korea's formation as a nation.[7] During the eighth century, Korea already had to struggle to assert its own primacy against the major cultural referent, which was China. And while Korean expatriate monk-scholars may have distinguished themselves in China, those who did not return to their homeland were noticeably absent in historical documentations, such as the *Chodangjip* (Collections of the Patriarch Hall), compiled in 952.[8] The value of *Chodangjip* to Korean Zen Buddhism is redoubtable, since it contains biographies and the teachings of eight Silla masters.[9] Missing from this distinguished list is Musang or Master Kim (680–756), a Chan master of two of the earliest schools in China, who was famous in Tibet. Also missing is Wŏnch'uk (613–696), one of Xuanzang's (602–664) chief disciples. Both were expatriate monk-scholars who never returned to Korea.[10] Conversely, those who returned were celebrated and went on to establish Zen schools and lineages. As Faure maintains in his work on Chan master Musang, culture, religion and nationalism interacted, and Buddhism became a pawn in this politicocultural game.[11]

The persistent identification of Buddhism with nationalism in modern and premodern Korea presents itself as a critical subtext that we must reckon with in the consideration of the image of Korean Zen, especially given the prevailing influence of Japanese Zen in the West. As the face of Korean Zen in the

West, the image of Seung Sahn as Zen master is indivisible from the image of Korean Zen that he imparts through his teachings of the "Don't Know Mind." But before considering this subtext of cultural and national pride, let us turn first to Seung Sahn's two-pronged strategy of rhetoric and practice in the formation of a new image of Zen in the West.

Seung Sahn and the Image of Korean Zen

Known to his American and European disciples as Dae Soen Sa Nim (Honored Zen Teacher), Seung Sahn taught a brand of Zen that became known as "Don't Know Mind." When he died on November 30, 2004, at Hwagyesa Temple in Seoul, Korea, he was surrounded by his disciples who had flown in from all corners of the world to be by his side. Credited for having transmitted Korean Zen to the West, Seung Sahn has been called the "Korean Bodhidharma" by his countrymen, in reference to the Indian monk who was said to have brought meditation to China. By all accounts, Seung Sahn arrived in Providence, Rhode Island, in 1972 with little money or English.[12] In a commemorative book celebrating his sixtieth birthday, he described those early days, "No eyes, no ears, no nose, no tongue . . . A good retreat!" That retreat turned into a twenty-year sojourn, in which Seung Sahn went on a trailblazing path that saw the proliferation of temples, books, and students all over America and Europe. The magnitude of his energy and drive to spread Korean Zen is perhaps best captured by an old Korean nun who had known both Zen Master Kobong and his young disciple, then known as Haengwŏn: "Haengwŏn Sunim is always making something! Haengwŏn Sunim is always making temples, making pagodas, making books, making students, making Zen centers, making this, going to this country, going to that country. Always making something! But my teacher Kobong Sunim never made anything. He never even . . . opened . . . his . . . mouth."[13]

Like premodern Korean monks, Seung Sahn saw himself as being tasked with the universal transmission of the Dharma. But if premodern Korean monks participated in the universal transmission both spatially and temporally, ultimately tracing their path back to India and the Buddha himself,[14] Seung Sahn does it by means of a temporal and spatial turn outward to the West before returning to the East near the end of his life. Indeed, the story of Seung Sahn might have turned out differently had he not returned to Korea. Perhaps, taking a lesson from Musang's and Wŏnch'uk's lack of legacy in Korea, as noted above, Seung Sahn returned. Back in the East, not alone, but with his American and European disciples in tow, Seung Sahn took his Dharma to other parts of

Asia, where he began a fundraising effort to build a temple on one of the mountains in Korea. Musangsa, the international temple of the school in Korea, was established in 2000, three years before Seung Sahn's death.[15]

But even before Seung Sahn's return to Korea, it was evident that he had had his eye on the kind of image that he would leave behind. In 1976, he published a biography of himself—though to be more precise, the official story is better seen as a piece of self-constructed hagiography written by him in collaboration with his American disciples, primarily for a Western audience. A close look at this "biography" reveals hagiographic topoi that clearly were intended to locate him within the Korean Zen lineage and, beyond that, to the Sinitic arc of premodern Buddhist influences and a time when Korean monk-scholars made significant contributions to Chinese Buddhism.[16]

The Official Biography

In the biography that Seung Sahn charged his disciples to write, we are given the basic information of his early life. We learn that he was born in 1927 to a Protestant Christian family; that in 1944, he fought in the Korean Independence movement to liberate Korea from Japan; and that he renounced the world and found enlightenment upon reading the *Diamond Sutra* (K. *Geumgang gyeong;* C. *Jingang jing*). We are then given a detailed account of his retreat into the mountains for a hundred days, a period during which he was said to have eaten only pine needles and had terrifying visions of tigers and demons. Of the visions of delight, he wrote: "Sometimes Buddhas would come and teach him a sutra. Bodhisattvas would appear in gorgeous clothing and tell him that he would go to heaven. Sometimes he would keel over from exhaustion and Kwanseum Bosal would gently wake him up. By the end of eighty days his body was strong. His flesh had turned green from the pine-needles."[17]

On the ninety-ninth day he had an "out-of-body" experience and understood that "the rocks, the river, everything he could see, everything he could hear, all this was his true self."[18] The biography also recounts how he met his teacher, the Zen master Kobong, who had instructed him to "only keep this don't know mind. That is true Zen practice." He had predicted then, "Someday Korean Buddhism will spread to the world through you."[19] Several patterns consistent with hagiographic accounts of Chan and Korean Zen masters can be readily identified here: a recourse to the fabulous; a repetition of the paradigm of enlightenment through the *Diamond Sutra;* and an identification with the Korean Sŏn lineage.

The Fabulous

We are alerted to the trope of the fabulous in Seung Sahn's biography when we are told of visitations by tigers, demons, and buddhas. This trope is a common motif in accounts of Chan patriarchs in the *Jingde chuandeng lu* chronicles and the *Chodangjip*. In *Jingde chuandeng lu*, we are told that when Master Fa-yung left the mountains, "birds and animals cried for months. In front of the temple four great paulownia trees suddenly withered away in the middle of the summer."[20] Of Mazu Daoyi, we are told that he could touch his nose with his tongue, and on the soles of his feet were wheel-shaped marks, both of which were associated with Sakyamuni Buddha.[21] And in *Chodangjip*, we are told that Master Toui was born after thirty-nine months in his mother's womb.[22] Also, Master Teng Yin-feng, a disciple of Mazu, died standing on his hands in front of Diamond Cave at Mount Wutai.[23] Or, consider the earlier *Biographies of Eminent Monks*, which tells us that the monk Huizhu lived on pine needles.[24] Or, to take a more representative Zen master of modern times, Hanam (1876–1944) was said to have secluded himself in a monastery for twenty-five years, where he died with his legs crossed, seated in meditation.[25] These hagiographies offer the student of Buddhism an idealized paradigm of the Zen spiritual experience.[26] As John Kieschnick points out, all this is part of a reconstruction of the ideal image of the monk by their biographers who compiled them for sundry reasons, among which are proselytization and even the pure pleasure of reading.[27] The fabulous aspects of Seung Sahn's biography clearly fall into this paradigm of the fantastical in Buddhist hagiography. His visitations by buddhas and bodhisattvas, and even his diet of pine needles, are intended to point not only to his asceticism but more important, to the connection between himself and past Zen patriarchs by foregrounding these very same paradigmatic patterns of spiritual experience. Quite clearly, his official biography shows us that Seung Sahn's self-image is carved after the image of past Zen masters.

Paradigm of Enlightenment: Diamond Sutra

Another distinct pattern consistent with hagiographic accounts of Chan and Korean Zen masters can be readily identified here: Seung Sahn's personal narrative places it within a paradigm of enlightenment that is special to the Korean Sŏn tradition. Chinul (1158–1210), an early and key systematizer of the Korean Sŏn tradition had achieved enlightenment when he read the *Platform Sutra*.[28] In this Chan text, the sixth patriarch describes his spiritual enlightenment upon hearing the *Diamond Sutra*. The biographers of Chinul, who had incorporated the *Hwaŏm* (*Hua*) theory into the Sŏn schools and was instrumental in bringing *hwadu* (head phrase) into the practice, tell us that Chinul, on account of this, would often encourage people to recite the *Diamond Sutra*.[29] This textual reference to the *Diamond Sutra* thus signals its textual importance within Korean Zen, and further asserts Korean Zen's historical association with the sutra.[30] More critically, it serves to align Seung Sahn's enlightenment with the sixth patriarch's own enlightenment through the sutra, where the image of Zen master Seung Sahn is represented as a repetition (with a difference, no doubt) of the image of past Zen patriarchs. The textual reference to the *Diamond Sutra* is thus intended to affirm the pedigree of Seung Sahn which, according to the chart produced by the school's publication arm, then lists him as the seventy-eighth patriarch. The construction of this lineage reprises the myth of origins with Sakyamuni Buddha at its fount and Mahakashyapa as the first patriarch.[31] It thus serves to codify Seung Sahn's place in the lineage and formalize in strategic ways his status and role as the seventy-eights patriarch and possibly as the last-generation embodiment of Buddha's teaching and virtues.

The referencing of the *Diamond Sutra* also underscores another important strategic move. It appeals to the august tradition of Korean Sŏn and the authority of its eminent teachers, which includes Bodhidharma, for his teaching of the "Don't Know Mind." In a 1984 roundtable session with his disciples, Seung Sahn reaffirmed the pristine roots of the Korean Sŏn lineage as going back to the Buddha, and underlined at the same time the authority of the school he has founded:

> So what kind of roots does our school have? A long time ago in India one man appeared and obtained enlightenment: Sakyamuni Buddha. That's our root. Then the twenty-eighth patriarch, Bodhidharma, came to China. At that time there were already many kinds of Buddhism being taught, including the sutras, but Bodhidharma brought something new: the teaching of how to correctly perceive mind, or Zen meditation. When he came to China he didn't bring anything. He only taught "don't know . . . So the transmission of this "don't know" teaching came from China and Korea and then here to the United States. The teachings of Bodhidharma are the roots of American Zen.[32]

Clearly, what we have here is a master narrative that attempts to revise Korean Zen tradition as one long, unbroken lineage of patriarchs leading to the legendary Bodhidharma and further to the Buddha. Although one who is familiar with Zen's cultural history may dismiss this as "nothing new," since Zen masters routinely promote their own lineage of teachers and patriarchs, doing so in this case would overlook the importance of the context in which this conversation took place. The round-table session presented a formal occasion where Seung Sahn properly pried his disciples away from their prior image of Zen and immersed them in the new image by a radical reconstruction of their roots and their lineage.[33] It must also be remembered that it is these Western disciples and other potential ones who ultimately concerned Seung Sahn, and not the scholars whose enterprise it is to debunk the myths that he constructs. Indeed, Seung Sahn's strategy could be summed up in this way: if America was already immersed in a Zen discourse shaped by the Japanese, then Seung Sahn would reimmerse them in another shaped by the Koreans. By the deliberate omission of Japan's role in the formation of American Zen, Seung Sahn clearly intends to impress upon his disciples that his image of Zen, supported by this master narrative, is the more authentic one. Further, what Seung Sahn's biographical narrative does is to consolidate the image of Korean Zen, and by extension, the authority of the school he founded in the West.

Seung Sahn and Korean Sŏn

The consolidation of Seung Sahn's authority as the seventy-eighth embodiment of Sakyamuni's teachings and as Korean Zen master is another important strategic move in his biography. After locating his place within the "transnational" Buddhist lineage that starts with the historical Buddha, he now moves into a specific location within the Korean Zen tradition and the development of the Nine Mountain Sŏn schools. Seung Sahn does this by inserting himself into another salient pattern in the hagiographies of Korean Zen patriarchs: leadership and participation in the resistance to Japanese influence. By mentioning his own involvement in the Korean independence movement, Seung Sahn situates his own life story and struggles within the long Korean tradition of national and Buddhist resistance, first against Sinitic incursions and hegemony, and then against Japanese invasions and occupation.

The close involvement of Buddhist monks in the nation's liberation movement is well documented. We are told that when Hideyoshi invaded the Korean peninsula (1592–1598), it was the monks' militia that first turned back the Japanese threat. The national Chogye Order, the officially recognized Buddhist order, also formed a Monks' Militia for National Defense in which all monks must participate to this day.[34] Seung Sahn's retelling of his own involvement in the Korean independence movement thus reaffirms his Korean identity and his place within the Korean Sŏn tradition. This important detail points strongly to the subtext of cultural and national pride that underlies the making of the Korean Zen image in an America already accustomed, if not immersed, in one shaped by Japanese Zen.

Cultural and National Pride

Seung Sahn's own references to Korean-Japanese tensions appeared often within a personal narrative, where he speaks of growing up in colonized Korea, having to learn Japanese in school, and being made to live as a second-class citizen in his own country. This narrative not only made its way into his official biography, as has been shown above, but also into texts published by the Kwan Um School.[35] We also learn that as abbot of Hwagyesa, he founded the United Buddhism Association, a community of laypeople committed to the revival of Korean Buddhism. He was also on the Board of Directors of the Chogye Order which, in the mid-fifties and sixties, sought to reform its own house and reverse policies (such as the marriage of monks) brought about by Japanese domination of Buddhist matters in Korea. Seung Sahn would also spend another nine years in Japan administering to the large Korean community there.[36] All this—framed as anecdotes leading to his renunciation and to his search for a solution to the "immense suffering"—suggests that Seung Sahn's image of Zen is indivisible from his own resistance to the image of Zen imposed on Korea by Japan during its occupation. But it must be pointed out that this subtext of national and cultural pride arising from a history of neighborly competition had never interfered in his relations with his Japanese Zen counterparts. His best friend remained the Soto Zen master Taizan Maezumi, and he himself had never been disparaging about Japanese Zen.

Still, one could easily imagine the cultural and national pride that Seung Sahn must have felt when he returned to Korea in the 1990s, with his Western disciples in tow. But Seung Sahn went beyond showing his country to his disciples; he got them to stay and build a temple on one of Korea's mountains.[37] Whether his disciples were aware of the temple's significance is uncertain, but, as shown earlier, Seung Sahn was cognizant of the "career moves" by Korea's Zen patriarchs. By modeling himself after the great premodern Korean masters who went to China, attained enlightenment after meeting many famous Zen masters, then built a great temple on one of the mountains, and established a school, Seung Sahn—in spite of being a globetrotting, "funky" Zen master—was performing within the cultural paradigm of his lineage. By doing so, it would appear that he was reasserting Korea's claim, as premodern Korean Buddhists had done more than a thousand years before, to being the authentic and more pristine root of Buddhism. And in presenting the master narrative of Korean Zen's lineage to his Western disciples, he had also spatially extended the historical competition between Korea and Japan to the West.

The Familiar in the New

Seung Sahn's success in penetrating the American market can be attributed to the fact that the image he projected was both different and reassuringly familiar. As mentioned earlier, his image operates on two levels: a rhetoric of difference charted through the distinction of the Korean Zen lineage, as we have seen, and a practice that draws on the well-tried and the familiar, as see in Seung Sahn's teachings and practice. Seung Sahn has often said that in spite of the many names that he had given his teachings—Primary Point, Only Go Straight, Donno, Just Do It—there is really only one teaching—the Don't Know Mind. Seung Sahn has often described it as clear mind that perceives "sugar as sweet, sky as blue." When I spoke to his disciples, they spoke of what is unique to them about the school, and why they had chosen it over the other schools available to them. They were remarkably uniform in their responses. Kwan Sah Sunim, a monk residing at the Providence Zen Center, said, "The directions in our school are very clear. Seung Sahn was always concerned about how the Don't Know Mind can help us function every day. His kongans are designed to help us live moment to moment with clarity."[38] Andrzej Stec, a Polish Dharma teacher, explained, "Seung Sahn did not want to stop at *mu*, as Japanese Zen did. For him, it is how the Don't Know Mind can help us day to day. He took it a step beyond the Japanese Zen schools which emphasize the attainment of *mu* [C. *wu*]."[39] Another long-time disciple of Seung Sahn would push it further. "Japanese Zen is very attached to *satori*, but what is the function of *kensho*? Get enlightenment, get enlightenment, but then what?"[40]

Certainly, one could protest that Japanese Zen schools do more than just aim for "*satori*,"[41] but as the interviews with Seung Sahn's key disciples consistently evidenced, they are "immersed" in a certain understanding of Zen that is different from that shaped by the Japanese. In practice, Seung Sahn also offered some familiar material by an adroit blending of Japanese and Korean Zen practices. For example, instead of adhering to the traditional Korean Zen practice of using a single *kōan* throughout a student's career, he opted instead for a more elaborate system of *kōan* training, such as the *Ten Gates Collection*, a system that was more closely modeled on Japanese Rinzai models.[42] Also, in Korea, meditation retreats last for the ninety days of summer and winter, but in America, in addition to these long retreats, Seung Sahn also offered weekend, three-day, and one-week retreats, which were more like a Japanese *sesshin*. Stec explains, "In Asia, monks and nuns work within a cultural context. But in America, context is missing. And Seung Sahn clearly saw that too much rule would not work in this environment. His aim was to throw out the net as wide as possible to catch the big fish."[43]

The organization of the school's hierarchy, conforming to stages of training, seniority, and levels of attainment, shows further evidence of this skilful blending of the new and the familiar. For example, the monastic robes—which would have been worn only by monks in Korea—are also permitted to be worn by Dharma teachers in Seung Sahn's schools. As one of the monks explained to me:

> The system is a way of offering candy. Seung Sahn saw that the American mindset responds to these incentives, and in fact needs these markers of achievement. So in our system, after you train for a few years, and have taken the ten precepts, you get this title, then after another few more years, you get some other title, and so forth. Dharma teachers and monks and nuns fall under this system of hierarchy.[44]

But far more radical than the permission to wear monastic robes by those not ordained is the presence of married Dharma teachers. This is clearly a concession, in view of Seung Sahn's own stance against married clergy in Korea. But his willingness to adjust the strictures of traditional monastic discipline for his new American disciples again points to his larger goal of throwing his net as wide as possible. By adapting this aspect of Japanese Zen style where monks could—and do—marry, Seung Sahn makes tacit acknowledgment of the successful immersion of Japanese Zen in America.

Alterations to the Image

Early on, Seung Sahn introduced the ritualistic reading of his correspondence with his students, whereby a letter from a student would be read, followed by his reply. This took place as part of morning and evening practice at all his residential Zen centers. This correspondence between the Zen master and his students had come about because Seung Sahn was always traveling from center to center.[45] The letters and his answers to them were collected into "kong-an books." *Only Don't Know* (1999), *Dropping Ashes on the Buddha* (1976), *The Whole World Is a Single Flower* (1992) are some of these books regularly read at these sessions. What is striking about these dialogues is that they clearly follow a pattern of dialogues between master and disciple found in the collection of letters written by the Chan master Dahui Zonggao (1089–1163) to his students.[46] Seung Sahn's letters, which remain the only material repository left today of that dynamic exchange between master and student, now function as important, historical records. But by virtue of being ritually performed, these texts undergo a process whereby they become sacred. These documented records of his teachings and his exchanges with his students—each of whom was asking on behalf of another who had similar questions and concerns—became a means by which a new student with his or her own queries and doubts entered into a relationship with the late Zen master. In being performed ritually twice a day after the morning and evening sittings, these texts served as the closure of an elaborate ritual. Under such circumstances, where the texts become performative ones within a ritualistic setting, something else happens to the text. The hermeneutic meaning becomes irrelevant. It is read without discussion and concluded with *hapchang* (hands put together, J. *gassho*). In this context, it is the non-hermeneutic relations that gain importance in this process, as the text interacts with other ancient texts and other similarly enacted rituals held elsewhere in another part of the Buddhist world.

In introducing this ritual to his students, Seung Sahn was teaching his students to perform his image of Zen, and by doing so, to uphold the Zen master's image, as well. As I had claimed at the start, the image of Korean Zen in the West has become synonymous with the image of Seung Sahn.[47] By ritualizing the correspondence between him and his students, these texts all but attain sacred status. In doing so, the image of Seung Sahn is also being performed in the way he wants to be remembered and honored for the reading of the letters between master and disciple recalls the paradigmatic exchange of ancient Zen masters and disciples, and in this single stroke, reinserts the Zen master back into his lineage even as he becomes even more alive in their presence.

A Zen Patriarch in a Modern Age?

What Seung Sahn's biography sets out to achieve, as I have shown, is to locate the master within the larger Sinitic Buddhist tradition, and specifically within Korean Zen tradition by referencing key patterns in hagiographical accounts of Buddhist monks. But modernity and the fabulous make strange bedfellows. Despite Seung Sahn's attempts to control the image presented in the official biography while he was alive, such a fabulous image sits not a little strangely in the technology-savvy era of the Internet. In fact, the image of Seung Sahn encounters a modern problem that the pre-Internet Chan and Sŏn patriarchs could not have imagined—moment-to-moment accessibility.

This unprecedented accessibility of the modern Zen master to his disciples can be attributed to several factors, of which expedience and necessity are key. A well-known story still circulating in the Kwan Um School of Zen is of Seung Sahn's early days in America. When he first arrived in Providence, he came face to face with the "wild hippies" that he had only heard of in Korea. He quickly saw that much of the formality and rituals that typically inform interactions between Zen master and disciples in a Zen monastery in Korea could not prevail in the West. For example, traditionally a certain distance between Zen master and audience was maintained by means of a high chair that the Zen master ascends to give his sermon to the audience, who would be seated on the floor. Any subsequent interaction between Zen master and teacher took place in a question-and-answer format during the Dharma session. And in a formal retreat, a Sŏn monk gets to see the master perhaps once or twice throughout an entire ninety-day retreat period.[48] In America, this distance and formality was quickly abandoned. Seung Sahn invited students into his kitchen and cooked noodles for them. He sat with them on the floor in a circle, ate with them, and was available to his students at all times. He experimented with his teaching style in order to reach out to his Western students. Stephen Mitchell says of Seung Sahn, "Zen Master Seung Sahn is a born teacher, an astonishingly adept and fertile inventor of skillful means. In the early days, just after he came to America, he would change his slogan every few months. One month it was 'Only go straight,' then, two months later, it was 'Just do it.' Then it was 'Don't check other people's minds.'"[49] Dae Bong, who knew him for twenty-seven years and was one of his closest disciples said, "He never took a vacation, was available to his students, even at one A.M., when students knocked on his door. Being a monk means living for other people. Do together-action."[50] Even when Seung Sahn began traveling from center to center across America and the globe, he kept in close contact by encouraging his students to write letters to him.

The problem is that this "together-action" also has the effect of taking away some of the shine from the image of a Zen master in that he becomes human, even ordinary. This is an important point because of the impact it has on the reception of the image of Seung Sahn in the West. One example might suffice to illustrate this. When Seung Sahn lay dying in the hospital, he received many calls inquiring about his health. Dae Bong recalled:

> Towards the end of his life he was quite ill; he couldn't travel anymore. He was in the hospital for six weeks. We slept there with him. When people called up to enquire about his health, the Korean abbot who was there would say, "He's in Hong Kong at the moment!" The thinking was that enlightened people don't die. Or they sit up straight and die. Western students had no problem with that. Asian ones had a problem with that. He's sick because he lived with us. The delusion that appears in Asia is that great Zen masters don't get sick. Well, Buddha died because he ate bad food.[51]

This remark by Seung Sahn's Western disciple is particularly telling. It points to a disjunction between the Asian reception of the Zen master's image and the Western one. The suggestion here appears to be that students of Seung Sahn who come from Asia, where a formal and ritualistic relationship between master and disciple are, more or less, still apparent were in complete denial of the Zen master's death, or expected his body to stay in a certain position after death. The source of this disjunction in perception could be summed up in this way: Seung Sahn's image of himself as Zen master—one designed to be in alignment with the historical lineage of Zen patriarchs—is at odds with the "funky" image that he—by necessity or expedience—projected in his interactions with American students. To his students, he was warm, funny, and accessible. Students reflecting on those days say, "He was making a lot of the form as he went along, closely watching the young American mind and finding the right remedies for the sometimes powerful imbalances."[52]

Seung Sahn, in tacit acknowledgement of the image he engendered, has referred to himself as the "funky Zen master." Yet this all-too-human image is clearly at odds with the elevated idealized image that he was trying to create through his biography. As I suggested earlier, the image of Zen patriarchs of yore is a reconstructed one; a combination of fact, yarn, and lore in which their "greatness" appears to emanate from the great distance, and from the inaccessibility of the person behind the image created in the hagiographies and scholarly writings. Seung Sahn did not have the benefit of either. He had had to write his own "biography" and to cross cultural and language chasms by closing the distance between himself and his American students. In the end, he appeared as human as those around him. He got sick like everyone else, and he died.

This all-too-human image was also a product of the many YouTube minishows that featured the Zen master. Leaving little to the religious imagination, the arrival of the Zen master in the living room provides a wonderful opportunity for preaching the Dharma, but at the same time it also threatens to strip away some of the "magic" of the image that Seung Sahn had hoped to create through the official biography. The Zen master who is all too human and always accessible presents, as such, a conundrum in that the image that emerges—despite his own valiant efforts to control it—is clearly at odds with the self-constructed image of the Zen master, where the important signifiers such as the antinomian behavior and the surreal circumstances surrounding birth, enlightenment, and death signify a special "enlightened" being worthy of reverence, awe, and even worship. These signifiers of quasi-divine status had long fed the religious and cultural imagination of Buddhist Asia. For Seung Sahn's Western disciples, this kind of image clearly holds no allure.

Concluding Remarks

The image of Seung Sahn is still in the making. In Dharma lectures given by his disciples—many of whom continue to teach the "Don't Know Mind" in the different Zen centers across the globe—stories about the Zen master and stories by him are repeated and generated anew. In some instances, they have begun to gain a folkloric quality, and in other instances, they have attained a fabulous quality as each of the disciples—perhaps because they are still missing him—plumb the depths of their memory to tell stories of their beloved Zen master. They eagerly add and embellish every detail, aware that they have become custodians of the image that their Zen master has left behind. But each of the disciples in his or her own way is trying to protect a personal image of Zen master Seung Sahn. More than that, they are protective of the image of Seung Sahn for the fact that their own image is the one that will be imparted to those who have never met him, and who will, therefore, be dependent on these stories for a sense of their Zen master.

As I have shown, the image of Korean Zen in the West is indivisible from the image of the Seung Sahn as Zen master. Through his official biography, we see that the Zen master has modeled his image after Zen patriarchs of the Korean Sŏn tradition. Distinct patterns and tropes point to paradigms and models familiar to the Chan tradition. With these clearly marked signifiers, such as the role of the *Diamond Sutra* and the Buddhist monks' resistance to Japanese influence in religious and political matters, Seung Sahn has shaped an image for himself that references not only his Korean identity but also his role and status as the seventy-eighth patriarch in a lineage that allegedly goes back to the historical Buddha.

Seung Sahn's ambition was to spread the Dharma to the West. As the quotation at the start of the chapter suggests, he intended to teach the bone of the Buddha's teachings. But the politicocultural reality in the East and in the West taught him a lesson that premodern Korean monks had already learned as they faced times of Chinese xenophobia, and struggled to have a distinct Korean Buddhist practice. The latter became more urgent when the Japanese threatened to influence Korean Buddhist practice in the course of its occupation. By the time Seung Sahn arrived in America in 1972, he found that American Buddhism was already dominated by Japanese Zen. He had to compete, yet again, for a distinct image of Korean Zen that could be welcomed and accepted in America. In trying to get to know his Western students, he was willing to abandon some of the ritualistic formality of the Korean Sŏn tradition while coopting some of the Japanese Zen practices already familiar to his Western students. It was by an adroit rhetorical strategy of promoting himself or his own self-image that he sought to claim the difference. In aligning the Korean Zen image with his own self-image, he offered Korean Zen as a viable—if not better—option to Japanese Zen, even as he adapted traditional Korean Zen practices to its new home and reappropriated parts of Japanese Zen practice. As Dae Bong noted, "He was going to the West with great cultural pride. But he learned from his students. He was more affected by us. He was the best student, that's why he was the Zen master."[53] When his school, the Kwan Um School of Zen, officially opened in 1983, he had within ten years trail-blazed across America and was already beginning to spread the Dharma to Europe. In appreciation for his lifetime of teaching, Seung Sahn also received the title Great Master from the Chogye Order of Korean Buddhism, the highest honor the order confers.

In the process he became more human, perhaps, at least when compared to the official image that had been carved out for him through his biography. It has been only five years since he died, and his Dharma talks are regularly invoked and made present once again through YouTube, RealPlayer, and other Web sites. The Web has indeed kept the teachings of the Zen master alive and present. But as I suggested earlier, the advantages of YouTube's and other picture shows are double-edged. In order for an image to flourish, it depends as much on absence as it does on presence. The "reality" of Bodhidharma was captured for posterity in only a couple of "Zen" strokes on rice paper, where the famous eyes lurking under the dark, flying eyebrows serve to remind devotees of his legendary commitment to enlightenment, and to evoke unlimited leaps in religious imagination. The "reality" of a Zen master on YouTube might do the same, but it might also have the effect of curtailing some of that awe. But this is speculation at best. Five years after Seung Sahn's death, he continues today to be remembered and loved by his disciples. And the multiple media in which he has become available has continued to win him new disciples. The image he left behind of himself is still in the process of being shaped, but insofar as the image of Zen in the West is concerned, there is no doubt that the Zen master has succeeded in planting a new image of Zen—a distinctly Korean one that goes by the name of the "Don't Know Mind."

NOTES

1. Dale S. Wright, *Philosophical Meditations on Zen Buddhism* (Cambridge: Cambridge University Press, 1998), p. 50.

2. Wright, *Philosophical Meditations on Zen Buddhism*, p. 80.

3. "Imagining 'Korean Buddhism': the Invention of a National Religious Tradition," in *Nationalism and the Construction of Korean Identity*, edited by Hyung Il Pai and Timothy R. Tangherlini (Berkeley: Institute of East Asian Studies, University of California, 1998), p. 84; and Robert E. Buswell, Jr., ed., *Currents and Countercurrents:*

Korean Influences on the East Asian Buddhist Tradition (Honolulu: University of Hawaii Press, 2005), p. 8.

4. Seo Kyung-Bo, *A Study of Korean Zen Buddhism Approached through the Chodangjip* (Seoul: Poryŏn'gak, 1973).

5. Seo, *A Study of Korean Zen Buddhism*, p. 401.

6. Seo, *A Study of Korean Zen Buddhism*, p. 398.

7. Bernard Faure, "Chan Master Musang: A Korean Monk in East Asian Context," in *Currents and Countercurrents: Korean Influences on the East Asian Buddhist Tradition*, edited by Robert E. Buswell, Jr. (Honolulu: University of Hawaii Press, 2005), p. 153.

8. The *Chodangjip* was discovered in 1920 at the Haein Monastery, Mount Kaya, and consists of twenty numbered volumes engraved on wooden blocks containing the records and deeds of more than 250 patriarchs., They comprise accounts of the Indian, Chinese, and Korean Zen masters who lived at the end of Sakyamuni's life and the end of the Tang Dynasty (483 B.C.E.—952 C.E.). The *Chodangjip* was lost in China, except for one volume containing thirty-six songs of a number of patriarchs, which was found in the Dunhuang, and is now in the British Museum. See Seo, *A Study of Korean Zen Buddhism*, p. 4.

9. Seo, *A Study of Korean Zen Buddhism*, p. 4.

10. Faure, "Chan Master Musang," p. 155.

11. Faure, "Chan Master Musang," p. 153.

12. Interviews with members of Providence Zen Center (September 2008).

13. Quoted in Hyak Gak Sunim's Inka Speech (2001). http://www.kwanumeurope.org/article.php?s=3&a=46.

14. Robert E. Buswell, Jr., "Introduction," in *Currents and Countercurrents*, p. 10.

15. The new temple at Mount Gyeryong in the center of South Korea has attracted a substantial Korean lay practice.

16. John Jorgensen, "Korea as a Source for the Regeneration of Chinese Buddhism: The Evidence of Chan and Sŏn Literature" in Buswell, ed., *Currents and Countercurrents*, pp. 73–110.

17. Seung Sahn, *The Whole World Is a Single Flower* (Boston: Charles E. Tuttle, 1992), p. 228.

18. Mu Seong Sunim, *Thousand Peaks: Korean Zen—Tradition and Teachers* (Providence: Primary Point Press, 1987, 1991), p. 213. See also *The Teaching of Zen Master Seung Sahn: Dropping Ashes on the Buddha*, compiled and edited by Stephen Mitchell (New York: Grove Weidenfeld, 1976), p. 232; and Seung Sahn, *The Whole World Is a Single Flower*, p. 229.

19. Mu, *Thousand Peaks*, p. 216.

20. Chang Chung-Yuan, trans., *Original Teachings of Chan Buddhism: Selected from Transmission of the Lamp* (New York: Vintage, 1971), p. 26.

21. Chang Chung-Yuan, trans., *Original Teachings of Chan Buddhism*, p. 148. Also, see footnote 4 on p. 177.

22. Recounted in Seo, *A Study of Korean Zen Buddhism*, p. 90.

23. Seo, *A Study of Korean Zen Buddhism*, p. 111.

24. Seo, *A Study of Korean Zen Buddhism*, p. 35.

25. Seo, *A Study of Korean Zen Buddhism*, p. 399.

26. Robert E. Buswell, Jr., *The Zen Monastic Experience* (Princeton: Princeton University Press, 1992), p. 5.

27. John Kieschnick, *The Eminent Monk: Buddhist Ideals in Medieval Chan Hagiography* (Honolulu: University of Hawaii Press, 1997), p. 68.

28. Korean Sŏn tradition traced its lineage to Mazu Daoyi (709-788), founder of the Hung-chou school. Eight of the mountain schools of Sŏn were founded by Korean disciples of major Chan masters. Of these eight, seven were founded by disciples of first-generation successors of Mazu Daoyi. See Robert E. Buswell, Jr., *Korean Approach to Zen: The Collected Works of Chinul*, translated. with an introduction by Buswell (Honolulu: University of Hawaii Press, 1983), p. 9.

29. Buswell, *Korean Approach to Zen*, p. 29.

30. Charles Muller, "A Korean Contribution to the Zen Canon," in *Zen Classics: Formative Texts in the History of Zen Buddhism*, edited by Steven Heine and Dale Wright (New York: Oxford University Press, 2005), p. 45.

31. Seung Sahn, *The Compass of Zen* (Boston: Shambhala, 1997), p. 393.

32. "The Roots of American Buddhism," in Second Annual Congress of the Kwan Um School of Zen in Primary Point Article Archive. Volume 1, 1984 http://www.kwanumzen.org/primarypoint/.

33. See Dale Wright, *Philosophical Meditations on Zen Buddhism* (New York: Cambridge University Press, 2000).

34. Mu, *Thousand Peaks*, p. 11. Also see Seo, *A Study of Korean Zen Buddhism*, pp. 385–411, for Japanese influence on Korean Buddhism during its occupation.

35. Primary Point Press is the publications division of the Kwan Um School of Zen.

36. Mu, *Thousand Peaks*, p. 218.

37. Mu, *Thousand Peaks*, p. 218.

38. Interview at Providence Zen Center, September 2008.

39. Interview at Providence Zen Center, September 2008.

40. Interview with Dae Bong Sunim, October 2008.

41. See Miura Isshu and Ruth Fuller Sasaki, *The Zen Kōan: Its History and Use in Rinzai Zen* (Orlando, Florida: Harvest Books, 1966) for an "after-*satori*" training within the Japanese Rinzai *koan* system.

42. Robert E. Buswell, Jr., correspondence, December 2008.

43. Interview at Providence Zen Center, September 2008.

44. Ibid.

45. Mu, *Thousand Peaks*, p. 219.

46. Buswell, correspondence, December 2008. See J. C. Cleary, *Swampland Flowers: The Letters and Lectures of Zen Master Ta Hui* (Boston: Shambhala, 1997, 2006).

47. Other than the Zen master Kusan, who came to America in 1971 for a brief period of time, Seung Sahn was the only Korean Zen master who stayed behind and established a school.

48. Please see Buswell's *Zen Monastic Experience* for further details of the rigors and formalities of a typical Sŏn monastery.

49. Kwan Um School of Zen, *Only Doing It for Sixty Years*, edited by Diana Clark (Cumberland, R.I.: Kwan Um School of Zen, 1987), p. 20.

50. Interview with Zen master Dae Bong, October 2008.

51. Interview with Zen master Dae Bong, October 2008.

52. Kwan Um School of Zen, *Only Doing It for Sixty Years*, p. 103.

53. Interview with Zen master Dae Bong, October 2008.

Index

Aitken, Robert, 241
Amitabha Sutra, 37
Avatamsaka Sutra, 35–36

Baizhang Huaihai, 3, 69, 117, 139
   Extensive Record of, 21, 23
   and hagiography, 7, 9–10
   as iconoclast, 10–15
   life of, 4–7
   as patron saint of Chan
      monasticism, 6, 9, 10, 16–20
   rules of purity of, 16, 18
   as teacher, 20–25
Baizhang Mountain, 6, 13–14, 16
Banjin Dōtan, 170
Brahmajala Sutra, 81–83

Caodong, *see* Sōtō Zen
Chan, 91–92
   history of, 3, 8, 16, 61, 100–101
   lineage in, 33–34, 64, 66–67,
      117–118, *see also under* Zen
      practices
Chang, Garma C. C., 92
Chanlin sengbao zhuan, 72–73
Chanyuan qinggui, 18, 20

Chodangjip, 269, 272
Chogye Order, 274–275
Ciming Quyuan, 136

Dae Bong, 279, 282
Dahui Zonggao, 91, 122, 277
   and awakening, 102–108
   and Chan, 95–98
   early life of, 94–95
   as iconoclast, 98
   teachings by, 109–110
   works by
      Annalistic Biography, 95
      Chan Arsenal of Master Dahui
         Pujue, 93, 96
      Chronological Biography, 94
      Dahui's Letters, 92–93
      Recorded Sayings (Yulu) of Chan
         Master Dahui Pujue, 93, 98
"Daitō Kokushi's Admonition,"
   226
Daoxin, 36
Daiun Harada, 242
Dharani, 38
Dharma transmission, 149, 156,
   162

Dōgen
   and Caodong school, 119, 143
   and early Chan masters, 118–119
   in Echizen, 119–120, 128
   and Eiheiji Temple, 119–120, 122, 126
   and Ejō, 120, 122, 126
   and fly whisk, 140
   and Gien, 128
   and Giun, 121, 122
   and Hongzhi Zhengjue, 119, 120, 125, 126–129
   and *honkadori*, 118, 138
   and Rujing, 118–119, 140
      as model, 120–121, 128–131, 133–135, 137
      in critique of, 125
   works by
      Eihei kōroku, 119–120, 123–125, 127, 135
      "Genjōkōan," 40
      Hōkyōki, 142
      Manuals of Zen Meditation, 130
      Shōbōgenzō, 120–122, 127
Dongshan Liangjie, 33, 119, 121
   and five ranks, 53–54
   and Hongzhi Zhengjue, 41, 44–45, 47–48, 49
   and "Jewel Mirror Samadhi," 50–53
   and his use of kōans, 43–50
   Recorded Sayings by, 33, 35, 37, 41
   and *Shōbōgenzō*, 40, 47
   training in suchness, 35–43

Ekkei, 184–185
Emperor Xiaozong, 92
Emperor Xuanzong, 4, 5

F.A.S. Society, 217, 218, 226, 232, 234
   and "Vow of Humankind," 218, 226, 229
Faure, Bernard 234, 269
Fayan Wenyi, 68, 69
Fozu tongcan ji, 67

Gong'an, see Kōan
Gong'an collections, *see* Kōan collections
Gonggong Mountain, 5, 10
Guishan Lingyou, 6, 13, 35, 37–38, 118, 122
   and *Guishan jingce*, 19

Haengwŏn, 270
Hakuun Yasutani Roshi, 242–245
Heart Sutra, 226
Hisamatsu Shin'ichi
   and calligraphy and tea ceremony, 217, 231–232
   and Formless Self (True Self), 219–228
   and the "Great Doubt Block," 218–219, 221, 231
   life of, 217, 219
   on "Oriental Nothingness," 217, 222
   and the Vietnam War, 234
   and WWII, 217, 228, 232, 233
   Zen to bijutsu by, 231
Hongzhi Zhengjue, *see under* Dōgen and, Dongshan and, Menzan and
Hongzhou school, 3, 10
Hsu Yun, 92
Huangbo Xiyun, 6, 117
Huayan Sutra, 24, 36, 37, 69
Hwagyesa Temple, 270, 275

inka, 242, 243, 262
Ikegami Shōzan Rōshi, 219

Jingde chuandeng lu, 9, 17, 33, 37, 248, 254, 267, 272

Kaiyuan Monastery, 5
Kant, Immanuel, 224
Katsudo Fukan, 167
Kenninji Temple, 168
Kenzei, 168
Kitahara Ryūtarō, 227

Kōan, 91–92, 102–103, 105–107
Kōan collections, 11
   Biyan lu, see *Blue Cliff Record*
   Blue Cliff Record, 9, 13, 14, 20, 46–47, 53, 110, 122, 155, 172
   Book of Serenity, 41, 44, 45, 48–49, 127
   Wumen guan, 9
Kobong, 270–271
Korean Sŏn lineage, 268, 271, 273, 281
Koryu Osaka Roshi, 240, 242
Kōshōji Temple, 121
Kuroda Institute for the Study of Buddhism and Human Values, 244–245
Kwan Um School, 275, 278, 282
Kyoto University, 217, 219, 231

Lebang wenlei, 75–77
Letan Monastery, 6
Lingyin Monastery, 64–65
Linji Yixuan (J. Rinzai), 6–7, 117
   and *Linji lu*, 98, 109, 110
Linji school, 96, 102, 105, 109, 117, 119
Long, Philomene, 254–255
Longshu jingtu wen, 73–75
Lotus Sutra, 64, 69, 73, 74, 81

Mahaprajnaparamita sutra, 157
Manpakuji, 150, 153
Manzan Dōhaku, 149–150, 157, 162, 167, 173
Mazu Daoyi, 3, 4, 5–6, 10, 11–12, 42, 117
Menzan Zuihō
   as Abbott
      at Zenjōji Temple, 159, 167
      at Kūinji Temple, 160–161, 167
      at Ryūkeiin Temple, 161
   compared to peers, 173–175
   and Dōgen, 148–150, 161, 168
   at Eifukuan, 167
   and Hongzhi Zhengjue, 171–172
   impact of, 175–178
   and *Kenzeiki*, 168–169
   and *kyōsaku*, 165–166
   at Rōbaian, 156, 157, 158
   and *Shōbōgenzō*, 148–149, 156–157, 160, 170
   works by
      Source Texts Cited in the Shōbōgenzō, 157, 170, 175
      Additional Record of Historical Research Concerning the Pure Rules for the Monks Hall of Sōtō, 162, 171, 174
      Buddha Samadhi, 159, 162
      Record of the Activities of the Founder of Eihei, 157, 174
      Record of Traps and Snares, 183, 194, 202
      Sermons of [the Abbot of the Temple of Mount] Kenkō, 163–164
      Standards for Walking Meditation, 162, 166–167
Mokurai Sōen, 185, 198
Mount Tiantai, 63, 73, 81
Mount Tiantong, 119, 120, 126, 128–129, 140
Musō Soseki, 92, 106

Nanquan Puyuan, 6, 42, 69
Nanyang Huizhong, 35–37
Nianfo, 77–79, 83
Nine Mountain Sŏn schools, 274
Nirvana Sutra, 69
Nishida Kitarō, 219, 235
Niutou Farong, 69
Nyogen Senzaki, 241
Nyojō goroku, 130, 140–142, see also under Dōgen, and Rujing

Ōbaku Zen, 150, 153, 159
Orategama I, 92
Ōtomo Inaba, 156

Pang Yun, 10
Platform Sutra, 70
Pure Land, 61, 65, 73–80, 83

Qin Gui, 101
Qisong, 72

Reirin Yamada Roshi, 241
Rentian baojian, 76–77
Rinzai Zen, 159, 165, 171, *see also under* Linji school
Ruizhu Shaocheng, 96
Ryōun, 153

Samantabhadra, 76
Scotus Erigena, 224
Seung Sahn Sunim
   in America, 270, 276, 281
   and the *Diamond Sutra*, 271, 273
   and the "Don't Know Mind," 270, 276, 281
   and hagiography, 272, 279–280
   and "Japanese Zen," 268–269, 277, 281
   life of, 271
   works by
      Only Don't Know, 277
      Dropping Ashes on the Buddha, 277
      The Whole World Is a Single Flower, 277
Shaku Sōen
   address at World's Parliament of Religions, 192–193
   autobiographies by, 186–187
   biographies of, 188–191
   early life, 184
   early practice of, 185
   image of, 186–187
   and impact of Uemura Soto's Death, 201–202
   and Keiō College, 188–191
   lectures in the U.S., 193
   and *Rōhatsu sesshin*, 185
   stance on war, 195–196, 199–201
   views on colonialism, 196–198
   works by
      Diary of a Journey to the West, 188–189
      Journal on Defeating Demons, 187, 200
      Sermons of a Buddhist Abbot, 187, 193, 199
      Shaku Sōen zenshū, 186
Shincha-kai, 231
Shōbōgenzō, see works by Dōgen, Dongshan and, Menzan and
Shungai Tōsen, 185
Shunryu Suzuki, 256–258
shutaidō, 225
Song gaoseng zhuan, 9, 61–64, 66, 68, 72
Sonnō Sōeki, 154–156
Sōtō Zen, 119, 125, 148, 240, 242, *see also under* Chan and lineage, 34, 97
Suzuki, D.T., 11, 242–243, 251

Taizan Maezumi, 275
   and alcoholism, 245–246, 256–258, 259–261
   and Baian Hakujun Kuroda Roshi, 240, 243
   death of, 246–247, 259, 261–262
   Dharma heirs of
      Beck, Charlotte Joko, 245
      Glassman, Bernard "Bernie," 232, 242, 262
      Loori, John Daido, 250, 256
      Mathiessen, Peter, 253–255, 257
      Merzel, Dennis Genpo, 251
   on Dōgen, 241, 250
   and "free-love," 245, 256, 258
   life of, 240–241, 244, 246
   name of, 240, 254
   teishō by, 244, 250
   and WWII, 240, 242
   works by
      On Zen Practice: Body, Breath, and Mind, 249
      The Hazy Moon of Enlightenment, 250
      The Way of Everyday Life, 244, 250
      Appreciate Your Life: The Essence of Zen Practice, 250, 252

Teachings of the Great Mountain: Zen Talks by Taizan Maezumi, 250
Tassajara Zen Mountain Center opening, 243
Tathata, 34
Tenkei Denson, 120
Tiansheng guangdeng lu, 72
Tiantai Deshao, 68, 69, 73
Tiantai school, 73, 77
Tokiwa Gishin, 217, 231
  Zen and the Fine Arts, trans. of *Zen to bijutsu*, 231
  Transmission of the Lamp, see *Jingde chuandeng lu*

Uemura Sōkō, 201
United Buddhism Association, 275

Weixin, 74, 77, 78
Wŏnch'uk, 269, 270
Wuliang shoujing, 74
Wumen Huikai, 92

Xitang Zhizang, 6
Xuedou Zhongxian, 13

Yanagida Seizan, 217
Yasukuni Shrine, 234
Yi Qing, 54
Yongming Monastery, 64–65
Yongming Yanshou, 59
  and Bodhisattva Practice, 79–83
  as Chan Master, 66–73
  identity of, 60–61
  and King Yama, 75
  as promoter of blessings, 61–66

as Pure Land Master, 73–79
works by
  Fozu tongji, 77
  Shou pusa jiefa bingxu, 81
  Wanshan tonggui ji, 64–66, 70, 78
Yongsong, 269
Yuanwu Keqin, 13–14, 97, 100, 102–107
Yuanzhi, 118
Yunmen, 124, 129
Yunqi Zhuhong, 92, 104–105
Yunyan Tansheng, 34–35, 37–43, 45

Zen at War, 196
Zen Center of Los Angeles, 242–245, 250, 258
Zen in America (or American Zen), 241–245, 246, 251
  and Phillip Kapleau, 242
  and Sean Murphy, 254
Zen practices
  kanbun sermons, 126, 134–135
  kanna practice, 159–160, 165
  kōan study, 241, 244, 253
  sesshin, 185, 253, 276
  shikantaza, "just sitting," 242, 250, 253
  zazen, 122, 128, 130, 132, 142, 166, 167, 243, 249, 250–251, 253, 254, 257
Zenshuji Temple, 241
Zen War Stories, 196
Zhantang Wenjun, 97, 99
Zhang Shangying, 100, 102
Zhanran, 35–36
Zhaozhou, 123–124
Zhuangzi, 183
Zongjing lu, 64, 69–70, 72, 82
Zutang ji, 10, 14